ANDREW BENDER
TIMOTHY N HORNYAK

TOKYO
CITY GUIDE

Cherry blossoms in full bloom at Shinjuku-gyōen (p114)

JOHN BAN

Tokyoites inhabit a singular capital inimitably yoking past and future, where Zen temples nestle in sci-fi cityscapes and centuries-old madness for cherry blossoms coexists with an insatiable desire for nonstop novelty.

Old and new are forever juxtaposed in Tokyo: its residents are at home both donning loincloths to shoulder a portable Shinto shrine through Asakusa's religious festivals and piloting humanoid fighting machines in Akihabara's robot sport tournaments. Tradition, happily, is not ossified, but feted along with innovation.

The workaholic stereotype is very true – death from overwork is legally recognised in Japan – but stroll through a neon-lined row of Shinjuku *yakitori* (grilled chicken) joints on the weekend, or any cherry grove in spring, and you'll see that people take pleasure very seriously here. There is ever-flowing sake, deep respect for freshly filleted fish, heartfelt karaoke, and constant curiosity about how outsiders view this archipelago at the end of the world.

Orderly, efficient Tokyo works stunningly well for a metropolis its size, yet it has about as many masks as there are hostess clubs in Kabukichō. Peeling back each facade reveals a city that's far less Western than first impressions suggest; nearly everything Tokyoites do, from taking out the trash to cheering a ball game, is profoundly un-Western. Their reverence for ritual, courtesy and the power to *ganbaru* (persevere) gives this superdense megalopolis a calm at the heart of the storm. This is *wa* – social harmony – and it's the force that makes Tokyo more a series of one-of-a-kind experiences than a collection of sights.

TOKYO LIFE

Tokyo never stops. Change trains during rush hour at Shinjuku Station and you'll experience Tokyo at its most dizzying, with rivers of people pouring from the platforms. Gaze out from the observation deck at the nearby Metropolitan Government Offices and you'll see a vast labyrinth of a city that seems to continue forever. This city of nearly 13 million people (expand that to 33 million if you include the greater metropolitan area) has been constantly reinventing itself following natural disaster, war and an endless architectural construction-demolition cycle.

What Tokyo lacks in greenery and historic structures is made up for by an almost playful chameleon character, with new redevelopment zones transforming neighbourhoods like Marunouchi, Roppongi and Shiodome into chic new centres of entertainment, business and media. Grand schemes, such as plans to restore Tokyo Station to its original 1914 glory and construction of the 634m-tall Tokyo Sky Tree, are changing the urban landscape. Meanwhile, the new Fukutoshin subway line is funnelling people between Ikebukuro and Shibuya, and a new high-speed rail link will cut travel time between central Tokyo and Narita Airport to 36 minutes as of July 2010.

Social pressures are often the subject of beery talk in *izakaya* (Japanese-style pubs). Two pillars of Japan's politics and economy crumbled in 2009–10 as the conservative Liberal Democrats lost their 54-year lock on political power to the Democratic Party of Japan, and Japan Airlines filed for bankruptcy. The rise of China and India is putting Japan's famed technological prowess in the shadows. Tokyo is now relying on the appeal of Japanese pop culture, video games, animation and environmental technologies to retain its international influence. The country's large but fragile economy is struggling to return to a solid growth footing following the 2008–09 recession.

To drum up business, the government is luring more travellers to Japan. The most popular are those with a curiosity for the culture, and Tokyoites delight at trying to explain their foods, social etiquette or the writing system. Tokyoites are as intensely interested in themselves as outsiders, and devour articles on the sex lives of the elderly, the schoolgirl prostitution scandal or trends in yoga for pets. Turn on the TV and you'll see infantile buffoonery on the variety shows and firemen belting out their best *enka* blues on the national karaoke program. Beneath its staid corporate face, the city is a child at heart. Tokyo's *joie de vivre*, frantic pace and pure energy never let up.

FRANK DEIM

Bright lights, big city – the classic meeting place outside the Studio Alta building (p109)

HIGHLIGHTS

FRANK DEIM

CENTRAL TOKYO

The geographical and spiritual heart of the city, central Tokyo is home to the lofty heights of the Imperial Palace, the shopping mecca of Ginza, the world's largest fish market in Tsukiji and the geek capital of Akihabara.

ERIC WHEATER

FRANK DEIM (TOKYO INTERNATIONAL FORUM, ARCHITECT RAFAEL VINOLY, 1996)

❶ Ginza Yon-chome Crossing
Famous department stores by day, a neon canyon by night (p56).

❷ Kōkyo (Imperial Palace)
Get just about as close as you can to Japan's incredibly reclusive royal family (p50).

❸ Tokyo International Forum
Gaze through the glass ceilings of one of the world's most significant postmodern buildings (p53).

❹ Tsukiji Central Fish Market
Be caught up in commerce in action before your sushi breakfast (p63).

1 **Omote-Sandō**
Shop till you drop along brand-store-lined boulevards (p139).

2 **Takeshita-dōri (Takeshita Street)**
Seek out a good deal on platform shoes and knee-high socks in Tokyo's youth fashion capital (p105).

3 **Yoyogi-kōen (Yoyogi Park)**
Take a picnic or watch weekend buskers (p107).

4 **Meiji-jingū (Meiji Shrine)**
Absorb the peace and quiet at this historic urban sanctuary (p105).

5 **Shibuya Crossing**
Get lost in the bright lights of this singular streetscape (p101).

MARTIN MOOS

SHIBUYA & HARAJUKU

From the craziest pop cultures and the wildest street fashions to the chicest boutiques and the trendiest night spots, always hip Shibuya and Harajuku are a mind-blowing introduction to the urban jungles of modern Tokyo.

RACHEL LEWIS

BRENT WINEBRENNER

ANTHONY PLUMMER

For a rare glimpse of old Edo amid a seemingly endless sea of concrete, head to the adjacent districts of Asakusa and Ueno, which retain the few scant remnants of Shitamachi (low city).

FRANK DEIM

FOTOSEARCH / PHOTOLIBRARY

NOBORU KOMINE

1 Sensō-ji (Sensō Temple)
Search for peace and enlightenment at this historic Tokyo temple (p83).

2 Sumida-gawa (Sumida River) Cruise
Cruise along Tokyo's ancient waterways in search of old Edo (p65).

3 Festivals in Asakusa
Watch the streets come alive with *mikoshi* (portable shrines) or samba (p85).

4 Hanami (blossom viewing) in Ueno-kōen (Ueno Park)
Savour the sweet scent of Tokyo's iconic *sakura* blossoms (p77).

5 Tokyo National Museum
10,000 years of Japanese art history under one roof (p78).

WILL ROBB

SHINJUKU

Tokyo's biggest transport hub, Shinjuku assaults the senses with towering buildings of steel and glass, heaving masses of commuters and mazelike cityscapes lit up by blazing neon.

MICHAEL COYNE

ANTHONY PLUMMER

❶ Shinjuku Station
The world's busiest train station frustrates and fascinates (p109).

❷ Kabukichō
Tokyo's night-time playground for all things naughty, gaudy and bawdy (p113).

❸ Golden Gai
Get lost in a labyrinth of intimate retro bars (p114).

❹ Shinjuku-gyōen (Shinjuku Park)
Seek order and perfection in a traditional Japanese garden (p114).

① National Art Center, Tokyo
Kurokawa Kishō's futuristic building entices with its undulating glass front (p93).

② Roppongi's Architecture
Roppongi's pastiche goes from tacky to the futuristic (p90).

③ Tokyo Midtown
Splurge on fine shopping and dining in the capital of class (p91).

④ View from Mori Art Museum/ Tokyo City View
Come for contemporary art, stay for views across the metropolis (p91).

SIMON RICHMOND

ROPPONGI

Tokyo's most infamous playground for expats is morphing into one of its major centres for art, architecture and high-end shopping.

MERTEN SNIJDERS (MAMAN BY LOUISE BOURGEOIS, 2002)

SIMON RICHMOND

BERNHARD LIMBERGER / LOOK-FOTO / PHOTOLIBRARY

SIMON RICHMOND

ODAIBA

A huge swath of reclaimed land floating in the middle of Tokyo Bay, the constructed island of Odaiba is a futuristic pleasure district for Tokyoites looking for a quick getaway or retail therapy.

① Venus Fort
Shop, shop and shop until you can't shop anymore (p151).

② Ō-edo Onsen Monogatari
Soak your travel-worn bones in natural mineral pools (p126).

③ Fuji Television Japan Broadcast Headquarters
Scratch your head in confusion after spotting some of Tokyo's weirder designs (p135).

MICHAEL TAYLOR (FUJI TELEVISION BUILDING, ARCHITECT TANGE KENZO, 1996)

ANTHONY PLUMMER

❶ Refuel in Style
Take a *kōhii* (coffee) break anywhere near Yebisu Garden Place (p144).

❷ Hotel Claska
Sleep in style in a neighbourhood devoted to design (p217).

❸ Meguro Riverside Promenade
Hunt for funky boutiques under the cherry trees (p144).

MARK HEMMINGS

EBISU, DAIKANYAMA & MEGURO

Although Ebisu, Daikanyama and Meguro are off the radar screens of most travellers, these high-class neighbourhoods are home to some of the city's finest dining and most sophisticated bars and clubs.

CLASKA   SIMON RICHMOND

SIMON RICHMOND (*ROBOT SOLDIER, SHACHIMARU KUNIO*)

OLIVER STREWE

MATSUNAKA TAKEYA / PHOTOLIBRARY

OUTER NEIGHBOURHOODS

Not all of Tokyo's sights are concentrated around the centre of town. With a bit of planning, you can take in a sumō match or visit the famous Ghibli Museum.

❶ Ghibli Museum
Head out west to catch the spirit of *Spirited Away*, at director Miyazaki Hayao's museum (p113).

❷ Shibamata
Return to the Shōwa Era in movie character Tora-san's neighbourhood (p86).

❸ Toden Arakawa Line
Traverse under-visited northern Tokyo by one-car trolley (p118).

❹ Sumō Wrestling
Watch the big guys go at it in Ryōgoku, east of the Sumida River (p123).

❺ Shimo-Kitazawa
Western suburb and centre for counter-culture and college fashions (p103).

WILL ROBB

ADINA TOVY AMSEL

EXCURSIONS

If you're hankering to escape the city crowds, it doesn't require much effort or time. Some worthwhile day trips can be had outside the capital.

BOB CHARLTON

WILL ROBB

❶ Hakone
View Mt Fuji from a cable car or pirate boat (p236).

❷ Daibutsu (Great Buddha), Kamakura
Japan's second-largest Buddha is ensconced amid dozens of temples (p242).

❸ Tōshō-gū, Nikkō
Unesco World Heritage Site saluting history's most renowned shōgun (p233).

❹ Rural Onsen
Journey as the Japanese do, to idyllic countryside hot springs (p228).

CONTENTS

THE AUTHORS

Andrew Bender

France was closed, so after college Andy left his native New England to work in Tokyo. It ended up being a life-changing journey, as visits here so often are. He's since mastered chopsticks, the language, karaoke and taking his shoes off at the door, appeared in Japanese TV commercials, earned his MBA, and worked with Japanese companies on both sides of the Pacific in fields from finance to film production. His writing has appeared in *Travel + Leisure*, *Forbes*, the *Los Angeles Times* and many airline magazines, plus over a dozen other Lonely Planet titles. In an effort toward ever greater trans-oceanic harmony, Andy also consults on cross-cultural issues from his current base in Los Angeles. Find out more at www.wheres-andy-now.com.

Timothy N Hornyak

A native of Montreal, Tim Hornyak moved to Japan in 1999 after watching Kurosawa's *Ran* too many times. Since then, he has written on Japanese culture, technology and history for titles including CNET News, *Scientific American* and *Far Eastern Economic Review*. He has played bass in a rock band in Tokyo, lectured on Japanese robots at the Kennedy Center in Washington and travelled to the heart of Hokkaidō to find the remains of a forgotten theme park called Canadian World. As the author of *Loving the Machine: The Art and Science of Japanese Robots*, his favourite robot is Astro Boy, but he firmly believes that the greatest Japanese invention of all time is the onsen.

We've heard even the most intrepid of travellers say that they're intimidated by Tokyo, so let's dispense with the fears first: language barrier, illegible signs and menus, crowds, high prices, getting lost. Yes.

And no. A little preparation (hint: you're reading it now) goes a long way. While it's true that Japanese generally speak less English than do people in many other Asian countries, English signage and picture menus are increasingly common. Moments of peace can be had even in the most unexpected places (subway cars are typically silent). One quickly figures out the gap between need-to-spend and want-to-spend and, if you're standing on a street corner trying to make sense of a map, don't be surprised if a stranger approaches offering help.

Now that that's out of the way, get ready to be wowed.

A trip to Tokyo can be as organised or as spontaneous as you'd like. Accommodation can be booked online ahead of time, and there is no shortage of guided city tours (see p261) to help you catch your bearings. Reservations at higher-end restaurants are helpful, but otherwise Tokyo is perhaps best experienced by simply putting down the guidebook, getting lost in the crowds and finding your own secret corner of the city.

WHEN TO GO

Tokyo is one of the world's most exciting cities, regardless of when you visit. If you take a quick look at the calendar of festivals (see right), you'll realise that Tokyo hosts a number of big events every single month.

Weather can be a factor. Summers (late June through August) are stiflingly hot and humid, and winter chill (December to February) can severely limit your outdoor time, although the skies tend to be clear in winter and snows not too bad. Spring (April and May) and autumn (October to November) tend to have the most reliably pleasant weather. See p18 for information about cherry blossom and autumn foliage seasons.

Otherwise you might want to time your visit so you can catch one of several annual sumō tournaments, which take place in January, May and September (see p207), or perhaps a baseball game or two (p208), which are played from March to October.

Virtually all businesses, restaurants and sights shut down for the New Year's holiday (31 December to 3 January). Make reservations well in advance if you plan to be in Tokyo during the big travel holidays of Golden Week (29 April to 5 May) or the newly designated Silver Week (around 21 Sep).

FESTIVALS

Old Edo was home to an abundance of *matsuri* (festivals), which originated in farming communities as expressions of the Shintō religion. Spring festivals were held to supplicate the local gods and to secure a plentiful harvest, while autumn festivals were held in thanks and celebration of a rich harvest. Summer and winter festivals were less common, though this changed with the rise of large urban settlements, where they were held in the hope of circumventing pestilence and plague. Today, Tokyo's civic calendar is jam-packed with *matsuri* as well as a mix of events from traditional flower viewings to trade shows covering everything from motorcycles to design.

For a list of Japan's national holidays, see p259.

THINGS TO PACK

- Seasonally appropriate, 'smart casual' clothing. Tokyo is very fashion-forward. Leave the athletic wear at home unless you plan on working out.
- Business attire in conservative colours, if you're going on business.
- Comfortable walking shoes. See p20 for shoe etiquette.
- Handkerchief: to dry your hands, not wipe your nose. Many public washrooms don't have paper towels or dryers.
- See p259 for information about bringing medications into Japan.
- Try to fit your belongings in a small to medium-sized suitcase. Japanese hotel rooms may be smaller than you're used to, and smaller bags will be easier to manage on public transport.

January & February

SHŌGATSU (NEW YEAR'S HOLIDAY)
1 to 3 Jan

While Tokyo comes to a virtual halt on the first few days of the year (also referred to as O-Shōgatsu, 'Honourable New Year'), the city's large Shintō shrines and Buddhist temples swell with visitors; Sensō-ji (p83) and Meiji-jingū (p105) are good places to start. Although both of these places get extremely crowded – Meiji-jingū gets millions of visitors alone – it can be a particular thrill to be part of the crowds of people from all walks of life, many of whom are dressed in fine kimono and purchasing seasonal trinkets.

You may also want to stop in at Yasukuni-jinja (p59), where the shrine's dramatic nō (stylised dance-drama) is performed in honour of the shrine's god. On 2 January, you should consider a visit to the Imperial Palace (p50) as the emperor and imperial family make a brief appearance in one of the inner courtyards – it's one of the very rare occasions when visitors are allowed a glimpse into imperial life behind bullet-proof glass.

SEIJIN-NO-HI (COMING-OF-AGE DAY)
15 Jan

Arrows fly at Meiji-jingū (p105) during traditional archery displays in the celebration of the world of the grown-up.

SETSUBUN
3 or 4 Feb

Setsubun marks the first day of spring in the traditional calendar, a shift once believed to bode evil and bring disaster. To ward off the oncoming evil, temples erupt into metaphysical food fights as rowdy suppliants throw tiny sacks of roasted beans and shout, *'Oni wa soto! Fuku wa uchi!'* ('Devil out! Fortune in!').

HARI-KUYŌ
early Feb

Women mourn the passing of broken pins and needles by burying their beloved sartorial pals in cubes of tofu or in radishes at Sensō-ji (p83).

March & April

HINA MATSURI (GIRLS' DAY)
3 Mar

Homes and public spaces are decorated with squat dolls in the traditional dress

top picks

QUIRKY EVENTS

- Setsubun (February; left)
- Hari-kuyō (February; left)
- Design Festa (May and November; p19 & p20)
- Takigi Noh (July or August; p19)
- Samba Carnival (August; p19)

of the *hina* (princess). Around this time, dolls made by children are set adrift on the Sumida River (Map p122) from Sumida-kōen near Azuma-bashi. There's also a Boys' Day held in May (see p18).

UME HANAMI
late Feb

Before the riot of cherry blossoms comes to town, the plum trees do their own number, the first sign that winter is ending. Popular viewing spots are Koishikawa Kōrakuen (p62) and Yushima Tenjin (p82).

HIWATARI MATSURI
mid-Mar

Mountain monks take the lead in this festival in Mt Takao (p231) by walking over hot coals. If you're feeling invincible (or drunk), you're also welcome to try.

ST PATRICK'S DAY PARADE
mid-Mar

www.inj.or.jp/stpatrick_e.html
Around 17 March, tens of thousands line the Omote-Sandō (Map p106) for the wearin' and drinkin' of the green.

TOKYO MOTORCYCLE SHOW
late Mar

At Tokyo Big Sight (Map p127) the biggest motorcycle show in Japan has been letting the good times roll since the 1970s.

HANAMI (CHERRY-BLOSSOM VIEWING)
usually early Apr

See the boxed text on p18 for the best spots for these blossom-viewing parties.

TOKYO INTERNATIONAL ANIME FAIR
late Mar or early Apr

www.tokyoanime.jp/en
Tokyo's International Anime Fair at Tokyo Big Sight (Map p127) brings in everyone from the 17-year-old animephile living next door to big-screen voice actors and some 170

TOKYO IN BLOOM

Owing to the seasonal nature of Japanese culture, monitoring the progress of spring blossoms and autumn foliage is an obsession up and down the archipelago – the national news carries maps of their progress. Even though Tokyo is largely hemmed in by concrete, blossom viewing and leaf peeping are still a big deal.

Hanami

Cherry blossoms seem to burst out overnight some time between the end of March and the beginning of April, representing the climax of spring. *Hanami* (cherry-blossom viewing) parties begin with the earliest buds and endure to the last clinging blossoms. Both daytime parties and moonlit soirees are standard, as crowds flood the parks with beer and good humour.

Hama Rikyū Onshi-teien (p65) There are about 100 cherry trees here, including a few wild varieties. A small admission fee keeps the crowds at bay.

Shinjuku-gyōen (p114) A prime cherry-blossom attraction, this garden has several varieties of cherry trees, including the spectacular *yaezakura* (double-blossoming cherries).

Ueno-kōen (p77) *Hanami* explosion as enthusiasts vie for the best angle on Ueno's 1000 flowering trees.

Yasukuni-jinja (p59) There are more than 1000 cherry trees in the grounds of the shrine; check out the cherry trees lining the nearby Imperial Palace moat as well.

Yoyogi-kōen (p107) There is plenty of space here to stretch out and admire the park's 500 or so cherry trees.

Zōjō-ji (p94) About 100 trees are found here at Shiba-kōen, with the temple for a backdrop.

Kōyō

During the *kōyō* (autumn foliage season), which runs from about mid-October to early November, Tokyo's trees virtually explode in colour. Look especially for the maple, which goes through a minor spectrum of yellows and oranges before climaxing in a fiery red. Some of the best spots include the following:

Kitanomaru-kōen (p51) This grassy expanse is a great place for an autumn stroll and/or a picnic.

Koishikawa Kōrakuen (p62) A lovely pond and surrounding gardens make this park one of Tokyo's best foliage spots.

Shinjuku-gyōen (p114) This sprawling garden's many leaf-peeping locales include the Western-style garden.

Ueno-kōen (p77) As popular for autumn foliage as for cherry blossoms.

Yasukuni-jinja (p59) The tree-lined walkway leading to this temple explodes in a fury of autumn colours.

Yoyogi-kōen (p107) This sprawling park is dotted with picturesque ginkgo, zelkova and cherry trees.

---

exhibitors. Sorry, *cos-play* (costume play) is sadly not permitted inside as the decorum of this bit of the event is surprisingly serious – in an anime sorta way.

HANA MATSURI   1st week in Apr

Happy birthday Buddha celebrations happen across Japan. Look for the parade of children in Asakusa, pulling a white papier-mâché elephant.

May & June

OTOKO NO HI (BOYS' DAY)   5 May

This is the male counterpart to Hina Matsuri (see p17). Homes where boys live fly *koino-bori* (banners or windsocks in the shape of a carp), a symbol of strength, never-ending struggle and other masculine virtues.

KANDA MATSURI   mid-May
www.kandamyoujin.or.jp

One of the city's three big *matsuri*, this festival features music, dancing and a healthy dose of sake. The highlight is the parade of *mikoshi* (portable shrines) through the streets of Kanda (see Kanda Myōjin, p68).

SANJA MATSURI   mid-May

Another one of the city's three big *matsuri*, this three-day festival attracts around 1.5 million spectators to Asakusa-jinja (p85). The highlight is watching half-naked men (and women, although not half-naked) carry more than 100 *mikoshi* around the shrine and neighbouring Sensō-ji. The crowd sheds its reserve and things get rowdy, so grab a beer or two and feel free to jump into the action and let it all hang out – so to speak.

DESIGN FESTA mid- to late May
www.designfesta.com
At Tokyo Big Sight (p136), this two-day arts and design fair brings in more than 2700 exhibitors (professionals and amateurs alike) and some 50,000-plus visitors, making it the biggest art event in Asia. Also held in mid-November (see p20).

IRIS VIEWING early to mid-Jun
Mizumoto-kōen (3-2 Mizumoto-kōen, Katsushika-ku) & Horikiri Iris Garden (2-19-1 Horikiri, Katsushika-ku)
These parks in eastern Tokyo show off more than 100 unique iris species. Saturdays and Sundays bring drum performances and larger crowds; weekdays are better for a quiet walk. These parks are best reached by taking the Keisei Line to Kanamachi Station.

SANNŌ-SAI mid-Jun
Tokyoites turn out to Hie-jinja (p87) for this *matsuri* with music and dancing and the usual frenetic procession of *mikoshi*, at the former protector shrine for Edo Castle.

July & August
INTERNATIONAL GAY & LESBIAN FILM FESTIVAL mid-Jul
www.tokyo-lgff.org; various venues
IGLFF has nearly 20 seasons beneath its belt, highlighting gay and lesbian cinema from Japan and around the world, with almost three dozen films and other programs.

SUMIDA RIVER HANABI last Sat in Jul
Summertime in Japan is synonymous with exhibitions of fireworks *(hanabi)*, which happen throughout the country. The ones on the Sumida-gawa are among the most spectacular around. Although you may have seen fireworks displays elsewhere, they probably haven't prepared you for the grandness of this one, which goes on, marvellously, for hours.

TAKIGI NOH Jul or Aug
As the summer weather starts to peak, shrines, temples and parks stage evening outdoor *nō* backlit by bonfires. Meiji-jingū (p105), Kichijoji Gesoji and Shinjuku are the usual spots for evening performances

within the city limits. This is a great bit of old Edo that has been preserved in modern Tokyo.

O-BON mid-Aug
For several days, Japanese city dwellers return to their ancestral provinces to gather with family and visit the graves of ancestors, marking the time when Buddhist teaching says the dead revisit the earth. *Bon-odori* (folk dances) by people in *yukata* (light cotton kimono) are held throughout Japan, but the one at Yasukuni-jinja (p59) is famous, illuminated by *bonbori* (paper lanterns).

FUKAGAWA HACHIMAN mid-Aug
The latest of the city's three big *matsuri* is famous for its traditional chant of 'wasshoi! wasshoi!' as spectators pour sacred water over the *mikoshi* carriers along the route. Needless to say, everyone gets wet, which is certainly welcomed if the August sun is beating down. Location: Tomioka Hachimangū (p123).

KŌENJI AWA ODORI last Sat & Sun in Aug
www.koenji-awaodori.com
Some 12,000 participants do the Fool's Dance along a 2km stretch. If you happen to find yourself along the parade route at Kōenji Station (Map pp48–9), you're welcome to break into your own rendition.

SAMBA CARNIVAL last Sat in Aug
This universally loved event, which is staged by the Nikkei Brazilians, features roughly 3500 dancers moving their fleshy way down Kaminarimon-dōri in Asakusa (Map p84) past half a million spectators. The dancing is top-notch and the judged competition is fierce, drawing dancers all the way from Rio.

September & October
TOKYO GAME SHOW late Sep
tgs.cesa.or.jp; Makuhari Messe
Get your geek on when the Computer Entertainment Suppliers Association stages this massive expo at a convention centre on the way to Narita Airport (Makuhari Messe is about 30 minutes east of Tokyo, via the JR Keiyō Line from Tokyo Station to Kaihin Makuhari Station).

NINGYŌ-KUYŌ
late Sep

Childless couples pray for children by offering dolls to Kannon, the Buddhist goddess of mercy. More interesting for spectators is the ceremonial burning by priests of all the dolls held in the temple precinct from the previous year. See Kiyōmizu Kannon-dō (p77) for more info.

TOKYO INTERNATIONAL FILM FESTIVAL
late Oct

www.tiff-jp.net

Bigger doesn't necessarily mean better when it comes to film festivals, though the TIFF – the biggest one in Asia – maintains its integrity by keeping a feature-length film competition at its core. The TIFF pays special attention to films from Asia, although there are always selections in English.

TOKYO METROPOLITAN CHRYSANTHEMUM FESTIVAL
late Oct to mid-Nov

Chrysanthemums are the flower of the season (as well as the flower of the imperial family), and this dazzling display in Hibiya-kōen (p56) is certainly cause for celebration, and has been ever since 1914. You can also catch dazzling chrysanthemum displays at Shintō shrines, including Meiji-jingū (p105) and Yasukuni-jinja (p59).

TOKYO DESIGNERS' WEEK
late Oct to early Nov

Video, furniture and fashion are a few of the genres represented at venues around the city, mostly in arts enclaves such as Aoyama, Harajuku and Roppongi. In 2009, some 300 exhibitors attended, representing 21 countries.

November & December

TOKYO JIDAI MATSURI (FESTIVAL OF THE AGES)
3 Nov

On National Culture Day, locals, dressed in splendid costumes representing figures from Japanese history parade around the Sensō-ji temple precincts in Asakusa (Map p84). This festival takes after a much bigger (and older) one in Kyoto, held a couple of weeks earlier.

SHICHI-GO-SAN (SEVEN-FIVE-THREE FESTIVAL)
early to mid-Nov

This adorable festival celebrates children of these tender ages, who were once thought to be in danger of imminent misfortune. Parents dress girls aged seven and three and boys aged five in wee kimono and head to Shintō shrines and Buddhist temples throughout town, grandparents often in tow. It's a prime photo opportunity.

KŌYŌ (AUTUMN FOLIAGE SEASON)

The city's trees undergo magnificent seasonal transformations during kōyō. See the boxed text, p18.

DESIGN FESTA
mid-Nov

www.designfesta.com

This enormous art and design festival at Tokyo Big Sight (p136) is held for a second time in mid-November. See also p19.

INTERNATIONAL ROBOT EXHIBITION
late Nov to early Dec

This biennial event organised by the Japan Robotics Association and friends featured 850-plus booths in 2009, at Tokyo Big Sight. The next event is scheduled for 2011.

TOKYO'S SHOE FETISH

Japan is fastidious about shoe habits, and shoe *faux pas* are about the surest way to start a visit on the wrong foot. Here are some important tips:

- Shoes are never worn in homes, or indoors at many restaurants, ryokan (traditional inns), shrines and temples.
- Remove shoes in a *genkan* (entryway inside the door). Shoes *are* worn in most other places.
- Step out of your shoes on the stone or tile surface inside the *genkan* and up onto the wooden or carpeted surface.
- Don't step on the stone or tile in your stocking feet.
- Place your shoes in a rack or locker, if provided.
- Many places provide slippers. If these are too small, you are not obligated to wear them.
- Slippers are not worn on tatami (straw floor mats).
- To put your shoes on again, place them on the stone surface and step down into them.
- Slip-on shoes are enormously helpful!

COSTS & MONEY

Tokyo, once known as an impossibly expensive city, has become a lot more affordable in the last 10 years – or at least prices have frozen, giving the rest of the world a chance to catch up. Truth be told, it's still possible to spend thousands of dollars on a five-star hotel room, and wine and dine on gourmet cuisine until your bank account is in the red, but Tokyoites are quick to point out that their city is as expensive as you want it to be. In fact, for every upmarket hotel or sophisticated restaurant in the capital, there are numerous affordable guesthouses and cheap noodle shops scattered about. All this means that, depending on currency fluctuations, a trip to Tokyo can well be better value than one to London, Paris or any other European capital.

Although shoestringers will have to part with a bit more cash than they're perhaps used to, it is possible to survive in Tokyo for around ¥5000 a day, if you sleep in dorms, subsist on noodles and rice, and limit your sight-seeing to reduce entrance and transport fees. More realistically, a budget of ¥10,000 to ¥15,000 will allow you to bed down in a private room, sample Tokyo's culinary offerings and snap a few hundred shots at sights around the city. If money is no object, then welcome to paradise – Tokyo is a fantasy come true.

Throughout this book, we have broken down sleeping and eating listings based on price. For instance, budget sleeps are rooms costing ¥6500 or less, midrange rooms cost between ¥6500 and ¥16,000, and top-end rooms will cost more than ¥16,000. Budget eats will cost around ¥1000 or less for lunch, and ¥2000 or less for dinner. A quality midrange meal can run upwards of ¥5000, while haute cuisine can easily run to ¥20,000 per person.

Generally speaking, anything that requires a lot of space costs a lot (eg bowling alleys, cinemas, domestic produce), so you can save a bit if you avoid these minor pleasures. Also, although most museums and cinemas don't generally offer discounts to adults, concessions are usually available to students, children and senior students, and the GRUTT pass is good value (see p80). And finally, you should know, too, that Tokyo's little-kept secret, the bargain lunch set, can sometimes put your foot in the door at places that might otherwise be beyond your budget.

HOW MUCH?

1L petrol ¥128
500mL bottled water ¥110
Onigiri (rice ball) ¥120
Cup of coffee in a cafe ¥450
Basic subway fare ¥160
2km taxi ride ¥710
Tokyo National Museum ticket ¥600
Souvenir T-shirt ¥2000
Kirin beer at a bar ¥700
Kirin beer from a vending machine ¥330

INTERNET RESOURCES

There is a vast treasure trove of Japan-related info on web. Before touching down in Tokyo, take a few moments to check out the following sites:

Hyperdia (www.hyperdia.com) Having problems finding your way around Tokyo? Resident expats use this English site to make sense of Tokyo's overwhelming transportation grid.

Japan National Tourism Organization (JNTO; www.jnto.go.jp/eng) This official government body offers an extremely comprehensive guide to tourism in Tokyo and the whole of Japan.

Japan Times (www.japantimes.co.jp) Tokyo's most widely circulated English-language newspaper is a great way to catch up on the latest Japan headlines.

Lonely Planet (www.lonelyplanet.com) Includes summaries on travelling in Tokyo, the Thorn Tree forum, travel news and links to the most useful travel resources on the web.

Metropolis (www.metropolis.co.jp) Japan's most popular English-language weekly magazine offers insights and listings about what's happening in Tokyo.

Tokyo Convention & Visitors Bureau (www.tcvb.or.jp) Targeted at business travellers, this website gives the basics.

Tokyo Notice Board (www.tokyonoticeboard.co.jp) From apartment listings to job openings, this weekly English-language classified zine is worth checking out.

Tokyo Tourism Info (www.tourism.metro.tokyo.jp) City-run portal that covers everything from upcoming events to self-guided walking tours.

HISTORY

IT CAME FROM THE SWAMP!

The monstrous metropolis that is Tokyo, population nearly 13 million, has come a long way from its origins as a collection of shallows and tidal pools at the mouth of the Sumida-gawa (Sumida River). Fertility was the focus of its first permanent inhabitants and this fecund swampland edging the Kantō plain was perfect for incubating new life. They were a pottery-producing culture who settled here during the late Neolithic Jōmon period (Jōmon means 'rope marks' for the design on pottery fragments discovered from this time) around 10,000 BC. These early Tokyoites lived as fishers, hunters and food gatherers, and likely benefited from the fauna-rich marshland that was left behind after what is now Tokyo Bay rose to cover most of the valley where Tokyo now sits.

Some 4000 years later, during the Yayoi period (400 BC to AD 250), wet-rice farming techniques were introduced from Korea. Shintō – Japan's native religion – also began to develop during this time. Shintō, similar to animism, involves the worship of gods who inhabit animals and objects in nature. By AD 300 Japan was already, more or less, a unified nation, with its cultural base in the Kansai area (around the present-day cities of Nara, Kyoto and Osaka), while the Kantō region remained a distant backwater. While the Roman Empire rose and declined, Edo (the old name for Tokyo) continued as a sleepy fishing village for another thousand years.

Meanwhile, the proto-Japanese nation came under the control of the Yamato clan (forerunners of the current imperial family), who claimed a handy direct descent from the sun goddess Amaterasu and introduced the title of *tennō* (emperor) around the 5th century. This was called the Kofun period, named for the earthen mounds in which the nobility were interred.

But the most important event in Japan's early history was the arrival of Buddhism in the 6th century, from India via China and Korea. Buddhism introduced a highly evolved system of metaphysics, codes of law and the Chinese writing system, a conduit for the principles of Confucian statecraft.

LIVE BY THE SWORD, DIE BY THE SWORD

Few would have guessed it, but Edo was to play a central role in Japan's life as a warrior state. The rise of the samurai was linked to how strong a hold the imperial court had over the nation. From the earliest days of the Yamato dynasty, it was the custom to relocate the capital following the death of an emperor (presumably to free the capital from the taint of death). However, this custom was altered in 710 with the establishment of Japan's first permanent capital at Nara.

By the end of the 8th century, the Buddhist clerical bureaucracy had become vast, threatening the authority of the imperial administration. The emperor responded by relocating the capital once again and establishing a new seat of imperial power at Heian-kyō (modern day Kyoto). From that point on, Kyoto generally served as the capital until the Meiji Restoration in 1868, when Tokyo became the new chief city.

TIMELINE

10,000 BC	AD 710	794
Tokyo area inhabited by pottery-making people during late Neolithic Jōmon period. The Kantō region around Tokyo is among the most densely settled in this era.	Japan's first permanent capital established at Nara, ending the practice of moving the capital following an emperor's death. The city is modelled on Chang'an, capital of Tang dynasty China.	Imperial capital moved to Heian-kyō, renamed Kyoto in the 11th century. It is laid out in a gridlike pattern and in accordance with traditional Chinese geomancy principles.

SAMURAI: THOSE WHO SERVE

The prime duty of a samurai, a member of the warrior class, was to give faithful service to his *daimyō* (feudal lord). In fact, the origin of the term 'samurai' is closely linked to a word meaning 'to serve'. Over the centuries, the samurai established a code of conduct that came to be known as *bushidō* (the way of the warrior), drawn from Confucianism, Shintō and Buddhism.

Confucianism required a samurai to show absolute loyalty to his lord. Towards the oppressed, a samurai was expected to show benevolence and exercise justice. Subterfuge was to be despised, as were all commercial and financial transactions. A real samurai had endless endurance and total self-control, spoke only the truth and displayed no emotion. Since his honour was his life, disgrace and shame were to be avoided above all else, and all insults were to be avenged.

From Buddhism, the samurai learnt the lesson that life is impermanent – a handy reason to face death with serenity. Shintō provided the samurai with patriotic beliefs in the divine status both of the emperor and of Japan – the abode of the gods.

Seppuku (ritual suicide), also known as hara-kiri, was a practice to which Japanese Buddhism conveniently turned a blind eye and was an accepted means of avoiding dishonour. Seppuku required the samurai to ritually disembowel himself, watched by an aide, who then drew his own sword and lopped off the samurai's head. One reason for this ritual was the requirement that a samurai should never surrender but always go down fighting. Since surrender was considered a disgrace, prisoners received scant mercy. During WWII this attitude was reflected in the Japanese treatment of prisoners of war – still a source of bitter memories.

In quiet moments, a samurai dressed simply but was easily recognisable by his triangular *eboshi,* a hat made from rigid black cloth.

The samurai's standard battle dress or armour (*yoroi* in Japanese, usually made of leather or maybe lacquered steel) consisted of a breastplate, a similar covering for his back, a steel helmet with a visor, and more body armour for his shoulders and lower body. Samurai weaponry – his pride and joy – included a bow and arrows (in a quiver), swords and a dagger.

Not all samurai were capable of adhering to their code of conduct – samurai indulging in double-crossing or subterfuge, or displaying outright cowardice, were popular themes in Japanese theatre.

Though the samurai are long gone, there are echoes of *bushidō* in the salaryman corporate warriors of today's Japan. Under the once-prevalent lifetime employment system, employees were expected to show complete obedience to their company, and could not question its decisions if, for example, they were transferred to distant Akita-ken.

The salaryman system has greatly changed in the past two decades with growth in part-time employees and corporate restructuring, but you can still see hordes of blue-suited warriors rushing to their duties every morning in train stations. Instead of swords, they wield business cards.

Next time you see a salaryman in his cups, spare a thought for these overworked drivers of the Japanese economy. Like the samurai of old, they are the bedrock of the social order.

From Kyoto's early days, a samurai class in the employ of the *daimyō* (feudal lords) emerged. The relationship was one of absolute service; samurai were sworn to do anything for the sake of their clan and lord, and were always prepared to die (see above). Much of Japan's subsequent history revolved around bloody struggles for power among the *daimyō* while the emperor mostly watched impotently from the sidelines in Kyoto.

The one interruption came when the warlord Minamoto no Yoritomo defeated the ruling Taira clan and established the first shōgunate in Kamakura (southwest of Tokyo) in 1185. Although the emperor remained the nominal ruler in Kyoto, the Minamoto clan ran a *bakufu* (military government) from Kamakura until 1333, when it was toppled by a rebellion and official power reverted to Kyoto.

1185	1457	1467
First shōgunate established at Kamakura under Minamoto no Yoritomo after defeating the ruling Taira clan; the Minamoto and Hōjō clans held power until Emperor Go-Daigo wrested power from the Hōjō in 1333.	*Waka* (31-syllable poem) poet Ōta Dōkan orders construction of first Edo Castle. Developed by shōgun Tokugawa Ieyasu in the 17th century, it became the largest fortress the world has ever seen.	Ōnin civil war devastates Kyoto; aristocrats flee to Ōta Dōkan's stronghold. The conflict begins the Sengoku Jidai, or Warring States period, which lasts to the early 17th century.

Near the mid-15th century, a *waka* (31-syllable poem) poet named Ōta Dōkan constructed the first castle at Edo on the site of an old fortress above Hibiya Cove. By 1467, when the disastrous Ōnin civil war was devastating the capital in Kyoto, many aristocrats and monks had fled the capital to become supplicants in Dōkan's secure eastern hold. This was a foretaste of Edo's explosive growth, but despite Dōkan's contribution to establishing the city, his overlord ordered his assassination.

BATTLE FOR SUPREMACY

By the time Portuguese traders and missionaries arrived in 1543, feudal lords had carved Japan into a patchwork of fiefdoms. One of the most powerful *daimyō*, Oda Nobunaga of the Chūbu region, near present-day Nagoya, was quick to see how the Portuguese could support his ambitious plans. He viewed their Christianity as a potential weapon against the power of the Buddhist clergy and made ample use of the firearms they introduced. By the time he was assassinated in 1581, Oda had united much of central Japan. Toyotomi Hideyoshi took over the job of consolidating power, but looked less favourably on the growing Christian movement, subjecting it to systematic persecution.

Toyotomi's power was briefly contested by Tokugawa Ieyasu, son of a minor lord allied to Oda. After a brief struggle for power, Tokugawa agreed to a truce with Toyotomi; in return, Toyotomi granted him eight provinces in eastern Japan, including all of the Kantō region and Edo. While Toyotomi intended this to weaken Tokugawa by separating him from his ancestral homeland Chūbu, the upstart looked upon the gift as an opportunity to strengthen his power. He set about turning Edo into a real city.

When Toyotomi Hideyoshi died in 1598, power passed to his son, Toyotomi Hideyori. However, Tokugawa Ieyasu had been busily scheming to secure the shōgunate for himself and soon went to war against those loyal to Hideyori. Tokugawa's forces finally defeated Hideyori and his supporters at the legendary Battle of Sekigahara in 1600, moving him into a position of supreme power. He chose Edo as his permanent base and began two-and-a-half centuries of Tokugawa rule.

BOOMTOWN EDO

In securing a lasting peace nationwide and ruling from Edo, Tokugawa Ieyasu laid the foundation for Tokyo's ascendancy as one of the world's great cities. In 1603 the emperor appointed him shōgun (military administrator), and the Tokugawa family ruled from Edo Castle (Edo-jō), on the grounds of the current Imperial Palace. It built up into the largest fortress the world had ever seen, with elaborate rituals shaping the lives of its many courtiers, courtesans, samurai and attendants. Edo would also grow to become the world's largest city, topping one million in the early 1700s and dwarfing much older London and Paris, as people from all over Japan flocked here to serve the growing military class.

This was the result of a canny move by the Tokugawa that ensured their hegemony. They implemented the *sankin kōtai* system of alternate residence. This demanded that all *daimyō* in Japan spend at least one year out of two in Edo. Their wives and children remained in Edo while the *daimyō* returned to their home provinces. This dislocating ransom policy made it difficult for ambitious *daimyō* to usurp the Tokugawas. The high costs of travelling back and forth with a large retinue eroded their financial power as well.

1600	1638	1853
Tokugawa Ieyasu, victor in the Battle of Sekigahara, establishes his capital in Edo, forming a shōgunate and beginning two-and-a-half centuries of peace under Tokugawa rule, known as the Edo period.	*Sakoku* national isolation policy; Japan cuts off all contact with the outside world save limited trade with the Dutch and Chinese off Nagasaki. The policy remains in place until the 1850s.	Black ships of the US navy arrive in Japan under the command of Commodore Matthew Perry, who succeeds in forcing Japan open to US trade at ports of Hakodate and Shimoda.

Society was made rigidly hierarchical, comprising (in descending order of importance) the nobility, who had nominal power; the *daimyō* and their samurai; the farmers; and finally the artisans and merchants. Class dress, living quarters and even manner of speech were all strictly codified, and interclass movement was prohibited.

When Tokugawa Ieyasu died in 1616, his ashes were briefly laid to rest in Chūbu before being moved to Nikkō (p233). Generations of Tokugawas made improvements to the vast Tōshō-gu Shrine dedicated to his memory there, transforming it into one of the grandest in all Japan. A smaller version stands in the large park Ueno-kōen (p77) in Tokyo.

The caste-like society imposed by Tokugawa rule divided Edo into a high city (Yamanote) and a low city (Shitamachi). The higher Yamanote (literally 'hand of the mountains') was home to the *daimyō* and their samurai, while the merchants, craftsmen and lower orders of Edo society were forced into the low-lying Shitamachi (literally 'downtown').

One distinguishing feature of those days was the pleasure quarters, where samurai would come to indulge in activities forbidden in the Yamanote: wine, women and song and not necessarily in that order. The most legendary of these districts was the Yoshiwara, to the northeast of present-day Asakusa.

Otherwise the typical residential neighbourhood of the Shitamachi featured squalid conditions, usually comprising flimsy wooden structures with earthen floors. These shanty towns were often swept by great conflagrations, which locals referred to as *Edo-no-hana*, or flowers of Edo; the expression's bravura sums up the spirit of Shitamachi. Under great privation, Shitamachi subsequently produced a flourishing culture that thumbed its nose at social hardships and the strictures of the shōgunate, patronising both the kabuki theatre and sumō wrestling, and generally enjoying a *joie de vivre* that the dour lords of Edo castle frowned upon. Today, the best glimpses we have into that time come from *ukiyo-e* (wood-block prints; see p35).

Another feature of Edo that has left its mark on today's Tokyo was the division of the city into *machi* (towns) according to profession.

Even today it is possible to stumble across small enclaves that specialise in particular wares. Most famous are Jimbōchō, the bookshop area; Kappabashi, with its plastic food and kitchen supplies; and Akihabara, which now specialises in electronics and manga (comic books), but in the past has been a bicycle retailing area, an area specialising in domestic household goods and a freight yard.

THE 'EASTERN CAPITAL' IS BORN

Edo's transformation from a grand medieval city into a world-class capital required an outside nudge, or *gaiatsu* (external pressure). This came in the form of a fleet of black ships, under the command of US Navy Commodore Matthew Perry, that sailed into Edo-wan (now known as Tokyo Bay) in 1853. Perry's expedition demanded, in the name of US President Millard Fillmore, that Japan open itself to foreign trade after centuries of isolation. Other Western powers were quick to follow in demanding the Japanese open treaty ports. The coming of Westerners heralded a far-reaching social revolution against which the antiquated Tokugawa regime was powerless. In 1867–68, faced with widespread antigovernment feeling and accusations that the regime had failed to prepare Japan for the threat of the West, the last Tokugawa shōgun resigned and power reverted to Emperor Meiji. In 1868 Meiji moved the seat of imperial power

1868	1872	1889
Meiji Restoration; Tokugawa shōgunate loyalists are defeated in civil war. The emperor casts off his figurehead role and assumes a position of supreme authority. Imperial residence moves to Edo, which is renamed Tokyo.	Japan's first train line connects Shimbashi in Tokyo with Yokohama to the southwest, with services between Osaka and Kōbe launched two years later, and Osaka-Kyoto services in 1877.	Constitution of the Empire of Japan promulgated. Based on a Prussian model of constitutional monarchy, the emperor wielded great power but shared it with an elected Diet (parliament).

TOKYO TOMES

- *Edo, the City that Became Tokyo* (2003) by Akira Naito – This beautifully illustrated history begins with primeval Edo, continues on to evil Edo, and concludes with the surrender of Edo Castle to the emperor. There are wonderful maps throughout.
- *Low City, High City* (1983) by Edward Seidensticker – Chronicles the decline of Edo from the 1860s to the 1920s. A follow-up, *Tokyo Rising*, charts the capital's postwar growing pains. *Tokyo Vice: An American Reporter on the Police Beat in Japan* (2009) by Jake Adelstein – A hard-nosed journalist probes Japan's organised crime.
- *Tabloid Tokyo: 101 Tales of Sex, Crime and the Bizarre from Japan's Wild Weeklies* (2005) by Mark Schreiber – This hilarious compilation of translated Japanese tabloid articles exposes the city's sordid underbelly. The sequel is *Tabloid Tokyo 2*.
- *Tokyo: Exploring the City of the Shogun* (2007) by Sumiko Enbutsu – A veteran Tokyo walker presents a delightful series of strolls through historic areas.
- *Tokyo Sights and Insights: Exploring the City's Back Streets* (1992) by Ryosuke Kami – A paean to vanishing neighbourhoods off the tourist path.

from Kyoto to Edo Castle, renaming the city Tokyo (Eastern Capital). This was known as the Meiji Restoration, and signified that power was restored to the emperor, and the imperial and political capitals were once again unified.

The Meiji Restoration was not an entirely peaceful handover of power. In Edo some 2000 Tokugawa loyalists put up a futile last-ditch resistance to the imperial forces in the brief Battle of Ueno. The struggle took place around the beautiful temple Kanei-ji (p78), which, along with Zōjō-ji (p94), was one of Edo's two mortuary temples for the Tokugawa shōgunate.

The word Meiji means 'enlightenment' and Japan's new rulers pushed the nation into a crash course in industrialisation and militarisation. In 1872 the first railroad opened, connecting Tokyo with the new port of Yokohama, south along Tokyo Bay, and by 1889 the country had a Western-style constitution.

In a remarkably short time, Japan achieved military victories over China (1894–95) and Russia (1904–05) and embarked on modern, Western-style empire building, with the annexation of Taiwan (1895), then Korea (1910) and Micronesia (1914).

Nationalists were also busy transforming Shintō into a jingoistic state religion. Seen as a corrupting foreign influence, Buddhism suffered badly – many valuable artefacts and temples were destroyed, and the common people were urged to place their faith in the pure religion of State Shintō.

During the Meiji period, and the following Taishō period, changes that were taking place all over Japan could be seen most prominently in the country's new capital city. Tokyo's rapid industrialisation, uniting around the nascent *zaibatsu* (huge industrial and trading conglomerates), drew job seekers from around Japan, causing the population to grow rapidly. In the 1880s electric lighting was introduced. Western-style brick buildings began to spring up in fashionable areas such as Ginza. In 1904 Mitsukoshi became Japan's first Western-style department store, and its annexe in Nihombashi (1914) was called the grandest building east of the Suez Canal. If the Meiji Restoration sounded the death knell for old Edo, there were two more events to come that were to erase most traces of the old city.

1923	1926	1944–45
Great Kantō Earthquake kills more than 140,000 and razes over half the city's wooden structures. An estimated 300,000 houses are destroyed, but the city's reconstruction plan is only partly realised due to money shortages.	Hirohito ascends the Chrysanthemum Throne to become the Shōwa emperor. Presiding over Japan's military expansion across East Asia and atrocities committed by Japanese forces, he is spared trial by Allied forces after WWII.	US firebombs Tokyo and drops two atomic bombs on Hiroshima and Nagasaki; US occupation begins. The American overlords embark on a successful program of demilitarisation and democratisation.

A CATFISH JUMPS – THE GREAT KANTŌ EARTHQUAKE

Japanese have traditionally believed that a giant catfish living underground causes earthquakes when it stirs. At noon on 1 September 1923 the catfish really jumped – the Great Kantō Earthquake caused unimaginable devastation in Tokyo. More than the quake itself, it was the subsequent fires, lasting some 40 hours, that laid waste to the city, including some 300,000 houses. A quarter of the quake's 142,000 fatalities occurred in one savage firestorm in a clothing depot. (There are some sombre reminders of the earthquake exhibited at the Kantō Earthquake Memorial Museum; see p121).

In true Edo style, reconstruction began almost immediately. The spirit of this rebuilding is perhaps best summed up by author Edward Seidensticker (see the boxed text, opposite): popular wisdom had it that any business which did not resume trading within three days of being burnt out did not have a future. Opportunities were lost in reconstructing the city – streets might have been widened and the capital transformed into something more of a showcase.

THE BEGINNING OF SHŌWA & WWII

From the accession of Emperor Hirohito (*Shōwa tennō* to the Japanese) and the initiation of the Shōwa period in 1926, Japanese society was marked by a quickening tide of nationalist fervour. In 1931 the Japanese invaded Manchuria, and in 1937 embarked on full-scale hostilities with China. By 1940 a tripartite pact with Germany and Italy had been signed and a new order for all of Asia formulated: the Greater East Asia Co-Prosperity Sphere. On 7 December 1941 the Japanese attacked Pearl Harbor, bringing the USA, Japan's principal rival in the Asia-Pacific region, into the war.

Despite initial successes, the war was disastrous for Japan. On 18 April 1942 B-25, bombers carried out the first bombing and strafing raid on Tokyo, with 364 casualties. Much worse was to come. Incendiary bombing commenced in March 1944, notably on the nights of the 9th and 10th, when some two-fifths of the city, mainly in the Shitamachi area, went up in smoke and 70,000 to 80,000 lives were lost. The same raids destroyed Asakusa's Sensō-ji (p83), and later raids destroyed Meiji-jingū (p105). By the time Emperor Hirohito made his famous capitulation address to the Japanese people on 15 August 1945, much of Tokyo had been decimated – sections of it were almost completely depopulated, like the charred remains of Hiroshima and Nagasaki after they were devastated by atomic bombs. Food and daily necessities were scarce, the population was exhausted by the war effort and fears of marauding US military overlords were high.

THE POSTWAR MIRACLE

Tokyo's phoenixlike rise from the ashes of WWII and its emergence as a major global city is something of a miracle. Once again, Tokyoites did not take the devastation as an opportunity to redesign their city (as did Nagoya, for example), but rebuilt where the old had once stood.

During the US occupation in the early postwar years, Tokyo was something of a honky-tonk town. Now-respectable areas such as Yūrakuchō were the haunt of the so-called *pan-pan* girls (prostitutes), and areas such as Ikebukuro and Ueno had thriving black-market zones. The remains of Ueno's black market can be seen in Ameyoko Arcade (p81), which is still a lively market.

1947	1952	1955
New constitution adopted, including Article 9 in which Japan renounces war and the possession of armed forces. Despite this, the SDF is eventually built up into a formidable military arsenal.	US occupation ends; Japan enters a period of high economic growth. The Korean War provides a shot in the arm for Japanese manufacturers, who supply US forces.	Liberal Democratic Party (LDP) founded; it goes on to hold a virtually uninterrupted monopoly on power into the 21st century despite recurring corruption scandals and deep-seated factionalism.

THE BUBBLE: 20 YEARS ON

When asked about the late-1980s bubble economy, some Tokyoites will say you had to wave tens of thousands of yen in the air just to get a taxi in Roppongi. People were paying record sums for golf memberships, ski apartments and European art in those heady days. It's been more than 20 years since the Nikkei 225 index hit a high of 38,916 points in December 1989, but the long hangover after the bubble lingers yet.

Today, as the Nikkei hovers around 10,000, some resort properties are worth only a third of their former value; deflation haunts prices like a pesky ghost. Meanwhile, corporate titans such as Japan Airlines have gone bust, and China is set to overtake Japan as the world's second-largest economy. The 1980s confidence in Japanese companies seems a forgotten dream.

The administration of Prime Minister Yukio Hatoyama is determined to cut wasteful spending and rein in the country's enormous public debt, thought to be about twice the size of GDP. Bureaucrats, once untouchable in their role of channelling money to pet projects, must now justify appropriations.

If there are rays of hope in this, one is that China is a huge new market for Japan. Another is that Japanese are big savers. They have continued to park their earnings in Japan Post Bank savings accounts, which end up funding government bonds. But as more companies shift production to China, industry in Japan is getting hollowed out. And as the population ages amid a low birth rate, more personal savings will be spent on retirement expenses, and less will go to bonds. Hatoyama will certainly need the skill of a magician to solve Japan's intertwined economic woes.

In 1947 Japan adopted its postwar constitution, with the now-famous Article 9, which barred the use of military force in settling international disputes and maintaining a military for warfare (although the nation does maintain a self-defence force).

By 1951, with a boom in Japanese profits arising from the Korean War, Tokyo rebuilt rapidly, especially the central business district, and the subway began to take on its present form. The once-bombed-out city has never looked back from this miraculous economic growth.

During the 1960s and '70s, Tokyo re-emerged as one of the centres of growing Asian nationalism (the first phase was in the 1910s and '20s). Increasing numbers of Asian students came to Tokyo, taking home with them new ideas about Asia's role in the postwar world.

One of Tokyo's proudest moments came when it hosted the 1964 summer Olympics. In preparation the city embarked on a frenzy of construction unequalled in its history. Many Japanese see this time as a turning point in the nation's history, the moment when Japan finally recovered from the devastation of WWII to emerge as a fully fledged member of the modern world economy.

Construction and modernisation continued at a breakneck pace through the '70s, with the interruption of two Middle East oil crises, to reach a peak in the late '80s, when wildly inflated real-estate prices and stock speculation fuelled what is now known as the 'bubble economy'. Based on the price paid for the most expensive real estate at the time, the land value of Tokyo exceeded that of the entire US, and Japanese companies went on a purchasing spree of international icons including Pebble Beach Golf Course, the Rockefeller Center and Columbia Pictures movie studio. When the bubble began to burst in 1989 with the crash of the stock market, the economy went into a protracted slump that was to last more than 20 years.

There were other, more disturbing, troubles in Japanese society. In March 1995 members of the Aum Shinrikyō doomsday cult released sarin nerve gas on crowded Tokyo subways, killing 12 and injuring more than 5000. This, together with the Kōbe earthquake of the same year, signalled the end of Japan's feeling of omnipotence, born of the unlimited successes of the '80s.

1964	1968–69	1972
Tokyo Olympic Games are held, marking Japan's postwar reintegration into the international community and the first time the Games are hosted by a non-Western country.	Tokyo University students take over administrative buildings to protest the Vietnam War. No one is allowed to graduate in the 1969 academic year and entrance examinations are cancelled.	Okinawa, captured and held by US forces in WWII, is returned to Japan. High concentration of US military bases on the islands has angered locals ever since.

CITY OF THE FUTURE

Tokyo has weathered a long hangover since the heady days of the bubble economy. The doldrums have finally given way to lacklustre growth and unemployment that flirts with record 5% highs, but the government maintains the economy is still on a recovery path.

The declining birth rate and population pose major problems for Tokyo and Japan – the birth rate for the capital is below 1% (even lower than the national average of 1.24%), while Japan's elderly continue to make up an ever-larger share of the population. Nobody really knows how the system will manage to support the 30% of the population that is projected to be over the age of 65 in the next 25 years. The workforce is shrinking, but there are few signs that Japan is ready to embrace Western-style immigration, recently making all foreign visitors to the country subject to fingerprinting and facial photography upon entry as part of its security policy.

The government may fear deception and fraud, but domestic headlines are rife with corporate malfeasance scandals, from revelations that buildings in Tokyo have been constructed with forged quake-resistance data to news that Japanese paper companies have been passing off unused paper as recycled material.

Japan is also struggling with its international role, particularly the leeway allowed by its 'Peace Constitution'; former Prime Minister Koizumi Junichirō's decision to deploy Self-Defense Force (SDF) troops to aid allies in the war in Iraq was met with massive protests. The Defense Agency was promoted to a fully fledged ministry and Japanese military cooperation with the US has escalated.

Japan's international image has suffered due to its so-called 'scientific' whaling program and a perceived lack of repentance over its wartime atrocities. The government has turned to Japanese pop culture products such as anime (animated film) and manga as a foreign policy tool in the hopes that popular cartoon heroes will convince people to embrace 'cool Japan'.

A GRAND OLD LADY GETS A MAKEOVER

If you pass through Tokyo Station before 2013, it will be undergoing a historic transformation. The capital's titulary train hub has pride of place before the Imperial Palace and the prestigious Marunouchi business district, and is also the city's main intercity rail link. Designed by Tatsuno Kingo and built in 1914, it survived the 1923 Great Kanto Earthquake, WWII bombing, and a postwar fire. It was also the site of a political assassination and the launch of the first *shinkansen* bullet train. Meanwhile, it has handled 1.75 million passengers a day in recent years. Tokyo Station is finally getting the facelift it deserves – just in time for its centenary.

For one, the elegant red brick building on the Marunouchi side, originally three stories tall until it was bombed in 1945, will be restored to its former height and glory with its rooftop domes rebuilt. It will house the Tokyo Station Hotel, which will be expanded and reopened as the premiere JR Group hotel. Within the ticket gates, the Ekinaka GranSta shopping complex will connect the Marunouchi and Yaesu sides of the station. The whole structure be made quake resistant.

To give Tokyo Station a 21st-century backdrop, skyscrapers housing shopping, dining and office space will stand on the ends of the Shinkansen areas and Yaesu side. The GranTokyo North and South towers, 43 and 42 stories respectively, will be linked by the 240m-long, sail-like GranRoof pedestrian deck, due to be completed in spring 2013. The Sapia Tower near the Nihonbashi exit will house another hotel, offices and university campuses.

The entire nine-year, ¥200 billion redevelopment project is akin to building a city within a city, and, naturally, it's been named Tokyo Station City. Goto Shinpei, a railway bureaucrat who a century ago called for a station design that would 'surprise the rest of the world,' would surely be proud.

1989	1995	2009
Death of Emperor Hirohito; Heisei era begins as Hirohito's son Akihito ascends the Chrysanthemum Throne; stock market decline begins, initiating a decade-long economic slump in Japan.	Doomsday cult Aum Shinrikyō releases sarin gas on the Tokyo subway, killing 12 and injuring more than 5000. Guru Shōkō Asahara is sentenced to death for Aum-related crimes in 2004.	LDP loses control of the House of Representatives to the opposition Democratic Party of Japan (DPJ), ending the LDP's virtually unbroken rule of Japan since 1955.

CRISIS AVERTED – FOR NOW

On 6 September 2006 Japan exhaled a long-held breath – news had just broken that a future emperor was born. Tipping the scales at 2.56kg, Prince Hisahito, son of Prince and Princess Akishino, was the first male child born into the moribund imperial family in more than four decades, averting a crisis of succession to the Chrysanthemum Throne.

Japanese had been debating a change to the 1947 Imperial Household Law to allow females to ascend the throne since reigning emperor Akihito's eldest son, Crown Prince Naruhito, has had no male children. The amendment might have made his young daughter, Princess Aiko, the first reigning empress since Empress Go-Sakuramachi in the 18th century; the succession laws were modified in the 19th century so that only men could be emperor.

Following Prince Hisahito's birth, a government bill to change the 1947 law was dropped, and the debate, which even included proposals to have concubines for imperial princes, was quietly shelved. Currently third in line for the throne, the baby prince will eventually face tremendous pressure from the arch-conservative Imperial Household Agency to produce a male heir and maintain the world's oldest continuous hereditary monarchy. But if, like most men in the imperial family, he only has daughters or no children at all, it will be déjà vu.

Meanwhile, mainstays of Japanese society have buckled under social and economic pressures. The conservative Liberal Democratic Party (LDP) lost its 54-year lock on political power in late 2009 to the opposition Democratic Party of Japan (DPJ), which elected Yukio Hatoyama prime minister. The LDP had only been out of power once since 1955 – an 11-month period in 1993–94 – so the change shocked many Japanese. In the business world Japan Airlines, Asia's largest carrier, filed for bankruptcy in early 2010 with ¥2.3 trillion in liabilities, a spectacular failure due to bloated management and the hangover from reckless spending during the bubble economy.

Little of this phases Tokyo, however it has continued to build new subway lines and redevelopment districts as well as a massive renovation of Tokyo Station (see the boxed text, p29) and the surrounding Marunouchi area. With that old Edo pluck, Tokyoites shrugged off losing their bid for the 2016 Olympics to Rio de Janeiro. The capital is now trying to lure more visitors while carving out a new role for itself as a centre of anime, manga, video games and other globally hot media.

ARTS

Tokyo's density has a sheer visual quality that sometimes makes it seem like a lurid anime or video-game backdrop. In its better moments it may resemble an *ukiyo-e*, such as when snow blanches the roof of Sensō-ji in Asakusa. That's when it's easy to see where the Japanese of old found inspiration in producing the wealth of traditional arts that Tokyo has helped foster. But the aesthetics of the built environment can also take the form of something as simple as the adorable, expressive graphics in advertisements or the way a department store clerk wraps a package.

If it's art with a capital A you're after, Tokyo is experiencing a renaissance. You'll find it in the large museums, in matchbox-sized galleries, decorating the streets, at train stations and convention halls, on hulking stages and in tiny underground theatres in quiet neighbourhoods, and a lot of it is really good.

CONTEMPORARY ARTS

Visual Arts

Tokyo has one of the world's most vibrant contemporary art scenes and dozens of galleries throughout the city at which to view it.

The opening of the Mori Art Museum in 2003 was something of a watershed for the contemporary arts. More than a dozen excellent art galleries are consolidated in buildings such as Complex in Roppongi (p90) and near the eastern bank of Sumida-gawa (p121). It's fair to say that the city's contemporary aesthetic heartbeat has never been heard more clearly.

Artists to look for include Miyajima Tatsuo, whose sculptures and installation pieces incorporate numeric LCD displays; Sugimoto Hiroshi, famous for his time-transcending photos (eg exposing the film to a movie screen while the entire movie runs); and Nara Yoshitomo and Murakami Takashi, both heavily influenced by manga (p70). The signature style of Kusama Yayoi is motifs of dots and nets, which make their way onto hanging art, sculptures and even clothing. Ishiuchi Miyako appeared in the Japan pavilion at the 2005 Venice Biennale, with her collection *Mother* exploring artefacts of her own mother's turbulent life in penetrating photographs. In 2009, the biennale honoured Yoko Ono for lifetime achievements in pioneering performance and conceptual art, citing such works as Cut Piece, a 1964 performance in which she asked audience members to cut pieces of her clothes off.

top picks

CONTEMPORARY ART VENUES

- National Art Center, Tokyo (p93)
- Kokuritsu Kindai Bijutsukan (National Museum of Modern Art; p51)
- Mori Art Museum (p91)
- Museum of Contemporary Art, Tokyo (p123)

Music

Tokyo has a huge, shape-shifting music scene supported by a local market of audiophiles willing to try almost anything. International artists make a point of swinging through on global tours, and the local scene surfaces every night in one of the city's thousands of 'live houses'.

Western classical music (p198) is performed by several outstanding local orchestras, such as the NHK Symphony Orchestra and the Tokyo Philharmonic Orchestra, and by visiting ensembles. Opera (p198) too has come to stay. Notable companies include the Fujiwara Opera, which specialises in French and Italian operas, and the Nikkai Opera, which mounts performances of Mozart and Wagner.

The jazz scene is enormous (see p197), as are the followings for rock, house, electronica and Latin jazz.

Mainstream music is dominated by the commercial J-Pop. Some of the biggest acts are young *aidoru* (idol) singers who owe their popularity to cute looks and a flood of media appearances. The all-girl group Morning Musume was a standard that many manufactured bands have copied, keeping things fresh by regularly 'graduating' some of its dozen-or-so members and holding auditions for new ones. The boy-band equivalent is SMAP, which has prospered since 1991 with about half as many members. Other current top J-Pop artists include part-Trinidadian singer Thelma Aoyama, the Korean-born Boa, Hamasaki Ayumi and long-time favourite Southern All Stars. Japanese bands also follow Western music trends such as hip hop and rap.

Tokyo is famous for its cutting-edge club-music scene. DJs here are numerous; some of the biggest names are Towa Tei, Satoshi Tomie, DJ Krush and DJ Kentaro.

Enka is a musical style popular among older generations but its nostalgic charm occasionally attracts younger audiences, too. Its lyrics and emotions emphasise themes of longing and tears, and musically it's usually languidly paced and in a musical scale that borrows from traditional Japanese music.

Tokyo is also one of the only cities in Asia where you may have the luxury of seeing up-and-coming performers playing in intimate venues. See p189 for more on where to go to check out the wide variety of music on offer.

And no discussion of the Tokyo music scene can be complete without a mention of karaoke. Karaoke started in Japan in 1971 and remains wildly popular, as a walk down just about any alley at night will evidence. Go with a group and you'll almost certainly be expected to perform; see p188. Most karaoke bars and karaoke boxes (private rooms with karaoke equipment) have at least a few English songs.

Commercial Theatre

Commercial theatre in Tokyo encompasses classical and contemporary dramas and musicals, both home-grown and imported, staged by large entertainment companies and starring well-known actors, singers and other celebrities. If you're struck by a sudden hankering for a Royal Shakespeare Company production of *Romeo and Juliet* or a Japanese-language performance of the *Phantom of the Opera* you might just be in luck.

Popular but quirky, the all-female Takarazuka troupe offers a musical experience that is unlike any other. Founded in 1913, partly as an inversion of the all-male kabuki theatre and partly as a form of entertainment for a growing male middle class with money to burn, Takarazuka combines traditional Japanese elements with Western musical styles. Interestingly, in light of its history, its most devoted admirers now comprise young women who swoon with romantic abandon over the troupe's beautiful drag kings. Takarazuka adopted its present revue format in the late 1920s, and except for the WWII years – during which the troupe proved an ideal propaganda tool – has continued to perform musicals and revues set in exotic locations.

Underground Theatre

Theatre the world over spent the 1960s redefining itself, and it was no different in Tokyo. The *shogekijō* (small theatre) movement, also called *angura* (underground), has given Japan many of its leading playwrights, directors and actors. Like their counterparts in the West, these productions took place in any space available – in small theatres, tents, basements, open spaces and on street corners.

Today's *shogekijō* takes on realistic themes, such as modern Japanese history, war and environmental degradation. Socially and politically critical dramas (such as those by Kaneshita Tatsuo and Sakate Yōji), psychological dramas (eg those by Iwamatsu Ryō, Suzue Toshirō and Hirata Oriza) and satirical portrayals of modern society (eg those by Nagai Ai and Makino Nozomi) have come to the fore and even attracted attention overseas.

Venues include the Suzunari Theatre outside the city centre in Shimokitazawa, and Die Pratze, near Kagurazaka Station in Tokyo. And there always seems to be at least one troupe performing English-language theatre. See p195 for listings.

Butō

In many ways, *butō* (contemporary dance) is Japan's most exciting dance form. It is also the newest, dating only from 1959, when Hijikata Tatsumi (1928–86) gave the first *butō* performance. *Butō* was born out of a rejection of the excessive formalisation that characterises traditional forms of Japanese dance and of an intention to return to the ancient roots of the Japanese soul.

Butō performances are best likened to performance art rather than traditional dance. During a performance, one or more dancers use their naked or seminaked bodies to express the most elemental and intense human emotions. Nothing is forbidden in *butō* and performances often deal with taboo topics such as sexuality and death. For this reason, critics often describe *butō* as scandalous, and *butō* dancers delight in pushing the boundaries of what can be considered tasteful in artistic performance.

Cinema

Japan boasts a vibrant, proud, critically acclaimed cinematic tradition. Renewed international attention since the mid-1990s has reinforced interest in domestic films, which account for an estimated 40% of box-office receipts – nearly double the level of most European countries. This includes not only artistically important works, but also films in the science-fiction, horror and 'monster-stomps-Tokyo' genres for which Japan is also known.

The golden age of Japanese cinema began with Kurosawa Akira's film *Rashōmon,* which won both the Golden Lion at the 1951 Venice International Film Festival and an Oscar for best foreign film.

The increasing realism and high artistic standards of the period are evident in such milestone films as *Tōkyō Monogatari* (Tokyo Story; 1953), by the legendary Ōzu Yasujirō; Mizoguchi Kenji's classics *Ugetsu Monogatari* (Tales of Ugetsu; 1953) and *Saikaku Ichidai Onna* (The Life of Oharu; 1952); and Kurosawa's 1954 masterpiece *Shichinin no Samurai* (The Seven Samurai), which was later remade into the classic Western movie *The Magnificent Seven.*

The 1960s gave the world such landmarks as Ichikawa Kon's *Chushingura* (47 Samurai; 1962), based on the Akō incident, and Kurosawa's *Yōjimbo* (1961).

TOKYO ON FILM

- *Tokyo Story (Tōkyō Monogatari;* 1953) – Ōzu Yasujirō's story of an older couple who come to Tokyo to visit their children only to find themselves treated with disrespect and indifference.
- *Godzilla (Gojira;* 1954) – It's become almost a cliché, but watch it again and you'll find a powerful metaphor in this city that spent the first half of the 20th century being beaten down and getting right back up again.
- *The Bad Sleep Well (Warui Yatsu Hodo Yoku Nemuru;* 1960) – Kurosawa Akira's first film after breaking from Toho studios centres on a protagonist who marries the boss's daughter as part of an intricate plan to avenge his father's death.
- *Tokyo Pop* (1988) – Fran Rubel Kuzui's breezy comedy about a lonely American songstress who finds redemption, fame and love in the here-today-gone-tomorrow world of J-pop.
- *Shall We Dance?* (1997) – A bored salaryman risks it all to learn the low-brow art of ballroom dancing. Footage includes some wistful shots of Tokyo at night.
- *Lost in Translation* (2003) – Tokyo takes on a muted gleam in Sofia Coppola's Oscar winner about two guests at the Park Hyatt, sharing a moment away from loveless marriages. Bill Murray is in finest deadpan form, and the movie made Scarlett Johansson a star.
- *Tokyo Godfathers* (2003) – Kon Satoshi's animated film uses a group of homeless men to explore the city's postbubble underside. They come across a baby and don't quite know what's hit them.
- *Nobody Knows (Dare mo Shiranai;* 2004) – Koreeda Hirokazu's slow and depressing, but somehow life-affirming, tale of four children forced to fend for themselves after their heinous mother abandons them. Based on true events.
- *Kamikaze Girls (Shimotsuma Monogatari;* 2004) – One of the daffiest buddy movies ever made, and the only one we know that pairs a country girl obsessed with Lolita outfits from Tokyo boutiques with a biker chick who spits to punctuate her sentences.
- *Train Main (Densha Otoko;* 2005) – After a shy *otaku* (supergeek) falls for a woman he defended from a drunkard, he turns to online pals for help with his feelings of love. This hit from director Masanori Murakami helped put *otaku* and Akihabara culture on the map.
- *Tokyo!* (2008) – This surrealistic romp by foreign directors Michel Gondry, Leos Carax and Bong Joon-ho is actually three stories, taking in sewer-dwellers, shut-ins and the challenge of finding good housing.

BACKGROUND ARTS

Up against TV and, later, video, cinema attendance in Japan declined through the 1980s, yet Japanese film-makers continued to set standards: Kurosawa garnered acclaim worldwide for *Kagemusha* (The Shadow Warrior; 1980), which shared the Palme d'Or at Cannes, and *Ran* (1985). Imamura Shōhei's heartrending *Narayama Bushiko* (The Ballad of Narayama) won the Grand Prix at Cannes in 1983. Itami Jūzō became perhaps the most widely known Japanese director outside Japan after Kurosawa with such biting satires as *Osōshiki* (The Funeral; 1985), *Tampopo* (1986) and *Marusa no Onna* (A Taxing Woman; 1988). Ōshima Nagisa scored critical success with *Senjo no Merry Christmas* (Merry Christmas Mr Lawrence) in 1983.

In the 1990s Japanese directors received top honours at two of the world's most prestigious film festivals: *Unagi* (Eel; 1997), Imamura Shōhei's black-humoured look at human nature's dark side won the Palme d'Or in Cannes and 'Beat' Takeshi Kitano took the Golden Lion in Venice for *Hana-bi* (Fireworks; 1997), a tale of life and death, and the violence and honour that links them. The undisputed king of current Japanese cinema, 'Beat' Takeshi is a true renaissance man of the media; he stars in and directs his films, and is an author, poet and frequent TV personality.

These days, a new generation of directors is emerging: Izuru Kumasaka, whose *Asyl-Park and Love Hotel* won Best First Feature at the 2008 Berlin Film Festival; Koreeda Hirokazu with *Dare mo Shiranai* (Nobody Knows; 2004), winner of the Best Actor prize at the Cannes Film Festival for its young star Yagira Yūya; and Kurosawa Kiyoshi with *Cure*.

Naturally, the world's blockbusters also screen widely in Tokyo. See opposite for cinemas.

Fiction

Most of Japan's national literature since the Edo period has been penned by authors who have written about or spent most of their lives in Tokyo. From Sōseki Natsume to Mishima Yukio to Murakami Haruki, the literature written in and about the metropolis has served as the

TOKYO FICTION

- *I Am a Cat* (1905–06) by Sōseki Natsume – Sōseki's best known for *Kokoro,* but this merciless turn-of-the-century narrative, told from the point of view of a cat, is way more fun.
- *Snow Country* (1948) by Kawabata Yasunari – Written in the years just before WWII, this novel by one of Japan's two Nobel Laureates tells the tale of a Tokyo dilettante's cruel, tragic affair with a mountain geisha.
- *The Sailor Who Fell from Grace with the Sea* (1963), and *After the Banquet* (1960) by Mishima Yukio – If you're looking for unsettling beauty, reach for the former. History buffs will want the latter tome, which was at the centre of a court case that became Japan's first privacy lawsuit.
- *A Personal Matter* (1964) by Ōe Kenzaburo – A 27-year-old school teacher's child is born brain-damaged. His life claustrophobic, his marriage failing, he dreams of escaping to Africa while planning the murder of his son.
- *Coin Locker Babies* (1980) by Murakami Ryu – A coming-of-age tale centred on the lives of Kiku and Hashi, two boys left to die in coin lockers by their mothers. Both survive. The latter part of the book follows Hashi through Toxictown, a futuristic danger zone. This is Murakami at his most poetic.
- *Norwegian Wood* (1987) by Murakami Haruki – Set in the late 1960s against the backdrop of student protests, *Norwegian Wood* is both the portrait of a young artist and an ode to first loves.
- *Kitchen* (1988) by Yoshimoto Banana – Yoshimoto gets a bad rap as a lightweight writer. It's true, *Kitchen* relentlessly chronicles Tokyo's fast-food menus and '80's pop culture, though underlying the superficial digressions are hints at a darker, deeper world of death, loss and loneliness.
- *Idoru* (1997) by William Gibson – This novel paints Tokyo's dark postearthquake future, after the grim reconstruction made possible by ominous nanotechnology. Shinjuku looms large, as does megawatt Akihabara.
- *Out* (1998) by Kirino Natsuo – A gritty thriller about downtrodden female employees of a *bentō* (boxed-lunch) factory who become a band of murderesses. Winner of Japan's grand prize for crime fiction.
- *Snakes and Earrings* (2003) by Kanehara Hitomi – This Akutagawa Prize–winner traces the downward spiral of a woman spellbound by a mysterious tattoo artist.
- *1Q84 (2009–10)* by Murakami Haruki – A nod to Orwell, this serialised tale about an assassin who finds herself in an alternate-reality Shibuya quickly became the top-selling book in Japan.

playground of the national imagination. Not surprisingly both of Japan's Nobel Laureates, Kawabata Yasunari and Ōe Kenzaburo, spent the bulk of their writing lives in Tokyo (Ōe eventually left to escape the Japanese press).

And the trend continues as a new generation of Tokyo writers takes the stage. In April 2004 the Akutagawa Prize – one of the nation's most prestigious – was awarded to the two youngest Japanese writers to have ever received it, both of them women: 19-year-old Kanehara Hitomi and Wataya Risa, aged 20. The previous youngest winners included Ōe Kenzaburo and current Tokyo governor Ishihara Shintarō, who were both 23 when they won. But in recent years, foreigners such as Iranian Shirin Nezammafi have been nominated. Chinese novelist Yang Yi became the first non-native Japanese speaker to take home the Bungakukai Shinjinsho, or new author's prize, in 2008.

Poetry

While Japanese traditional poetry, such as the 17-syllable haiku or the 31-syllable *waka,* is most closely associated with the ancient capital of Kyoto, it has a history in Tokyo as well. Japan's most famous poet of all time, Matsuo Bashō, led a literary society here and began his journey to write his renowned work *Oku no Hosomichi* on the banks of the Sumida-gawa. Today it's not uncommon to see large busloads of retirees setting off on haiku composition trips, often to inspired locations such as the stops on Bashō's journey through northern Japan. Haiku remains extremely popular and its five-seven-five syllable structure is also used in the media to construct ad slogans.

Contemporary poetry in Tokyo is alive and well and read mostly by the dedicated. One exception to this trend is Tanikawa Shuntarō *(Map of Days, Naked),* whose inspired verse has earned him not only a loyal following, but interviews in fashion and pop culture magazines. Also of note is Shiraishi Kazuko *(Let Those Who Appear),* whose rowdy, lyrical poetry has earned her comparisons to American Beat poet Allen Ginsberg.

TRADITIONAL ARTS

You don't have to visit a museum to see old art forms in Tokyo. From kabuki-attired pitchmen in TV ads to lacquered mousepads to *sensu* (folding fans) emblazoned with corporate logos, traditional arts and crafts are everywhere in the capital, and are subject to continuous innovation.

top picks

TRADITIONAL ART VENUES

- Bijutsukan Kōgeikan (Crafts Gallery; p51)
- Musée Tomo (p94)
- Tokyo Kokuritsu Hakubutsukan (Tokyo National Museum; p78)
- Ukiyo-e Ōta Memorial Art Museum (p107)

Painting

From AD 794 to 1600, Japanese painting borrowed from Chinese and Western techniques and media, ultimately transforming these towards its own aesthetic end. By the beginning of the Edo period (1600–1868), which was marked by a wide range of painting styles attracting enthusiastic patronage, Japanese art had come completely into its own. The Kanō school, initiated more than a century before the beginning of the Edo period, continued to be in demand for its depiction of subjects connected with Confucianism, mythical Chinese creatures or scenes from nature. The Tosa school, which followed the *yamato-e* (Japanese world) style of painting (often used on scrolls during the Heian period from 794–1185), received commissions from nobility eager for scenes from ancient classics of Japanese literature.

Finally, the Rimpa school (beginning from around 1600) absorbed the earlier styles of painting and progressed beyond conventions to produce a strikingly decorative and delicately shaded form of painting. The works produced by a trio of outstanding artists from this school – Tawaraya Sōtatsu, Hon'ami Kōetsu and Ogata Kōrin – rank among the finest from this period.

Wood-block Prints

Far from the Chinese-inspired landscapes and religious-themed paintings, *ukiyo-e* (literally 'pictures of the floating world') were for the common people, used in advertising or in much the same way posters are used today. The subjects of these wood-block prints were images of everyday life, characters in kabuki plays (p37) and scenes from the 'floating world', a term derived from a Buddhist metaphor for life's fleeting joys.

Edo's particular floating world revolved around pleasure districts such as the Yoshiwara. In this topsy-turvy kingdom, an inversion of the usual social hierarchies imposed by the Tokugawa shōgunate, money meant more than rank, actors and artists were the arbiters of style, and prostitutes elevated their art to such a level that their accomplishments matched those of the women of noble families.

The vivid colours, novel composition and flowing lines of *ukiyo-e* caused great excitement when they finally arrived in the West; the French came to dub it 'Japonisme'. *Ukiyo-e* was a key influence on Impressionists and post-Impressionists (eg Toulouse-Lautrec, Manet and Degas). Yet among the Japanese, the prints were hardly given more than passing consideration – millions were produced annually in Edo, often thrown away or used as wrapping paper for pottery. For many years, the Japanese continued to be perplexed by the keen interest foreigners took in this art form.

The compact but exceptional Ukiyo-e Ota Memorial Art Museum (p107) has rotating exhibitions, while the Edo-Tokyo Museum (p121) has a section describing *ukiyo-e* and how they were made.

Ceramics

Japan has one of the world's great ceramic traditions, from early Jōmon earthenware to the humble aesthetic of the tea ceremony and brightly coloured vessels sold overseas for big prices. Tokyo is not a significant centre for ceramic making, but has some great venues to learn about ceramic styles and their appreciation.

Various museums around town host ceramics exhibitions – Tokyo Kokuritsu Hakubutsukan (Tokyo National Museum; p78) is a particularly good example. Department-store art galleries are also good places to catch a show. The remarkable online gallery www.e-yakimono.net has all the information you need about ceramic styles and appreciation.

BACKGROUND ARTS

Folk Crafts

The *mingei* (folk crafts) movement was launched in the early 20th century as an attempt to counter desire for cheap mass-produced goods and promote the works of ordinary craftspeople instead. Central to the *mingei* philosophy is *yo no bi* (beauty through use), where everyday objects should bring pleasure through their aesthetics, touch and ease of use.

Mingei movement leaders included potters Hamada Shoji (1894–1978) and Kawai Kanjirō (1890–1966), the eccentric genius potter and painter Munakata Shikō (1903–75), Serizawa Keisuke (1895–1984) for his amazing textiles and the British-born potter Bernard Leach (1887–1979).

To see some *mingei* works, visit the Crafts Gallery (p51) of Kokuritsu Kindai Bijutsukan (National Museum of Modern Art).

Ikebana

Key differences between ikebana (flower arranging) and Western forms of flower arranging are the illusion of space, the interplay between the flowers and the vessels or baskets used to display them, and the sense of balance created when a flower is placed just so. The popularity of ikebana is evident in the eye-pleasing creations in the city's shop windows and the *tokonoma* (sacred alcoves) of its private residences. Bamboo baskets, remarkable for their complexity and delicacy, are popular for use in ikebana.

See p207 for information about ikebana classes.

Tea Ceremony

First things first: the tea ceremony is not about drinking tea (well, only a little). As much a philosophy as an art, *sadō* (the way of tea), combines a host of related arts and crafts: ceramics, kimono, calligraphy, ikebana, food, traditional architecture and garden design.

Originally the pastime of samurai and Zen priests, *sadō* placed great emphasis on the aesthetic qualities of simplicity and naturalness, which together with humility create a spirit called *wabi-sabi*. Tea-master Sen no Rikyū codified the practice in the Momoyama period. Today a proper tea ceremony takes place in a tea room of 4½ tatami mats. Seasonal ikebana and scroll paintings, the selection of ceramics and utensils used in the preparation and serving of the tea, the sweets accompanying the tea, and the design of the adjoining garden should all unite to create an 'only-in-this-moment' experience.

Opportunities to participate in a full tea ceremony are exceedingly rare anywhere in Japan; if you are invited, *accept* (but not so eagerly as to show immodesty). Otherwise, many places around town offer the same sort of whisked green tea *(matcha)* with a sweet in far less formal settings. The teahouse at Hama Rikyū Onshi-teien (p65) is particularly lovely, located in the centre of a pond. Inquire at shrines, temples and smaller museums for other options.

Nō

Nō originated from the combination of indigenous Shintō-related dance and mime traditions, and dance forms that originated elsewhere in Asia, and it really came to the fore in Kyoto between 1350 and 1450. Rather than a drama in the usual sense, a *nō* (dance-drama) seeks to express a poetic moment by symbolic and almost abstract means: glorious movements, grand and exaggerated costumes and hairstyles, sonorous chorus and music, and subtle expression. Actors frequently wear masks while they perform before a spare, unchanging set, which features a painting of a large pine tree.

Most *nō* plays centre around two principal characters: the *shite,* who is sometimes a living person but more often a demon or a ghost whose soul cannot rest; and the *waki,* who leads the main character towards the play's climactic moment. The elegant language used is that of the court of the 14th century.

Some visitors find *nō* rapturous and captivating; others (including many Japanese) find its subtlety all too subtle. If you are going to take in a *nō* performance, familiarise yourself with the story and characters beforehand. If all else fails, the intermissions of *nō* performances are punctuated by *kyōgen* (short, lively comic farces).

For performance information, see p194.

Kabuki

If *nō* has a history of catering to the elites, with themes of the afterlife and classical Japanese legend, kabuki originated as art for the common people, with dialogue, lively music, breathtaking costumes, an absence of masks, casts of dozens and stagecraft that was – and remains – unique in the world of theatre.

Although kabuki is most closely associated with Edo, it began in Kyoto around 1600 when a charismatic shrine priestess called Okuni and her troupe started entertaining crowds with a new type of dance people dubbed 'kabuki', a slang expression that meant 'cool' or 'in vogue'.

Okuni's dancers were not above prostituting their talents and when fights for the ladies' affections became a bit too frequent, order-obsessed Tokugawa officials declared the entertainment a threat to public morality. Women's kabuki was banned and troupes of adolescent men took over the female roles, a development that only fed the flames of samurai ardour. Finally, in 1653, the authorities mandated that only adult men with shorn forelocks could perform kabuki, which gave rise to one of kabuki's most fascinating and artistic elements, the *onnagata* (an actor who specialises in portraying women).

Over several centuries, kabuki has developed a repertoire of popular themes, such as famous historical accounts and stories of love-suicide, while also borrowing copiously from *nō* (opposite), *kyōgen* and bunraku (below). Many kabuki plays border on melodrama, while others vary from stories of bravery to elaborate dance pieces.

Unlike Western theatre, kabuki is actor-centred. Kabuki actors are born to the art form – the leading families of modern kabuki go back many generations – and training begins in childhood. Sons often follow their fathers into the *yago* (kabuki acting house) to train in order to perpetuate an ancestor's name on stage. Thus the generations of certain families (eg Bando and Ichikawa) run into the double digits. The Japanese audience takes great interest in watching how different generations of one family perform the same part. Actors today enjoy great social prestige, and their activities on and off the stage attract as much interest as those of film and TV stars.

Ingenious features of kabuki include the revolving stage (a kabuki invention), the *hanamichi* (a raised walkway connecting the stage to the back of the theatre, which is used for dramatic entrances and exits), *koken* (on-stage assistants) and *hikinuki* (on-stage costume changes).

Another unique aspect of kabuki is the *kakegoe*, enthusiastic fans who shout out the name of the *yago* of their favourite actors at pivotal moments such as well-known lines of dialogue or poses called *mie*. Actors note they miss this reinforcement when performing overseas (but don't try it yourself!). While Ginza's Kabuki-za theatre is being rebuilt throughout 2013, the Shinbashi Embujō (p194) will be the premiere Kabuki theatre spot in Tokyo.

Puppet Theatre

Japan's traditional puppet theatre developed at the same time as kabuki, when the *shamisen* (a three-stringed lute), imported from Okinawa, was combined with traditional puppetry techniques and *jōruri* (narrative chanting). Bunraku, as it came to be known in the 19th century, addresses many of the same themes as kabuki, and in fact many of the most famous plays in the kabuki repertoire were originally written for the puppet theatre. Bunraku involves large puppets – nearly two-thirds life size – manipulated by up to three black-robed puppeteers. The puppeteers do not speak; a seated narrator tells the story and provides the voices of the characters, expressing their feelings with smiles, weeping and starts of surprise and fear. Although bunraku is most closely associated with Osaka, the best place to see it in Tokyo is the New National Theatre (Shin Kokuritsu Gekijō; p198).

Rakugo

A traditional Japanese style of comic monologue, *rakugo* (literally 'dropped word') dates back to the Edo period. The performer, usually in kimono, sits on a square cushion on a stage. Props are limited to a fan and hand towel. The monologue begins with a *makura* (prologue), which is followed by the story itself and, finally, the *ochi* (punch line, or 'drop', which is another pronunciation of the Chinese character for *raku* in *rakugo*). Many of the monologues in the traditional *rakugo* repertoire date back to the Edo and Meiji periods, and while well known, reflect a social milieu unknown to modern listeners. Accordingly, many practitioners today also write new monologues addressing issues relevant to contemporary life.

ARCHITECTURE

Tokyo's awesome built environment looks part Legoland, part sci-fi video-game backdrop, part heaving neon anarchy. Disasters and lax planning laws have obliterated most heritage buildings and modern ones are scrapped and rebuilt every 20 years or so, giving the cityscape an inspired heterogeneous character similar to an immense Escher print. Unlike Kyoto, laid out under grid-based Chinese geomancy principles, the city of Tokyo evolved concentrically around Edo Castle, and its medieval design has a strong labyrinthine dimension; several excellent English-language books explore these themes (see p26). The resulting cityscape is a fantastic mishmash of impermanent structures grafted onto ancient patterns, so old and new are always right before your eyes.

FOREIGN INFLUENCES

Until the end of the Edo period, the city's houses and shops were almost entirely constructed of wood, paper and tile, and early photos show a remarkable visual harmony in the old skyline. Japan first opened its doors to Western architecture with the Meiji Restoration (1868). Japanese architects immediately responded to these new influences, but some 20 years later, a nationalistic push against the influence of the West saw a resurgence in the popularity of traditional Japanese building styles.

This ambivalence towards Western architecture continued until after WWI, when foreign architects, such as Frank Lloyd Wright, came to build the Imperial Hotel in Tokyo (since demolished for safety reasons, although the facade can be seen at Meiji Mura, a culture-history park near Nagoya, two hours from Tokyo on the bullet train). Wright introduced the International Style, characterised by sleek lines, cubic forms and materials such as glass, steel and brick. Other pre-WWII monoliths still stand in Marunouchi and Yūrakuchō opposite the east side of Hibiya Park; American bombers spared them and they were used for postwar command facilities.

After WWII the aggressively sculptural stone and concrete work of French architect Le Corbusier exerted strong influence on Japanese architects, and by the mid-1960s Japanese architects were beginning to attract attention on the world stage for their unique style.

EARLY STYLE ICONS

The best known of Japan's 20th-century builders was Tange Kenzō (1913–2005). The mixing of Le Corbusier and traditional Japanese forms can be seen in Tange's buildings, including the National Gymnasium (1964; p107) in Yoyogi-kōen, Hanae Mori Building (p132) and Sōgetsu Kaikan (1977; p89). His skyscraping Tokyo Metropolitan Government Offices (1991; p109) was modelled after the great European cathedrals – look up from the plaza below and see if it doesn't remind you of Notre Dame in Paris. Also look out for the Fuji TV Headquarters (1996; p135) in Odaiba; its latticelike frame suspends a giant orb that looms like the Death Star over Tokyo Bay.

In the 1960s architects such as Shinohara Kazuo, Kurokawa Kisho, Maki Fumihiko and Kikutake Kiyonori began a movement known as Metabolism, which promoted flexible spaces and functions at the expense of fixed forms in building. Kurokawa's Nakagin Capsule Tower (Map p64; 8-16-10 Ginza, Chūō-ku; Ōedo Line to Tsukijishijō) is a seminal work, designed as pods that could be

TEMPLE OR SHRINE?

They may seem the same, but Buddhist temples and Shintō shrines are two different beasts. The quickest way to distinguish them is by checking their entrances. The main entrance of a shrine is a *torii* gate, usually composed of two upright pillars, joined at the top by two horizontal crossbars, the upper of which is normally slightly curved. *Torii* are often painted a bright vermilion. In contrast, the *mon* (main entrance gate) of a temple is often a much more substantial affair, constructed of several pillars or casements, joined at the top by a multitiered roof. Temple gates often contain guardian figures, usually *Niō* (deva kings). Keep in mind, though, that shrines and temples sometimes share the same precincts (often a small shrine can be found on temple grounds), and it is not always easy to tell where one begins and the other ends. This reflects the flexible attitude Japanese often take toward religion.

removed whole from a central core and re-placed elsewhere. His last great work, the National Art Center in Roppongi (2006), weaves undulating vertical forms into a strikingly latticed, organic structure.

Shinohara finally came to design in a style he called Modern Next, incorporating both modern and postmodern design ideas combined with Japanese influences. This style can be seen in his Centennial Hall (1987) at the Tokyo Institute of Technology, an elegant and uplifting synthesis of clashing forms in shiny metal cladding. Maki, the master of minimalism, pursued design in a modernist style while still emphasising elements of nature – such as the roof of his Tokyo Metropolitan Gymnasium (1990; p207), which takes on the form of a sleek metal insect. Another Maki design, the Spiral Building (1985; p132) is a favourite with Tokyo residents for its user-friendly design, gallery space, cafe and shops.

Isozaki Arata, who originally worked under Tange, also promoted the Metabolist style before becoming interested in geometry and postmodernism. His work includes the Cultural Centre (1990) in Mito, about an hour from Tokyo, which contains a striking geometric, snakelike tower clad in different metals, and the Museum of Contemporary Art in Los Angeles.

Kikutake, meanwhile, went on to design the Edo-Tokyo Museum (1992; p121). This enormous structure encompasses almost 50,000 sq metres of built space and reaches 62.2m (the height of Edo Castle) at its peak.

Another Tokyo architect to break into the international scene recently is Taniguchi Yoshio. He had some important commissions in Japan – including the Gallery of Hōryū-ji Treasures (p79) at Tokyo Kokuritsu Hakubutsukan (Tokyo National Museum) – but his first overseas project was as big as they get: the 2004 renovation and expansion of the Museum of Modern Art (MoMA) in New York.

top picks

CONTEMPORARY BUILDINGS

- **Asahi Flame** (1989; Map p84) Famously capped by a representation of a golden flame come to be known as the 'golden turd', Philippe Starck's late Bubble-era design is one of Tokyo's most recognisable modern structures.
- **Tokyo Metropolitan Government Offices** (1991; p109) Tange Kenzo's city hall has both heft and airiness; great, free observatories mean it's popular too.
- **Fuji Television Japan Broadcast Center** (1994; p135) The signature building of Odaiba, a fantasy in geometry.
- **Museum of Contemporary Art, Tokyo** (1995; p123) Yanagisawa Takahiko's wild design feels like an experiment in outrageous geometry. Steel and concrete blend harmoniously into the surrounding urban park.
- **Tokyo International Forum** (1996; p53) This wonder of glass in Yurakuchō looks like the hull of a ship.
- **Prada Aoyama Building** (2003; p132) Jacques Herzog and Pierre de Meuron's creation is a marvel of white-on-white, encased in a crystalline honeycomb.
- **Roppongi Hills** (2003; p90) Jon Jerde created a phenomenon of East-meets-West, ancient-meets-future and stark beauty-meets-crass commercialism.
- **National Art Center, Tokyo** (2006; p93) Kurokawa Kisho's last great work is an undulating meshwork embracing seven large exhibition halls unsupported by columns.
- **Mode Gakuen Cocoon Tower** (2008; p133) This award-winning educational spire in Nishi-Shinjuku designed by Tange Associates stands out with its webby, curvy facades.
- **Tokyo Sky Tree** (pp48–9) When complete in late 2011, this 634m-tall broadcasting tower will be the tallest structure in Japan. You can see it going up east of Asakusa by Oshiage station.

NEXT GENERATION BUILDERS

In the 1980s a second generation of Japanese architects began to gain recognition within the international architecture scene, including Ito Toyo, Hasegawa Itsuko and Andō Tadao. This younger group has continued to explore both modernism and postmodernism, while incorporating the renewed interest in Japan's architectural heritage. One of Ito's most striking recent designs, built in 2004, TOD's Omote-sandō Building (Map p106; 5-1-15 Jingūmae, Shibuya-ku) looks as if it was wrapped in surgical tape. Andō's architecture utilises materials such as concrete to create strong geometric patterns that have so regularly appeared in Japan's traditional architecture. Two of his landmarks are around Omote-sandō: Collezione (6-1-3 Minami-Aoyama, Minato-ku) and Omote-sandō Hills (Map p106; 4-12 Jingūmae, Shibuya-ku). See also p131.

Across the street from Omote-sandō Hills is the new Christian Dior store (5-9-11 Jingūmae, Shibuya-ku) by a young protégée of Ito's, Sejima Kazuyo, together with her partner Nishizawa Ryūe in the firm SANAA. They and others like them are quietly becoming the next generation of great Japanese architects; projects include museums in Spain, in New York and in Toledo, Ohio, USA.

Sejima and Nishizawa picked up the prestigious Pritzker Architecture Prize for 2010. Judges praised their design simplicity, saying, 'SANAA's architecture stands in direct contrast with the bombastic.'

ENVIRONMENT & PLANNING

Comprehensive pollution laws (introduced in 1967), one of the best public-transport systems in the world and an ongoing commitment to recycling programs continue to make Tokyo one of Asia's most environmentally viable supercities.

Adding to the liveability of the city are the numerous parks that dot the landscape. There are thousands ranging from pocket parks to riverside promenades and sprawling affairs dating back to samurai times, frequented year-round as the city's mild climate makes them accessible and the marked changes in seasons make them appealing.

THE LAND

Tokyo is famously earthquake prone because it lies at the junction of the Eurasian, Pacific and Philippine tectonic plates. To compound the problem, much of the city and many crowded residential areas are built on loosely consolidated landfill, which could theoretically mix with underground water during a big tremor, causing portions of the city to collapse.

On 17 January 1995 the city of Kōbe (about 600km from Tokyo) was devastated by an earthquake measuring 7.2 on the Richter scale, and it left Tokyoites wondering 'what's in store for us?'

Although imperceptible earthquakes happen nearly every day in Japan, the last one to give Tokyo a major shakedown was the 7.9-magnitude 1923 Great Kantō Earthquake (p27). Thankfully, Tokyo today is not the city it was in 1923. Its architects have been leaders in designing buildings to withstand earthquakes; some skyscrapers are on rollers or casters, others are reinforced at intervals. Yet the prospect of another major quake remains a grim one, and the devastation in Kōbe served as a reminder that no amount of earthquake preparation is too much. Meanwhile, more and more skyscrapers are going up in Tokyo due to relaxed building codes.

The government's Meteorological Agency launched a quake warning system in 2007 that broadcasts alarms 10 to 20 seconds before strong shocks are expected to hit an area based on preliminary vertical tremors. So far, its prediction rate has had mixed success.

To learn about earthquake safety, visit the Ikebukuro Bōsai-kan (p115).

GREEN TOKYO

Tokyo has an excellent recycling system duly enforced by garbage collection services. In apartments, homes and businesses, all garbage must be separated into burnable, nonburnable and recyclable bags. Garbage that is not appropriately bundled is simply not picked up.

Foreign visitors are often surprised at the lack of garbage bins in public places. Eating while walking in Japan is almost never done, except at fairs or the occasional ice-cream cone. Otherwise, the rule is to hold on to your rubbish (trash) until you get home. Under duress, train stations and convenience stores usually have bins, typically separated into those for paper (sometimes newspapers and magazines), cans, bottles, and other rubbish, with handy pictures.

Overall awareness of environmental problems is mixed in resource-poor Japan. While some Japanese manufacturers lead the pack when it comes to products that save energy (Toyota's Prius was the first mass-produced gasoline-electric hybrid vehicle), others are ridiculously wasteful when it comes to packaging – it's common to find, say, a bag of marshmallows or cookies with each item sealed individually in plastic.

Meanwhile, climate change has forced large cities such as Tokyo to institute public campaigns to lower surface temperatures through measures such as installing rooftop gardens. Laws passed in 2002 require all new and reconstructed buildings to include a roof garden. The measures were adopted to combat Tokyo's infernal summer heat – temperatures have risen 3°C in the last hundred years – and also to beautify its concrete expanse.

Another strategy is keeping air-conditioner use to a minimum by dressing down in summer – the government's popular Cool Biz fashion campaign has seen stuffy bureaucrats, politicians and businessmen renounce their suits and ties in the sweltering months for open-neck short-sleeve shirts. The Warm Biz campaign encourages them to dress more warmly to save on heating costs.

URBAN PLANNING & DEVELOPMENT

Tokyo has looser building restrictions than many giant cities, and this is evident in its chaotic, ugly sprawl. In Japan, buildings are regarded as disposable commodities and usually junked after 20 years, and the country has long been criticised for its failure to protect historic structures from the wrecking ball – landowners have inordinate power to decide what kind of buildings will go up on their property, often only a tiny slice of land.

Tokyo's neglect to limit businesses to certain zones began after WWII, when reconstruction was paramount. But in 2006 the Tokyo Metropolitan Government finally moved to protect the skyline surrounding three early-20th-century buildings – the Diet, the State Guest House and the Meiji Memorial Picture Gallery. It was probably too little too late, but the declining birth rate means that more space will open up and the ordinance may serve as a precedent for better planning and preservation.

Tokyo is also encouraging the renovation of decrepit office buildings and boosting train services to reduce congestion. In 2008 it launched yet another subway line, the Fukutoshin Line running between Ikebukuro and Shibuya. Meanwhile, it is trying to revitalise the centre of the city by redeveloping Tokyo Station into a city within a city (see the boxed text, p29).

GOVERNMENT & POLITICS

Based in Shinjuku, the Tokyo Metropolitan Government is the bureaucracy running the metropolis, which has the 127-member Metropolitan Assembly as its legislature and a governor. However, Tokyo's 23 inner wards, or *ku*, have autonomous local governments with their own elected assemblies and mayors. Within Tokyo and surrounding the 23 wards are 26 cities, five towns and eight villages, all of which have their own assemblies.

Local politics in Tokyo is very much overshadowed by national politics because the Japanese parliament, the Diet, is located here, too. It's divided into two houses: the lower, House of Representatives, and the upper, House of Councillors. The party that controls the majority of seats is the ruling party and has the right to appoint the prime minister, who appoints a cabinet.

Since 1955, the Diet has been dominated by the conservative Liberal Democratic Party (LDP) but the opposition Democratic Party of Japan took control of the powerful House of Representatives in 2009, with reform-minded Yukio Hatoyama becoming prime minister. See p87 for information about tours of the National Diet.

ECONOMY

Although it looked as if Japan was going to take over the world economically through the 1980s, by the 1990s its economy was in a certifiable recession and remained so until very recently. Unemployment hovered around 5% (high by national standards), homelessness rose (visible in major encampments in districts such as Ueno and Shinjuku), corporations approached bankruptcy and bank loans turned into bad debts. The result: deflation, increased public debt and growing concern over how to support a greying populace (Japan has one of the world's oldest populations, with life expectancies more than 77 years for men and 85 for women).

2005 marked the beginning of a turnaround for Japan, with land values in Tokyo rising for the first time since 1991. Though the 2008–09 global recession clawed back some gains, by late 2009 exports were on the rise and the national economy was back on a fragile but clear recovery path.

MEDIA

Tokyo is Japan's media capital. *Terebi* (TV) networks based here include NHK (the national broadcaster), Fuji TV, Nippon TV, TBS and TV Asahi; their headquarters are destinations for Japanese visitors. Breakfast broadcasts vary from sober reporting of world news to chipper chatter about the latest pop-star gossip. Daytime TV focuses on cooking and chat shows for housewives, and late-afternoon anime for kids. Infotainment, variety and quiz shows are popular night-time fare.

top picks

NEWS SITES

- Japan Times (www.japantimes.co.jp)
- Mainichi Daily News (http://mdn.mainichi.jp)
- Nikkei Net (http://e.nikkei.com/e/fr/freetop.aspx)
- Kyodo News (http://home.kyodo.co.jp)
- Asahi Shimbun (www.asahi.com/english)
- Japan Today (http://www.japantoday.com)

Programming from overseas is typically dubbed, but many Japanese TVs have a 'bilingual' button for watching shows in their original language.

Japanese are voracious readers and the country's newspapers have the world's highest circulation rate. Major *shimbun* (newspapers) include the liberal *Asahi Shimbun,* the conservative financial daily *Nihon Keizai Shimbun* (aka *Nikkei*) and the more populist *Mainichi Shimbun,* right-wing *Sankei Shimbun* and *Yomiuri Shimbun,* which boasts the world's largest circulation. Sports newspapers are targeted at male readers (often with racy photos to match), and the lurid *shūkanshi* (weekly tabloids) compete intensely for the most sensational stories – you'll see them advertised on trains citywide. See p261 for English-language publications.

The quality of Japanese journalism depends heavily on the news provider. A typical government corruption scandal might first surface as a scoop in a more aggressive weekly tabloid, be picked up by TV variety shows, then appear in mainstream newspapers before finally making headlines on conservative NHK. The public broadcaster's coverage of politics tends to be staid and safe.

In all media, however, granting anonymity to sources is extraordinarily common; even eyewitnesses to traffic accidents will have their faces blurred or voices distorted in a TV news report. Though there is a high degree of press freedom in Japan, social mores and systems such as exclusionary press clubs mean mainstream media are generally better at roles such as reporting breaking news than investigative journalism and criticism. Freelance journalists and independent media struggle against company-centred thinking but have small, dedicated readerships.

Despite their traditional love of newspapers and NHK, Japanese are increasingly relying on the internet and mobile phones for news and other information. Japanese online forum 2channel (http://2ch.net, in Japanese) can log more than three million posts in a single day, covering everything from political scandals to suicide notes and hate speeches, and is the largest site of its kind on the net; its popularity is gaining on traditional media.

NEIGHBOURHOODS

top picks

What's your recommendation? www.lonelyplanet.com/tokyo

NEIGHBOURHOODS

The target of relentless Allied firebombing during WWII, old Edo burnt to the ground in a fiery maelstrom. However, as Japan transformed itself into one of the world's largest and most dynamic economies, the modern city of Tokyo quickly rose from the ashes. Today the greater Tokyo area numbers upwards of 33 million people, and is regarded by demographers as the largest metropolitan area in the world.

Lacking the geometric precision of gridded cities, the urban complexity of Tokyo can be absolutely mind-blowing to the uninitiated. In fact, even Tokyoites joke among themselves that getting lost in their own city is a matter of course. However, the key to breaking down Tokyo into manageable pieces is to simply view the capital as an amalgamation of minici-

'the urban complexity of Tokyo can be absolutely mind-blowing to the uninitiated'

ties. Despite its fairly repetitious facade of stale concrete, blazing neon and jumbled electrical wires, Tokyo is actually made up of distinct neighbourhoods, each of which is distinguished by its own unique character and flair.

Like Edo before it, Tokyo has long thought of itself in terms of the high city and the low city. The high city, or Yamanote, home of the shōgun (and the nobles and samurai who served him), was a rarefied place, while the low city, or Shitamachi, was reserved for the commoners.

If you look at a JR (Japan Rail) transit map today, you'll notice a green ring around the city centre. This is the JR Yamanote Line, which loops around the heart of the city, connecting east and west, old and new. Among a slew of other political, cultural and economic factors, public transport has eliminated the distinctions between the high city and the low city. However, the unique heritage and idiosyncrasies of Tokyo's minicities are still very much alive, and a quick stroll through each of the neighbourhoods is still the best way to get acquainted with the many faces of the capital.

We begin at the centre of it all, the Imperial Palace, which is the geographical and spiritual heart of both Tokyo and Japan. Next we head east towards Sumida-gawa (Sumida River, the eastern boundary of Yamanote) and Ginza, which retains its high-stepping airs as the most prestigious shopping district in the country. Just to its south, the Tsukiji Central Fish Market is one of the grandest in the world, while the up-and-coming Shinagawa district is further south along Tokyo Bay.

Iidabashi and Kagurazaka anchor the areas north and northwest of the Imperial Palace. Northeast of the Imperial Palace lies Akihabara, giving way to the remnants of Edo's rough-and-tumble low city, namely the historic Shitamachi of Asakusa and the modern district of Ueno. Crossing the river brings us to Ryōgoku, seat of sumō culture, and the southeasterly manmade island of Odaiba, which has no intention whatsoever of taking you back to old Edo.

Southwest of the Imperial Palace is the government district of Akasaka and the pleasure-district-turned-design centre of Roppongi. In the southwesterly corner are the fashionable residential areas of Ebisu and Meguro, though class gives way to youth in the adjacent fashion hubs of Harajuku and Shibuya. Continuing north, we finish our tour at the high-rise-meets-low-rise cacophony of Shinjuku and Ikebukuro, two of the city's most important financial and commercial districts.

Indeed, the appeal of Tokyo lies in its multitude of layers, all of which must be peeled back in order to fully delve into the core of the city. From the highfalutin boutiques of Ginza and the trendy street fashions of Harajuku, to the cheery fishmongers of Ueno and the chanting monks of Asakusa, Tokyo will lay siege to your senses from the moment you set foot on its streets.

IKEBUKURO &
TAKADANOBABA
(p115)

UENO
(p77)

ASAKUSA
(p83)

AKIHABARA
& KANDA
(p66)

SHINJUKU
(p109)

IIDABASHI
& AROUND
(p59)

SUMIDA
RIVER - EAST
(p121)

IMPERIAL
PALACE &
MARUNOUCHI
(p50)

AKASAKA
(p87)

HARAJUKU
& AOYAMA
(p105)

GINZA
(p56)

SHIBUYA
(p101)

TSUKIJI &
SHIODOME
(p63)

ROPPONGI
(p90)

EBISU,
DAIKANYAMA
& MEGURO
(p95)

Tōkyō Bay

SHINAGAWA
(p119)

ODAIBA
(p126)

Tōkyō
Bay

0   2 km
0   1 mile

ITINERARY BUILDER

Planning an itinerary through the world's largest megalopolis is no small task, especially since Tokyo can take several lifetimes to fully explore. Each of Tokyo's neighbourhoods are best thought of as cities unto themselves, adding layers of complexity to a capital defined by both tradition and modernity. However, most of its top sights can be checked off in a few days, though you should slow down and save enough time to savour a fine Japanese meal, or take in one of the capital's numerous cultural attractions. Indeed, the beauty of Japan is often revealed in the subtle nuances that lie behind the dense crowds and blazing neon.

AREA	ACTIVITIES	Sights	Museums
	Central Tokyo	Imperial Palace (p50) Yasukuni-jinja (p59) Tsukiji Central Fish Market (p63)	Bridgestone Museum of Art (p54) Shōwa-kan (p61) Kite Museum (p55)
	Shibuya, Harajuku & Aoyama	Shibuya Crossing (p101) Meiji-jingū (p105) Aoyama architecture walking tour (p131)	Nezu Museum (p108) Ukiyo-e Ōta Memorial Art Museum (p107) Nihon Mingei-kan (p104)
	Asakusa & Ueno	Sensō-ji (p83) Nippori to Ueno walking tour (p129) Shibamata (p86)	Tokyo National Museum (p78) Shitamachi Museum (p80) Taiko Drum Museum (p86) Japanese Sword Museum (p112)
	Shinjuku, Ikebukuro & Northwest Tokyo	Tokyo Metropolitan Government Offices (p109) Shinjuku-gyōen (p114) Toden Arakawa tram ride (p118)	Sompo Japan Museum of Art (p113) Ghibli Museum (p113) Mori Art Museum (p91) Suntory Museum of Art (p91)
	Roppongi & Akasaka	Roppongi Hills & Tokyo Midtown (p90 & p91) National Diet Building (p87) Zōjō-ji (p94)	National Art Center, Tokyo (p93) Edo-Tokyo Museum (p121) National Museum of Emerging Science & Innovation (p126)
	Odaiba, Shinagawa & Sumida River – East & Ebisu	Ryōgoku Kokugikan (p121) Sengaku-ji (p119) Kiyosumi Teien (p123)	Museum of Maritime Science (p128) Meguro Parasitological Museum (p99) Yamatane Museum of Art (p95)
	Daikanyama & Meguro	Daien-ji (p97) Institute for Nature Study (p99) Meguro Wedding Hall (p99)	Tokyo Metropolitan Museum of Photography (p97)

HOW TO USE THIS TABLE

The table below allows you to plan a day's worth of activities in any area of the city. Simply select which area you wish to explore, and then mix and match from the corresponding listings to build your day. The first item in each cell represents a well-known highlight of the area, while the other items are more off-the-beaten-track gems. Here, Central Tokyo refers to the neighbourhoods of Imperial Palace, Maranouchi, Ginza, Shiodome, Tsukiji, Iidabashi, Akihabara and Kanda.

Eating	Shopping	Entertainment
Marunouchi Building restaurants (p175)	Akihabara Electric Town (p66)	Shimbashi Embujō Theatre (p194)
Ten-Ichi (p161)	Ginza department stores (p139)	Milonga Nueva (p187)
Kyūbey (p162)		La Qua Spa (p204)
Maisen (p173)	Omote-Sandō (p139)	Attic Room (p187)
Kyūsyū Jangara (p174)	Takeshita-dōri (p148)	Shidax Village (p188)
Fonda de la Madrugada (p173)	Tōkyū Hands (p146)	Muscle Theatre (p195)
Asakusa Imahan (p166)	Kappabashi-dōri (p142)	Sumida-gawa Cruise (p65)
Komagata Dojō (p166)	Traditional Crafts Museum (p85)	Ueno-kōen (p77)
Daikokuya (p166)	Ameyoko Arcade (p81)	
New York Grill (p175)	Japan Traditional Craft Center (p115)	New York Grill & Bar (p183)
Sandaya Honten (p175)	Kinokuniya Bookshop (p134 & p58)	Kabukichō (p113)
Omoide-yokochō (p176)	Shinjuku electronics stores (p149)	Golden Gai (p114)
Inakaya (p167)	Axis (p143)	Agave (p184)
Hu Tong San La Ju (p168)	Tolman Collection (p143)	Love Net (p188)
Nirvana New York (p168)	Japan Sword (p143)	Sake Plaza (p186)
Tomoegata (p178)	Venus Fort (p151)	Ō-edo Onsen Monogatari (p126)
Tsukiji Tama Sushi (p178)	Decks Tokyo Beach (p151)	
Eataly (p171)	MISC (p145)	Yebisu Garden Cinema (p191)
Kimukatsu (p171)	Beams (p145)	Tableaux Lounge (p187)
Bombay Bazaar (p171)	Kamawanu (p144)	Buri (p186)

GREATER TOKYO

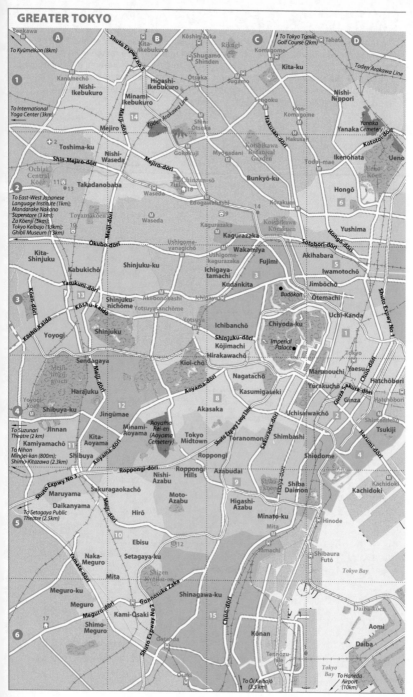

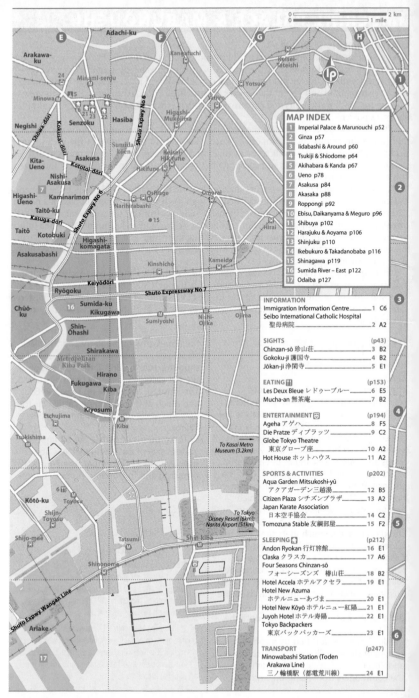

MAP INDEX

INFORMATION

Immigration Information Centre 1 C6
Seibo International Catholic Hospital
　聖母病院 2 A2

SIGHTS (p43)

Chinzan-sō 珍山荘 3 B2
Gokoku-ji 護国寺 4 B2
Jōkan-ji 浄閑寺 5 E1

EATING 🍴 (p153)

Les Deux Bleue レドゥーブルー 6 E5
Mucha-an 無茶庵 7 B2

ENTERTAINMENT 🎭 (p194)

Ageha アゲハ 8 F5
Die Pratze ディプラッツ 9 C2
Globe Tokyo Theatre
　東京グローブ座 10 A2
Hot House ホットハウス 11 A2

SPORTS & ACTIVITIES (p202)

Aqua Garden Mitsukoshi-yū
　アクアガーデン三越湯 12 B5
Citizen Plaza シチズンプラザ 13 A2
Japan Karate Association
　日本空手協会 14 C2
Tomozuna Stable 友綱部屋 15 F2

SLEEPING 🏠 (p212)

Andon Ryokan 行灯旅館 16 E1
Claska クラスカ 17 A6
Four Seasons Chinzan-sō
　フォーシーズンズ 椿山荘 18 B2
Hotel Accela ホテルアクセラ 19 E1
Hotel New Azuma
　ホテルニューあづま 20 E1
Hotel New Kōyō ホテルニュー紅陽 21 E1
Juyoh Hotel ホテル寿陽 22 E1
Tokyo Backpackers
　東京バックパッカーズ 23 E1

TRANSPORT (p247)

Minowabashi Station (Toden
　Arakawa Line)
　三ノ輪橋駅（都電荒川線）.................. 24 E1

The geographical and spiritual heart of Tokyo and Japan is the Imperial Palace, which has been the centre of national affairs since the year 1600. Under the watch of shōgun Tokugawa Ieyasu and his descendants, the city of Edo expanded at a breakneck pace, on its way to becoming a military stronghold and one of the world's largest cities. Edo Castle (Edo-jō), which grew to include the thick stone walls and expansive moat that remain today, became the focus of the shōgun's power.

Although few other vestiges of the castle survived Allied bombing, its imposing grounds still house the reconstructed Imperial Palace. However, in truth most of the area's power broking takes place a short walk away in adjacent Marunouchi. Here, government ministries, national financial institutions and corporate headquarters attend to the daily ebb and flow of this economic powerhouse.

The historic Yamanote has greatly expanded beyond this tract of land, though the Imperial Palace and Marunouchi recall the era when the high town was the command post of a nation. The monolithic ministry and insurance-industry buildings fronting the palace survived WWII, and still carry out their original functions. At nearby Tokyo Station, legions of salarymen (office workers) pass through the turnstiles, each devoting their time and energy to keeping Japan's financial gears churning and fresh faces of other regions of Japan continue to arrive, becoming part of the throbbing metropolis.

Once you've arrived at Tokyo Station, the western exit will take you out towards the Imperial Palace. It is an easy, accessible five-minute walk through Marunouchi's rows of banks and blue suits to one of the most open spaces in the city, within which lives the most cloistered family in Japan. The eastern exit takes you to Yaesu and more of the financial district around Nihombashi.

IMPERIAL PALACE AREA

KŌKYO (IMPERIAL PALACE) Map p52
皇居

The Imperial Palace is the permanent residence of Japan's emperor and imperial family. Unlike their royal counterparts in the UK, life in the Imperial Palace is rigidly controlled by a secretive organisation known as the Imperial Household Agency, which keeps any potential scandals under wraps.

Completed in 1968, the palace itself is a somewhat staid, contemporary reconstruction of the Meiji Imperial Palace, which was targeted by aerial bombers during WWII. However, on these grounds once stood Edo Castle, which in its time was the largest castle in the world. The first Edo Castle was home to a prominent feudal lord, though the grounds were abandoned following his assassination in 1486. In 1590 Tokugawa Ieyasu chose the grounds as the site for an unassailable castle from which the shōgun was to rule all Japan until the Meiji Restoration.

Edo Castle was fortified by a complex system of stone walls, moats, watch towers and armouries. However, this didn't stop the commoners from rising up, and by

the time Commodore Perry and the black ships (see p25) brought about the end of shōgunal rule in 1868, large sections of the old castle had already been destroyed. The Emperor Meiji took up power in Edo, and much of the remaining castle was torn down to make way for the new Imperial Palace.

The grounds of palace are off limits to visitors except on 2 January (New Year's holiday) and 23 December (the Emperor's birthday) and to a limited number of visi-

---

TRANSPORT: IMPERIAL PALACE & MARUNOUCHI

Train The brick-fronted Tokyo Station is a major transit hub, served by Narita Express (from the airport, p248) and many JR Lines, including the Yamanote and Chūō Lines. Yūrakuchō Station, one stop south on the Yamanote Line, may be more convenient to some destinations.

Subway The Marunouchi Line runs along the east side of the Imperial Palace and connects with Tokyo Station. The Toei Mita, Chiyoda and Hanzōmon Lines also have stops near Tokyo Station and around the Imperial Palace.

tors on official 1¼-hour guided tours (☎ 3213-1111; sankan.kunaicho.go.jp/english; admission free, 🕐 10am & 1.30pm Mon-Fri) in Japanese with an English audio guide. These tours must be applied for well in advance (the schedule opens on the first day of the month prior to the tour). It's advisable to have someone in Tokyo make the application, as participants must present a permission card mailed from the Imperial Household Agency.

If you don't enter the palace in one of these ways, it is possible to wander around the perimeter and visit the gardens (see Higashi Gyoen, below), from where you can catch a glimpse of the palace's most famous landmark, the double-barrelled bridge, Nijū-bashi.

HIGASHI-GYŌEN (IMPERIAL PALACE EAST GARDEN) Map p52
東御苑

☎ 3213-2050; admission free; 🕐 9am-4.30pm Mar–mid-Apr, Sep & Oct, 9am-5pm mid-Apr–Aug, 9am-4pm Nov-Feb, closed Mon & Fri & for imperial functions; ⊕ Marunouchi, Tozai, Chiyoda or Hanzōmon Line to Ōtemachi (exits c13b or c8b)
Higashi-gyōen is the only corner of the Imperial Palace proper that is regularly open to the public, and it makes for a pleasant retreat from the grinding hustle and bustle of Tokyo. Here you can get up-close-and-personal views of the massive stones used to build the castle walls, and even climb the ruins of one of the keeps, off the upper lawn. Although entry is free, the number of visitors at any one time is limited, so it never feels crowded.

Entry here is through one of three gates: Ōte-mon on the east side and Hirakawa-mon and Kitahanebashi-mon on the north side. Most people enter through Ōte-mon, which is situated closest to Tokyo Station, and was the principal entrance to Edo Castle for more than 200 years. Here you may want to make a stop at the Museum of Imperial Collections, which mounts small exhibits of the 5000-plus artworks held within the palace.

KITANOMARU-KŌEN (KITANOMARU PARK) Map p52
北の丸公園

⊕ Hanzōmon, Shinjuku or Tōzai Line to Kudanshita (exit 2), Tōzai Line to Takebashi (exit 1b)
This large park north of the Imperial Palace grounds is home to a few noteworthy mu-

seums as well as the Nihon Budōkan (☎ 3216-5123; 2-3 Kitanomaru-kōen). Westerners know the 14,000-plus-seat Budōkan as Tokyo's legendary concert hall for big acts from the Beatles to Beck, but it was originally built as the site of martial arts championships (judō, karate, kendō and aikidō) for the 1964 Olympics (budō means 'martial arts'). These arts are still practised and exhibited here today.

Southeast of the Budōkan is Kagaku Gijitsukan (Science Museum; ☎ 3212-2440; www.jsf.or.jp/eng; 2-1 Kitanomaru-kōen, Chiyoda-ku; adult/student/child ¥600/400/250; 🕐 9.30am-4.50pm), which features a good selection of exhibits aimed primarily at children and teenagers. There is little in the way of English explanations, but there is an excellent bilingual guidebook (¥200) available. Even without a guidebook or an understanding of Japanese, you can still stand inside a soap bubble and visit the 'methane boy' (he emits exactly what you think he emits).

In the south of the park, facing the Imperial Palace East Garden, is the Kokuritsu Kindai Bijutsukan (National Museum of Modern Art, Tokyo; MOMAT; ☎ 5777-8600; www.momat.go.jp/english; 3-1 Kitanomaru-kōen, Chiyoda-ku; adult/senior & under 18yr/university student ¥420/free/130, 1st Sun of month free; 🕐 10am-5pm Tue-Thu, Sat & Sun, 10am-8pm Fri). All pieces date from the Meiji period onwards and impart a sense of a more modern Japan through portraits, photography and grim wartime landscapes. Its collection of more than 9000 works is arguably the best in the entire country.

Situated conveniently nearby, the Bijutsu-kan Kōgeikan (Crafts Gallery; ☎ 5777-8600; www.momat.go.jp/english; 1 Kitanomaru-kōen, Chiyoda-ku; adult/senior & under 18yr/university student ¥200/free/70, 1st Sun of month free; 🕐 10am-5pm Tue-Sun), which stages excellent changing exhibitions of mingei crafts (see p36): ceramics, lacquerware, bamboo, textiles, dolls and much more. Artists range from living national treasures to contemporary artisans. Its red-brick building is an important cultural property in its own right – it dates from 1910, when it was the headquarters of the imperial guards, and was then rebuilt after its unfortunate destruction in WWII.

The gate at the northern end, Tayasu-mon, dates from 1636, making it the oldest remaining gate in the park.

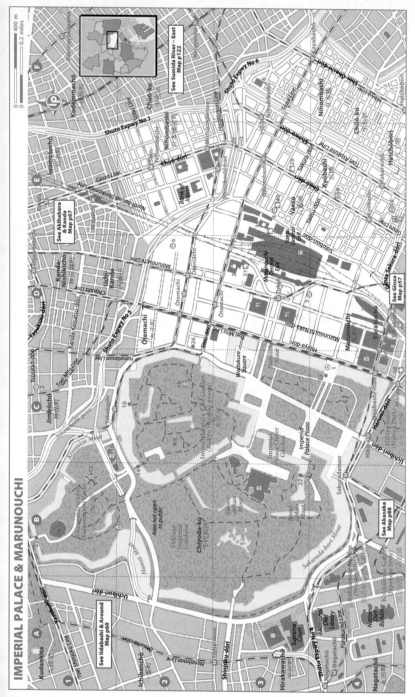

IMPERIAL PALACE & MARUNOUCHI

52

IMPERIAL PALACE & MARUNOUCHI

MARUNOUCHI AREA

TOKYO INTERNATIONAL FORUM
Map p52

東京国際フォーラム

☎ 5221-9000; 3-5-1 Marunouchi, Chiyoda-ku; admission free; ◉ JR Yamanote Line to Yūrakuchō, Yūrakuchō Line to Yūrakuchō (exit D5)

Located between Tokyo and Yūrakuchō Stations, the Forum is one of Tokyo's architectural marvels. Architect Rafael Viñoly won Japan's first international architecture competition with his design that matches a building with this sort-of-trapezoidal lot, hemmed in by train tracks on the east side. Completed in 1996, the Forum sits on land that had been the site of the Tokyo Metropolitan Government Offices (p109), which moved to its present location in Shinjuku.

The eastern wing looks like a glass ship plying the urban waters, while the west wing is a cavernous space of vaulted steel and glass. At night, the eastern glass hall is lit by hundreds of precisely placed beams, and takes on the appearance of a space colony. Although it's used mainly for its meeting halls and convention venues, many events are open to the public, and casual visitors are free to wander its courtyard-cum-sculpture garden and the glass eastern wing.

Take the lift to the top floor of the eastern wing and walk down via the many catwalks. There are restaurants, cafes and shops.

IDEMITSU MUSEUM OF ARTS Map p52

出光美術館

☎ 3213-9402; www.idemitsu.co.jp/museum; 9th fl, 3-1-1 Marunouchi, Chiyoda-ku; adult/high school and junior high student/child ¥1000/700/free; ◐ 10am-5pm Tue-Sun, to 7pm Fri; ◉ JR Yamanote Line to Yūrakuchō, subway Chiyoda or Toei Mita Line to Hibiya (exit A1 or B3)

This excellent collection of Japanese art, sprinkled with Chinese and Korean pottery and a few stray Western pieces, is the result of the lifetime passion of petroleum magnate Idemitsu Sazo. As there is no permanent display, exhibits change every few months, highlighting the complete depth of Idemitsu's collection. There are broad views across to the grounds of the Imperial Palace.

NIHOMBASHI AREA

NIHOMBASHI Map p52

日本橋

◉ Ginza Line to Mistukoshimae (exits B5 or B6) or Nihombashi (exits B11 or B12)

Even with the bronze lions guarding it, you could be forgiven for walking right past this

CHŌME THE WAY TO GO HOME...

Finding a place from its address in Tokyo can be difficult, even for locals. The problem is twofold: first, addresses are given within a district rather than along a street (only major streets have names or numbers); and second, building numbers are not necessarily consecutive, as prior to the mid-1950s numbers were assigned by date of construction. During the US occupation after WWII, an attempt was made to impose some 'logic' upon the system, and main streets were assigned names, though the city reverted to its own system after the Americans left.

Tokyo, like most Japanese cities, is divided first into *ku* (wards – Tokyo has 23 of them), which in turn are divided into *chō* or *machi* (towns) and then into numbered *chōme* (pronounced *cho*-may), areas of just a few blocks. Subsequent numbers in an address refer to blocks within the *chōme* and buildings within each block. In English, addresses are most often written, for example, '3-5-1 Marunouchi, Chiyoda-ku, Tokyo'– the '3' refers to the *chōme*, the '5' narrows down the field to a single block within the *chōme*, and the '1' indicates a specific building, all within the Marunouchi district of Chiyoda ward. A number followed by 'fl' (in this book, and sometimes 'F' in Japanese address) indicates the floor within the building, and a 'B' (as in B1fl) before that number indicates it's a below-ground level. Note that when written in Japanese the order is reversed ('Tokyo, Chiyoda-ku, Marunouchi 3-5-1'). Of course!

Generally you have to ask for directions. Numerous *kōban* (police boxes) are there largely for this purpose. Businesses often include a small map on their advertisements or business cards, or most are happy to email you a map. It was not too long ago that you needed this map to show to a taxi driver, but nowadays if you have the address they can generally get you there by means of a navigation system. If you're arriving by train or subway, be sure to also get the closest exit number from the station. We've provided transit information throughout this guidebook, including exit numbers where useful.

Otherwise, you can pick up a bilingual road atlas (Kodansha publishes the excellent *Tokyo City Atlas*) or buy a map that shows every building in every *chōme*. More and more there are also directional signs in English to important locations.

granite bridge under an expressway, where Chūō-dōri meets the river Nihombashi-gawa. Still, it bears mention for its historic significance. Nihombashi (Japan Bridge) was the point from which all distances were measured during the Edo period (p24), the beginning of the great trunk roads (the Tōkaidō, the Nikkō Kaidō etc) that took *daimyō* (feudal lords) between Edo and their home provinces. To see a replica of the original wooden bridge, visit the Edo-Tokyo Museum (p121).

BRIDGESTONE MUSEUM OF ART
Map p52
ブリヂストン美術館
☎ 3563-0241; www.bridgestone-museum.gr.jp/en; adult/under 15yr/student/senior ¥800/free/500/600; ☯ 10am-8pm Tue-Sat, 10am-6pm Sun; ⊚ Ginza or Tozai Line to Nihombashi (Takashimaya exit), Ginza Line to Kyōbashi (Meidi-ya exit) or JR Yamanote or Marunouchi Line to Tokyo (Yaesu Central exit)

Tokyo has a love affair with all things French, so it shouldn't come as too much of a surprise that French impressionist art looms large in the civic imagination. The Bridgestone Corporation's collection, which was previously kept as a private collection by Bridgestone founder Ishibashi Shōjiro, is one of the best French impressionist col-

lections you will find in all of Asia. Though European painting is undoubtedly the main attraction (think Renoir, Ingres, Monet, Corot, Matisse, Picasso, Kandinsky et al), the museum also exhibits sculpture and some works by Japanese impressionists as well as European pieces that employ abstract or neoclassical aesthetics.

NATIONAL FILM CENTRE Map p52
東京国立近代美術館フィルムセンター
☎ 5777-8600; www.momat.go.jp; 3-7-6 Kyōbashi, Chūō-ku; screenings adult/student ¥500/300, exhibition only ¥200/70; ☯ gallery 11am-6.30pm Tue-Sun, check website for screening times; ⊚ Ginza Line to Kyōbashi (exit 1), Toei Asakusa Line to Takarachō (exit A4)

Under the auspices of the National Museum of Modern Art, Tokyo (p51) in Kitanomaru Kōen, the National Film Centre is an archive of films both Japanese and foreign, as well as books, periodicals, posters and other ancillary materials. There are screenings almost every day of classic films at bargain prices (tickets in regular cinemas are easily three times the cost here) and usually one film per day has English subtitles. A rotating selection of archival materials – sometimes keyed to a film series – can be seen in a gallery on the 7th floor, though signage is not typically in English. If the location of this museum seems random (ie in a modern business district) know that this is where some of Japan's first cinemas were in the Meiji Period. For more information about Japanese classic films, see p32 and for screenings of contemporary films, see p191.

KITE MUSEUM Map p52
凧の博物館

☎ 3275-2704; www.tako.gr.jp/eng/museums_e/tokyo_e.html; 5th fl, 1-2-10 Nihombashi, Chūō-ku; adult/child ¥200/100; ⊙ 11am-5pm Mon-Sat; ⊕ Ginza, Tōzai or Toei Asakusa Line to Nihombashi (exit C5)

In Japan, even the humble kite can be an art form. Enthusiastic, English-speaking staff can guide you and your kids through a sample of the 300 or so kites in the small but jam-packed galleries, including brilliantly painted kites based on folk characters, wood-block prints or samurai armour. None are particularly old (they're made of paper, after all), but they're amazing to admire nonetheless. If you'd like to design your own (¥260 per kite), phone ahead to reserve. The Kite Museum is located above the restaurant Taimeiken (たいめいけん), just beyond Finn McCool's Irish pub.

TOKYO STOCK EXCHANGE Map p52
東京証券取引所

☎ 3665-1881; www.tse.or.jp; 2-1 Nihombashi Kabutocho, Chūō-ku; admission free; ⊙ 9am-4pm Mon-Fri, except holidays; ⊕ Tōzai Line to Kayabachō (exit 11), Ginza or Toei Asakusa Line to Nihombashi (exit D2)

The Tokyo Stock Exchange (TSE) has been operating since 1878, and today it is the world's second-largest capital market after the New York Stock Exchange. The two main indices of the TSE are the benchmark Nikkei (an index of 225 companies selected by the *Nihon Keizai Shimbun,* Japan's leading economic daily) and the broader TOPIX index, which covers all 1600 companies on the TSE's prestigious 1st Section.

Though the Tokyo Stock Exchange no longer echoes with the flurry of unbridled activity (the trading floor closed in 1999, and now all trading is by computer), a visit is a good introduction to the world of capitalism. You can walk through the visitors galleries on your own with an English-language audio guide, or inquire about the daily 40-minute guided English-language tour, with video presentation (reservations required).

Drinking p182; Eating p161; Shopping p139; Sleeping p215
Proudly reigning alongside Fifthth Avenue, Beverly Hills and the Champs-Élysées, Ginza is one of the most famous upmarket shopping districts in the world. Lined with brand-name shops and luxury boutiques, Ginza is as much a lifestyle as a destination. Japan's economy may not be what it once was, but you'd scarcely know from the alphabet soup of international name brands here (Armani, Bulgari, Chanel, De Beers etc). There are clusters of department stores throughout Tokyo, but Ginza's have long been the leaders.

Even if Ginza has lost a bit of its glamour over the past few years – particularly since Omote-Sandō, Aoyama, Ebisu and Daikanyama have become increasingly trendy – its history still imparts an aura. The 'silver seat' (it's where the mint once was) was one of the first areas of Tokyo to modernise following the Meiji Restoration (p25) and Ginza retains a European air that is atypical of urban Japan. With brick buildings, wide boulevards, tree-lined streets, gas street lamps and other past emblems of Western modernity, Ginza is indeed a rarity in the urban jungle of Tokyo.

Ginza's sights are more experiential than monumental. The department stores here are shopping extravaganzas, to be sure, but even if you're not looking to drop a single yen they can make a great cultural study: traditional Japanese products and kimono displayed as if in art galleries, in-store art galleries that actually *are* art galleries, and wildly bustling food floors called *depachika* (p162). See p139 for details of these stores. With its pricey real estate, Ginza is also the place where some of Japan's most prominent companies lavish space on flagship showrooms. Amid all of this are some prestigious stand-alone art galleries. And all of this can be seen for free.

Ginza is also well suited for a leisurely stroll or for lingering over a cup of coffee. It's at its best on Saturdays and Sundays when the silver-painted main street, Chūō-dōri, closes to motor vehicles, allowing the alleyways and lanes to come alive with pedestrians.

Ginza is bounded to the west and north by the Imperial Palace, Marunouchi and Nihombashi. To the east and south are Tsukiji and Shiodome, where you'll find fish and grocery markets alongside soaring skyscrapers. Ginza itself, almost completely encircled by the Shuto Expressway, is about as grid-like as Tokyo gets. Within these confines, the neat rows of squares make for easy navigation through the boutiques, galleries and cafes. The main points of orientation are Sukiyabashi Crossing (by the Sony Building, where Harumi-dōri meets the expressway overpass) and Ginza Yon-chome Crossing (by Mitsukoshi Department Store, where Harumi-dōri meets Chūō-dōri).

SONY BUILDING Map p57
ソニービル

☎ 3573-2371; www.sonybuilding.jp; 5-3-1 Ginza, Chūō-ku; admission free; ⏰ 11am-7pm; ◉ Marunouchi, Ginza or Hibiya Line to Ginza (exit B9)
SItuated right on Sukiyabashi Crossing is the Sony Building, which attracts gadget hounds in search of gizmos that have yet to be released. On the first four floors of this mid-century international-style mini-skyscraper, kids will love the free Playstation games, while adults tend to lose an

hour or so perusing all the latest audio and video accessories.

HIBIYA-KŌEN (HIBIYA PARK) Map p57
日比谷公園

admission free; ◉ Chiyoda, Hibiya or Toei Mita Line to Hibiya (exits A5 or A13)
Built around the turn of the 20th century at the height of Meiji era, this leafy park situated just west of Ginza was Tokyo's first Western-style park. At the time, Western design was the fashion, and it doesn't take long to notice the similarities to public spaces in London, Paris and New York. If you're in need of a break on a quiet afternoon, find your way to one of the two ponds for a nice cup of tea at a pavilion.

HOUSE OF SHISEIDO Map p57
ハウスオブ資生堂

☎ 3571-0401; www.shiseido.co.jp/house-of-shiseido; 7-5-5 Ginza, Chūō-ku; admission free;

TRANSPORT: GINZA

Train The JR Yamanote Line stops at Shimbashi Station, which borders Ginza to the southwest, and Yūrakuchō Station to the northwest.

Subway The Ginza, Hibiya and Marunouchi Lines connect at Ginza Station, in the heart of Ginza.

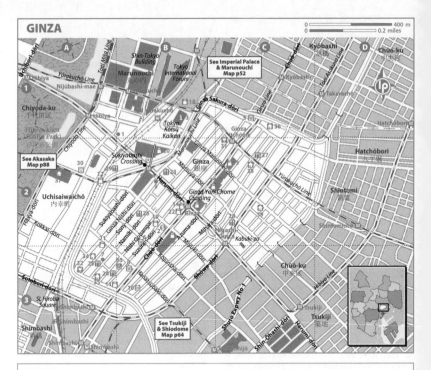

GINZA

⊙ 11am-7pm Tue-Sun; ⊙ JR Yamanote Line to Shimbashi (Ginza exit), Toei Asakusa Line to Shimbashi (exits 1 & 3)
Underwritten by the cosmetics giant Shiseido, this space is also a true classic Ginza concoction: soft-sell corporate promo.

Most people will be drawn by the alluring, wonderfully displayed themed exhibitions (past ones have included speciality handbags and cosmetics for men), and along the way you might find yourself distracted by advertising icons of the history of Shiseido.

BOOKSHOPS

Japanese are voracious readers and are spoilt for choice when it comes to literature shops. That said, few bookshops have much of a selection in English. Here are some notable retailers with English and Japanese selections.

If you're looking specifically for manga, see the Akihabara listings (p141) in the Shopping chapter.

Blue Parrot (Map p116; ☎ 3202-3671; www.blueparrottokyo.com; 3rd fl, 2-14-10 Takadanobaba, Shinjuku-ku; ⏰ 11am-9.30pm; ⊕ JR Yamanote Line to Takadanobaba, Waseda exit, or Tōzai Line to Takadanobaba, exit 6) A fabulous resource of English books, magazines, DVDs, children's books and internet access.

Good Day Books (Map p96; ☎ 5421-0957; www.gooddaybooks.com; 3rd fl, 1-11-2 Ebisu, Shibuya-ku; ⏰ 11am-8pm Mon-Sat, 11am-6pm Sun; ⊕ JR Yamanote Line to Ebisu, east exit, or Hibiya Line to Ebisu, exit 1) The best selection of used English-language books in Tokyo, with a wide range of paperbacks, hardcovers and magazines.

Issei-dō (一誠堂書店; Map p67; ☎ 3292-0071; www.isseido-books.co.jp; 1-7 Kanda-Jimbōchō, Chiyoda-ku; ⏰ 10am-6.30pm Mon-Sat; ⊕ Toei Mita or Toei Shinjuku Line to Jimbōchō, exits A5 or A7) An antiquarian bookseller with a wonderful selection of old texts. The 2nd floor has many well-weathered volumes in English.

Kinokuniya (紀伊國屋書店; Map p110; ☎ 5361-3301; www.kinokuniya.co.jp; Takashimaya Times Square, 5-24-2 Sendagaya, Shinjuku-ku; ⏰ 10am-8pm; ⊕ Shinjuku, south exit) One of the best selections of English-language titles on the 6th floor, with another nearby branch east of Shinjuku Station.

Maruzen (丸善; Map p52; ☎ 5288-8881; Oazo Bldg, 1-6-4 Marunouchi, Chiyoda-ku; ⏰ 9am-9pm; ⊕ JR Yamanote Line to Tokyo Station, Marunouchi north exit) Established in 1869, this is Japan's oldest Western bookshop; this new four-storey branch has an eye-popping selection of English-language books on topics from J-pop to ancient Greek literature. Its founder is said to have invented Japanese curry rice – there's a restaurant serving the dish here.

GALLERY KOYANAGI Map p57
ギャラリー小柳

☎ 3561-1896; www.gallerykoyanagi.com; 8th fl, 1-7-5 Ginza; ⏰ 11am-7pm Tue-Sat; ⊕ Ginza, Hibiya or Marunouchi Line to Ginza, exit A9, or Yūrakuchō Line to Ginza-itchōme (exit 7)

Exhibits include serious heavy-hitters from Japan and abroad, like Sugimoto Hiroshi, Marlene Dumas and Olafur Eliasson. Enter in the alley behind Bank of Tokyo-Mitsubishi.

GINZA GRAPHIC GALLERY Map p57
ギンザ・グラフィック・ギャラリー

☎ 3571-5206; www.dnp.co.jp/gallery/ggg; 7-7-2 Ginza; ⏰ 11am-7pm Tue-Fri, 11am-6pm Sat; ⊕ Ginza, Hibiya or Marunouchi Line to Ginza (exit A2)

Monthly changing exhibits of graphic arts with a focus on advertising and poster art, mostly Japanese but with the occasional Western artist. The annual Tokyo Art Directors Conference exhibition takes place here in July.

SHISEIDO GALLERY Map p57
資生堂ギャラリー

☎ 3572-3901; www.shiseido.co.jp/e/gallery/html; 8-8-3 Ginza, Chūō-ku; admission free; ⏰ 11am-7pm Tue-Sat, 11am-6pm Sun; ⊕ JR Yamanote Line to Shimbashi (Ginza exit), or Toei Asakusa Line to Shimbashi (exits 1 or 3)

This gallery in the basement of the Shiseido Parlour Café is more experimental than the cosmetics company thereof. An ever-changing selection, particularly of installation pieces, lends itself well to the high-ceilinged space.

TOKYO GALLERY Map p57
東京画廊

☎ 3571-1808; www.tokyo-gallery.com; 7th fl, 8-10-5 Ginza; admission free; ⊕ Ginza Line to Shimbashi (exit 1)

Tokyo Gallery collaborates with the Beijing-Tokyo Art Project, and shows challenging, often politically pointed works by Japanese and Chinese artists.

NOTE: KABUKI-ZA THEATRE

Tokyo's Kabuki-za Theatre is the best place in town to view this signature Japanese art; however, it closed for renovation in April 2010 and was not due to reopen till spring 2013. Until then, look for kabuki performances at the Shimbashi Embujō Theatre (p194).

IIDABASHI & AROUND

Drinking p182; Eating p163; Shopping p140; Sleeping p216

The area north and west of the Imperial Palace is the bulk of the former Yamanote, now more a collection of contiguous neighbourhoods than one unified district. Roughly bordered by the grounds of the Imperial Palace to the east, the government and business district of Akasaka to the south and greater Shinjuku and Ikebukuro to the west and northwest, it spans the spectrum from historic gardens and samurai quarters to baseball stadiums, amusement parks, war memorials and soaring steel-and-glass skyscrapers. Iidabashi, Kagurazaka and Kudanshita are the main districts of interest to visitors.

North of the palace, Yasukuni-jinja is a controversial shrine to Japan's war dead that is plastered across the international headlines every time a Japanese politician stops by to pay respect. A pass through the onsite history museum is sobering, while another nearby museum, Shōwa-kan, recounts the WWII from the perspective of the home front. Despite the importance of WWII to many Western visitors, it's a subject rarely broached with Japanese hosts; these two museums together offer perhaps the best combination of geopolitical and everyday life views a visitor may get.

Northwest of the palace is Kōrakuen, which originally housed the pleasure gardens of Yamanote nobility. Today, it continues to be a place of amusement, especially since the neighbourhood is home to the Tokyo Dome, the fabled home of the Yomiuri Giants baseball team, the Japanese equivalent of the New York Yankees. Also in the shadow of the dome is Koishikawa Kōrakuen, a traditional Japanese garden that is no longer reserved for the highest of classes.

West of the palace is Kagurazaka, which offers up quaint old-Edo streetscapes and hide-and-seek alleys, which would provide the perfect setting for a romantic tryst or a shady backroom deal.

YASUKUNI-JINJA (YASUKUNI SHRINE) Map p60
靖国神社

☎ 3261-8326; www.yasukuni.or.jp; 3-1-1 Kudankita, Chiyoda-ku; shrine free, Yūshūkan adult ¥800, student ¥300-500; ⊗ 9am-5pm; ◉ Tōzai, Hanzōmon or Toei Shinjuku Line to Kudanshita (exit 1)

If you've kept up with international headlines, you might recall several news stories about citizens of China, Korea and other Asian nations taking to the streets when Japanese politicians (such as former Prime Minister Junichiro Koizumi) visited Yasukuni-jinja. Literally 'For the Peace of the Country Shrine', Yasukuni is the memorial shrine to Japan's war dead, around 2.5 million souls who died in combat. However, although the conservative right wing in Japan stands by its patriotic duty to honour its war dead, the complete story is just a little more controversial (to say the least).

To put things in perspective, it's important to fully understand the history of Yasukuni-jinja. Although the shrine only dates back to 1869, in the years leading up to and during WWII, it was chosen as Tokyo's chief Shintō shrine. During this time, Yasukuni-jinja became the physical representation of the Japanese government's jingoistic policy.

Of course, that's really only half the story told. Despite a postwar constitutional commitment to the separation of religion and politics, as well as a renunciation of militarism, in 1979 14 class-A war criminals (as determined by the US-led International Military Tribunal for the Far East), including Hideki Tojo (the WWII general), were enshrined here amid massive worldwide protests. Leading Liberal Democratic Party (LDP) politicians have also made a habit of visiting the shrine on the anniversary of Japan's defeat in WWII (15 August).

TRANSPORT: IIDABASHI & AROUND

Train The JR Chūō and JR Sōbu Lines stop at Iidabashi and Suidōbashi, which are located at the centre of this area.

Subway Useful stations include Iidabashi (Nanboku and Toei Ōedo Lines), Kōrakuen (Nanboku and Marunouchi Lines), Kagurazaka (Tōzai Line) and Kudanshita (Hanzōmon, Tozai and Toei Shinjuku Lines).

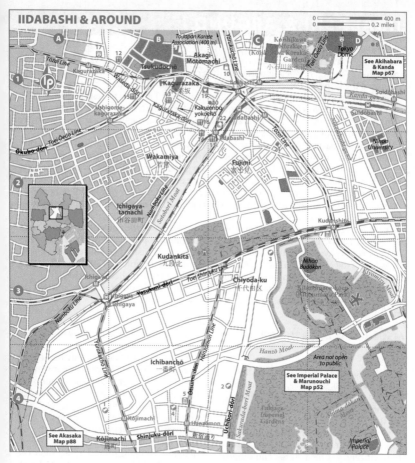

Regardless of your political leanings, Yasukuni is one of the most beautiful shrines in Tokyo. Its enormous *torii* (gate) at the entrance is, unusually, made of steel, while the second set is made of bronze. The beautiful inner shrine is laid out in the style of Japan's most important Shintō edifice, Ise Shrine (100km southeast of Kyoto), and there are often seasonal displays of ikebana in the inner courtyard. The grounds are charmingly home to a flock of doves, which balances out all the war hawks.

Beyond the inner shrine, visitors may come away with mixed feelings about the shrine's museum, the Yūshūkan, Japan's oldest museum (1882). It starts, fittingly enough for a war memorial, with stately cases depicting Japan's military heritage and traditions, punctuated by displays of swords and samurai armour, and art and poetry extolling the brave, daring and indomitable spirit of the Japanese people; and telling Japanese history through the Meiji Restoration (p25).

However, as you progress through Japan's late-19th- and early-20th-century overseas military conflicts (tussles with Russia, the occupation of Korea, and others) the exhibits become more controversial. The source of the most controversy is the section of the museum covering the 'Greater East Asian War', which you probably know as WWII. While the text of these galleries has been toned down from the statements of previous years, it's hard to imagine, for example, Chinese nationals being satisfied with the portrayal of the Nanjing Massacre (here called the 'Nanking Incident') of December 1937; no mentioned is made of those killed, estimated between 100,000 (from some Japanese sources) and 300,000 (from Chinese sources).

Other exhibits are fascinating and also harrowing. Note the *kaiten* (human torpedo), essentially a submarine version of the kamikaze aeroplane. You can listen to the final message of a *kaiten* pilot to his family – it's in Japanese but it's easy to hear how young he sounds. There's also the 'miracle coconut' inscribed and set afloat by a Japanese soldier in the Philippines shortly before his death in 1944. The coconut floated in the Pacific for 31 years before washing up very near his widow's home town – you can still make out the Japanese characters. The walls of the last few galleries of the Yūshūkan are covered with seemingly endless photos of the dead, enough to leave a lump in many throats and make one wonder about the value of any war.

As such, the feelings engendered by visiting a place of such solemnity can be mixed – the attached gift shop, selling gaily decorated biscuits, chocolates and curry, doesn't do much to dispel.

SHŌWA-KAN Map p60
昭和館

☎ 3222-2577; 1-6-1 Kudan-Minami, Chiyoda-ku; **adult/high school & university students/child ¥300/150/80;** ⏰ 10am-5.30pm; ◉ Tōzai, Hanzōmon or Toei Shinjuku Line to Kudanshita (exit 4)

This museum of WWII-era Tokyo gives a sense of everyday life for the common people. Galleries on the 6th and 7th floors are filled with many hundreds of artefacts: how people ate, slept, dressed, studied, prepared for war and endured martial law, famine and loss of loved ones. The personal perspective of this museum makes it much more accessible than the Yūshūkan. An English audio guide (free) explains the basics.

On the 5th floor are consoles where you can view a limited number of videos about the war in English, mostly news footage from Western media. There are a great many more videos in Japanese.

TOKYO DOME CITY Map p60
東京ドームシティ

◉ Marunouchi or Nanboku Line to Kōrakuen, JR Chūō or JR Sōbu Line to Suidōbashi (west exit)

On the grounds of the historic Kōraku-en Stadium (1937), the Tokyo Dome (aka 'Big Egg') opened with great fanfare in 1988 and has never looked back. Then again, it's hard to remain nostalgic about the past when you're home to the Yomiuri Giants, the most successful franchise in the history of Japanese baseball. The dome itself is an engineering marvel, especially considering that the Teflon roof is supported by nothing but air – the pressure is 0.3% higher indoors than out (what will the Japanese think of next?). If you're looking to catch the Yomiuri Giants in action, the baseball season typically runs from the end of March through October – see p208 for more details.

Gung-ho baseball fans will not want to miss the Japanese Baseball Hall of Fame & Museum (野球体育博物館; ☎ 3811-3600; 1-3-61 Kōraku, Bunkyō-ku; adult/child ¥500/200; ⏰ 10am-6pm Tue-Sun Mar-Sep, 10am-5pm Tue-Sun Oct-Feb), which chronicles baseball's rise from a hobby imported by an American teacher in 1872 to the national obsession it's become. From the establishment of college and professional baseball leagues in 1922 to the Japanese team winning the bronze medal at the 2004 Olympics, this museum walks you through the Japanese incarnation of the sport. Be sure to pick up the comprehensive English-language pamphlet. The entrance to the museum is adjacent to Gate 21 of the Tokyo Dome.

Tokyo Dome is surrounded by the amusement park Tokyo Dome Attractions (東京ドームアトラクションズ; ☎ 5800-9999; www.tokyo-dome.co.jp/e; 1-3 Kōraku, Bunkyō-ku; day pass adult/child ¥4000/3000; ⏰ 10am-9pm Mon-Fri, 9.30am-9pm Sat & Sun) with the usual assortment of coasters and spinners, as well as a healthy smattering of bars, restaurants and shops. If you don't want to invest in an all-day pass offering access to all of the rides, tickets are available for individual rides (¥200 to ¥1000) with no additional admission charge. Check the website for extended hours.

If none of that's your speed, check out La Qua Spa (p204), Tokyo's ritziest free-standing day spa.

KOISHIKAWA KŌRAKUEN (KOISHIKAWA KŌRAKU GARDEN)
Map p60

小石川後楽園

☎ 3811-3015; 1-6-6 Kōraku, Bunkyō-ku; adult/senior & child ¥300/free; ⏰ 9am-5pm; ⊚ Toei Ōedo Line to Iidabashi (exit C3)

This 70,000-sq-metre formal Japanese garden is one of Tokyo's most beautiful and least visited (by foreigners at least) – if you have the slightest interest in gardens, you should make a beeline here.

Established in the mid-17th century as the property of the Tokugawa clan, the garden incorporates elements of Chinese and Japanese landscaping, although nowadays the shakkei (borrowed scenery) also includes the other-worldly cool of the Tokyo Dome. The garden is particularly well known for plum trees in February, irises in June and autumn colours. Of special note is the Engetsu-kyo (Full-Moon Bridge), which dates from the early Edo period.

Kōrakuen means 'the garden of later enjoyment', which comes from a Chinese proverb about maintaining power first and enjoying it later – we assume this sounds better in Chinese.

KAGURAZAKA Map p60
神楽坂

⊚ Tōzai or Yūrakuchō Line to Iidabashi (exit B3)

Kagurazaka is worth a visit more for an atmospheric stroll than for any particular sights. Its intimate kakurenbo yokochō (hide-and-seek alleys) recall bygone days of Edo, or a city like Kyoto that wears its history on its sleeve. But this is Tokyo, which means that the denizens of the nearby government and business districts come to broker their power, and deals are being made behind the wooden facades and sliding gates of the expensive restaurants and nightspots.

From Sotobori-dōri, head up Kagurazaka Hill and turn right at Royal Host restaurant. The back alleys will be on your left in a few blocks.

JCII CAMERA MUSEUM Map p60
日本カメラ博物館

☎ 3263-7100; www.jcii-cameramuseum.jp; 25 Ichiban-cho, Chiyoda-ku; adult/child ¥300/free; ⏰ 10am-5pm Tue-Sun; ⊚ Hanzōmon Line to Hanzōmon (exit 4)

What's that? You didn't know that Japan is obsessed with photography? This museum, established in 1989 by the Japan Camera Industry Institute, takes it a step further. Designed for the equipment obsessed, the museum holds more than 10,000 cameras, of which as many as 600 may be on show at any one time. Highlights of the collection include the world's first camera, the 1839 Giroux daguerreotype (one of an estimated seven worldwide); and the Sony Mavica, a prototype for the original digital camera, from which images had to be downloaded to a floppy disk.

Behind the museum is the JCII photo salon (☎ 3261-0300; admission free; ⏰ 10am-5pm Tue-Sun) with a changing roster of photography exhibits.

Exiting Hanzōmon Station, walk around the Diamond Hotel. The photo salon is in this alley, while the museum entrance is through to the next street.

Eating p163; Sleeping p216

A morning visit to the Tsukiji Central Fish Market (below), arguably Tokyo's top attraction, will awaken all your senses. From the sights and sounds of fresh tuna being sliced up with samurai-like precision to the smells and tastes of a sushi breakfast so fresh it still wriggles in your mouth, Tsukiji is a world unto itself. Since most of the action takes place between the hours of 5am and 8am, you're either going to have to set the alarm clock for the wee hours of the morn or party all night long in the nearby pleasure district of Roppongi (p90).

Prior to 1923, the city's fish market was ensconced in Nihombashi as it had been throughout the Edo era. Of course the whole place smelled, well, fishy, and the market's well-off neighbours had grown weary of looking at its ugly facade. Fortunately for them (not so much for others), they got a reprieve when the deadly Great Kantō Earthquake flattened it. Though some of the more stubborn stall-keepers insisted on returning to the old location, the market was officially moved to the old naval lands at Tsukiji, where it is now the world's largest fish market.

South of Tsukiji, the gleaming skyscrapers of the Shiodome business district stand in stark contrast to the ramshackle market. Pretty much all of them were constructed in the new millennium.

The markets of Tsukiji rest on the banks of the Sumida-gawa (Sumida River) on what was once old naval lands. Heading away from Tsukiji to the northwest on foot via Harumi-dōri will land you in Ginza, while walking just a few minutes to the southwest will bring you to the gates of Hama Rikyū Onshi-teien, one of Tokyo's most expansive gardens. Shiodome is the cluster of tall buildings on the other side of the Shuto Expressway. Although this largely residential and commercial district doesn't attract as many tourists as the surrounding areas, it is home to one of the city's most appealing skylines.

TSUKIJI CENTRAL FISH MARKET Map p64
築地市場

www.tsukiji-market.or.jp; admission free; ☯ early morning, closed 2nd & 4th Wed of most months, Sun & public holidays; ◉ Toei Ōedo Line to Tsukijishijō (exit A1), Hibiya Line to Tsukiji (exits 1 or 2)

If it lives in the sea, it's probably for sale in the Central Fish Market, where acres and acres of fish and fish products change hands in a lively, almost chaotic atmosphere. Everything is allotted its own area, and a quick scan of the loading docks will reveal mountains of octopus, rows of giant tuna, endless varieties of shellfish and tank upon tank of live exotic fish.

The Tsukiji Market information centre (☎ 3541-6521; www.tsukijitour.jp; 2nd fl, 4-7-5 Tsukiji, Chūō-ku; ☯ 8.30am-3pm market days; ◉ Hibiya Line to Tsukiji, exit 2) has historic images of the market including reproductions of ukiyo-e (woodblock prints), and conducts tours of the market by advance reservation (from ¥8000, including breakfast). It's in the Kyōei (aka KY) building, at the corner of Harumi-dōri and Shin-Ōhashi-dōri.

In 2008 (the most recent year for which figures were available as we went to press), about 2072 tonnes of fish and seafood, worth over ¥1.74 billion (US$18.5 million),

were sold here daily; that's 567,162 tonnes worth some ¥478 billion (US$5 billion) annually. In 2009, a single, highly prized 128kg tuna from northern Japan sold for ¥9.63 million (that's over ¥75,000 per kilo!), though that pales in comparison to the 2001 record of ¥20 million.

If you are of a mind to visit the auctions, you can watch from a visitors gallery between 5am and 6.15am. Afterwards, you are free to visit the wholesalers market, and wander around the seemingly endless rows. By late morning the action has pretty well wound down, but you can still visit the Outer Market.

TRANSPORT: TSUKIJI & SHIODOME

Train Shimbashi Station (JR and subway lines) is the transit hub for Shiodome. Shimbashi is also the terminus for the Yurikamome Line for Odaiba.

Subway The best way to reach the fish market is to take either the Hibiya Line to Tsukiji Station, or the Toei Ōedo Line to nearby Tsukijishijō.

Water bus There is a Tokyo Cruise (p65) dock at the pier on the east end of Hama Rikyū Onshi-teien. Destinations include Asakusa and Odaiba.

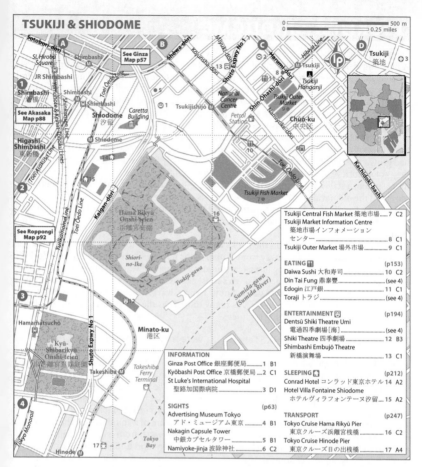

TSUKIJI & SHIODOME

0 — 500 m
0 — 0.25 miles

The wholesale stalls are set up to sell directly to restaurants, retail shops and other commercial enterprises. In fact, some of the hundreds of merchants have been in business for more than 20 generations! The hustle and bustle can be intoxicating, and as long as you're there before 8am, some kind of push and pull will doubtless be going on. Keep in mind, however, that the market shuts completely by 1pm for cleaning. Although the market is not as odoriferous as you might think, you still don't want to wear your nicest clothing (and especially not your best shoes).

Tradition has it that you should finish your visit here with a sushi breakfast from one of the many restaurants in the area. Daiwa Sushi (p164) is within the market itself and gathers long, long queues.

Between the Central Fish Market and the Outer Market is Namiyoke-jinja, the Shintō shrine where wholesalers and middlemen come to pray before work. Highlights are the giant gold parade masks used for the lion dance and the dragon-shaped taps over the purification basins.

CAUTION

Tsukiji Fish Market may be a major attraction for visitors, but it is also very much a working market. Out of respect for the workers, make sure that your sightseeing doesn't get in the way of commerce; groups in particular should not crowd around a stall. In addition, be very careful to stay out of the way of hand carts, and especially the hundreds of motorised carts which manoeuvre about the market at breakneck speed.

CRUISING THE SUMIDA RIVER

Though the heavily developed Sumida-gawa is no longer a quaint river, it is still famous for its 12 bridges, and a trip via *suijō bus* (water bus) is an excellent way to survey Tokyo's old geography and see the city from a different perspective.

Hinode Pier, the main pier for Tokyo Cruise (東京クルーズ; Map p64; ☎ toll free 0120-977-311; www.suijobus .co.jp) is in the Tsukiji/Shiodome area, and there is a secondary pier by Hama Rikyū Onshi Teien (below). The most popular destinations include upriver to Asakusa (p83; ¥760, 40 minutes from Hinode Pier and ¥720, 35 minutes from Hama Rikyū), and across Tokyo Bay to Odaiba (p126; ¥460, 20 minutes from Hinode Pier only). A special boat, the futuristic *Himiko*, designed by manga artist Matsumoto Reiji, makes the trip directly between Asakusa and to Odaiba (¥1520, one hour).

Schedules vary by departure point, but most boats leave once or twice per hour between 9.45am and 5.10pm (with occasional extended departures during summer); the website has complete details. English leaflets describe the dozen or so bridges you'll pass under en route.

If you have arrived too late to see the fish auctions, or maybe you just can't stand the thought of dead sea creatures, we can almost guarantee you will find something of interest in the Tsukiji Outer Market. With that said, if you hate food in general – well, there is not much we can do to help you.

The Outer Market concentrates on fruits and vegetables and does a brisk business of its own (2008 annual produce sales were upwards of ¥8.8 billion, almost US$94 million), yet it's neither as famous nor as breathtakingly busy as its inner counterpart. That's usually a blessing, given that it allows you time to browse not just the produce but alley after alley of noodle shops, tiny cafes and cooking-supply shops, not to mention seafood and sushi counters. In addition, you'll also find boots, baubles, baskets, plates, picks (of the tooth variety) and pottery, all at reasonable prices.

It can be quite an education to see how those Japanese foods that you have always loved are actually made, and to learn what all those tiny bowls and plates are used for. In short, the Tsukiji Outer Market is a one-stop shop for anything you need to prepare and serve that next great Japanese meal. Be sure to first check your home country's import restrictions if you plan to take any food products home with you.

There has been much talk and several proposals over the last decade about the fish market moving to some other location, but as we went to press the whole issue had gone back to the drawing board, thanks to a change in political whim. For now, Tsukiji stays were it is. We hope it stays.

HAMA RIKYŪ ONSHI-TEIEN (DETACHED PALACE GARDEN) Map p64
浜離宮庭園

☎ 3541-0200; adult/senior ¥300/150; ⏰ 9am-5pm; ⓞ Toei Ōedo Line to Shiodome (exits A2 or A3) or Tsukijishijō (exit A2)

Once a shōgunal palace extending into the area now occupied by the fish market, this sparse garden is one of Tokyo's finest. The Detached Palace Garden features a large duck pond with an island that's home to a charming tea pavilion, as well as some wonderfully manicured trees (black pine, Japanese apricot, hydrangeas, camellias etc), some of which are hundreds of years old. Besides visiting the park as a side trip from Ginza or Tsukiji, consider travelling by boat to or from Asakusa via the Sumida-gawa cruise aboard Tokyo Cruise (above).

ADVERTISING MUSEUM TOKYO Map p64
アド・ミュージアム東京

☎ 6218-2500; www.admt.jp; B1 fl, 1-8-2 Higashi Shimbashi, Minato-ku; admission free; ⏰ 11am-6.30pm Tue-Fri, 11am-4.30pm Sat & public holidays; ⓞ Ginza Line (exit 4), Toei Asakusa or JR Yamanote Line to Shimbashi (Shiodome Shio-site exit), Toei Ōedo Line to Shiodome (Shimbashi Station exit)

Dentsu, Japan's largest advertising agency, operates this museum of Japanese ads in the basement of the Caretta building. The collection covers wood-block printed hand-bills from the Edo period to sumptuous art nouveau and art deco Meiji- and Taisho-era works to the best of today. There's not a lot of English signage, but the strong graphics of many of the ads stand alone. If you see advertising as art, it's a spectacle, and there are video consoles to watch award-winning TV commercials from around the world.

Eating p164; Sleeping p216; Shopping p141

Otaku (geeks) are a storied Japanese breed, known for their obsession with electronics and manga (Japanese comics). Akihabara is also storied for the same reason. Long the province of electronics shops during Japan's postwar boom, the last decade has seen it flourish as a haven for manga-mania as well. From multistoreyed computer shops and back-alley discount camera stores, to shops creaking with manga and anime (Japanese animation) cafes, and the latest in geek fashions, Akihabara is one of Tokyo's most bizarre districts. Following the rapidly increasing global popularity of anime, *otaku* culture and all things Japanese, a visit to Akihabara is becoming something of a Tokyo staple.

With its street touts hawking cheap goods, electronic bells ringing with inimitable sound and fury, geeks of all ages decked out in anime garb, and a frenetic street scene of lights, beeps and endless pedestrian traffic, Akihabara can quickly overwhelm the senses. Of course part of the reason why you are in Akihabara is to stand at the ground zero of geekdom, though you can always manage to find respite in the neighbouring commercial and residential district of Kanda.

During the Edo period, the vibrant green banks of the Kanda-gawa were famously depicted in wood-block prints. Streets in the neighbourhood were lined with artisans' shops, and a residential district served as a rowdy, overcrowded home to workers and craftsmen. These days, however, Kanda's vital spirit has been channelled by the thousands of students who inhabit Ochanomizu, the area that lies north of Kanda proper. Nihon University and Meiji University, two of Japan's most prestigious private universities, are located nearby, and a couple of enclaves cater to them with clusters of shops as in days of old. Kanda's Jimbo-chō district is a haven for booksellers.

Akihabara is a stop on the JR Yamanote Line, north of Marunouchi (Tokyo Station) and south of Ueno. Electric Town (Denki-gai in Japanese) is just west of Akihabara Station, while Kanda is farther west, east of the grounds of the Imperial Palace.

AKIHABARA

AKIHABARA ELECTRIC TOWN (DENKI-GAI) Map p67
秋葉原電気街

◉ JR Yamanote or JR Sōbu Line to Akihabara (Denki-gai exit), Hibiya Line to Akihabara (exit 3)
What the Tsukiji Central Fish Market is to the food trade, Akihabara is to Japan's legendary electronics industry: bustling, busy and fun to watch, and you don't have to get up early in the morning to catch the action (afternoon is prime time). Akihabara can no longer claim exclusive rights to the title of the city's electronics centre (thanks to increased competition from denser hubs

like Shinjuku and Ikebukuro), yet it is still quite the scene. Akihabara is where many items are market-tested, so even if you have no intention of shopping now, it's worth a peek to see what you may be buying two years hence.

As the electronics business has moved elsewhere (Korea, China and Taiwan), Akihabara has turned to the boom market in cartoon manga, often pornographic, to round out its fiscal activity. If you like your pornography of the PG-13 variety, don't miss the opportunity to have a cup of coffee and curry rice in any of Akihabara's unique maid cafes (see p164). Superfans might consider visiting Tokyo Anime Center

TRANSPORT: AKIHABARA & KANDA

Train The JR Yamanote and Keihin-Tōhoku Lines both stop at Akihabara and Kanda. Akihabara is also served by the JR Sōbu Line, which runs from east to west across central Tokyo. Visitors won't have much need to use Kanda Station unless going to the hotels nearby. Ochanomizu Station on the JR Chūō and Sōbu Lines is convenient to other sights.

Subway Since the Hibiya Line stops a bit east of the main electronics neighbourhood, the JR is more convenient for Akihabara. For Kanda, the Marunouchi Line stops at Awajichō, close to the traditional restaurant neighbourhood, while Ochanomizu on the Marunouchi Line and Shin-Ochanomizu on the Chiyoda Line are convenient to other sights. To get to Jimbōchō, take either the Toei Shinjuku or the Hanzōmon Lines to Jimbōchō Station.

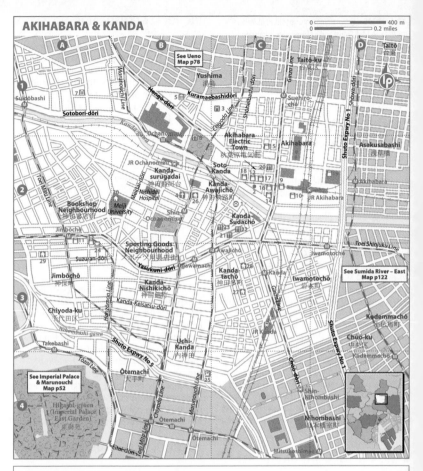

AKIHABARA & KANDA

(☎ 5298-1188; www.animecenter.jp; 4th fl, Akihabara UDX Bldg, 4-14-1 Soto-Kanda, Chiyoda-ku; admission free; ⊗ 11am-7pm; ⊕ JR Yamanote or JR Sōbu Line to Akihabara, Electric Town or Denki-gai exit), a rather underwhelming exhibition hall that springs to life when there are anime related special events.

KANDA & AROUND

ORIGAMI KAIKAN Map p67
おりがみ会館

International Origami Centre; ☎ 3811-4025; 1-7-14 Yushima, Bunkyō-ku; admin@origamikaikan.co.jp; admission free; ⊗ 9am-6pm Mon-Sat; ⊕ Maru-nouchi Line to Ochanomizu (exit 1), JR Chūō or Sōbu Lines to Ochanomizu (Hijiribashi exit)

This multistorey exhibition space and workshop is dedicated to this quintessentially Japanese art. In a shop/gallery on the 1st floor and a gallery on the 2nd, many of the works are so sculptural you'd mistake them for wood, and with patterns so intricate you'd mistake them for fabric, while on the 4th floor is a workshop where visitors can watch the process of dyeing and painting of origami paper. Although admission is free, origami lessons (offered most days in Japanese) cost ¥1000 to ¥2500 for one to two hours, depending on the complexity of that day's design. First-timers would do well to try for a class with the centre's director, Kobayashi Kazuo. It's best to request a reservation by email when you know your schedule.

KANDA MYŌJIN (KANDA SHRINE)
Map p67
神田明神

☎ 3254-0753; www.kandamyoujin.or.jp; 2-16-2 Sotokanda, Chiyoda-ku; admission free; ⊕ Maru-nouchi Line to Ochanomizu (exit 2)

Hidden behind the main streets, this little known but quite splendid Shintō shrine boasts vermillion-coloured halls surrounding a stately courtyard. It traces its history back to AD 730, though its present location dates from 1616. The *kami* (gods) enshrined here are said to bring luck in business and in finding a spouse. It is the home shrine of the Kanda Matsuri (Kanda Festival; p18) in mid-May, one of the largest festivals in Tokyo.

NICHOLAI CATHEDRAL Map p67
ニコライ堂

☎ 3295-6879; 4-1-3 Kanda-Surugadai, Chiyoda-ku; admission ¥300; ⊗ 1-4pm Apr-Sep, 1-3.30pm Oct-Mar; ⊕ Chiyoda Line to Shin-Ochanomizu (exit 2)

This Russian Orthodox cathedral is named for St Nicholai of Japan (1836–1912), who first arrived as chaplain of the Russian consulate in the port city of Hakodate (Hokkaidō) and through missionary work soon amassed about 30,000 faithful. The Tokyo building, complete with a distinctive onion dome, was first constructed in 1891. The original copper dome was, like parts of so many grand buildings, damaged in the 1923 earthquake, forcing the church to downsize to the (still enormous) dome that's now in place. If you're interested in attending worship services, enquire inside for times.

TOKYO WONDER SITE HONGO Map p67
トーキョーワンダーサイト本郷

☎ 5689-5531; www.tokyo-ws.org; 2-4-16 Hongo, Bunkyō-ku; admission free; ⊗ variable; ⊕ JR Sōbu Line to Ochanomizu (Ochanomizu-bashi exit) or Suidōbashi (east exit)

Operated by the Tokyo Metropolitan Government, Tokyo Wonder Site comprises three floors of galleries with the aim of promoting new and emerging artists. There is a regularly changing program of exhibitions, competitions and lectures in media ranging from painting to video art. Check the website before setting out.

YUSHIMA SEIDŌ (YUSHIMA SHRINE)
Map p67
湯島聖堂

☎ 3251-4606; 1-4-25 Yushima, Bunkyō-ku; admission free; ⊗ 9.30am-5pm Apr-Sep, 9.30am-4pm Oct-Mar; ⊕ Marunouchi Line to Ochanomizu (exit 2), JR Chūō or Sōbu Lines to Ochanomizu (Hijiribashi exit)

Established in 1632 and later used as a school for the sons of the powerful during the Tokugawa regime, Yushima Seidō is one of Tokyo's few Confucian shrines. There's a Ming dynasty bronze statue of Confucius in its black-lacquered main hall, which was rebuilt in 1935. The sculpture is visible only from 1 to 4 January and the fourth Sunday in April, but you can turn up at weekends and holidays to see the building's interior.

TOKYO POP

Heeding the call of Tokyo's youth subculture

MANGA & ANIME

Manga characters spring to life in Akihabara (p66)

top picks

ANIME

Ghost in the Shell (1995) Oshii Mamoru

My Neighbor Totoro (1988) Miyazaki Hayao

Grave of the Fireflies (1988) Takahata Isao

Neon Genesis Evangelion (1995-96) Anno Hideaki

Doraemon (1979-2005) Fujimoto Hiroshi

Giant robots, martial-arts superheroes and magical schoolgirls. Sound like pretty childish fare for entertainment? Just check the Japanese businessman on the train beside you as he opens a lurid manga (Japanese comic book) and delves into another samurai romance. In today's Japan, kids' entertainment is for kids of all ages.

Walk into any convenience store in Tokyo and pick up a phone directory-sized weekly manga anthology. You'll find about 25 tales of heady pulp fiction – comic narratives spanning everything from gangster sagas to bicycle racing to *shōgi* (Japanese chess), often with generous helpings of sex and violence. Anime (Japanese animation) can be even wilder: legions of saucer-eyed schoolgirls, cute fluorescent monsters and mechatronic superheroes go light years beyond Disney and Pixar. This onslaught of fantasy has also achieved critical mass overseas.

In 2004 manga accounted for 37% of all publications sold, though comic book sales have declined 20% over the past decade due to the low birth rate, proliferation of electronic diversions like mobile phones and the widespread availability of material through second-hand manga shops, libraries and cafes.

Anime has fared better. Japan's most revered animator Miyazaki Hayao enjoyed international acclaim by winning the 2003 Oscar for Best Animated Feature for *Spirited Away* – the most successful Japanese movie of all time in Japan. His 2008 *Ponyo* was another hit in Japan and the US, helped by an infectious theme song. Fans will want to visit the Ghibli Museum (p113) for a behind-the-scenes look at the art of this unique Japanese genre. However, overseas sales have been struggling largely due to the proliferation of file-sharing internet sites; illegal copying has not hurt manga as badly.

To gauge the economic might of manga and anime, you could attend the Tokyo International Animation Fair (www.tokyoanime.jp/en/index.php; March at Tokyo Big Sight; p136). It's a one-stop hit for proving exactly how big anime is in Japan. Some estimates suggest that nearly 5000 titles of anime are currently produced annually, covering features, TV episodes and Original Video Animation (OVAs; animation released directly to retail sale on DVD). The number of booths, companies and buyers at the Tokyo International Animation Fair supports these estimates.

Less corporate in its orientation is Comiket (www.comiket.co.jp; short for 'Comic Market') which is held twice a year in Tokyo (August and December, also at Tokyo Big Sight). This is a massive gathering of fan-produced amateur manga known as *dōjinshi*. To the untrained eye, *dōjinshi* looks like 'official' manga, but most are parodies of famous manga characters. Complete subgenres exist here, from gag-strips to sexual re-imaginings of popular titles. The last decade witnessed many a famous manga artist emerge from this sprawling subculture.

Also at Comiket one can experience the *cos-play* phenomenon: 'costume play', where fans dress up in their favourite character's attire. It's a bit nerdy, but the Japanese kids take it to another level. Your scepticism may melt into admiration.

There are hundreds of anime/manga stores throughout Tokyo. Current districts to explore include Nakano, where many second-

> 'Experience the cos-play phenomenon: 'costume play', where fans dress up in their favourite character's attire'

hand collectors' stores have sprouted. A major chain is Mandarake (p141), with a superstore in Nakano that will require many hours of your time.

But if you want to dive in and truly get lost, head to Akihabara. Akihabara's Electric Town is still the electronics district par excellence, but there has been a massive increase in anime/manga stores lining the strip. Mandarake has a new superstore here, but a visit to Tokyo Anime Center (p66) is worthwhile if you only have a few minutes to spare in Akihabara – it sells souvenir anime and manga goods like T-shirts. Several Akihabara retailers deal in the more perverse *(hentai)* end of the spectrum with PC games, magazines and DVDs. If you see lots of images of helpless-looking cartoon girls around the entrance, chances are it's a *hentai* shop. And don't be surprised if you see cute, anime-esque (and real) girls dressed as French maids at Akihabara Station – sipping coffee while chatting with doe-eyed maids is the latest *otaku* pastime (see@Home Café, p164). Life imitating art? Yes, but there's really no distinction if you're a real *otaku*!

Timothy N Hornyak

WILL ROBB (OSAMU TEZUKA)

Anime characters such as Astro Boy are wildly popular

JOCHEN TACK / ALAMY

Art collides with life in Shibuya (p101)

HYPERFASHION

Fashion takes on an entire new meaning in the trendy boutiques of Harajuku (p147)

You don't have to go far to see the far-out in Tokyo. Get off the train at JR Harajuku Station on a Saturday and you'll encounter a patchwork of subcultures if you walk to Yoyogi-kōen, but the most striking are the gosurori (Gothic Lolita) kids posing like vampires at noon on Jingū-bashi (Jingū Bridge). Think Halloween meets neo-Victorian with the odd glam rock accent and you'll get the idea. Those with the fake bandages and eye patches on their faces may be imitating broken dolls.

But whatever subgenre you find and wherever you go, visitors to Tokyo are often in awe of this city's incredible sense of style. From the chaotic get-up worn by Harajuku girls (and boys) to the sleek black shoes that click along the avenues in Ebisu, people here think carefully about design, trends and beauty.

Ever since the Edo period, this city has been Japan's most fashion-forward. Edokko (children of Edo) found a way to make chic the drab kimono imposed by the Tokugawa shōgunate, by crafting handsome pouches closed with sculptural clasps called *netsuke* to adorn their otherwise uniform appearance. Since the late 19th century, the Japanese have been eager adopters of Western fashions but have maintained their traditional dress for special occasions – it's common to see Japanese wearing kimono at weddings, and *yukata* (light summer kimono) for fireworks shows.

Japanese workaday wear ranges from the standard-issue salaryman suit (overwhelmingly dark blue or black) to ubiquitous uniforms like frumpy 'office lady' vests, to the skirts over jeans and thigh-high tights favoured by Tokyo girls. In the last couple

AKB48

You may have heard of Morning Musume, the eight-girl J-pop idol group that was big in the early 2000s. AKB48 carries the manufactured idol supergroup concept to the next level – it consists of about 50 fresh-faced young girls from all over Japan. Divided into three teams, the AKB48 girls have their own TV show and their own concert hall in Akihabara. Fans, mostly grown men, line up daily to see these young idols on stage.

of decades, Tokyo's fashion scene has been loosely organised around the work of Issey Miyake (p148), Yohji Yamamoto (p148) and, more recently, Rei Kawakubo of Comme des Garçons (p148), who show internationally in addition to maintaining their presence in Tokyo. Other designers include Koshino Hiroko, Sakabe Mikio and Utsugi Eri. Visionaries like Fujiwara Hiroshi, the renowned streetwear fashion arbiter, have a huge impact on what Japanese youth wear.

Young designers have initiated an antifashion movement in Japan, designing clothes meant to be worn with comfort inside and outside of the house. Sneaker and streetwear preachers A Bathing Ape (aka BAPE; p147), the creation of designer and Teriyaki Boyz DJ Nigo, has sold premium urban footwear at slick outlets that feel like shrines to j-hop, Japanese hip hop. Even casual wear may not be inexpensive compared to your home; Tokyo's parasite singles have money. Hot casual brand GDC (see p144), which groups labels like Ugly and Ventura, sells fab T-shirts for a cool ¥10,000. Districts in which to see the newest and most fashionable wares are Omote-sandô and Aoyama, Daikanyama and Shimo-kitazawa; see p147 for more details.

GREG ELMS

Pick up some fab sneakers at A Bathing Ape (p147)

GREG ELMS

Little Bo Peep and Madame Lash get in on the fun of cos-play (costume play) in Harajuku (p105)

FUN TECH

It may be the 30 buttons on your state-of-the-art Japanese toilet or a USB memory drive that looks exactly like a piece of sushi, or a new digital camera studded with Hello Kitty faces – Japanese are inimitable in their flair for tricking out ordinary gadgets with primo engineering and lots of fun, hot looks.

The humble photo booth has evolved beyond recognition in the *purikura* (print club), a mini graphics studio that can spit out extensively user-designed photo stickers and has enough room for you to change into your fave superhero costume. Parking garages are narrow towers – a vertical car-stacking machine – in which cars go up and down in revolving bays for maximum use of space. Arcades are ear-splitting, multilevel 'game centres' full of machines that make you bang *taiko* (drums), dance to a rhythm track or guide a pair of metal claws around a stuffed animal's neck. In addition to ranking your vocalist skills, karaoke music players count the number of calories burned per song. Inescapable vending machines dispense a cornucopia of consumer goods from underwear to steaming *rāmen* noodles. As the capital of the most automated society in the world, Tokyo is well suited for those who shun human interaction (p149).

Japan has long been an export powerhouse for cameras, stereos and cars, but now it's pinning its hopes on 'partner robots' to take up the slack as the workforce shrinks. Robot exhibitions are big in Tokyo (p20), and one of the hottest trends in consumer robots are the do-it-yourself kits that can be assembled into little soccer-playing humanoids (see Tsukumo Robotto Ōkoku, p141). These little electro-mechanical athletes and warriors compete in tournaments in Akihabara,

WILL ROBB

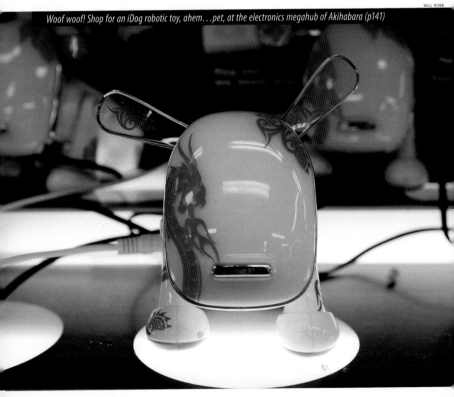

Woof woof! Shop for an iDog robotic toy, ahem…pet, at the electronics megahub of Akihabara (p141)

Fishing for sweets at a Shinjuku (p109) arcade

CHRIS HUTTY / ALAMY

Even flowers can be bought at a vending machine (p149)

TIMOTHY N HORNYAK

wowing kids and adults raised on a diet of comic-book heroes like Astro Boy. Only in Tokyo would millions gather to witness an 18m replica of a robot from the animated Gundam sci-fi series erected in a park in Odaiba in 2009.

Tokyoites are decidedly at home with machines and technology. Such is the reverence for tools that Asakusa's Sensō-ji (p83) holds annual thanksgiving rituals for long-serving needles that are attended by seamstresses, tattoo artists and the like. The animistic roots of Japan's passion for machines and desire to personalise them run deep, and residents of the capital are always eager to get the latest mobile phone and accessorise it with their favourite cartoon character hand straps. Indeed, riding a subway full of silent, phone-gazing commuters or walking by a *pachinko* (vertical pinpall game) parlour ringing with the clatter of metal balls and electronic sounds gives the impression that Tokyoites are immersed in a sea of electronic devices. If you need a break, step into an oxygen bar, sit back in a high-tech massage chair or sing a few rounds of karaoke. There's no escaping the machine in Tokyo.

'The animistic roots of Japan's passion for machines and desire to personalise them run deep'

DESIGN

Be inspired by the architectural genius of the National Art Center, Tokyo (p93)

WILL ROBB (NATIONAL ART CENTER, TOKYO, ARCHITECT KUROKAWA KISHO, 2006)

Tokyo brims with innovative Japanese designs – be it futuristic buildings, patterned handkerchiefs or sexy novelties like an electronic candlestick. Recent recipients of the state-sponsored Good Design Award include Panasonic Let's Note laptops, Nissin cup noodles and Series N700 shinkansen bullet trains. Fuelled by public hunger for new products, uniquely Japanese design is ubiquitous in Tokyo, from daily necessities sold at convenience stores to the latest products at exquisite design stores in Roppongi and the Omote-sandô area.

Clothing retailers for the masses like Muji (p139) and Uniqlo (p139) have inspired, practical duds that are simple without being bland; the former's amazing selection of no-name, generic umbrellas, batteries, toasters and even chocolates are a refreshing tonic to brand-saturated modern culture. Electronics junkies already know about Akihabara and its ever-thinning TV screens, mobile-phone accessories and robot stores (see p66); Tokyo also hosts Asia's largest design show, Design Festa (p19 and p20) with its own permanent gallery (p131). Professional exhibitions like Tokyo Designer's Week and 100% Design Tokyo draw the brightest designers and manufacturers from around Japan, as well as massive public attendance.

But the best places to find cool designs in Tokyo are the unexpected: an ergonomic, multifunction rice cooker that looks like a mini spaceship; an origami crane expertly poised on a ryokan pillow in welcome; or a tilting, three-wheeled moped for delivering pizza. The humble black *bentō* (boxed lunch), with its sections for fish, rice, vegies and other foods, is a nifty illustration of the way space is compartmentalised and maximised in a culture that makes do with overcrowding so remarkably well. Like *kata,* the progressive steps to learning a traditional art (such as karate or ikebana), design is more a fundamental part of life in Tokyo, an everyday expression of the highly prized qualities of beauty and functionality.

RACHEL LEWIS

All aboard the sleek shinkansen *(bullet train)*

Eating p165; Shopping p138; Sleeping p217

Forming part of the historic core of Shitamachi, Ueno has always proudly thumbed its nose at the high fashions and fickle trends of the high-class districts in Yamanote. Although rising real estate prices and recent gentrification have erased most vestiges of the old atmosphere, Ueno's Ameya Yokocho, which was once the site of the largest postwar black market, still holds true to its proud roots even if the goods are (more) legit now.

Historically, Ueno Hill was famous as being the site of a last-ditch defence of the Tokugawa shōgunate by an estimated 2000 loyalists in 1868. Devoted to preventing the restoration of the emperor, these adherents stationed themselves at Kanei-ji, a grand temple compound located up on the hill. They were duly dispatched by the imperial army, which prompted the subsequent Meiji government to decree that Ueno Hill would become one of Tokyo's first parklands.

Today, Ueno-kōen is the neighbourhood's foremost attraction and one of Tokyo's most famous leafy retreats. Boasting a wealth of museums, shrines, a kid-friendly zoo, some phenomenal cherry-blossom viewing (p18) and the de facto front garden of Tokyo University (Japan's most prestigious institution of higher learning), Ueno Park for an afternoon is the perfect antidote to the urban grind.

The sprawling Ueno Station is the nexus of the neighbourhood, with the greater Asakusa area to the east and Akihabara and Kanda to the south. In Ueno itself, all things lead to the park with its myriad art museums; to get here, take the Ueno-kōen (Ueno Park) exit from Ueno Station.

UENO-KŌEN (UENO PARK) Map p78
上野公園

☎ 3828-5644; ⏰ 5am-11pm; ◎ JR Yamanote Line, Ginza or Hibiya Line to Ueno (Ueno-kōen exit)

Tokyo's oldest public park has several names: its Sunday name, which no one ever uses, is Ueno Onshi Kōen; some locals dub it Ueno no Oyama (Ueno Mountain); and English speakers call it Ueno Park. Whichever you prefer, Ueno-Kōen makes for a pleasant city escape.

There are two entrances to the park: the main one takes you straight into the museum and art gallery area, a course that might leave you worn out before you get to Ueno's temples. For these, it's better to start at the southern entrance between JR Ueno Station and Keisei Ueno Station, and do a little temple-viewing en route to the museums. From the JR Station, take the Ikenohata exit and turn right. Just around the corner is a flight of stairs leading up into the park.

Situated slightly to your right at the top of the stairs is the mother of all meeting places, a statue of Saigō Takamori. Fans of the film *The Last Samurai* should note that Katsumoto, the character played by Ken Watanabe, was loosely based on Takamori, a Tokugawa loyalist who gained legendary status among the common Japanese. The Meiji government, capitalising on this fame,

posthumously pardoned Takamori and granted him full honours. Today he remains an exemplar of the samurai spirit in Japan.

Continue along the way, bear to the far left and follow a wide tree-lined path until you reach Kiyōmizu Kannon-dō, modelled after the landmark Kiyōmizu-dera (Kiyomizu Temple) in Kyoto. During Ningyō-kuyō (p20) those wishing to conceive a child leave a doll here for the Senjū Kannon (the 1000-armed Buddhist goddess of mercy), and the accumulated dolls are burnt ceremoniously each 25 September.

From the temple, continue down to the narrow road that follows the pond, Shinobazu-ike. Through a red *torii* (gate), located on an island in the pond, is Benten-dō, a memorial to Benten, a patron goddess of

TRANSPORT: UENO

Train The JR Yamanote Line stops at Ueno Station and is the best transport option for reaching Ueno Park. Okachimachi Station, one stop south, is more convenient for Ameya Yokocho (p81). The private Keisei Line terminates here, and has cheap connections to Narita Airport. For shopping in Nippori, take the Yamanote Line to Nippori Station.

Subway The Hibiya and Ginza Lines connect with Ueno Station and let you off near the park. If you're heading to Tokyo University or Yushima Tenjin, take the Chiyoda Line to Yushima.

UENO

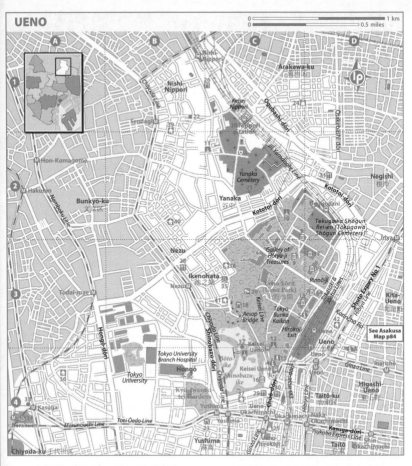

the arts. Behind the temple you can hire a small boat (☎ 3828-9502; row boats per hr ¥600, paddle boats per 30min ¥600; ⏰ 9am-6pm Mar-Nov) to take out on the water, weather permitting.

Make your way back to the road that follows Shinobazu-ike and turn left. Where the road begins to curve and leaves Shinobazu-ike behind, there is a stair pathway to the right. Follow this path and take the second turn to the left. This will take you into the grounds of Tōshō-gū (☎ 3822-3455), which was established in 1627 (the present building dates from 1651). This is a shrine which, like its counterpart in Nikkō, was founded in memory of Tokugawa Ieyasu (p24).

Inside, beyond the subdued worship hall, Ieyasu's shrine is all black lacquerwork and gold leaf. Miraculously, the entire structure has survived all of Tokyo's many disas-

ters, making it one of the few early Edo structures still extant. There's a good view of the 17th-century, five-storey pagoda Kanei-ji, now stranded inside Ueno Zoo, to your right as you take the pathway into the shrine. The pathway itself is fronted by a stone *torii* and is lined with 200 stone lanterns rendered as gifts by *daimyō* in the Edo period.

TOKYO NATIONAL MUSEUM (TOKYO KOKURITSU HAKUBUTSUKAN) Map p78
東京国立博物館
☎ 3822-1111; www.tnm.jp; 13-9 Ueno Kōen, Taitō-ku; adult/child & senior/university student ¥600/free/¥400, additional charges apply for special exhibitions; ⏰ 9.30am-5pm Tue-Sun; ◉ JR Yamanote, Ginza or Hibiya Line to Ueno (Ueno-kōen exit)

UENO

If you visit only one museum in Tokyo, make it this one. The Tokyo National Museum's grand buildings hold the world's largest collection of Japanese art, and you could easily spend many hours perusing the galleries here. The building dates from 1939, and is in the imperial style, which fuses Western and Japanese architectural motifs.

The museum has four galleries, the most important of which is the Honkan (Main Gallery). For an introduction to Japanese art history from Jōmon to Edo in one fell swoop, head to the 2nd floor. Other galleries include ancient pottery, religious sculpture, arms and armour, exquisite lacquerware and calligraphy.

The Gallery of Hōryū-ji Treasures displays masks, scrolls and gilt Buddhas from Hōryū-ji – in Nara Prefecture, said to be the first Buddhist temple in Japan (founded 607) – in a spare, elegant box of a contemporary building (1999) by Taniguchi Yoshio, who also designed the new building for New York's Museum of Modern Art. The Heiseikan (Heisei Hall) opened in 1993 to commemorate the marriage of Crown Prince Naruhito (p30), and it is used for exhibitions of Japanese archaeology as well as special exhibits.

Hyōkeikan (Hyōkei Hall) was built in 1909, with Western-style architecture that is reminiscent of a museum you might find in Paris, though inside it shows works from across East and South Asia and the Middle East. Normally these are in a fifth building, Tōyōkan (Gallery of Eastern Antiquities), which is closed for earthquake retrofitting and due to reopen in 2012.

NATIONAL MUSEUM OF WESTERN ART (KOKURITSU SEIYŌ BIJUTSUKAN) Map p78
国立西洋美術館

☎ 3828-5131; www.nmwa.go.jp; 7-7 Ueno Kōen, Taitō-ku; adult/student/child ¥420/130/free, permanent collection free 2nd & 4th Sat each month; ⏱ 9.30am-5pm Tue-Sun, to 8pm Fri; ◎ JR Yamanote, Ginza or Hibiya Line to Ueno (Ueno-kōen exit)

This museum has its roots in French impressionism, but runs the gamut from medieval Madonna and Child images to 20th-century abstract expressionist painting. All the big names are here, particularly Manet, Rodin, Miró and the Dutch Masters. It also hosts wildly popular temporary exhibits on loan from such stalwarts as the Museo del Prado in Madrid. The main building was designed by Le Corbusier in the late 1950s and is now on UNESCO's World Heritage list; a couple of additions have been made since.

Much of the original collection was amassed by Matsukata Kōjiro (1865–1950), president of a shipbuilding company and later a politician. He would travel frequently to Europe on business and bring back treasures to inspire up-and-coming Japanese painters. Some 400 of his works were impounded in France during WWII, and it was only after Matsukata's death that they were allowed to be shipped to Japan.

UENO ZOO (UENO DŌBUTSU-EN)
Map p78

上野動物園

☎ 3828-5171; www.tokyo-zoo.net/english/index .html; 9-38 Ueno-kōen, Taitō-ku; adult/child/student/senior ¥600/free/200/300; 🕙 9.30am-5pm Tue-Sun; 🚇 JR Yamanote, Ginza or Hibiya Line to Ueno (Ueno-kōen exit)

Japan's oldest zoo was established in 1882, and is home to lions and tigers and bears (oh my!). The biggest attractions are normally the giant pandas, but the zoo's only remaining panda, Ling Ling, passed away in 2008. As we went to press, a pair of new pandas was reportedly due to arrive from China in early 2011.

If you object to zoos in general, this one probably won't change your opinion, what with small enclosures for the animals and a facility that's generally showing its age. On the other hand it's larger than you'd think, given the obvious space constraints of Tokyo. Plus, all of the big-name animals from around the globe are well represented here.

If you're visiting the zoo with the kids, you can take a ride on the monorail to the petting zoo, where your precious ones can gently run their small, sticky hands over tame animals such as ducks, horses and goats.

NATIONAL SCIENCE MUSEUM (KOKURITSU KAGAKU HAKUBUTSUKAN) Map p78

国立科学博物館

☎ Mon-Fri 3822-0111, Sat, Sun & holidays 3822-0114; www.kahaku.go.jp; 7-20 Ueno-kōen, Taitō-ku; adult/child ¥600/free; 🕙 9am-5pm Tue-Sun, to 8pm Fri; 🚇 JR Yamanote, Ginza or Hibiya Line to Ueno (Ueno-kōen exit)

This large, sprawling, multistorey museum dedicated to the pursuit of science is packed with delights, especially if you're travelling with the little ones. Displays (eg of the forest or animals of the savannah) are imaginatively presented, some allowing kids to climb up, down, around and even within.

Other displays explain concepts of physics and mechanics by showing just how things like magnets do what they do. Also, don't miss the giant, life-sized replica of a blue whale that soars over the entrance to the museum. And of course, there are dinosaurs, dinosaurs and more dinosaurs…

There is English signage throughout, though it's not as extensive as the Japanese signage. An English-language audio guide is available (¥300). Note the different contact number for weekends and holidays.

SHITAMACHI MUSEUM Map p78

下町風俗資料館

☎ 3823-7451; 2-1 Ueno-kōen, Taitō-ku; adult/child/student ¥300/free/100; 🕙 9.30am-4.30pm; 🚇 JR Yamanote to Ueno (Shinobazu exit), Ginza or Hibiya Line to Ueno (exit 6), Chioyda Line to Yushima (exit 2)

This museum re-creates life in the plebeian quarters of Tokyo during the Meiji and Taishō periods through an exhibition of typical Shitamachi buildings. Take off your shoes and look inside an old tenement house or around an old sweet shop while soaking up the atmosphere of long-gone Shitamachi. For some more detailed info, pick up the English-language leaflets describing the various buildings in detail. On the first and third Sunday of the month, the museum stages *kamishibai* (narratives told by performers using lovely painted cards) and on the second Sunday are exhibitions of making traditional artificial flowers.

AMEYA YOKOCHŌ (AMEYOKO ARCADE) Map p78
アメヤ横町

🕙 10am-8pm; 🚇 Yamanote Line to Okachimachi (north exit) or Ueno (south exit), Ginza Line to Ueno Hirokōji (exit A5), Hibiya Line to Naka-Okachimachi (exit A5)

This unabashed shopping street is one of the few areas in which some of the rough readiness of old Shitamachi still lingers. Step into this alley paralleling the JR Yamanote Line tracks south of JR Ueno Station, and ritzy, glitzy Tokyo may seem

TOKYO FOR CHILDREN

Tokyo deliberately cultivates spaces for children. Parks, museums and other venues are designed with wee ones in mind. And, even on a limited budget, you'll find things here reasonably priced and accessible. The following should get you started:

Ghibli Museum (p113) Kids who are charmed by the animation of Miyazaki Hayao (*Ponyo*, *Spirited Away* etc) will want to make the trek out of town to visit this busy little museum.

Ikebukuro Earthquake Hall (Ikebukuro Bōsai-kan; p115) Younger children may be rattled, both literally and emotionally, by the simulations of earthquakes and fires, but it's important preparation for older kids.

Meguro Parasitological Museum (p99) This museum is ideal for kids who like big worms and other scary bugs.

Mori Art Museum (p91) This is a dramatic place to introduce kids to contemporary art. If they weary of the exhibits, excellent views await on the 52nd-floor observation decks.

Museum of Maritime Science (Fune no Kagaku-kan; p128) Filled with detailed model ships, hands-on displays and a cool pool for piloting remote-controlled submarines.

National Children's Castle (Kodomo-no-Shiro; Map p106; ☎ 3797-5666; www.kodomono-shiro.jp/english/index .html; adult/child ¥500/400; 🕙 variable; 🚇 JR Yamanote Line to Shibuya, east exit, or Ginza Line to Omote-Sandō, B2 exit) Has playrooms, puppet theatres, a swimming pool and a music lobby where kids can make all the noise they like and make friends with Japanese kids. The National Children's Castle Hotel (p223) next door was built especially for those with young children and can be a convenient refuge for travelling families. It's located on Aoyama-dōri.

National Museum of Emerging Science & Innovation (Miraikan; p126) Offers interactive exhibits where kids can manipulate robots and micromachines, and explore the principles of superconductivity.

RiSūPia (p128) Gamelike exhibits make learning about maths and physics fun.

Tokyo Disney Resort (Map pp48–9; www.tokyodisneyresort.co.jp/index_e.html; 1-day pass adult/child 12-17yr/child 4-11yr ¥5800/5000/3900, 2-day pass ¥10,000/8800/6900; 🚇 JR Keiyo Line to Maihama) The world's most successful theme park is home to kid-friendly Tokyo Disneyland, as well as the more adult-oriented Tokyo DisneySea.

Tokyo Metropolitan Children's Hall (Tokyo-to Jido Kaikan; Map p102; ☎ 3409-6361; www.fukushihoken.metro. tokyo.jp/jidou/English/index.html; 1-18-24 Shibuya, Shibuya-ku; admission free; 🚇 JR Yamanote Line to Shibuya, east exit) Boasts six kid-friendly storeys and a number of ingenious play areas – check out the human-body maze or get messy in the hands-on art studio where children can make pottery and origami. It's 300m northeast of Shibuya Station, next to Mitake-kōen.

Ueno Zoo (Ueno Dōbutsu-en; opposite) This fairly comprehensive zoo has all the usual lions and tigers and bears. If you've come with little ones, the real attraction here is the goat- and sheep-filled petting zoo.

There are a number of amusement parks, including the oldie-but-a-goody Hanayashiki Amusement Park (p130); the flashier Tokyo Dome City (p61); the rainy-day, Sega-operated Tokyo Joypolis (p127); the indoor amusements and food theme-parks of Namco Namjatown (p115); and one of the world's tallest Ferris wheels (p128) in Odaiba.

like a distant memory. The gravelly *irasshai* (Welcome) and *ikaga desu ka?* (How about buying some?) of fishmongers, fruit and vegetable sellers, knock-off-clothing vendors and a healthy smattering of open-air markets couldn't be further from Ginza or Aoyama.

Ameyoko earned its notoriety as a black-market district in the years following WWII, though today it's primarily a bargain shopping area. Simple shops spill out into the alleys, selling block after block of cheap clothing (for Japan, anyway), produce, dried fruit, dried *nori* (seaweed), dried mushrooms and dried squid.

Some of the same tourist items on sale in Ginza sell here at more reasonable rates. Shopkeepers also stand on less ceremony than those in other shopping areas in Tokyo, brazenly hawking their goods with guttural cries to the passing crowds. In the Ameyoko Center building, Chinese, Korean and Southeast Asian merchants have set up their own shopping arcade where you'll find exotic cooking spices, fresh seafood, durian fruit and other unusual imported items.

TOKYO UNIVERSITY (TOKYO DAIGAKU) Map p78

東京大学

Tōdai; ⊙ Chiyoda Line to Nezu (exit 2) or Yushima (exit 1)

Most kids in Japan dream of gaining admission to Tokyo University, Japan's most prestigious institution of higher learning. As with the Ivy League colleges and Oxbridge

in the US and UK, admission here practically assures later admission to the halls of power in both business and government. With that in mind, high-school students spend years studying at home and in cram schools for Tōdai's rigorous admission exam.

The campus itself is not beautiful, but does hold historical interest. In 1968–69 Tōdai became the centre of a national crisis when students thrice took over the main administrative building, Yasuda Hall, ousting the school's president and other administrators before finally being ousted themselves. In order to make an example of the students, police employed tear gas as well as blasting the students' stronghold with fire hoses on national TV in what came to be called the battle of Yasuda castle.

Today, students at Tōdai are a bit more tame, and have a reputation among the Japanese as being somewhat conservative, stodgy and eccentric in comparison to other university students. Regardless of their disposition, standing among the hallowed halls of Japan's top university is a memorable experience, even if only to rub shoulders with the future Japanese elite.

YUSHIMA TENJIN (YUSHIMA SHRINE)
Map p78

湯島天神

Yushima Tenmangū; ☎ 3836-0753; 3-30-1 Yushima, Bunkyō-ku; admission free; ⏰ 6am-8pm; ⊙ Chiyoda Line to Yushima (exit 1)

Across the way from Tokyo University, this particularly attractive Shintō shrine traces its lineage back to the 5th century. In the 14th century, the spirit of a renowned scholar was also enshrined here, which leads to Yushima Tenjin's current popularity: it receives countless pilgrims in search of academic success. Amid the buildings with their painted accents and gold trim (the latest reconstruction was in 1995), students hang messages written on wooden tablets called *ema*, left in hope that lofty exam scores will gain hopeful high-school students admission to the power generator across the street or universities nationwide.

ASAKUSA

Eating p166; Shopping p142; Sleeping p218

As the thriving core of the historic Shitamachi district, Asakusa (a-*sock*-sa) is where the spirit of old Edo proudly lives. The neighbourhood is centred on the imposing temple of Sensō-ji (also known as Asakusa Kannon-dō), which was founded in the 7th century, not only before Tokyo was Edo but also before Edo was even a glimmer of an idea. As Edo rose, Asakusa emerged as a bustling commercial centre and bawdy entertainment area, becoming the sturdy beat of Shitamachi's rowdy heart.

Sadly Asakusa had never fully recovered from the Great Earthquake of 1923 before it was flattened once again by aerial bombing in the closing months of WWII. Although the brightest lights have shifted elsewhere, this works to Asakusa's advantage: it retains a close-to-the-ground feeling of the common people not readily visible in other parts of town. Its main streets, Kaminarimon-dōri and the pedestrianised Nakamise-dōri, are undeniably of the 21st century (and well touristed), but just metres away is a glimpse of a bygone Japan that is difficult to experience outside places like Kyoto.

Here, more than any other district in Tokyo, you'll be rewarded by closing the book, ignoring the map and just getting lost in the side streets and back alleys. Up one street, you might find a charming ryokan (traditional Japanese inn), a fastidious *sembei* (rice cracker) maker or a smiling kimono seller, while down the next lane could be a marvellous public bath frequented by the *yakuza* (Japanese mafia). Asakusa is ripe for your own personal discovery. One area that may be a turn-off: west of Sensō-ji and south of Hanayashiki amusement park is a cluster of girlie theatres, a legacy of the days when striptease was popular in Asakusa – though it almost didn't succeed due to the popularity of female sword fighting!

Asakusa is bounded on the east by the Sumida-gawa (Sumida River) and by Ueno to the west. All of the destinations in this section are easiest reached via Asakusa Station on the Ginza Line. There is also an Asakusa Station on the Toei Asakusa Line, a slightly longer walk. From either subway station, head away from the river along Kaminarimon-dōri; the Kaminarimon Gate marks the entrance to Sensō-ji. Through the gate, the lively Nakamise-dōri shopping arcade leads straight to the temple.

SENSŌ-JI (SENSŌ TEMPLE) Map p84
浅草寺

☎ 3842-0181; 2-3-1 Asakusa, Taitō-ku; admission free; ☒ 24hr; ◉ Ginza Line to Asakusa (exit 1), Toei Asakusa Line to Asakusa (exit A5)

Asakusa's raison d'être, Sensō-ji enshrines a golden statue of Kannon, the goddess of mercy, which was miraculously fished out of the nearby Sumida-gawa by two fishermen in AD 628. In time a structure was built to house the image, which has remained on the spot through successive reconstructions of the temple, including a complete postwar reconstruction following the aerial bombings at the end of WWII.

The temple precinct begins at the majestic Kaminarimon (Thunder Gate), which houses a pair of ferocious protective deities: Fūjin, the god of wind, on the right; and Raijin, the god of thunder, on the left.

Straight on through the gate is the bustling shopping street Nakamise-dōri. Everything is sold here from tourist trinkets like purses made from obi (kimono sash)

fabric to Edo-style crafts and wigs to be worn with kimono. Along this route are also stands that specialise in salty, crunchy *sembei* and ningyō-yaki (snacks in the shape of pagodas, fish and more), made of pancake batter with a dollop of *anko* (bean paste) baked inside.

Nakamise-dōri leads north to another gate, Hōzō-mon, whose fierce guardians you must pass to reach the main temple compound. On the gate's back side, behind

TRANSPORT: ASAKUSA

Train The Tōbu Nikko Line terminates at Asakusa Station, offering the most convenient connections to Nikko (p231).

Subway The Ginza Line stops at Asakusa, just in front of Azuma-bashi. The Toei Asakusa Line also stops at a separate Asakusa Station nearby.

Water bus Azuma-bashi is the northern terminus of Tokyo Cruise (p65), connecting to Hinode Pier, Hama Rikyū and Odaiba.

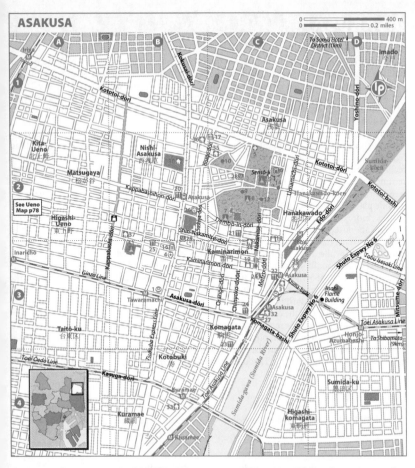

these guardians, are a pair of 2500kg, 4.5m-tall straw sandals crafted for Sensō-ji by some 800 villagers in northern Yamagata prefecture. Off the courtyard stands a 53m-high five-storey pagoda, a 1973 reconstruction of a pagoda built by Tokugawa Iemitsu. The current structure is the second-highest pagoda in Japan.

Before the *hondō* (main hall), smoke winds its way up from a huge incense cauldron around which supplicants stand wafting the smoke and its scent to their bodies and over their heads to ensure good health. The Kannon image (a tiny 6cm) is cloistered away from view deep inside the main hall, as is common in Buddhist temples in Japan. Nonetheless, a steady stream of worshippers makes its way to the temple, where the people

cast coins, pray and bow in a gesture of respect. Do feel free to join in (see the boxed text, p98).

Holy though it may be, Sensō-ji and its precincts are often very busy and distinctly not Zen-like, resounding with cameras and voices with accents from across the country and around the world. To escape the fray, just left of the pagoda is Dembō-in (伝法院), a subtemple of Sensō-ji that adjoins the residence of the chief priest. The garden here is said to have been designed in the late 18th century after Katsura-rikyu, the sprawling imperial villa in Kyoto. The pond in the centre of the garden is in the shape of the kanji character for 'heart', and other elements of classic temple garden design include a stone representing a dock, flowering trees

ASAKUSA

that cascade over the shore and a *horai* in the far corner, which represents the place of enlightenment. Here you can almost forget that you're in Tokyo, though you'll have to ignore the boxy buildings just outside the garden's confines. Dembō-in is officially closed to the public, but visitors can phone in advance (in Japanese) to arrange a visit. Visits without a reservation are not permitted.

ASAKUSA-JINJA (ASAKUSA SHRINE)
Map p84
浅草神社
2-3-1 Asakusa, Taitō-ku; admission free; ⊙ Ginza Line to Asakusa (exit 1), Toei Asakusa Line to Asakusa (exit A5)
The proximity of this Shintō shrine, behind Sensō-ji and to the right, testifies to the coexistence of Japan's two major religions. Asakusa-jinja was built in honour of the brothers who discovered the Kannon statue and is renowned as a fine example of an architectural style called *gongen-zukuri*. It's also the epicentre of one of Tokyo's most important festivals, the Sanja Matsuri (p18), a three-day extravaganza of costumed parades, some 100 lurching *mikoshi* (portable shrines) and stripped-to-the-waist *yakuza* sporting remarkable tattoos.

Niten-mon, the gate that marks one of the entryways to Asakusa-jinja, was erected in 1618 as a private entrance to the temple

for the Tokugawa shōgun. The gate was built here at the same time as Tōshō-gū (p233), which burned at this location and was moved to Ueno for fire prevention. The gate's weathered wooden pillars, plastered with votive papers left by Shintō pilgrims, and its enormous red paper lantern certainly merit a stop on your way out of the compound. Remarkably, Niten-mon is the only structure in the temple precinct to have survived Asakusa's various disasters.

TRADITIONAL CRAFTS MUSEUM (EDO SHITAMACHI DENTŌ KŌGEIKAN) Map p84
江戸下町伝統工芸館
☎ 3842-1990; 2-22-13 Asakusa, Taitō-ku; admission free; ⊙ 10am-8pm; ⊙ Ginza Line to Asakusa (exit 1), Toei Asakusa Line to Asakusa (exit A5)
Gallery Takumi, as this small hall is also known, is a great place to view dozens of handmade crafts that still flourish in the heart of Shitamachi. The gallery on the 2nd floor is crammed with a rotating selection of works by neighbourhood artists: fans, lanterns, knives, brushes, gold leaf, precision wood-working and glass just for starters. Craft demonstrations take place most Saturdays and Sundays around noon. If anything you see strikes your interest, staff can direct you to artisans or shops selling their work.

DETOUR: SHIBAMATA

Star Wars, Harry Potter, Chucky...all the movies in those series combined wouldn't come close to the whopping 48 films of *Otoko wa Tsurai Yo* (It's Tough Being a Man; 1968–1995). *Otoko wa Tsurai Yo* starred Tora-san (played by Atsumi Kiyoshi and directed by Yamada Yōji), the fedora-sporting, plaid blazer-wearing, awkward-in-love bloke who is to Japan what Archie Bunker is to America: a working-class everyman in a suburb just outside the big city. The films were set in Shibamata (柴又), at the eastern edge of Tokyo-to (Tokyo Metropolis), making a visit here must for Tora-san fans. Even if you've never heard of Tora-san, Shibamata's atmospheric streets and workaday feel make it a comfy-cosy throwback to the Shōwa Era.

Shibamata's main street, Taishakuten-sandō (帝釈天参道), feels like a film set lined with dozens of wood-built shops specialising in *unagi* (eel), *sembei* (rice crackers) and *kusa-dango* (sweet bean paste dumplings wrapped in leaves). The street ends at the small temple Taishakuten (帝釈天), which was founded in 1629 and boasts exquisite wood carvings.

At the lovely garden Yamamoto-tei (山本亭; ☎ 3671-8577; 7-19-32 Katsushika Shibamata, Katsuhika-ku; admission ¥100; 🕘 9am-5pm, closed 3rd Tue of month), where you can take a seat inside over a bowl of powdered green tea and a sweet (¥500) and contemplate this Kyoto-style classical garden, ranked fourth best in Japan by the *Journal of Japanese Gardening*. Nearby is a Tora-san Museum (寅さん記念館; ☎ 3657-3455; 6-22-19 Shiamata, Katsushika-ku; adult/child/senior ¥500/300/400; 🕘 9am-5pm, closed 3rd Tue of the month), which serious fans will want to visit, although there isn't much English signage. Finally, Yagiri no Watashi (矢切の渡し; Yagiri Ferryboat; one way adult/child ¥100/50, 🕘 9.30am-4.30pm mid-Mar–Nov & early Jan) has plied the Edo-gawa (separating Tokyo and Chiba-ken to the east) since the Edo Period. It's Tokyo's only remaining human-powered ferry.

To reach Shibamata, take the Toei Asakusa Line to Oshiage, and transfer at Keisei-Takasago to the Keisei Kanamachi Line (from Oshiage ¥180, about 20 minutes). Taishakuten-sandō begins about 100m from the station, past the statue of – guess who?

TAIKO DRUM MUSEUM (TAIKO-KAN)
Map p84

太鼓館

☎ 3842-5622; 2-1-1 Nishi Asakusa, Taitō-ku; adult/child ¥300/150; 🕘 10am-5pm Wed-Sun; 🚇 Ginza Line to Tawaramachi (exit 3)

More than 600 drums make up this collection, gathered from around the world, though only about 200 are available at any one time in the splendidly interactive drum on display. You have free rein to touch or play any instrument that doesn't have a mark – those with a blue dot should be handled carefully, while a red dot means 'off limits'. If you are inspired by the display, you can buy a Japanese-style drum and lots of other festival products at Miyamoto Unosuke Shoten (see the boxed text, p142).

KAPPABASHI-DŌRI (KAPPABASHI STREET) Map p84

合羽橋通り

🚇 Ginza Line to Tawaramachi (exit 3)

A 10-minute walk west of Sensō-ji, Kappa-bashi-dōri is the country's largest wholesale kitchenware and restaurant-supply district. Gourmet accessories include colourful, patterned *noren* (split doorway curtains), pots and pans, restaurant signage, tableware and a number of bizarre Japanese kitchen gadgets to make you go 'Hmmm?'

The drawcard for overseas visitors is the plastic models of food, such as you see in restaurant windows throughout Tokyo. Whether you want steak and chips, a lurid pizza, a bowl of *rāmen* or a plate of spaghetti bolognaise complete with an upright fork, you'll find it here.

AKASAKA

Drinking p182; Eating p167; Sleeping p220

During the Meiji era, Akasaka was the district of Tokyo that was most densely populated by geisha. These female companions, who were highly trained artists and mistresses of conversation, continued to occupy the area during both the world wars. During the American occupation, Akasaka's geisha houses served as the settings for notorious backroom deals that jump-started the economy, sealed political alliances and shaped the modern nation of Japan.

Although Tokyo's geisha are few and far between nowadays (if you want geisha, go to Kyoto), Akasaka remains as Tokyo's centre of both explicit and exclusive power. With the National Diet Building just a few minutes' walk away in the Nagatachō area, Akasaka fills with bureaucrats, politicians and high-powered businessmen at the end of the day. The geisha houses may be gone, but Akasaka's backstreets and late-night bars still echo with political murmurings and business deals.

Politics aside, Akasaka is also home to Hie-jinja, which comes alive in the spring when the cherry blossoms complement its row of rust-red *torii*, and in autumn when children in traditional costumes arrive for Shichi-go-san (p20). Sannō-sai (p19), one of Tokyo's most exuberant *matsuri* (festivals) takes place here in mid-June, offering an excellent chance to see one of the rowdy, colourful processions of *mikoshi*.

Akasaka is situated southwest of the Imperial Palace, due north of Roppongi and west of Aoyama. The neighbourhood is centred on Hie-jinja, though the pull of the National Diet Building to the shrine's east is strong.

HIE-JINJA (HIE SHRINE) Map p88
日枝神社

☎ 3581-2471; www.hiejinja.net/eindex.htm; 2-10-5 Nagatachō, Chiyoda-ku; admission free; Ⓔ Ginza or Namboku Line to Tameike-sannō (exit 5 or 7)

This Shintō shrine traces its roots to the sacred Mt Hiei, northeast of Kyoto, and it has been the protector shrine of Edo Castle since it was first built in 1478. The present site dates from 1659, though the shrine was destroyed in the 1945 bombings and later rebuilt in 1967.

These days, the shrine is chiefly known as the host of one of Tokyo's three liveliest *matsuri,* Sannō-sai (p19). Given the shrine's protector status, the festival was regularly attended by the shōgun, and even now the route of the festival's *mikoshi* terminates at the Imperial Palace.

When the festival's not on, the shrine makes for a colourful yet quiet break. A highlight is the walk up through a 'tunnel' of *torii*, especially dramatic on a sunny day. The shrine is also great for a visit when the cherry blossoms are out or the leaves are changing.

Oh, and if you're wondering about the carved monkey clutching one of her young, she is emblematic of the shrine's ability to offer protection against the threat of a miscarriage.

NATIONAL DIET BUILDING Map p88
国会議事堂

☎ 3581-3111; www.sangiin.go.jp; 1-7-1 Nagatachō, Chiyoda-ku; Ⓨ 8am-5pm Mon-Fri, closed national holidays; Ⓔ Yūrakuchō, Hanzōmon or Namboku Line to Nagatachō (exit 1), Marunouchi or Chiyoda Line to Kokkai-gijidōmae (exit 1)

Built on a site once inhabited by feudal lords, the National Diet was completed in 1936 with its landmark pyramid-shaped dome. The chambers – the Shūgi-in or House of Representatives (the Upper House) and the Sangi-in or House of Councillors (the Lower House) – have witnessed fist fights and wrestling matches over the occasional hot-button issue. Recently things have been a bit more sedate.

Free 60-minute tours (☎ 5521-7445) of the Sangi-in are available when the Diet is not in session (ring the day before to confirm); they take in the public gallery, the emperor's room (from where he addresses the Diet at the start of each session) and

TRANSPORT: AKASAKA

Subway The Yūrakuchō, Hanzōmon, Namboku, Chiyoda, Marunouchi and Ginza Lines all converge in the Akasaka area. Akasaka-mitsuke is the most central station here, and nearby are Nagatachō, Akasaka and Tameike-Sannō Stations.

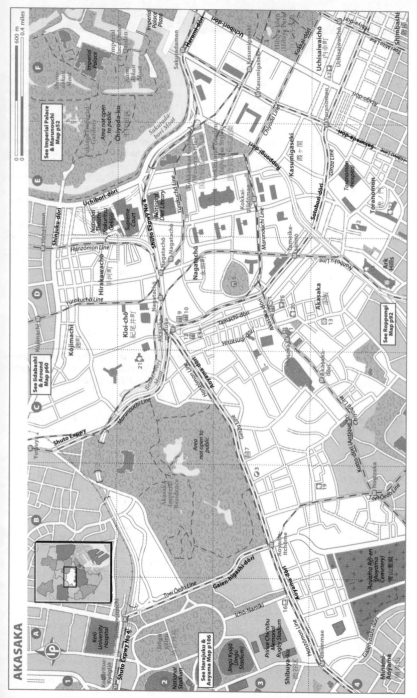

AKASAKA

AKASAKA

central hall (featuring a floor mosaic of a million pieces of marble and murals depicting the four seasons). Although an English pamphlet is available, there is no guarantee that English-speaking guide will be available when you arrive. For the tours, it is best to arrive after 9am to avoid the largest tour groups. And unless you're here for a protest, leave your red headbands, which are de rigueur among demonstrators, in your suitcase.

HOTEL NEW ŌTANI Map p88
ホテルニューオータニ
☎ 3265-1111; www.newotani.co.jp/en/tokyo/index.html; 4-1 Kioi-chō, Chiyoda-ku; ◉ Ginza or Marunouchi Line to Akasaka-mitsuke (Exit D)
The New Ōtani was a showplace when it opened in 1964 to coincide with the Tokyo Olympics. Even though the mantle of tippy-top hotel has since gone elsewhere, it remains worth visiting for its 400-year-old garden (admission free; ◷ 6am-10pm), which once belonged to a Tokugawa regent, and for the New Ōtani Art Museum (☎ 3221-4111; guests free,

nonguests from ¥500; ◷ 10am-6pm Tue-Sun), which displays a decent collection of modern Japanese and French paintings as well as wood-block prints. Otherwise, visitors may be blown away by the hotel's sheer mass: two towers, 1479 guest rooms, nearly three dozen banquet rooms and 38(!) restaurants and bars. Be sure to pick up a map. You can stay here, too (p220).

SŌGETSU KAIKAN Map p88
草月会館
☎ 3408-1151; www.sogetsu.or.jp/english/index.html; 7-2-21 Akasaka, Minato-ku; ◷ 9.30am-5.30pm Mon-Fri; ◉ Ginza, Hanzōmon or Toei Ōedo Line to Aoyama-itchōme (exit 4)
Sōgetsu is one of Japan's leading schools of avant-garde ikebana offering classes in English (p207). Even if you have no interest in flower arranging, it's worth a peek in for the building (1977) designed by Tange Kenzō, and the giant, climbable piece of installation art, by the revered Japanese-American sculptor Isamu Noguchi, that occupies the lobby.

Drinking p182; Eating p167; Shopping p143; Sleeping p221

Since the end of WWII, Roppongi has garnered a notorious reputation as a den of sin: American soldiers on leave, wet-behind-the-ears foreigners fresh off the plane, Chinese prostitutes, Russian strippers, Nigerian bouncers and plenty of hungry women and hungrier men on the prowl. Many self-respecting Tokyoites and long-term foreign residents won't go near the place at night, but it's hard to deny that a good time is usually had by those who do. Dancing and flirting until the wee hours of the morning is the standard course of action in Roppongi, as are spending big and drinking hard.

Daytime was always a different story. Even 10 years ago, any Tokyoite could tell you exactly what went on during the day in Roppongi – nothing. Yet in 2003 everything changed following the opening of Roppongi Hills, a masterfully designed shopping/dining/office/residential/hotel/gallery/museum complex. A visually stunning project aimed at redefining the cultural landscape of the neighbourhood, Roppongi Hills is now one of the capital's principal landmarks, joined in 2007 by Tokyo Midtown, an equally impressive feat of urban architecture with similar aspirations, and the fabulous National Art Center, Tokyo.

These developments are – slowly – transforming Roppongi from a sleazy pleasure quarter into a high-class neighbourhood with all the bourgeois trimmings. Roppongi Hills and Tokyo Midtown may be mere steps from the liquor-soaked clubs, but they're a world away in attitude.

Roppongi lies between Aoyama to the west and the well-to-do residential neighbourhoods of Azabu and Shirokane to the south, en route to Meguro and Shinagawa. To the north is stately Akasaka. This section also covers the Shiba area to the east, which links up with Shiodome.

Roppongi Crossing (Roppongi kōsaten), where Roppongi-dōri meets Gaien-Higashi-dōri in the shadow of the expressway, is the reference point for all things Roppongi. Roppongi Hills lies west along Roppongi-dōri (Nishi-Azabu crossing is a few minutes further on foot), while Tokyo Midtown is a few blocks north along Gaien-Higashi-dōri.

ROPPONGI HILLS Map p92
六本木ヒルズ

☎ 6406-6000; Roppongi 6-chōme; admission free; Ⓢ Hibiya or Toei Ōedo Line to Roppongi (exit 1)

Opened in 2003 to an incredible amount of fanfare, Roppongi Hills was the dream of real-estate developer Mori Minoru, who long envisaged a transformation of Roppongi. Since then, an incredible amount of lofty praise has been vaulted at the complex, which is arguably the most architecturally arresting sight in Tokyo – architects including Jon Jerde, Maki and Associates, and Kohn Pedersen Fox Associates worked on the various buildings. The result is a feast for the eyes, enhanced by public art such as Louise Bourgeois' giant, spiny alfresco spider called *Maman* and the benches-cum-sculptures along Keyakizaka-dōri.

With expertly drawn lines of steel and glass, expansive tree-lined public spaces and a healthy smattering of the city's top bars, restaurants and shops, Roppongi Hills stands as a testament to a new concept in urban planning. Rather than building larger and taller residential towers, it is argued developers should instead focus on usable space that can better serve the community. And

although most Tokyoites can't even dream about owning a high-rise apartment at the city's most prestigious address, Roppongi Hills is a destination in its own right.

The centrepiece of the complex is the 54-storey Mori Tower, which is home to some of the world's leading companies, as well as the Mori Art Museum and Tokyo City View observatory. At the base of the tower is the marvellous Grand Hyatt Tokyo (p221) and some 200 shopping, drinking and dining establishments including internationally known brands and chefs (eg Joël Robuchon). On the plaza below, the TV Asahi network headquarters adjoin an ancient samurai garden and the Roppongi Hills Arena, where you can often catch outdoor performances. Just beyond, the brand-name shops ascending Keyakizaka are nothing short of marvels of modern design.

TRANSPORT: ROPPONGI

Subway The Hibiya and Toei Ōedo Lines both run through Roppongi. The Hibiya Line drops you closer to Roppongi Crossing, Roppongi's main intersection, and Nishi-Azabu.

Try ascending into Roppongi Hills from the subway Hibiya Line, via escalators through the cylindrical building Metro Hat. Other-worldly indeed.

MORI ART MUSEUM Map p92
森美術館

☎ 5777-8600; www.mori.art.museum; Mori Tower, Roppongi 6-chōme; admission varied; 🕙 10am-10pm Wed-Mon, 10am-5pm Tue; ⊚ Hibiya or Toei Ōedo Line to Roppongi (exit 1)
Perched on the 52nd and 53rd floors of Mori Tower in the Roppongi Hills complex, the high ceilings, broad views and thematic programs of this museum have somehow managed to live up to all the hype. Contemporary exhibits are consistently beautifully presented and run the gamut from Chinese artist-cum-rabble-rouser Ai Wei Wei to the theme of medicine and art.

Admission varies but is usually around ¥1500 to ¥1800 for adults, and includes entry to Tokyo City View (☎ 6406-6652; www .tokyocityview.com; adult/child/student ¥1500/500/1000; 🕙 9am-1am), on the 52nd floor. There are observatories atop other tall buildings in town, but none can match Roppongi Hills for its central location and undeniable cool factor; weather permitting you can also visit a new rooftop Sky Deck (additional ¥300, 🕙 10am-8pm).

The museum is subject to closure between exhibitions, but Tokyo City View is open daily.

TOKYO MIDTOWN Map p92
東京ミッドタウン

☎ 3423-8000; www.tokyo-midtown.com/en; Minato-ku; admission free; ⊚ Hibiya or Toei Ōedo Line to Roppongi (exit 8)
Like Roppongi Hills, Tokyo Midtown (2007) is a composite urban district of ultramodern buildings surrounding a historic Japanese garden. Following the same design and urban planning lines that made Roppongi Hills so successful, the Tokyo Midtown complex brims with sophisticated bars, restaurants, shops, art galleries, a hotel and leafy public spaces. Escalators ascend alongside man-made waterfalls of rock and glass, bridges in the air are lined with back-lit *washi* (Japanese handmade paper), and planters full of soaring bamboo draw your eyes through skylights to the lofty heights of the towers above.

Separate from the myriad opportunities for parting with serious cash is Hinokichō-kōen. Formerly a private garden attached to an Edo Period villa, Hinokichō was reopened as a public park for the benefit of visitors to Tokyo Midtown. Adjacent to the park, Midtown Garden is a cherry tree-lined grassy space that makes a perfect spot for a picnic. In the middle of Midtown Garden is sort of a geometric clamshell of a building, 21_21 Design Sight (☎ 3475-2121; www.2121designsight.jp; 9-7-6-Akasaka, Minato-ku; adult/child ¥1000/free, student ¥500-800; 🕙 11am-8pm Wed-Sun), constructed by Pritzker Prize–winning architect Andō Tadao, curated by fashion designer Issey Miyake and featuring temporary exhibits of cutting-edge art and design.

Tokyo Midtown is also home to the Suntory Museum of Art (below), as well as the glamorous Ritz-Carlton Tokyo (p221).

SUNTORY MUSEUM OF ART Map p92
サントリー美術館

☎ 3479-8600; www.suntory.com/culture-sports/ sma; Tokyo Midtown, 9-7-4 Akasaka, Minato-ku; admission varied; 🕙 10am-6pm Sun & Mon, 10am-8pm Wed-Sat, closed between exhibitions; ⊚ Hibiya or Toei Ōedo Line to Roppongi (exit 8)
From the time of its original opening in 1961, the Suntory Museum of Art has subscribed to an underlying philosophy of lifestyle art. Rotating exhibitions focus on the beauty of useful things: Japanese ceramics, lacquerware, glass, dyeing, weaving and such. Its new Midtown digs by architect Kuma Kengō are at turns understated and breathtaking. Admission is free for children and junior-high-school students.

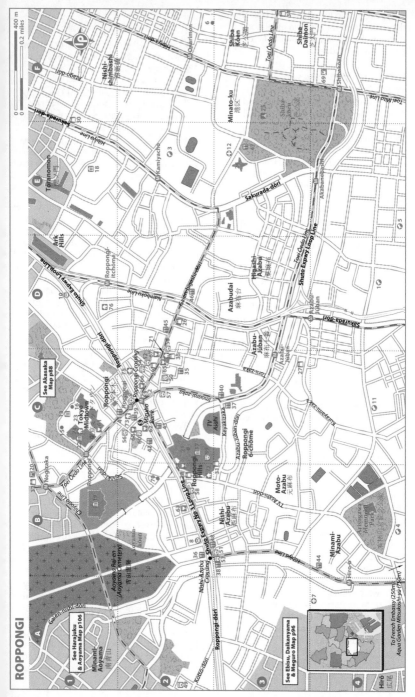

ROPPONGI

NATIONAL ART CENTER, TOKYO Map p92
国立新美術館

NACT; ☎ 6812-9900; www.nact.jp; 7-22-1 Roppongi, Minato-ku; admission varies; 🕙 10am-6pm Sat-Mon, Wed & Thu, 10am-8pm Fri; 🚇 Chiyoda Line to Nogizaka (exit 6)

This architectural marvel designed by Kurokawa Kishō, which opened in 2007 as Japan's fifth national-class museum, has no permanent collection but boasts the country's largest exhibition space for visiting shows, which have included Renoir, Modigliani and the Japan Media Arts Festival. The NACT is also worth visiting for its awesome undulating glass facade mesh, its cafes atop giant inverted cones and the great gift shop. Building admission is free.

NOGI-JINJA & GENERAL NOGI'S RESIDENCE Map p92
乃木神社 & 旧乃木邸

☎ 3478-3001 or 5413-7015 (Minato-ku office); 8-11-32 Akasaka; admission free; 🕙 shrine 6am-5pm; 🚇 Chiyoda Line to Nogizaka (exit A1), Hibiya or Toei Ōedo Line to Roppongi (exit A7)

A short walk from the urbanity that is Tokyo Midtown, this shrine on the grounds of the home of a Meiji-era general is a relaxing break. The shiny black wooden house is open to the public only on 12 and 13 September, but the rest of the year you can peek through its windows and notice the mash-up of Japanese and Western styles that defined the Meiji period; think a tatami room with a Western fireplace.

TOKYO TOWER Map p92
東京タワー

☎ 3433-5111; www.tokyotower.co.jp/english; 4-2-8 Shiba-kōen, Minato-ku; adult/child ¥820/460; ⏰ observation 9am-10pm; ◎ Toei Ōedo Line to Akabanebashi (Akabanebashi exit)

Built during the postwar boom of the 1950s when Japan was struggling to create a new list of monuments symbolising its modernity, Tokyo Tower resembles the Eiffel Tower, albeit 13m taller. The similarities stop there, however as the Tokyo Tower was painted bright orange and white in order to comply with international aviation safety regulations.

Truth be told, Tokyo Tower is something of a shameless tourist trap, though it's good fun if you go with the right attitude. Lifts whisk visitors up to the observation deck, which provides some stunning views of the sprawling megalopolis that is Tokyo. The 1st floor boasts an enormous aquarium (adult/child ¥1000/500), while the 3rd floor is home to a wax museum (adult/child ¥870/460) that retains some degree of retro-popularity.

ZŌJŌ-JI (ZŌJŌ TEMPLE) Map p92
増上寺

☎ 3432-1431; Shiba-kōen; admission free; ⏰ dawn-dusk; ◎ Toei Ōedo Line to Akabanebashi (Akabanebashi exit)

Behind Tokyo Tower is this former funerary temple of the Tokugawa regime, one of the most important temples of the Jōdō (Pure Land) sect of Buddhism. It dates from 1393, yet like many sights in Tokyo its original structures have been relocated and were subject to war, fire and other natural disasters. It has been rebuilt several times in recent history, the last time in 1974.

Nevertheless, Zōjō-ji remains one of the most monumental temples in town. The main gate, Sanmon, was constructed in 1605, and its three sections were designed to symbolise the three stages one must pass through to achieve nirvana. The giant bell (1673; 15 tonnes) is considered one of the great three bells of the Edo period. On the temple grounds there is a large collection of statues of the bodhisattva Jizō, said to be a guide during the transmigration of the soul.

MUSÉE TOMO Map p92
智美術館

☎ 5733-5311; 4-1-35 Toranomon, Minato-ku; adult ¥1300, student ¥500-800; ⏰ 11am-6pm Tue-Sun; ◎ Hibiya Line to Kamiyachō (exit 4b)

This marvellous museum may be one of Tokyo's most elegant and tasteful. It is named for Kikuchi Tomo, whose collection of contemporary Japanese ceramics wowed them in Washington and London before finally being exhibited in Tokyo. Exhibitions change every few months and might include highlights of the Kikuchi collection or a special study of raku pottery; you can bet that the displays will be atmospheric and beautiful. The museum is behind the Hotel Ōkura.

EBISU, DAIKANYAMA & MEGURO

Drinking p182; Eating p170; Shopping p144; Sleeping p221

Home to a smart, stylish set of young professionals, wealthy families and privileged expats, Ebisu is one of Tokyo's best-kept secrets. The entire neighbourhood, which screams status, privilege and excellent breeding, offers up some of the city's most cosmopolitan eateries and lounges. Quick to scoff at the teen trends and fickle fashions of nearby Harajuku and Shibuya, Ebisu is cool, classy and always sophisticated.

Up the hill and to the west of Ebisu is Daikanyama, which is characterised by a matrix of funky restaurants and bars run by eccentric proprietors, crazy buildings designed by local visionaries and unique shops defying classification. Equally prestigious as an Ebisu address, Daikanyama is something of a Ginza for high-class shoppers and diners in-the-know.

One stop south from Ebisu on the JR Yamanote Line is Meguro, which has recently begun to gentrify to match its northern neighbours. Meguro boasts some unique sights, including the haunting Daien-ji temple, the Meguro Museum of Art, Tokyo and the frankly icky Meguro Parasitological Museum, beyond which is MISC, an up-and-coming design district of lively shops (p145). There's also a lovely promenade along the Meguro-gawa. A short ride to the east are the forests of the Shizen Kyōiku-en, a nature reserve right in the middle of the big city.

If you have even the slightest love for that deliciously malty alcoholic beverage known in Japanese as *biiru*, don't miss the Beer Museum Yebisu, which has a bargain tasting room that serves up copious amounts of their brew. Also of note in Ebisu is the Tokyo Metropolitan Museum of Photography, a point of pilgrimage for devout shutterbugs (and there are a lot of them in Japan!).

Ebisu and Daikanyama are located south of Harajuku, Shibuya and Aoyama and southwest of Roppongi. Shinagawa is due east, across the narrow southern end of the JR Yamanote Line. From the JR Ebisu Station, the east exit opens onto the Yebisu Sky Walk, a series of conveyor belts that eventually deposits you in the courtyard of Yebisu Garden Place. This is the side of Ebisu designed for visitors, tourists and hardcore shoppers. If you want to see where locals live and play, head for the west exit and up the hill towards glitzy Daikanyama.

From Meguro Station, Daien-ji, Meguro Gajoen, the design district and the Meguro Museum of Art are west of the station, while the Tokyo Metropolitan Teien Art Museum and Shizen Kyōiku-en are east along Meguro-dōri.

EBISU

BEER MUSEUM YEBISU Map p96
恵比寿麦酒記念館
☎ 5423-7255; www.sapporobeer.jp/english/when/museum/museum.html; 4-20-1 Ebisu, Shibuya-ku; adult/under 12yr/12-19yr ¥500/free/300; ⏰ 11am-7pm Tue-Sun, last entry 5pm; ◉ Hibiya or JR Yamanote Line to Ebisu (main exit)

Yes, this is the site of the original Yebisu brewery (1889; now owned by the giant brewer Sapporo). And yes, inside are giant pot-bellied beer vats, antique signage, cute beer ads and a cheesy magic vision theatre. But really you've come for the tasting room, where you can try cheap draughts of everything from weizen and ale to porters and stouts – a four-glass tasting set costs ¥400.

YAMATANE MUSEUM OF ART (YAMATANE BIJUTSUKAN) Map p96
山種美術館
☎ 3239-5911; www.yamatane-museum.or.jp; 3-12-36 Hirō, Shibuya-ku; adult/child/student

¥1000/free/800, special exhibits extra; ⏰ 10am-5pm Tue-Sun; ◉ Hibiya Line to Ebisu (exit 2), JR Yamanote Line to Ebisu (main exit)

This exceptional collection of *nihonga* (Japanese-style paintings) includes some 1800 Japanese works dating from the Meiji Restoration and onwards, of which a small selection is on display at any one time; exhibits change approximately seven or

TRANSPORT: EBISU, DAIKANYAMA & MEGURO

Train The JR Yamanote Line stops at Ebisu and Meguro Stations. Daikanyama is served by the Tōkyū Tōyoko Line, a privately run line that starts in Shibuya.

Subway The Hibiya Line runs through Ebisu and connects with the main JR station, and on to Naka-Meguro, near Daikanyama and the Meguro-gawa. Meguro is served by the Namboku and Toei Mita Lines. Some locations east of Meguro are closest to Shirokanedai Station on the Namboku Line.

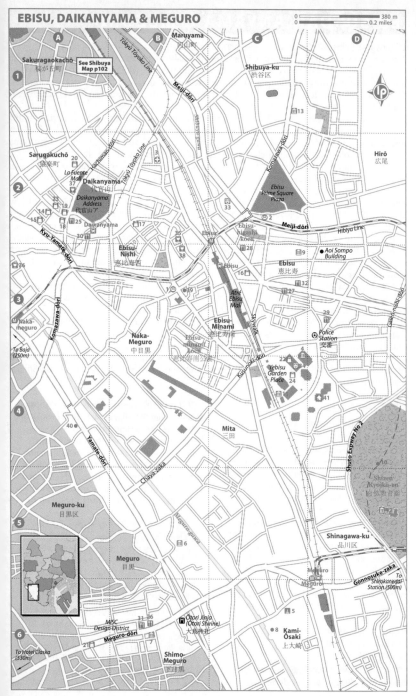

EBISU, DAIKANYAMA & MEGURO

0 ——————— 380 m
0 ——————— 0.2 miles

A   **B**   **C**   **D**

Maruyama
円山町

Sakuragaokachō
桜が丘町

See Shibuya
Map p102

1

Shibuya-ku
渋谷区

🏛13

Hirō
広尾

Sarugakuchō
猿楽町

20

La Fuente
Mall 37

Daikanyama
代官山

Daikanyama
Address

2

23

14 ▢ 19
15 ▢ ▢ 25 Daikanyama
18 代官山
30

Ebisu-
Nishi
恵比寿西

Ebisu
Prime Square
Plaza

33

🏛 2

Meiji-dōri

Hibiya Line

Ebisu-
higashi-
kōen

Ebisu

28

Ebisu
恵比寿

🏛9 ● Aoi Sompo
Building

▢36

Kyu-yamate-dōri

35

38

16 ▢

🏛27

🏛32

Ⓜ Naka-
meguro

▢39

 Atré
Ebisu
Mall

29

3

To Baja
(250m)

Naka-
Meguro
中目黒

Ebisu-
Minami
恵比寿南

● Police
Station
交番

22

24

Ebisu-
minami-
kōen
恵比寿南公園

Yebisu
Garden
Place

Skywalk

🏛

41

4

40 ●

Mita
三田

Chaya-zaka

Shuto Exprwy No 2

Ao

Shizen
Kyoiku-en
自然教育園

Meguro-ku
目黒区

Meguro-gawa

🏛2

5

Meguro
目黒

🏛6

Shinagawa-ku
品川区

Meguro

🏛5

To Hotel Claska
(530m)

MISC
Design District

31 26

Ⓜ Meguro
Meguro

Gonnosuke-zaka
To
Shirokanedai
Station (500m)

Ōtori Jinja
(Ōtori Shrine)
大鳥神社

● Kami-
Ōsaki
上大崎

6

21

Meguro-dōri

Shimo-
Meguro
下目黒

EBISU, DAIKANYAMA & MEGURO

eight times per year. Two names to look for: Hayami Gyoshū (1894–1935), whose *Dancing Flames* is an important cultural property; and Okumura Togyū (1889–1990), whose *Cherry Blossoms at Daigoji Temple* is a masterpiece in pastel colours. In 2009 the museum moved to these new surrounds.

TOKYO METROPOLITAN MUSEUM OF PHOTOGRAPHY Map p96
東京都写真美術館
☎ 3280-0099; www.syabi.com; 1-13-3 Mita, Meguro-ku; admission ¥500-1650; 🕙 10am-6pm Tue-Sun; 🚇 Hibiya or JR Yamanote Line to Ebisu (main exit)

In a corner of Yebisu Garden Place, this five-storey museum chronicles the history and contemporary use of still and moving images, and holds 23,000 works, roughly 70% of them Japanese. Displays often comprise exceptional work by photographers from both Japan and abroad, and there's an extensive library of photographic literature from throughout the world. Ticket prices are based on how many exhibits you see.

NADIFF A/P/A/R/T Map p96
ナヂフアパート
☎ 3446-4977; 1-18-4 Ebisu, Shibuya-ku; admission free; 🕙 noon-8pm; 🚇 Hibiya or JR Yamanote Line to Ebisu (main exit)

You never quite know what's going to be on show at this arts foundation (its name is an abbreviation for 'New Art Diffusion'), but you can be sure it will reflect the latest in Japanese style and taste. In its contemporary building hidden in Ebisu's backstreets, there are gallery spaces upstairs and down and a little cafe-gallery-event space on the 4th floor, while the ground floor is home to a bookshop of arts and architecture. With your back to the Aoi Sompo building, head down the street and follow the signs on electrical poles to the alley to your left.

MEGURO

DAIEN-JI (DAIEN TEMPLE) Map p96
大円寺
☎ 3491-2793; 1-8-5 Shimo-Meguro, Meguro-ku; admission free; 🕙 9am-5pm; 🚇 JR Yamanote, Namboku or Mita Line to Meguro (west exit)

Established sometime around 1615, this small, photogenic temple hemmed in by trees commemorates stillborn and miscarried children, as well as aborted foetuses. Located in the rear of the temple precinct is a separate tribute to the 14,700 people who died in the fire of 1772, which, in addition to flattening most of the wooden houses in surrounding Meguro, burned the original temple structure to the ground.

TEMPLE & SHRINE ETIQUETTE

Visitors to Tokyo are often nervous about committing some dreadful faux pas at a Buddhist temple or Shintō shrine. Relax – as with most other aspects of their lives, the Japanese are not particularly rigid in these matters and certainly wouldn't judge a foreign visitor for not adhering to ritual.

If photography is forbidden, it will be posted as such; otherwise, it is permitted and you should simply use your discretion when taking pictures so as not to interfere with other visitors.

It may surprise overseas visitors that many Japanese do not practise one religion exclusively. Rather, in a great many families the custom is to visit a Shintō shrines for certain life rites (eg blessing of a new baby or a traditional wedding ceremony) and Buddhist temples for others (usually associated with the afterlife). In fact, Buddhist temples and Shintō shrines are often found in the same precincts.

Shintō Shrines

Just past the *torii* (gate) at most larger Shintō shrines is a *chōzuya* (trough of water) with long-handled ladles perched on a *hishaku* (rack) above. This water can be used to purify yourself before entering the sacred precincts. Some Japanese forgo this ritual and head directly for the main hall. The traditional way to purify oneself is to take a ladle, fill it with fresh water from the tap or basin, pour some over one hand, transfer the ladle and pour water over the other hand, then pour a little water into a cupped hand, rinse your mouth and spit the water out. Make sure that any water you have used for washing or rinsing goes on to the ground beside the trough (not into the trough, which would make it impure).

Once you have purified yourself, head to the *haiden* (hall of worship), which sits in front of the *honden* (main hall) enshrining the *kami* (god or gods). Here you'll often find a thick rope hanging from a gong, in front of which is an offerings box. Toss in a coin, ring the gong by pulling on the rope (to summon the deity), bow twice, place your hands in the prayer position to pray silently, clap twice, bow once more and then back away. Some Japanese believe that a ¥5 coin is the luckiest offering at a temple or shrine (the word for ¥5, *go-en*, is a homonym for fate), and that the blessing engendered by the offering of a ¥10 coin will come in the future (since 10 can be pronounced '*tō*' in Japanese, which also means 'far').

Many shrines sell *ema* (small votive plaques), on which you can write a wish before hanging it on a rack for the purpose. Your wish does not have to be in Japanese.

Buddhist Temples

Unless the temple contains a shrine, you will not have to purify yourself before entry. The place of worship in a temple is in the *hondō*, which usually contains a Buddhist altar and one or more Buddha images. The standard practice is to toss some change into the offering box, which sits in front of the altar, step back, place your hands together, pray and then bow to the altar before backing away.

Most temples sell *omikuji* (fortunes written on little slips of paper). These usually cost ¥100. Either pay an attendant or place the money in an honour-system box. Fortunes are dispensed randomly from a special box containing sticks with different numbers written on their ends. Shake the box until one stick pops out of a hole in the box's top. Show this to the attendant and you will be given a fortune matching the number on the stick (remember to return the stick to the box!). This will be written in Japanese under one of four general headings: *dai-kichi* (big luck), *kichi* (luck), *sho-kichi* (small luck) and *kyō* (bad luck). *Kichi* is considered best – your luck is good, but getting better – whereas *dai-kichi* implies that it's great now but otherwise all downhill. *Sho-kichi* is moderately grim and *kyō* is the worst.

Some fortunes are translated into English, or you can ask someone on the temple grounds to read your fortune for you. Once you've read it, fold the fortune and tie it to a nearby tree branch so that the wind can disperse the bad luck; there's always a tree nearby festooned with the white fortunes, or sometimes there's a clothesline-type contraption for the same purpose.

At both shrines and temples, you can buy amulets called *omamori* – for traffic safety, academic success, good health, safe pregnancy and more – usually for ¥300 to ¥500. *Omamori* run the gamut from minimalist paper or wooden charms to small but elaborate brocade bags embroidered with the name of the shrine or temple and your wish.

Another popular memento is *shūin-chō* (pilgrimage books; around ¥1000), which are blank fanfold books; purchase one at the first shrine or temple you visit, and then have it inscribed at each subsequent shrine or temple (around ¥300), usually with lovely calligraphy.

As you enter, you'll come across some red-bonneted *jizō* figures (small stone statues of the Buddhist protector of travellers and children). Further into the temple precinct and completely lining one of its walls are *Arhat* (atonement) statues of the Go-hyaku-rakan (the 500 followers of Buddha). Each of these exquisite stone markers were made to appease the souls that departed in the great fire, and each has its own design and facial expression. Water is often placed in front of the statues to ease the degree of the victims' suffering.

MEGURO WEDDING HALL (MEGURO GAJOEN) Map p96
目黒雅叙園
☎ 3491-4111; 1-8-1 Shimo-Meguro, Meguro-ku; admission free; 🕐 24hr; 🚇 JR Yamanote, Namboku or Toei Mita Line to Meguro (west exit)

One look at the ads on virtually any subway car will tell you that wedding halls are big business in Tokyo. For better or for worse, Gajoen is one of the biggest, and as a study in anthropology you can hardly beat it. 'Wedding hall' doesn't do justice to its many storeys of chapels, banquet halls, expensive restaurants and hotel rooms. The impossibly long corridor connecting them is lined with friezes of geisha and samurai, and often festooned with flowers, while floor-to-ceiling windows look out on a drop-dead gorgeous hillside garden. Even if there aren't wedding bells in your future, it's definitely worth stopping by for a look.

MEGURO MUSEUM OF ART, TOKYO
Map p96
目黒区美術館
☎ 3714-1201; www.mmat.jp; 2-4-36 Meguro, Meguro-ku; adult/concession ¥1000/700; 🕐 10am-6pm Tue-Sun; 🚇 JR Yamanote, Namboku or Mita Line to Meguro (west exit)

Half local, half global, one part of this museum exhibits the work of Meguro artists, while the other is dedicated to international fine art and craft exhibits (think the work of Charles and Ray Eames). The building is a delight – it's airy, spacious and well lit compared with many other Tokyo art museums, which can want for space – and there's a coffee shop with pleasant views of the grounds.

Take the west exit of Meguro Station, walk straight ahead down Meguro-dōri and turn right just after crossing Meguro River (Meguro-gawa). Walk along the river and the museum is on your left, past the tennis court and swimming pool.

MEGURO PARASITOLOGICAL MUSEUM Map p96
目黒寄生虫館
☎ 3716-1264; 4-1-1 Shimo-Meguro, Meguro-ku; admission free; 🕐 10am-5pm Tue-Sun; 🚇 JR Yamanote, Namboku or Mita Line to Meguro (west exit)

Yeah, ew. Probably the grossest museum in Japan, this spot was established in 1953 by Satoru Kamegai, a local doctor concerned by the increasing number of parasites he was encountering in his practice due to unsanitary postwar conditions. The grisly centrepiece is an 8.8m-long tapeworm found ensconced in the body of a 40-year-old Yokohama man. Although there's not a lot of English signage, little explanation is necessary (or even welcomed) as you can easily see how some of these nasties might set up house inside you. Fun for the whole family! Entrance is on the ground floor of a small apartment building.

SHIROKANEDAI

INSTITUTE FOR NATURE STUDY (SHIZEN KYŌIKU-EN) Map p96
自然教育園
☎ 3441-7176; www.kahaku.go.jp/english/visitor_info/shizenen/index.html; 5-21-5 Shirokanedai, Minato-ku; adult/under 18yr & senior ¥300/free; 🕐 9am-4.30pm Tue-Sun Sep-Apr, 9am-5pm Tue-Sun May-Aug, last entry 4pm year-round; 🚇 Namboku Line to Shirokanedai (exit 1)

Although the 200,000 sq metres of this land was the estate of a *daimyō* some six centuries ago and was the site of gunpowder warehouses in the early Meiji period, you'd scarcely know it now. Since 1949, this garden has been part of the Tokyo National Museum (p78) and aims to preserve the local flora in undisciplined profusion. There are wonderful walks through its forests, marshes and ponds, making this one of Tokyo's least known and most appealing getaways. And there is a bonus: admission is limited to 300 people at any one time.

TOKYO METROPOLITAN TEIEN ART MUSEUM Map p96
東京庭園美術館

☎ 3443-0201; www.teien-art-museum.ne.jp; 5-21-9 Shirokanedai, Minato-ku; admission varies by exhibition, garden only adult/child/senior/student ¥200/free/100/160; ⊗ 10am-6pm, closed 2nd & 4th Wed of the month; ⊛ Namboku Line to Shirokanedai (exit 1)

Although this museum hosts art exhibitions (eg Meissen porcelain or pottery by important Japanese artists), its appeal lies principally in the building itself – it's an art deco structure built in 1933, designed by French architect Henri Rapin. The interior details remain alluring, including etched tile trim, light fixtures sculpted to look like peaches and pumpkins, and the 'perfume fountain', sort of an early aromatherapy device. The house was originally home to Prince Asaka-no-miya (1887–1981), Emperor Hirohito's uncle, who was pardoned for his part in the Nanjing Massacre (see p59). It became a museum in 1983. It sits in the southwest corner of the Shizen Kyōiku-en (separate entrance and admission).

SHIBUYA

Drinking p182; Eating p171; Shopping p145; Sleeping p222

Step out of Shibuya Station after dark and you'll find yourself in the Tokyo of your dreams. At Shibuya Crossing, a mind-blowing spectacle of neon and giant screens, streets radiate out like a starburst, and the crowd is a mix of diligently acquired elegance and adolescent exuberance. Much like New York's Times Sq and London's Piccadilly Circus, Tokyo's Shibuya Crossing is visual and aural candy at its best.

If the truth be told, Shibuya is not rich in history, and its paltry handful of sights pales in significance compared to those found in adjacent neighbourhoods. However, Shibuya is perhaps the best neighbourhood in Tokyo to take in the beating pulse of modern Japan by simply browsing, shopping, dining and watching outrageous get-ups that have recently come off the runways at Tokyo's fashion shows. You will be rewarded here by putting down the guidebook and getting lost in the sea of rampant consumerism.

Shibuya is studded with department stores that vie for the patronage of cash-loaded young Japanese looking for their own unique fashion identity. The offshoots of the Tōkyū and Seibu department stores tend to be funkier than in other parts of the city, though the Tōkyū Hands (p146) is perhaps the gem among all of them.

Shibuya, the neighbourhood, is at the centre of Shibuya ward, with nearly a million people within its bounds. Harajuku borders it to the north, Aoyama and Roppongi lie to the east and the sophisticated Ebisu and Daikanyama are just south. The studenty suburb of Shimo-Kitazawa, a short train ride northwest, feels like Shibuya on a smaller scale.

The most famous meeting place in Tokyo, which lies in front of Shibuya Station, is the statue of Hachikō the dog. This famous pooch even has his own exit from the station named after him, which is in fact the exit you should use for all of the sights listed in this section.

HACHIKŌ STATUE Map p102
ハチ公像
Ⓢ JR Yamanote or Ginza Line to Shibuya (Hachikō exit)

In the 1920s, a professor who lived near Shibuya Station kept Hachikō, a small akita dog, who came to the station every day to await the return of his master, Professor Ueno of Tokyo University. The good professor died while at work in 1925, but the dog continued to show up and wait at the station until his own death 10 years later. Hachikō's faithfulness was not lost on the Japanese, who built a statue to honour his memory. The story is more interesting than the statue itself, but Hachikō is perhaps Tokyo's most famous meeting spot. The proud pooch is usually surrounded by hip-looking Tokyoites with mobiles in hand, coordinating the festivities to follow.

SHIBUYA CROSSING Map p102
渋谷交差点
Ⓢ JR Yamanote or Ginza Line to Shibuya (Hachikō exit)

Adjacent to Hachikō Plaza is arguably one of the coolest intersections you will ever see in your life. Made famous in the West following Sofia Coppola's Lost in Translation, Shibuya Crossing is remarkable for its throngs of people, blazing neon lights and enormous video screens, which sometimes display live videos of the street scene below. The sheer energy of the place is enough to stop you dead in your tracks while you loudly proclaim to yourself, 'Wow – I'm in Tokyo!'

TOBACCO & SALT MUSEUM Map p102
たばこと塩の博物館
☎ 3476-2041; www.jti.co.jp/Culture/museum/Welcome.html; 1-16-8 Jinnan, Shibuya-ku; adult/child ¥300/100; ◷ 10am-6pm Tue-Sun; Ⓢ JR Yamanote Line or Ginza Line to Shibuya (Hachikō exit)

For years, smokers have found solace in Tokyo's cafes and bars, and for much of that time the government was in the business of supplying them through a tobacco monopoly. That company has since been privatised to Japan Tobacco Inc, which is

TRANSPORT: SHIBUYA

Train The JR Yamanote Line stops at Shibuya Station. You can also connect here to suburban private trains operated by the Tōkyū and Keiō Inokashira Lines.

Subway The Ginza, Hanzōmon and Fukutoshin Lines stop at Shibuya.

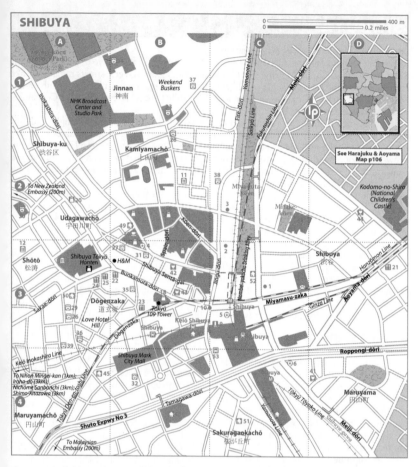

the owner of this museum, a shrine to the bitter leaf, complete with pipes, paraphernalia and wood-block prints.

Downstairs is a homage to Japanese modes of salt production, which until recently was conducted by cumbersome harvests from a reluctant sea. Among the exhibits is a grey, crystalline salt cylinder whose circumference could match that of a small whale. English signage is sadly limited, though the visual power of the exhibits here speaks for itself.

BUNKAMURA Map p102
文化村

☎ 3477-9111; www.bunkamura.co.jp; 2-24-1 Dōgenzaka, Shibuya-ku; admission varies by event; ⏰ varied; 🚇 JR Yamanote or Ginza Line to Shibuya (Hachikō exit)

Bunkamura means 'culture village' and it was Japan's first cross-cultural centre. Spin-the-globe exhibits feature the work of artists from Grandma Moses and Monet to Munakata Shikō, as well as photographic displays by the likes of Man Ray. It's also a busy theatre, art-house cinema and concert hall. It's about seven minutes' walk from Shibuya Station (turn right at the Shibuya 109 building).

TOGURI MUSEUM OF ART Map p102
戸栗美術館

☎ 3465-0070; www.toguri-museum.or.jp; 1-11-3 Shōto, Shibuya-ku; adult/child/student ¥1000/400/700; ⏰ 9.30am-5.30pm Tue-Sun; 🚇 JR Yamanote or Ginza Line to Shibuya (Hachikō exit), Keiō Inokashira Line to Shinsen

SHIBUYA

A few minutes' walk from Bunkamura (opposite), the Toguri displays about 100 pieces at a time from its 7000-piece collection of fine Japanese, Korean and Chinese porcelain. Special exhibits include styles such as Imari and Nabeshima ware for connoisseurs of Japanese pottery and those who'd like to become connoisseurs. The galleries are reasonably sized, there's a pretty garden and the residential neighbourhood is so quiet that you'd never guess you're just steps away from Shibuya's hustle and bustle.

LOVE HOTEL HILL Map p94
ラヴホテルヒル

Ⓡ JR Yamanote Line or subway Ginza Line to Shibuya (Hachikō exit)
Anyone who thinks that Japan is all about raked pebble gardens, geisha in kimono and Zen meditation hasn't strolled through Love Hotel Hill. Just west of central Shibuya, this neighbourhood offers one of the largest concentrations of love hotels in Tokyo, where men and women out on the prowl hope the night will end.

Depending on your tastes, you can bed down in a variety of themed hotels ranging

from miniature Gothic castles and kitschy Arabian palaces to traditional Japanese-themed inns and Balinese-inspired resorts. Although choosing where to go is the best part of visiting a love hotel (well, aside from the actual act itself), our personal favourite is a particular Caribbean-themed love hotel with fake palm trees at the bedside – we'll leave it to you to find it!

To reach Love Hotel Hill, take the road up Dōgenzaka to the left of the Shibuya 109 building. At the top of the hill, on the side streets that run off the main road, is the main concentration of love hotels. Of course, the best way to get around this area is to meet a nice Japanese guy or girl to show you around!

SHIMO-KITAZAWA off Map pp48-9
下北沢

A quick train ride northwest of Shibuya, Shimo-Kitazawa is one of Tokyo's most popular pockets for clothing and accessories for young people, cafes and live music for young people, and, er, young people for young people. It's thanks to its location at the crossroads of two suburban train lines

DETOUR: NIHON MINGEI-KAN

Arguably the most important Japanese art movement in the first half of the 20th century was called *mingei* (folk crafts; see p36). The collection at the lovely Nihon Mingei-kan (日本民芸館; Japan Folk Crafts Museum; off Map pp48–9; ☎ 3467-4527; www.mingeikan.or.jp/english/; 4-3-33 Komaba, Meguro-ku; adult ¥1000, student ¥200-500; ✆ 10am-5pm Tue-Sun) numbers some 17,000 pieces. Most are from Japan, but there are also pieces from Europe, Africa and other Asian countries. The museum's pioneers were Yanagi Sōetsu, Hamada Shōji and Kawai Kanjiro, three of the leaders of the *mingei* movement itself; the impressive building (1936) was Yanagi's house. In addition to changing exhibits of *mingei*, the museum also sponsors an annual competition of new works.

Take the Keiō Inokashira Line to Kobama-Tōdai-mae station and then walk west (the train tracks will be on your left). When the road turns right (about five minutes), the museum is on your right. Note that it closes between exhibitions.

and a number of universities. There's even a bit of a counterculture vibe, but keep in mind that this is Tokyo, not Goa.

The narrow streets of Shimo-Kitazawa (Shimokita to its friends) are barely passable by cars, meaning a streetscape like a dollhouse version of Shibuya, minus the shiny brand names and giant department stores. While there are no big-name sights or landmarks, Shimokita gets by just fine on its bargain-priced hipster shopping,

restaurants and entertainment venues, and a lively street scene all afternoon and evening, especially on weekends. See p146 and p173 to get you started, but this is one neighbourhood where losing yourself in the lanes is more than half the fun.

Shimo-Kitazawa can be reached via the Keiō Inokashira line from Shibuya (¥130, five minutes) or the Odakyū line from Shinjuku (¥150, eight minutes). Most of the action begins outside the south exit (南口).

HARAJUKU & AOYAMA

Drinking p182; Eating p173; Shopping p147

Few districts in Tokyo can offer as many contrasting styles and personalities as the adjacent neighbourhoods of Harajuku and Aoyama. The living, breathing souls of Harajuku are the aptly named 'Harajuku girls', who have been vaulted onto the global stage following the smash hit 'Rich Girl' by American pop singer Gwen Stefani. Although Harajuku girls don't typically live here (Harajuku is in fact one of the most expensive strips of real estate in Tokyo), they are certainly an easily identifiable breed. With camera in hand, be sure to take a stroll down Takeshita-dori, or stop by the informal Sunday afternoon *cos-play* (costume play) fashion show on the bridge, Jingū-bashi, over the train tracks – you'll certainly photograph some interesting characters!

Just across the bridge, to the west, enter the grand, calming, tree-lined precincts of Meiji-jingū, and you'll quickly be transported back to old Japan. This serene shrine, which would probably be more at home in ancient Kyoto than in ultra-modern Tokyo, is one of the undeniable highlights of any trip to the capital.

East of the bridge, the shopping boulevard of Omote-Sandō is home to the haute-est of haute couture, much of it housed in eye-popping contemporary buildings that set standards for the world. If you have one opportunity to shop in Tokyo (and your budget has no limits), make it here.

At the boulevard's other end is Aoyama, domain of chic boutiques and ersatz Parisian cafes. Here, too, are fine museums, galleries and design shops, most notably the newly reopened Nezu Museum.

Omote-Sandō links Harajuku with Aoyama, which lies at the centre of the greater Shibuya ward, through the district officially known as Jingūmae. To the south is Shibuya, the broad expanse of Yoyogi Park is to the west, and to the east are Aoyama Cemetery and Roppongi.

HARAJUKU STATION AREA

MEIJI-JINGŪ (MEIJI SHRINE) Map p106
明治神宮

☎ 3379-5511; www.meijijingu.or.jp; Kami-zono-chō, Yoyogi, Shibuya-ku; admission free; 😊 dawn-dusk; ◉ JR Yamanote Line to Harajuku (Omote-Sandō exit), Chiyoda Line to Meiji-Jingūmae (exit 3)

Tokyo's grandest Shintō shrine, this 1920 edifice enshrines the Emperor Meiji and Empress Shōken, under whose rule Japan ended its isolation from the outside world. Destroyed in WWII bombings and reconstructed in 1958, the shrine buildings occupy just a corner of the precinct's 70 forested hectares. In fact, its 100,000 trees are said to have been donated by 100,000 visitors from all over Japan.

Meiji-jingū might be a reconstruction of the original, but unlike so many of Japan's postwar reconstructions, it is altogether authentic. The main structure was built with *hinoki* cypress from the Kiso region of Nagano prefecture, while the cypress for the huge *torii* was imported from Alishan in Taiwan. If you're there when a wedding is on, the procession is photographic gold.

The grounds are also home to the Meiji-jingū Gyōen (Map p106; admission ¥500; 😊 9am-4.30pm), a lovely strolling garden. It was once

the property of two *daimyō* families, after it came under imperial control, Meiji himself designed the garden as a gift to the Empress Shōken. There are peaceful walks to the pond and teahouse and a good dose of privacy at weekdays, and spectacular irises and satsuki azaleas in season.

TAKESHITA-DŌRI (TAKESHITA STREET) Map p106
竹下通り

◉ JR Yamanote Line to Harajuku (Takeshita-dōri exit)

This teeming alley, which lies at the heart of Harajuku, represents Tokyo's propensity for both teenage kitsch and subcultural fetish. Boom boxes blare at full volume while young, angst-decorated adolescents browse through racks of cheap versions of

TRANSPORT: HARAJUKU & AOYAMA

Train The JR Yamanote Line stops at Harajuku Station.

Subway The Chiyoda Line runs beneath Omote-Sandō, stopping at Omote-Sandō and Meiji-jingūmae Stations. The Fukutoshin Line also stops at Meiji-jingūmae Station. The Ginza and Hanzōmon Lines both stop at Omote-Sandō Station.

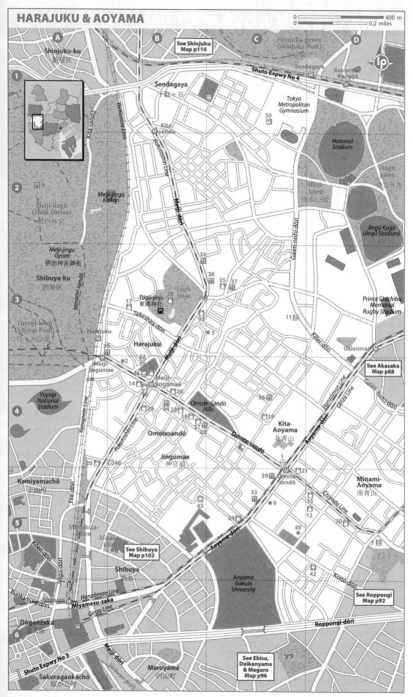

0 —————— 400 m
0 —————— 0.2 miles

Shinjuku-ku
新宿区

See Shinjuku
Map p110

Shinjuku-gyoen
(Shinjuku Park)

Sendagaya

Kokuritsu-
Kyogijo

Shuto Expwy No 4

Sendagaya
千駄ヶ谷

Kita-
sando

Tokyo
Metropolitan
Gymnasium

50

National
Stadium

Yamanote Line

Kita-sando

Meiji-jingu
Kaikan

Meiji-jingu
(Meiji Shrine)
明治神宮

Meiji-jingu
Gyoen
明治神宮御苑

Shibuya-ku
渋谷区

Fukutoshin Line

Jingu
gaien
神宮外苑

Meiji-dori

Meiji
koen
明治公園

Jingu Kyujo
(Jingu Stadium)

Minami-sando

31

38 25 37

28 Togo-
jinja

Togo-jinja
東郷神社

17

Takeshita-dori

Prince Chichibu
Memorial
Rugby Stadium

Gaienmae M

11

Gaien-nishi-dori

3

Yoyogi-koen
(Yoyogi Park)

35

Harajuku

Harajuku

Killer-dori

Meiji-
jingumae M

2

14

Meiji-
jingumae

26

See Akasaka
Map p88

Yoyogi
National
Stadium

Yamanote Line

29

34 23

Omote-Sando
Hills

36

Kita-
Aoyama
北青山

19

18

37

Omotesando

Omote-sando

Hanzomon Line

Ginza Line

Aoyama-dori

Galen-higashi-dori

Jingumae
神宮前

1

Minami-
Aoyama
南青山

20

40

39 Omote-
sando M

Kamiyamacho
上山町

43

33

Chiyoda Line

15

12

9

30

Fire-dori

24

49

7

Miyashita-
koen

Miiake-
koen

See Shibuya
Map p102

Aoyama-dori

42

Kotto-dori

Shibuya
渋谷

Koen-dori

Aoyama
Gakuin
University

See Roppongi
Map p92

Hanzomon Line

Miyamasu-zaka

Ginza Line

Bunkamura-dori

Shibuya

Dogenzaka
道玄坂

Shibuya

Roppongi-dori

Meiji-dori

Shuto Expwy No 3

Sakuragaokacho
桜ヶ丘町

Maruyama
円山町

See Ebisu,
Daikanyama
& Meguro
Map p96

the day's latest trend. This is the place to look for outrageously gaudy jewellery, punk accessories, trendy hair boutiques, fast-food joints and cuddly toys. Also see p147.

JINGŪ-BASHI (JINGŪ BRIDGE) Map p106
神宮橋

JR Yamanote Line to Harajuku (Omote-Sandō exit)

If the weather's good, on Saturday and (especially) Sunday afternoons this bridge between the station and Meiji-jingū becomes the epicentre of the Harajuku *cosplay* scene. Legions of bizarrely dressed teens parade before photographers as if they were on a Milan catwalk. From Lolitas and goths to French maids and anime characters, you never really know what will appear here! However, don't expect to see anything at other times.

YOYOGI-KŌEN (YOYOGI PARK)
Map p102
代々木公園

admission free; dawn-dusk; JR Yamanote Line to Harajuku (Omote-Sandō exit)

Sunday in Yoyogi-kōen used to be one of Tokyo's prime attractions, when local bands gathered to give free concerts on the park's pathways and kids in wild hair-dos and 1950s get-ups gathered to gyrate to recorded rock'n'roll. Even if it's no longer what it once was, performers do still gather (see the boxed text, p197). In any case, with lots of open spaces and some flowering trees, Yoyogi-kōen is not a bad place for a picnic or playing some sport on the grass. It's also worth a stop to view an early masterpiece by architect Tange Kenzō, the National Gymnasium, which was built for the 1964 Olympics.

UKIYO-E ŌTA MEMORIAL ART MUSEUM Map p106
浮世絵太田記念美術館

☎ 3403-0880; www.ukiyoe-ota-muse.jp; 1-10-10 Jingūmae, Shibuya-ku; adult ¥700-1000, student Tue-Fri ¥200-500, Sat & Sun student free-¥250; 10.30am-5.30pm Tue-Sun; JR Yamanote Line to Harajuku (Omote-Sandō exit), Chiyoda Line to Meiji-jingūmae (exit 5)

This cosy museum, which asks that you trade your shoes for a pair of slippers at the door, has an excellent collection of *ukiyo-e* (wood-block prints). The original collector, Ōta Seizo, former head of the Toho Life Insurance Company, began to buy *ukiyo-e* when he realised that many important examples of Japanese wood-block prints belonged to foreign museums, making it impossible for Japanese to view many of the genre's masterworks. The museum usually displays no more than a few dozen works at a time from its collection of over 10,000 prints, including those by masters of the art such as Hokusai and Hiroshige. Note that the museum closes between the 27th and the end of each month.

Downstairs from the museum is a branch of the shop Kamawanu (p144), which specialises in beautifully printed *tenugui* (traditional towels).

OMOTE-SANDŌ STATION AREA

NEZU MUSEUM Map p106
根津美術館

☎ 3400-2536; www.nezu-muse.or.jp; 6-5-1 Minami-Aoyama, Minato-ku; adult/child/student ¥1000/free/800; 10am-5pm Tue-Sun; Chiyoda, Ginza or Hanzōmon Line to Omote-Sandō (exit A5)
This museum reopened in autumn 2009 after a 3½-year renovation, and Tokyo is all the more fortunate for it. The new main gallery space, by architect Kuma Kengō, is based on traditional Japanese architecture but using modern materials. It displays a rotating selection of the museum's renowned collection of Chinese, Japanese and Korean antiquities. Among are seven designated national treasures and 87 important cultural properties. Some new,

high-tech presentation technology was innovated for the museum as well, including special LED bulbs that show off the colours of the works and are easy on the eyes, as well as saving energy. Solar panels further cut down on energy costs.

The museum building is just the half of it. Beyond the galleries is a spectacular strolling garden, a designated landmark in its own right, with peaks and dales, teahouses, a contemporary cafe (also designed by Kuma) and sculptures cleverly integrated into the garden paths. A hurried walk through it can take 15 minutes, but why would you want to rush?

WATARI MUSEUM OF CONTEMPORARY ART (WATARI-UM)
Map p106
ワタリウム美術館

☎ 3402-3001; www.watarium.co.jp, in Japanese; 3-7-6 Jingūmae, Shibuya-ku; adult/student ¥1000/800; 11am-7pm Tue & Thu-Sun, 11am-9pm Wed; Ginza Line to Gaienmae (exit 3)
This progressive and often provocative museum was built in 1990 to a design by Swiss architect Mario Botta. Exhibits are always cutting-edge and sometimes arty-farty – think push-the-envelope photos by Larry Clark, or vacuum-cleaner ballets choreographed by visiting Scandinavians. There's an excellent art bookshop called On Sundays (☎ 3470-1424; variable) where you can browse through an enormous collection of obscure postcards.

SHINJUKU

Drinking p182; Eating p174; Shopping p149; Sleeping p223

Shinjuku is anything but camera shy. Here Bill Murray caught his first, jet-lagged glimpses of Tokyo in *Lost in Translation*, and Ridley Scott was rumoured to have drawn inspiration for his cult classic *Blade Runner*. More than any other neighbourhood, Shinjuku represents Tokyo's sensory overload and breakneck pace. Its neon canyons crackle with an energy drawn from somewhere in the future, and its laissez-faire attitude draws 20- and 30-something party people to tiny nightspots stacked storeys high.

Shinjuku's raison d'être is its enormous commuter train station, which is the second largest in the world, and services an estimated 3.5 million passengers each day. This station also effectively divides Shinjuku into two very distinct neighbourhoods. The west side, Nishi-Shinjuku, which was once the site of a sizeable reservoir, is now dominated by skyscraping office towers, luxury hotels and the imposing Tokyo Metropolitan Government Offices, all connected by wide avenues that are definitely more New York than old Edo. A few important museums populate these skyscrapers, alongside the offices.

Not to be outdone by its higher-stepping other half, Shinjuku's east side is spontaneous chaos, an area to wander with your neck craning up and around. Chief attractions here include the shrine Hanazono-jinja, site of a great Sunday morning flea market, and the colourful if sleazy Kabukichō and Golden Gai entertainment areas. Tokyo's gay district, Shinjuku-nichōme, is also located in East Shinjuku, and is perhaps one of the liveliest gay neighbourhoods in Asia. Just beyond, the park Shinjuku-gyōen remains one of Tokyo's favourite spots for cherry-blossom viewing in the spring, and a calming respite at other times.

Shinjuku is bordered by Harajuku to the south, greater Akasaka and Iidabashi to the east and Takadanobaba to the north, as the JR Yamanote Line heads toward Ikebukuro.

Shinjuku Station is the city's biggest transit hub and the one everyone warns you about: take the wrong exit and you may find yourself a half-hour away from your destination. We've even included a map of it in this section (Map p110). Yes, it is daunting, but here are some general guidelines. The classic rendezvous point is opposite the station's east exit, across Shinjuku-dōri, in front of the Studio Alta building with its huge video screen. Continuing through the side streets away from the station, you'll reach Yasukuni-dōri with its neon buildings, and beyond that the bawdy district of Kabukichō. Isetan (p150) and other top department stores and Shinjuku-nichōme are to the east via Shinjuku-dōri or Yasukuni-dōri (Shinjuku-sanchōme Station is the closest station for these locations).

If you're heading for the skyscrapers, there is a pedestrian tunnel towards Tochōmae Station on the Toei Ōedo Line, which may be the easier stop depending on your destination. There's also a south exit, which is the closest access to Shinjuku-gyōen and the Takashimaya Times Square shopping complex.

WEST OF SHINJUKU STATION (NISHI-SHINJUKU)

TOKYO METROPOLITAN GOVERNMENT OFFICES Map p110

東京都庁

☎ 5321-1111; www.metro.tokyo.jp; 2-8-1 Nishi-Shinjuku, Shinjuku-ku; admission free; observatories 9.30am-11pm, north observatory closed 2nd & 4th Mon of the month, south observatory closed 1st & 3rd Tue of the month; Toei Ōedo Line to Tochōmae (exit A3)

Known as Tokyo Tochō, this grey granite complex designed by Tange Kenzō has stunning, distinctive architecture and great views from the 202m-high observatories (☎ 5320-7890) on the 45th floors of the twin towers of Building 1. On a clear day, look west for a glimpse of Mt Fuji. Don't worry if one of the observatories happens to be

TRANSPORT: SHINJUKU

Train The JR Yamanote Line, JR Chūō Line and several other commuter lines stop at Shinjuku Station. The private Keio and Odakyū Lines come in handy for destinations west of the Yamanote Line.

Subway The Marunouchi, Toei Shinjuku and Toei Ōedo Lines run through Shinjuku. For west Shinjuku, Tochō-mae Station on the Toei Ōedo Line is more convenient.

SHINJUKU

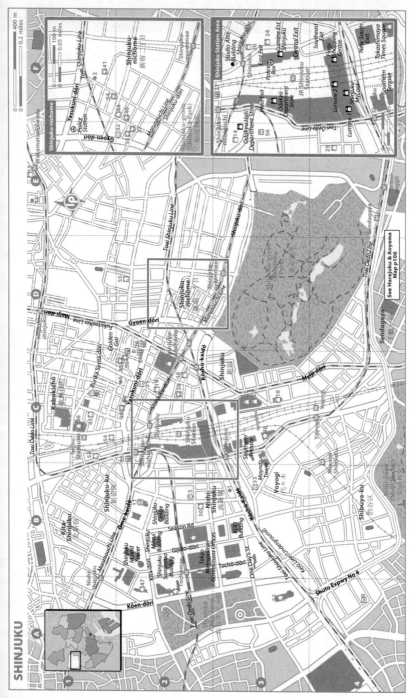

SHINJUKU

closed during your visit; the views are virtually the same.

Back on the ground, stand in the Citizens Plaza and look up at Building 1 and see if it does not remind you of a computer-chip version of the great cathedrals of Europe. There's even a 'rose window', only this being Tokyo the rose is replaced by a gingko leaf, in honour of the city's official tree. With several modern sculptures scattered about, this is a good spot for a picnic lunch.

TOKYO OPERA CITY Map p110
東京オペラシティ

☎ 5353-0770; www.operacity.jp; 3-20-2 Nishi-Shinjuku, Shinjuku-ku; admission free; Ⓞ Keio New Line to Hatsudai (north exit)
Since opening in 1997, Tokyo Opera City has been recognised as one of the world's most acoustically perfect concert halls, and this in a city that embraces classical music with fervour. It's also one of the most architecturally daring, like a giant indoor A-frame.

Even if you are unable to make it to a concert, Tokyo Opera City is called home by two of Tokyo's best art spaces. The two storeys of the Tokyo Opera City Art Gallery (☎ 5353-0756; www.operacity.jp/ag; 3rd fl; admission varies by exhibition; Ⓨ 11am-7pm Tue-Thu & Sun, 11am-8pm Fri & Sat) showcase temporary exhibits from new and established Japanese artists to fashion in Antwerp. Meanwhile the NTT Intercommunication Centre (ICC; ☎ 0120-144-199; www.ntticc.or.jp; 4th fl; admission varies by exhibition; Ⓨ 10am-6pm Tue-Sun) has an excellent collection of cutting-edge works and installations that address the myriad intersections of art and technology. Its

111

superlative video library includes important works by artists such as Idemitsu
Mako, Bill Viola and Nam June Paik, while
installations on display include dreamy
pieces such as works by Laurie Anderson,
and Mikami Seiko's *World, Membrane and
the Dismembered Body,* designed especially for the museum's eerie, echo-free
chamber.

JAPANESE SWORD MUSEUM Map p110
刀剣博物館
☎ 3379-1386; 4-25-10 Yoyogi, Shibuya-ku;
adult/student ¥525/315; ⏰ 9am-4.30pm Tue-Sun;
Ⓔ Keio New Line to Hatsudai (east exit)
In 1948, after American forces returned the
katana (Japanese swords) they'd confis-
cated during the postwar occupation, the
Ministry of Education established a society

TOKYO FOR FREE

If you've been here for a few days, you've probably learned that yen is easy enough to spend quickly in the metropolis.
To balance your budget, consider the many things to do that are completely free. These suggestions will cost no more
than the train ticket to get to them.

For an idea of current goings-on, including some freebies, check the website of Japan National Tourism Organization (JNTO; www.jnto.go.jp).

Parks

Unlike Tokyo's gardens, most of Tokyo's parks are free (Shinjuku-gyōen is the big exception to this rule), and provide a
welcome escape from the omnipresent concrete and urban sprawl. Just grab a *bentō* (boxed lunch) and/or some baked
bread and you have yourself a picnic. Good spots are Kitanomaru-kōen (p51) near the Imperial Palace, Yoyogi-kōen
(p107) near Harajuku, Ueno-kōen (p77) and Hibiya-kōen (p56) near Ginza.

Galleries

Most private galleries don't charge admission. Indeed, these galleries are often rented by individual artists who are
delighted to help cultivate interest in their work. Ginza and Harajuku are the best places to hunt for them. Department store galleries (on upper floors) are another good bet – if these are not free, admission is often cheaper than a
museum entry fee.

Temples & Shrines

Shrines are almost always free in Tokyo and most temples charge only to enter their *honden* (main hall). Sensō-ji (p83)
in Asakusa and Meiji-jingū (p105) in Harajuku are two good places to start.

Company Showrooms

So they're really just another form of advertising, but some showrooms in Tokyo are like small museums and most
have hands-on displays and test-drives – all for free. Auto enthusiasts will love Toyota Mega Web (p128) in Odaiba,
and just about everyone will find something intriguing at the Sony Building (p56) in Ginza. Other showrooms can be
found in Ginza, Shinjuku and Harajuku.

Tsukiji Central Fish Market

Wander the world's biggest fish market (p63) for hours at no cost.

Skyscrapers

Several skyscrapers have free observation floors – Tokyo Metropolitan Government Offices (p109), Shinjuku Sumitomo Building (p133) and Tokyo Big Sight (p136).

Bookshops

Unlike in some other countries, in Japan no one will object to you spending hours reading books and magazines on
display in bookshops. There's even a word for the practice: *yomitachi* (a standing read). See the boxed text, p58, for
listings.

to preserve the feudal art of Japanese sword-making. There are about 120 swords with their fittings in the collection, of which about a third are on view at any one time. The museum also showcases crafts of tempering and polishing steel. Its location, in a residential neighbourhood, is not obvious, but if you ask for the Token Hakubutsukan, someone should be able to help you.

SOMPO JAPAN MUSEUM OF ART
Map p110

損保ジャパン東郷青児美術館

☎ 5777-8600; www.sompo-japan.co.jp/museum/english/index.html; 42nd fl, 1-26-1 Nishi-Shinjuku, Shinjuku-ku; adult/student ¥500/300; ⏰ 10am-6pm Tue-Sun; ⊕ JR Shinjuku (west exit)

The private museum of the Sompo Japan insurance company concentrates heavily on the lithography, sculpture and painting of Tōgō Seiji (1897–1980), whose subjects, most often women, resemble luminescent anime figures set against backdrops that hover between cubist and art deco. Tōgō was closely associated with the Sompo Japan's forerunner, Yasuda Fire & Marine Insurance Company, and donated many of his works to the museum. The museum also caused a stir in the 1980s bubble, when it purchased Van Gogh's *Sunflowers* for ¥5 billion; there are also a limited number of works by Gauguin, Cézanne and Van Gogh. The museum's 42nd floor location has excellent views.

EAST SHINJUKU
KABUKICHŌ Map p110
歌舞伎町

⊕ JR Yamanote Line to Shinjuku (east exit)

Tokyo's most notorious red-light district, which lies east of Shinjuku Station and north of Yasukuni-dōri, is made up of soaplands (bathhouse that offer sexual services), love hotels, peep shows, pink cabarets, porn booths, 'nurse' pubs, prostitutes and strip shows, all well attended by drunken salarymen out for the night. Female voices wail out invitations in accents from the Philippines, Thailand and China as well as Japan, while Japanese punks eke out a living passing out ads for karaoke boxes and peep shows. For the ladies, there are 'men's' bars, with photos of foppish Japanese blokes with shaggy hair dyed along the spectrum from platinum to auburn, peering out from backlit signs and waiting to do for the gals what hostess bars do for the guys.

Remarkably, the area is generally safe (and much more interesting) to walk through at night, though it's wise to go with a friend or more or you may find yourself the object of unwanted, and irritating, attention (both for males and females). However, most places are aimed solely at Japanese clients, hence foreigners are generally not permitted.

GOLDEN GAI Map p110
ゴールデン街

🚇 Marunouchi or Toei Shinjuku Line to Shinjuku-sanchōme (exit B3)

This ramshackle block of tiny bars became golden just in time for the '64 Olympics. By day, there's not much to see here except for dozens of stray cats. But by night, the closet-sized bars, some accessed by stairways steep enough to bruise your shins as you ascend, light up and fill up, mostly with off-duty office workers. There's been much speculation about the demise of Golden Gai's rickety structures and narrow alleyways, but for the moment it seems a new generation is buying in and quietly setting up shop. See p182 for recommended spots.

HANAZONO-JINJA (HANAZONO SHRINE) Map p110
花園神社

☎ 3200-3093; 5-17 Shinjuku, Shinjuku-ku; admission free; 🕑 24hr; 🚇 Marunouchi or Toei Shinjuku Line to Shinjuku-sanchōme (exits B3 or B5)

During the day merchants from nearby Kabukichō come to this Shintō shrine to pray for the solvency of their business ventures, but at night the spotlights come on, legions of high-school kids and salary-men show up, and action spills over from nearby Golden Gai and from further-away Yasukuni-dōri. On Sunday the grounds become a marketplace (🕑 8am-4pm), where you'll find bargains on knick-knacks and, possibly, some antiques.

SHINJUKU-GYŌEN (SHINJUKU PARK) Map p110
新宿御苑

☎ 3350-0151; www.shinjukugyoen.go.jp; 11 Naito-chō, Shinjuku-ku; adult/under 6yr/6-15yr ¥200/free/50; 🕑 9am-4.30pm Tue-Sun; 🚇 Marunouchi Line to Shinjuku-gyōenmae (exit 1)

Though Shinjuku-gyōen was designed as an imperial retreat (completed 1906), it's now definitively a park for everyone. The wide lawns and diverse design (the garden applies French, English and Japanese horticultural principles) make it a favourite for urbanites in need of a quick escape. To make an afternoon of it, head for the east side where the glassed-in greenhouse displays subtropical waterlilies the size of party platters. Alternatively, park yourself in the southern part of the park in the traditional teahouse. Expect lots of company during cherry-blossom season; however, Shinjuku Park is easily one of the top blossom-viewing spots in Tokyo.

IKEBUKURO & TAKADANOBABA

Eating p176; Shopping p150; Sleeping p225

Ikebukuro has long been the ugly stepsister to Shinjuku and Shibuya, never mind the glitzy neighbourhoods to the southeast, and it's the one Yamanote Line hub that many Tokyoites will admit to looking down upon. Its chief purpose is transit (and there is a lot of it on subways, JR and commuter rail), mostly connecting Tokyo with Saitama-ken (Saitama Prefecture) to the north. There's a cacophony of big-box department stores and electronics dealers to serve commuters, though those alone don't merit a visit.

What Ikebukuro lacks in charm it makes up in decent lodgings, and transit links make it a convenient place to stay. The neighbourhood of Takadanobaba, adjacent to Waseda University, one of Japan's top schools, is a couple stops south and brims over with international restaurants for student budgets.

The bright lights of Shinjuku are further south, to the east are quiet lowland residential districts and to the west are Tokyo's more remote wards. The JR Yamanote Line runs smack through the middle of Ikebukuro, dividing it into east and west. Like Shinjuku, Ikebukuro's east and west sides have different identities: the west end has the lion's share of bars and good restaurants.

IKEBUKURO

SUNSHINE CITY Map p116

サンシャインシティ

☎ 3989-3331; admission free; ◉ JR Yamanote Line to Ikebukuro (east exit)

A complex of four buildings east of the station, Sunshine City is visited by shoppers and for Namco Namjatown (☎ 5950-0765; www .namjatown.jp; 2nd fl, World Import Mart bldg; adult/child admission ¥300/200, passport ¥3900/3300; ◐ 10am-10pm). The main activities are carnival-style rides and attractions. Foodies will prefer the food 'theme parks' dedicated to adventures in gyoza (pan-fried dumplings), ice cream and desserts, and the rest can escape to the 'healing forest' for massage. The passport gets you into Namjatown as well as most of the attractions, though some still cost extra, as do food and treatments. Check the website or the Namjatown map for attractions that don't require knowledge of Japanese.

Other Sunshine City highlights include the observatory (adult/child ¥620/310; ◐ 10am-9.30pm) atop the office tower Sunshine 60, one of the tallest buildings in Japan (guess how many storeys it has?), and the quiet Ancient Orient Museum (☎ 3989-3491; Bunka Kaikan Centre; admission ¥500; ◐ 10am-5pm), which features art and antiquities from Iran, Iraq, Uzbekistan and especially Syria.

IKEBUKURO EARTHQUAKE HALL (IKEBUKURO BŌSAI-KAN) Map p116

池袋防災館

☎ 3590-6565; 2-37-8 Nishi-Ikebukuro, Tōshima-ku; admission free; ◐ 9am-5pm Wed-Mon, closed 3rd Wed of month; ◉ JR Yamanote or Marunouchi Line to Ikebukuro (Metropolitan exit)

Quick: what should you do in case of an earthquake? What if your house is on fire? This facility operated by the Tokyo Fire Department prepares you for these and other disasters by means of videos (available in English) and incredibly realistic simulations; it's hard not to be rattled once the room starts a-shaking. A visit here is important preparation if you're planning on living in Japan. Even if you're not, it's an important insight into a possibility that's never far from the mind of any Japanese.

JAPAN TRADITIONAL CRAFT CENTER Map p116

全国伝統的工芸品センター

☎ 5954-6066; www.kougei.or.jp/english/center .html; 1st fl, Metropolitan Plaza Bldg, 1-11-1 Nishi Ikebukuro, Toshima-ku; admission free; ◐ 11am-7pm; ◉ JR Yamanote or Marunouchi Line to Ikebukuro (Metropolitan exit)

Operated by the Japanese Ministry of Economy, Trade and Industry, this showroom is less a museum and more a valuable resource for working artisans and crafts

TRANSPORT: IKEBUKURO

Train Ikebukuro is one of the hubs of the JR Yamanote Line, and the terminus of the Tōbu and Seibu lines.

Subway The Marunouchi Line terminates at Ikebukuro, while the Yūrakuchō and Fukutoshin Lines run through it.

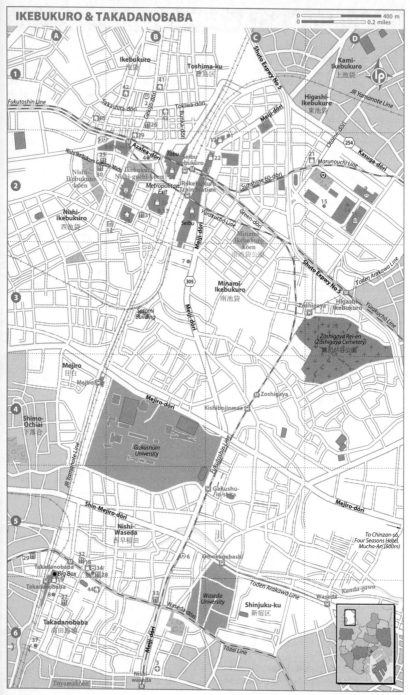

0   400 m
0   0.2 miles

Fukutoshin Line

Ikebukuro
池袋

Toshima-ku
豊島区

Kami-
Ikebukuro
上池袋

Higashi-
Ikebukuro
東池袋

JR Yamanote Line

Sakashita-dōri

Gekijō-dōri

Tokiwa-dōri

Bunka-dōri

Meiji-dōri

Ōtone-dōri

Marunouchi Line

Kasuga-dōri

(254)

Nishi-Ikebukuro Michi

Ikebukuro
Nishi-guchi-kōen

Azalea-dōri

Tōbu

Seibu
Ikebukuro

Ikebukuro
Train Station

Sunshine 60-dōri

Shuto Expwy No 5

Nishi-
Ikebukuro-
kōen

Metropolitan
Exit

Seibu

Yūrakuchō Line

Green-dōri

Nishi-
Ikebukuro
西池袋

Minami-
Ikebukuro-
kōen
南池袋公園

Shuto Expwy No 5

Toden Arakawa Line

Meiji-dōri

Minami-
Ikebukuro
南池袋

Zōshigaya

Higashi-
Ikebukuro

Yūrakuchō Line

Satomi
Building

Zōshigaya Rei-en
(Zōshigaya Cemetery)
雑司ヶ谷公園

Mejiro
目白

Mejiro

Mejiro-dōri

Zōshigaya

Kishibojinmae

Shimo-
Ochiai
下落合

JR Yamanote Line

Gakushūin
University

Fukutoshin Line

Gakushū-
in-shita

Mejiro-dōri

Shin-Mejiro-dōri

Nishi-
Waseda
西早稲田

To Chinzan-sō,
Four Seasons Hotel,
Mucha-An (500m)

Takadanobaba

Big Box

Ōtokagebashi

Takadanobaba

Toden Arakawa Line

Waseda

Kanda-gawa

Takadanobaba
高田馬場通

Waseda-dōri

Waseda
University

Shinjuku-ku
新宿区

Meiji-dōri

Tōzai Line

Nishi-
waseda

Toyamakōen

IKEBUKURO & TAKADANOBABA

collectors. You'll find on display more than 130 different types of crafts, ranging from lacquerwork boxes to paper, textiles to earthy pottery. You can also buy much the same from the discriminating collection. Also see p151.

GOKOKU-JI Map pp48-9
護国寺
☎ 3941-0764; admission free; ☒ dawn-dusk;
◉ Yūrakuchō Line to Gokokuji (exit 1)
Declared an important cultural property, Gokoku Temple gets surprisingly few visitors. One of the few surviving Edo temples, it dates from 1680 and was built by the fifth Tokugawa shōgun for his mother. Exiting the temple grounds and turning to the left, you'll reach Toshimagaoka Goryo, an imperial mausoleum that is closed to the public.

RIKUGI-EN Map pp48-9
六義園
☎ 3941-2222; 6-16-3 Hon-Komagome; admission ¥300; ☒ 9am-5pm; ☒ JR Yamanote Line to Komagome (south exit)
Rikugi Garden is a fine garden with landscaped views unfolding at every turn of the pathways that criss-cross the grounds.

The garden is rich in literary associations: its name is taken from the six principles of *waka* (31-syllable poems), and the landscaping evokes famous scenes from Chinese and Japanese literature.

TAKADANOBABA AREA

CHINZAN-SŌ Off Map pp48-9
椿山荘
☎ 3943-1111; www.chinzanso.com; admission free; ☒ 10am-9.30pm; ◉ JR Yūrakuchō Line to Edogawa-bashi (exit 1a), Toden Arakawa Line to Waseda
This lovely, hilly 66,000-sq-metre strolling garden was part of the estate of a Meiji-era politician and statesman, and lining its many pathways are a number of antiquities transported from all over Japan. Most notable is a 16.7m three-storey pagoda, estimated at nearly a millennium old, which was transported from the Hiroshima area, as well as lanterns, monuments and *torii*. We don't particularly love the contemporary construction of hotels and wedding halls around it, but all that is forgotten in the garden's lovely soba shop Mucha-an (p177).

CLANG-CLANG! CHIN-CHIN!

Given Tokyo's tangled streets, it's hard to imagine that streetcars were common here until the 1960s. The Toden Arakawa Line (都電荒川線) is the last remaining streetcar within central Tokyo, arcing across the city's north side between Minowabashi in the east and Waseda, near Takadanobaba, in the west. It was due to be demolished along with the other streetcar lines, but public outcry preserved it, and it's been in municipal hands since the 1970s. Apart from being about the cheapest ride in Tokyo (one way ¥160, 50 minutes; day pass ¥400), it's also a great way to observe the city up close and personal.

Cheery, historical trams that look like they could be friends of Thomas the Tank Engine depart Minowabashi Station (三ノ輪橋駅), a short walk from Minowa Station (三ノ輪駅) on the Hibiya Line. An interesting detour on that walk is the Buddhist temple Jōkan-ji (浄閑寺; Map pp48–9), where many of the souls who perished in the 21 fires that raged through the nearby Yoshiwara pleasure quarters (see p24) are enshrined, and where courtesans who had outlived their usefulness were rolled up straw mats and tossed over the temple's stone walls late at night – dead or alive. The temple's cemetery is one of Tokyo's eerier ones: you can see funerary urns inside the pedestal beneath the central *Jizō* image (see the boxed text, p60).

Once you've boarded the tram, the route is lined with cherry trees, homes with hanging laundry, pocket parks and plenty of the sort of everyday street life that most visitors – and many Tokyoites – don't get to observe. During cherry blossom season, it's worth getting off at Asukayama Station (飛鳥山駅) for *hanami* (cherry blossom viewing; see p18) in the park, and train *otaku* will want to alight at Arakawa Shako-mae (荒川車庫前), where a couple of antique streetcars can be inspected up close. The Arakawa Line takes its nickname (*chin-chin densha*) from the sound its bells make before the cars leave each station, although *chin-chin* has another meaning that will make young boys laugh (see p154).

The train terminates at Waseda (早稲田), from where it is a lovely cherry-tree-lined walk of under 10 minutes to Chinzan-sō (p117).

SHINAGAWA

Eating p177; Sleeping p226

Long the forgotten quarter of Tokyo, Shinagawa has been more in the limelight in recent years thanks to its status as a *shinkansen* (bullet train) stop and a slew of new corporate headquarters, hotels and residences by the redeveloping waterfront. While none of this marks it as a top-tier attraction, there are some worthwhile sights within easy reach of the massive JR Shinagawa Station, as well as some rewarding restaurants to visit.

Shinagawa is near the southern end of the Yamanote with the Tsukiji and Shiodome area to the north and Meguro and Ebisu to the west.

SENGAKU-JI Map p119

☎ 3441-5560; 2-11-1 Takanawa, Minato-ku; admission free; ⏰ 7am-6pm Apr-Sep, 7am-5pm Oct-Mar; 🚇 Toei Asakusa Line to Sengakuji (exit A2)

This temple of the Sōtō Zen sect is included in Tokyo's sights mostly for the story that surrounds it, that of the 47 *rōnin* (masterless samurai), also called the Akō Incident. With its theme of paying the supreme sacrifice in the name of loyalty, this story, also called The Akō Incident, has captured the Japanese imagination like no other, and has been adapted into countless films and plays (usually by the name *Chūshingura*).

These *rōnin* plotted for two years (1701–03) to wreak vengeance on the man who caused what they believed to be the unjust and humiliating death of their master, Lord Asano of Akō province. They sought revenge even knowing that they, too, would have to forfeit their lives. After having brought the head of his enemy to their master's grave, 46 of the *rōnin* were condemned to commit *seppuku* (ritual suicide by self-disembowelment) in the samurai fashion – the 47th apparently escaped this communal fate on a technicality.

The cemetery here is quite dramatic as there always seems to be incense burning; you can buy your own to add for ¥100. There is also a new museum (adult/child/student ¥500/250/400; ⏰ 9am-4pm) on the premises;

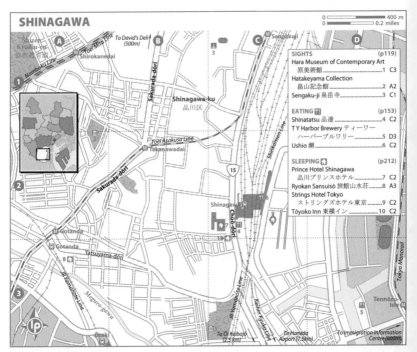

SHINAGAWA

0 ————— 400 m
0 ————— 0.2 miles

Train Shinagawa is on the JR Yamanote Line and is served by the Keikyū Line to Haneda Airport. If you're heading west on the *shinkansen* (to Odawara, for Hakone and beyond), it is a much more manageable station than Tokyo.

Subway Shinagawa Station is not on any subway lines. However, the Nanboku and Toei Mita Lines serve Shirokanedai, and the Toei Asakusa Line serves Takanawadai and Sengakuji, all of which are useful for nearby attractions and restaurants.

there's not much English explanation, but a video presentation in English is available.

HARA MUSEUM OF CONTEMPORARY ART Map p119
原美術館
☎ 3445-0651; www.haramuseum.or.jp; 4-7-25 Kita-Shinagawa, Shinagawa-ku; adult ¥1000, student ¥500-700; ⊗ 11am-5pm Tue & Thu-Sun, 11am-8pm Wed; ⊚ JR Yamanote Line to Shinagawa (Takanawa exit)
This museum is one of Tokyo's more adventurous art spaces, though given that exhibitions change often, it is a good idea to check what's on before making your way out here. The Bauhaus design and the cafe, which overflows into a delightful garden, are attractions in themselves.

HATAKEYAMA COLLECTION Map p119
畠山記念館
☎ 3447-5787; www.ebara.co.jp/socialactiv ity/hatakeyama/english/; 2-20-12 Shirokanedai, Minato-ku; adult/student ¥500/300; ⊗ 10am-5pm Tue-Sun Apr-Sep, 10am-4.30pm Tue-Sun Oct-Mar; ⊚ Toei Asakusa Line to Takanawadai (exit A2)
This undervisited museum should be high on the list for anyone with an interest in Japanese ceramics and the tea ceremony. It was the private collection of Hatakeyama Issei, an industrialist who dedicated himself to the way of tea and also designed the museum. You'll find seasonal displays of priceless works of teaware from the Muromachi, Momoyama and Edo periods, some of them important cultural property. The muted lighting in the exhibit hall seems inspired by the mock-up of a teahouse in the corner (you can have tea here for an additional ¥400). It's all reached via a lovely garden.

Eating p178; Sleeping p226

The area across the Sumida-gawa from central Tokyo is relatively off the radar for most foreign visitors, perhaps because it's more a collection of districts than one single unit. Even so, there are a few noteworthy attractions for anyone interested in getting off the beaten track and exploring a different side of Tokyo – in both geography and attitude. Of particular note is Ryōgoku, the centre of sumō culture, with its large number of sumō *heya* (stables). And the nearby Edo-Tokyo Museum, which gives a marvellous presentation of city history, is always a big hit with anyone looking for a glimpse of old Edo.

To the south, the neighbourhoods of Kiyosumi and Fukagawa retain a Shitamachi feel that's not gussied up for tourist consumption, with some old gardens and temples. Stroll Eitai-dōri east of Monzen-nakachō Station on the 1st, 15th and 28th of each month for a street market with lots of local colour. Kiyosumi is also where you'll find the Museum of Contemporary Art, a remarkable building with consistently smart exhibitions. Perhaps because of this museum, or because rents remain relatively low, private galleries from other parts of Tokyo have begun to move here.

Ryōgoku is a quick train ride from Akihabara or a quick taxi ride from Asakusa. Kiyosumi and Fukagawa are neighbours on the south side in Kōtō-ku, just across the Sumida-gawa from Ginza.

RYŌGOKU

RYŌGOKU KOKUGIKAN Map p122
両国国技館

☎ 3623-5111; www.sumo.or.jp/eng/index.html; 1-3-28 Yokoami, Sumida-ku; admission free; ☷ 10am-4.30pm Mon-Fri; ◎ JR Sōbu or Toei Ōedo Line to Ryōgoku (west exit)

Just north of JR Ryōgoku Station is this sumō stadium with its adjoining Sumō Museum (☎ 3622-0366). Fifteen-day *basho* (sumō tournaments) take place here three times a year (January, May and September), while three other tournaments are held in other cities in March, July and November. Together, these *basho* decide who will be the *yokozuna* (grand champion).

Although small, the museum displays a rotating selection of interesting artefacts of sumō history and art (mostly wood-block prints). When sumō tournaments are on at the stadium, only those holding tickets to the matches can enter the museum.

For details on watching tournaments, see p207. For details on eating *chanko-nabe*, the delicious and nutritious stew that is consumed in massive quantities by sumō wrestlers, see Tomoegata (p178).

EDO-TOKYO MUSEUM Map p122
江戸東京博物館

☎ 3626-9974; www.edo-tokyo-museum.or.jp; 1-4-1 Yokoami, Sumida-ku; adult/child ¥600/free, student ¥300-450; ☷ 9.30am-5.30pm Tue-Sun, to 7.30pm Sat; ◎ Toei Ōedo Line to Ryōgoku (exit A4), JR Sōbu Line to Ryōgoku (west exit)

This massive, futuristic building is by far the best city-history museum we've ever encountered. The permanent collection on the upper floors starts with a reconstruction of half of the bridge at Nihombashi (p53), on either side of which are thorough histories of Edo and Tokyo respectively, mostly with excellent English signage. Highlights are too numerous to mention, but we like the sections on the lodgings of the *daimyō*, wood-block printing, the evolution of kabuki and Tokyo's headlong rush to Westernise. There are often special exhibits, but the extent of the permanent collection is usually enough to overwhelm most visitors.

KANTŌ EARTHQUAKE MEMORIAL MUSEUM Map p122
東京都復興記念館

☎ 3622-1208; Yokoami-kōen, Sumida-ku; admission free; ☷ 9am-4.30pm Tue-Sun; ◎ Toei Ōedo Line to Ryōgoku (exit A1)

This museum presents sombre exhibits about the 1923 earthquake that destroyed

TRANSPORT: SUMIDA RIVER – EAST

Train The JR Sōbu Line is a main approach to Ryōgoku.

Subway The Toei Ōedo Line connects the Ryōgoku, Kiyosumi and Fukagawa districts via Ryōgoku, Kiyosumi-Shirakawa and Monzen-Nakachō Stations. The Hanzōmon and Tōzai Lines also serve the last two stations, respectively.

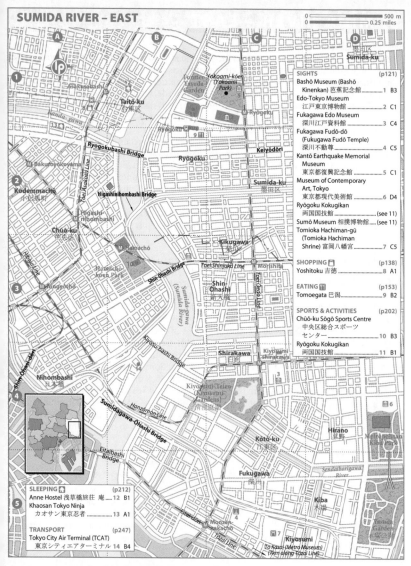

0   500 m
0   0.25 miles

more than 70% of the city and killed more than 50,000 people. Maps chart the course of the devastating fires, while cases display glassware, eyeglasses, binoculars, tools and other objects convoluted by heat. There is also a harrowing collection of photographs and paintings of the aftermath. The museum has generalised to cover other disasters to strike Tokyo prefecture, including WWII air raids and the volcanic eruption on one of the prefecture's southern islands. The museum sits in Yokoami-kōen (Yokoami Park), with other memorial buildings and a garden dedicated to quake victims.

A pleasant walk connects the park and the Ryōgoku Kokugikan (p121) through the Yasuda garden (Map p122; admission free; 9am-4pm), once the site of the Edo home of a *daimyō*.

KIYOSUMI & FUKAGAWA

KIYOSUMI TEIEN (KIYOSUMI GARDEN) Map p122

清澄庭園

☎ 3641-5892; 3-3-9 Kiyosumi, Kōtō-ku; adult/child/senior ¥150/free/70; 9am-5pm; Toei Ōedo or Hanzōmon Line to Kiyosumi-shirakawa (exit A3)

This marvellous garden was the first location to be designated a site of scenic beauty by the Tokyo Metropolitan Government – and it's easy to see why. The origins of Kiyosumi Teien date back to 1721 when it was a villa for a *daimyō*. Although the villa itself was destroyed in the 1923 earthquake, the property thereafter was purchased by Iwasaki Yatarō, founder of the Mitsubishi Corporation. He was able to use company ships to transport prize stones here from all over Japan – count all 50 (they're numbered). They're set around a pond ringed with Japanese black pine, hydrangeas, Taiwan cherries and other plants designed to bloom at different times of the year.

MUSEUM OF CONTEMPORARY ART, TOKYO Map p122

東京都現代美術館

MOT; ☎ 5245-4111; www.mot-art-museum.jp; 4-1-1 Miyoshi, Kōtō-ku; adult/child ¥500/free, student ¥250-400; 10am-6pm Tue-Sun; Hanzōmon or Toei Ōedo Line to Kiyosumi-shirakawa (exit B2)

Dedicated to showcasing postwar artists and designers from Japan and abroad, MOT also holds some 3800 pieces exhibited in rotation in its permanent collection gallery, by the likes of David Hockney, Sam Francis and Andy Warhol, as well as by Japanese artists such as Yokō Tadanori. The building's stone, steel and wood architecture by Yanagisawa Takahiko is a work of art in its own right – highlights include a sunken garden, V-shaped structural supports, and a water-and-stone promenade.

The museum is in Metropolitan Kiba Park. It takes about 10 well-signposted minutes on foot from the subway station.

FUKAGAWA FUDŌ-DŌ (FUKUGAWA FUDŌ TEMPLE) Map p122

深川不動尊

Fukagawa Fudō Hall; ☎ 3461-8288; 1-17-13 Tomioka, Kōtō-ku; admission free; Tōzai or Toei Ōedo Line to Monzen-nakachō (exit 1)

The history of this giant temple dates from 1703 as a sub-temple of Shinshō-ji in the city of Narita, one of the head temples of Shingon Buddhism. The main image, which is housed in a recently constructed inner hall, is Fudōmyō – a venerable Buddha depicted in murals by Nakajima Chinami (2004). On the 2nd floor is a gallery depicting all 88 temples of the 1400km pilgrimage route on the island of Shikoku; it is said that offering a prayer at each alcove has the same effect as visiting each temple. One of the best times to visit is around 3pm, when priests read sutras in a thunder of *taiko* drums and fire.

TOMIOKA HACHIMAN-GŪ (TOMIOKA HACHIMAN SHRINE) Map p122

富岡八幡宮

☎ 3462-1315; 1-20-3 Tomioka, Kōtō-ku; admission free; Tōzai or Toei Ōedo Line to Monzen-nakachō (exit 1)

Next door to Fukagawa Fudō-dō, this large shrine dates from 1627, and is

VISITING A SUMŌ STABLE

Sumō stables, called *heya* or *beya* in Japanese, are where the *sumōtori* (wrestlers) live and train. There are over 50 *heya* in Ryōgoku, along with shops catering to their clothing needs as well as restaurants. *Heya* are not normally in the business of hosting guests, but a few of them occasionally open to allow visitors to observe training sessions. Some things to know:

- Times of visits are limited. Stables close during tournaments and for one to three weeks immediately before and afterwards.
- Training usually begins around 6am and finishes by 10am, with the lower-ranking wrestlers training earliest. The best time to see the wrestlers is usually around 8.30am. For most visitors, a half-hour visit is sufficient.
- Most *heya* prefer visits arranged in advance. See p208 or ask at tourist information offices about which *heya* are open and how to arrange a visit (and don't be a no-show or cancel at the last minute).
- Discipline is a key element of sumō training, and you should also exercise discipline as a visitor. Sit quietly outside the *dohyō* (ring) and do not make noise or take photographs without permission.

closely associated with the world of sumō. Around the back of the main building is the *yokozuna* stone, carved with the names of each of these champion wrestlers. Also of note are two treasured *mikoshi* (portable shrines), used in the Fukagawa Hachiman festival in mid-August. The current *mikoshi* date from 1991, and are encrusted with diamonds and rubies – look in the eyes of the phoenix and other birds on top.

A flea market takes place here on the 15th and 28th of most months, from around 8am to sunset.

FUKAGAWA EDO MUSEUM Map p122
深川江戸資料館

☎ 3630-8625; 1-3-28 Shirakawa, Kōtō-ku; adult ¥300, student ¥50-300; 9.30am-5pm, closed 2nd & 4th Mon of month; Toei Ōedo or Hanzōmon Line to Kiyosumi-shirakawa (exit A3)

This museum re-creates a 17th-century Edo neighbourhood complete with a fire lookout tower, life-sized facades and buildings you can enter. Explore the shops like the greengrocer's and rice shop, or slip off your shoes to enter the tenement homes and handle the daily utensils and children's toys. Be sure to note the Inari shrine and the *kura* (mud-walled storehouses) where belongings were kept for protection from fire and, just as big a danger, Edo's legendary humidity.

BASHŌ MUSEUM (BASHŌ KINENKAN) Map p122
芭蕉記念館

☎ 3631-1448; 1-6-3 Tokiwa, Kōtō-ku; admission ¥100; 9.30am-5pm Tue-Sun; Toei Ōedo Line to Morishita (exit A1)

Although it now takes just a matter of minutes from the central Nihombashi

MATSUO BASHŌ

Matsuo Bashō (1644–94) was born in what is now Mie prefecture in western Japan. By the age of 10 he had begun to compose haiku, the seasonal-themed Japanese poetry that has five syllables in the first line, seven in the second and five in the third. In 1671 he published his first set of poems and by 1680 he was the leader of a literary circle in Edo. In 1681 one of his disciples planted a *bashō* (banana tree) by Matsuo's cottage here in Fukagawa; the cottage came to be known as Bashō-an (Banana House) and from that Matsuo took his pen name.

Bashō soon embarked on an additional career as a travel writer. He wandered the length of his homeland, documenting what he saw – Edo's own Mark Twain, Bill Bryson or Pico Iyer. Here is one of his most famous verses, from 1686:

Furu-ike ya
kawazu tobikomu.
Izu no oto.

The ancient pond
a frog leaps in.
The sound of the water.

In 1689 he departed Fukagawa to research what would become one of his most famous works, *Oku no Hosomichi no Tabi* (The Narrow Road to the Deep North), then later travelled to the Kyoto area where he wrote *Saga Nikki* (Saga Diary). Upon returning home to Fukagawa, he wrote the verse:

Moon viewing at my hut.
Let me hang on the pillar
like a banana leaf.

In 1694 he took one last journey, to the great city of Osaka, where he fell ill. His last poem before dying that October:

On a journey, ailing
My dreams roam about
Over a withered moor.

The above haiku are translated from Japanese and don't conform exactly to the 5-7-5 rule, but one of haiku's great legacies is its easy adaptability to other languages. To try one in English, use the 5-7-5 syllabication, include a reference to the season and throw in a twist, so that by the end of the haiku, readers are transported somewhere they couldn't anticipate.

DETOUR: METRO MUSEUM

Under the tracks in the eastern suburb of Kasai, the Metro Museum (off Map pp48–9; ☎ 3878-5011, 6-3-1 Higashi-Kasai, Edogawa-ku; adult/child ¥210/100, 🕙 10am-5pm Tue-Sun) chronicles the history of the Tokyo Metro from the first subway in 1927 (it connected Asakusa with Ueno) to the opening of the Fukutoshin Line in 2008. Visitors can pile into a couple of early Ginza and Marunouchi Line cars along with mannequins in period costumes, watch a 3D video of how tunnels are built and marvel at a multilevel model train set (shows at 11am, 1pm, 2pm and 3.30pm).

While the primary target of this museum is tots, there are some cool activities for those grown-ups who haven't outgrown their fascination with rolling stock. The best is the simulator like the one Metro drivers actually train on. Little of the signage is in English, so you may want to have a Japanese-speaking friend along.

To reach the Metro Museum, take the Tōzai Line to Kasai, and head out the east entrance for Kan-nana-dōri. The museum entrance is across the street, under the tracks on the south side.

district, Fukagawa was considered a very remote area of Edo in 1680 when the revered haiku poet Matsuo Bashō (opposite) arrived here. At this small, plain museum, you can see some scrolls of poetry written by Bashō and those inspired by him, as well as souvenirs of his journeys. There's no English signage, but nonetheless it's a unique opportunity to enter his world. There's a small garden out back, or walk out to the Sumida-gawa and take a left for a lookout where you can view the skyscrapers while contemplating Bashō's long-lost Edo.

ODAIBA

Eating p178; Shopping p151

On Odaiba, you could be forgiven for thinking that you're not in Tokyo anymore. The name of this conglomeration of artificial islands means 'fortification', and indeed that's why the Tokugawa shōgunate ordered them built in the mid-1800s, after the arrival of the black ships (p25). It later served as a shipping terminal, but it wasn't until the Bubble Era of the 1990s that it reached its present status as a destination for shopping and fun, mixed in with a giant convention centre and corporate headquarters.

Reaching Odaiba is a journey – as much in length as in attitude. Most visitors board the conductorless train Yurikamome around Shimbashi. As it loops you across the width of Tokyo Bay via the Rainbow Bridge, Odaiba's futuristic buildings beckon while the skyline you just left continues to tempt. Once on Odaiba, the streetscape of futuristic buildings, elevated walkways above and wide avenues below is unlike anything you left behind.

The architectural centrepiece of the island is the Fuji TV Broadcast Centre (p135), whose 25th-floor observation deck opens onto views of the city. Malls like Decks Tokyo Beach and Venus Fort (p151) dominate the rest of the landscape, with big-name shops, theme dining and game arcades. If you're looking for some non-retail therapy, however, the National Museum of Emerging Science and Innovation, the Museum of Maritime Science and Ō-edo Onsen Monogatari are all excellent alternatives.

The Yurikamome Line train connects Shimbashi to Toyosu on the Yurakuchō Line via Odaiba. The Rinkai Line train also bisects Odaiba. Most of Odaiba is navigable by foot, though jumping on and off the Yurikamome can be convenient. The western part of the island, fronted by Odaiba Kaihin-kōen (Odaiba Marine Park), is home to luxury hotels, shopping and arcades, and a great number of eateries. The museums and other attractions generally lie to the east.

Ō-EDO ONSEN MONOGATARI (Ō-EDO ONSEN STORY) Map p127
大江戸温泉物語

☎ 5500-1126; www.ooedoonsen.jp/higaeri/english/index.html; 2-57 Aomi, Kōtō-ku; adult ¥1900-2900, child ¥1400-1600; ⏰ 11am-9am; ⓨ Yurikamome Line to Telecom Center, Rinkai Line to Tokyo Teleport (free shuttle bus)

Public bathing in onsen (hot springs) is a Japanese obsession (see p203), and, believe it or not, they've managed to find an actual hot spring 1400m below Tokyo Bay. Of course, Ō-edo Onsen is so much more than just a mere hot springs complex. Something of Disneyland-meets-health-spa, this bathing theme park re-creates an old Japanese downtown area, selling old-timey foods, toys and souvenirs. Wander around in your yukata (light cotton kimono) and you'll fit right in. Sure it's kitschy, but what the hey…

Bathing opportunities (most separated by gender) include indoor and outdoor pools, a foot bath, a bed of hot stones and the opportunity to be buried in hot sand. Massage services are available, as are relaxation spaces in case all that pampering makes you sleepy. Bathing products and rental of towels and yukata are included.

Admission prices are highest between 11am and 6pm, and lowest between 5am and 8am; there's a surcharge of ¥1700 per person between 2am and 5am. Visitors with tattoos will be denied admission.

NATIONAL MUSEUM OF EMERGING SCIENCE & INNOVATION (MIRAIKAN) Map p127
未来館

☎ 3570-9151; www.miraikan.jst.go.jp; 2-41 Aomi, Kōtō-ku; adult/child ¥600/200; ⏰ 10am-5.30pm Wed-Sun; ⓨ Yurikamome Line to Fune-no-Kagakukan or Telecom Center

In the 20th century, '2001' had overtones of the future. Miraikan means 'hall of the future', so it's somehow fitting that that 2001 was the year this futuristic building opened.

TRANSPORT: ODAIBA

Train Odaiba is on the Yurikamome Line from Shimbashi, which crosses the majestic, 918m-long Rainbow Bridge, and connects to Toyosu on the Yurakuchō Line on the other end. An ¥800 day pass makes sense unless you plan to make a simple round trip. The Rinkai Line also approaches from the south and east. See listings for individual stops.

Water bus Tokyo Cruise (p65) stops at Odaiba Marine Park and Palette Town.

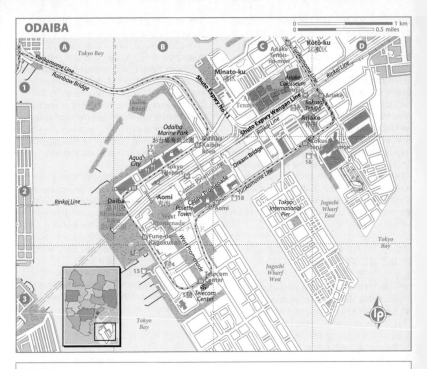

ODAIBA

Since then, it's been a favourite of travellers with kids. Robotics (check out Asimo), information and environmental technology figure prominently, as do the newest in the life sciences. The Gaia dome theatre/planetarium, in its own orb, almost always books out – get a reservation when you arrive. The green building itself is as futuristic as its exhibits: glass of different degrees of clarity has been used for different parts of the exterior shell (to allow for the capture of natural light) and 'through holes' and 'wind gardens' provide ventilation.

TOKYO JOYPOLIS Map p127
東京ジョイポリス
☎ 5500-1801; http://tokyo-joypolis.com; 3rd to 5th fl Decks Tokyo Beach, 1-6-1 Daiba, Minato-ku; adult/child admission ¥500/300, passport ¥3500/3100; Ⓜ Yurikamome Line to Odaiba Kaihin-kōen
On a rainy day or when your (inner) children just want to go for a spree, this three-

storey indoor amusement park, operated by game-maker Sega, is just the ticket. Of the 20 or so attractions, virtual reality and action rides like the Spin Bullet (like a spinning roller coaster), the snowboard-like Halfpipe Canyon and bobsled-themed Storm G are the most popular. For others, including many on the top (5th) floor, Japanese is helpful. Lines are shortest on weekdays when kids are in school. Note that some rides have minimum height requirements, all clearly spelled out in an English pamphlet or on the website. Separate admission and individual ride tickets (most from ¥500) are available, but if you plan to go on more than a half-dozen attractions the unlimited 'passport' makes sense.

MUSEUM OF MARITIME SCIENCE (FUNE NO KAGAKU-KAN) Map p127
船の科学館
☎ 5500-1111; www.funenokagakukan.or.jp; 3-1 Higashi Yashio, Shinagawa-ku; adult/child ¥700/400; ⊚ Yurikamome Line to Fune-no-Kagakukan
This museum is shipshape, literally. From the outside it looms like an ocean liner by the water's edge, and inside are four floors of excellent displays related to every aspect of ships; don't miss the stunningly crafted replicas of Japanese ships, and try the navigation simulator. Outside, the 83.7m ice-breaker *Sōya* is preserved. The museum is full of activities for kids, including a pool next door used for swimming and demonstrations and instruction of small craft. There's limited English signage, but an English audio guide is available (¥500).

RISŪPIA Map p127
リスーピア
☎ 3599-2600; risupia.panasonic.co.jp; Panasonic Center Tokyo, 3-5-1 Ariake, Kōtō-ku; adult/child ¥500/free; ⊚ Yurikamome Line to Kokusai-tenjijō Seimon or Ariake

The 'ri' stands for *rika* (science), the 'sū' for *sūgaku* (mathematics) and the 'pia' is short for 'utopia', and if that seems a contradiction, it won't after you visit this nifty museum. RiSūPia is operated by Panasonic on two floors of its Odaiba showroom building. The 1st floor (no charge) is the Quest gallery, where principles of maths and science are illustrated through science museum-type exhibits; check out the RiSū Earth, a 'glowing globe of knowledge' that you spin to reveal important historical figures in science.

It's worth investing the ¥500 to go to the 3rd-floor Discovery Field, where game-style exhibits include playing 'air hockey' with prime numbers, trying to sort coloured foam balls in a hopper as the lighting colour changes, and assembling foam blocks into shapes before time runs out – which is more challenging than it looks.

There are excellent explanations throughout in both Japanese and English. Note: RiSūPia can be crowded on weekends and holidays.

TOYOTA MEGA WEB Map p127
トヨタメガウェブ
☎ 3599-0808; www.megaweb.gr.jp; 1 Aomi, Kōtō-ku; admission free, virtual test drives ¥600; ⊙ 11am-9pm; ⊚ Yurikamome Line to Aomi (main exit), Rinkai Line to Tokyo Teleport (main exit)
In the Palette Town development, Mega Web was designed to display the wares of the Toyota Motor Corporation. Yes, it's a showroom, but against all odds it's actually also fun. Test drive vehicles (advance reservation required) or poke around in the History Garage with cars from the Golden Age. Some facilities close earlier; call ahead to confirm.

Next door, don't miss one of the world's tallest Ferris wheels (Dai-kanransha), which is as high as the second viewing platform of the Eiffel Tower (the one in Paris, not Tokyo Tower!).

WALKING TOURS

NIPPORI, YANAKA & UENO-KŌEN

Spared from aerial bombing during WWII, the neighbourhoods of Yanaka and Nippori (near Ueno) are imbued with the slowness of a former age. This is one of the city's most rewarding strolls, featuring the colourful shopping street of Yanaka, a walk lined with small Buddhist temples, and one of Tokyo's most important cemeteries, culminating with the museums of Ueno Park.

1 Yanaka Ginza (谷中ぎんざ) Exiting left from Sendagi Station, cross the street and turn right at the post office, bear left, make a quick right, and you'll be transported back 50 years. Yanaka Ginza *shōtengai* (shopping street) is the kind of place that dominated Tokyo's neighbourhoods in the mid-Shōwa era, and this one is plenty *genki* (healthy), with shops continuing to sell tea, crafts, basketry and everyday wear. Pick up street foods and rice crackers made before your eyes, but be sure to dispose of refuse where you bought your snacks. Yanaka Ginza can also be reached from Nippori Station (turn left and after a couple hundred metres head down the stairs). Head up the stairs and turn right after the Indian restaurant to continue.

2 Sandara Kōgei (さんだら工芸屋) Along this narrow street that's lined with Buddhist temples (feel free to take a peek in if you feel like it), you'll pass the under-renovation Asakura Chōsō Museum (p82), shortly after which retail therapy of the Shitamachi variety can be all yours at this quaint little family-run basket shop, which sells a variety of traditional baskets as well as rustic Japanese crafts.

3 Kannon-ji (観音寺) Belonging to the Shingon sect, this Buddhist temple features a comforting representation of the female incarnation of the bodhisatva known as Kannon (the deity of mercy), as well as a small cemetery from where you can steal views of the modern city beyond. It also has a connection with the tale of the 47 samurai in *Chūshingura* (see Sengaku-ji, p119), perhaps the most famous story of Japanese history. As you continue toward Yanaka Rei-en, you'll find a handful of small shops selling Buddhist religious objects. Bear left at the Daily Yamazaki convenience store toward the cemetery.

4 Yanaka Rei-en (谷中霊園) Even if you normally don't have a morbid bent, a stroll through this historical and rather scenic cemetery (p108) is an excellent way to catch a glimpse of old Edo. With your camera in hand, spend some time wandering through row upon row of ancient tombstones while keeping an eye out for the rather territorial cats in residence. A central point of interest is the family tomb of a branch of the Tokugawa family (see Boomtown Edo, p24).

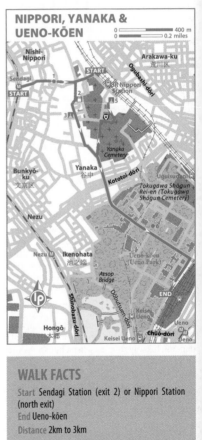

WALK FACTS

Start Sendagi Station (exit 2) or Nippori Station (north exit)

End Ueno-kōen

Distance 2km to 3km

Time One to 1½ hours (without museum visits)

Fuel stop Snacks on Yanaka Ginza

5 Tennō-ji (天王寺) At the far end of the cemetery, the Heaven's King Temple belongs to the Tendai sect, one of the most important Buddhist traditions in Japan. The highlight of this small but tranquil temple is the large Buddha image occupying the central courtyard inside a modernist enclosure. Cast in 1690, and modelled after the Great Buddha (p243) in Kamakura, this rather solemn statue has weathered the many disasters of both old Edo and modern Tokyo.

6 Ueno-kōen (上野公園) Walk back through the cemetery with Tennō-ji behind you, and bear left when you reach the street. Cross the street at Kototoi-dōri, and at the next light bear to the left. In a couple of blocks you will see the Tokyo National Museum (p78) grounds on your left, and the other museums and access to Ueno Station are across the street on your right.

SHITAMACHI

If you squint a little, Shitamachi (or the Low City) still looks something like the settings depicted in the wood-block prints famously produced here in Edo times. Luckily, the area retains much of its traditional working-class feel – sort of a rough, gruff, friendly spirit distinctly different from other zones of re-invention-addicted Tokyo. If you haven't already, be sure to detour to visit the landmark Sensō-ji.

1 Chingodō (鎮護堂) Founded in 1883, this odd, peaceful little subtemple of Sensō-ji pays tribute to *tanuki*, raccoon dogs that figure in Japanese myth as mystical shape-shifters and merry pranksters, and who were said to be found in great numbers here. *Tanuki* are normally depicted with enormous testicles on which they can fly. They frequently pop up in Japanese woodcuts such as Utagawa Kuniyoshi's *The Seven Wonders of the Clowning Raccoon*, in which the *tanuki* is shown cheerily dancing his way round a geisha house. As you enter, also notice the *jizō*, statues protecting travellers and children. There are often stalls set up along the stretch of road outside Chingodō, selling workaday clothing, shoes and festival accessories.

2 Hanayashiki Amusement Park (花やしき) This nostalgia-inducing amusement park (☎ 3842-8780; 2-28-1 Asakusa; adult/child ¥900/400, rides pass ¥2200/1900; ☒ 10.30am-6pm Wed-Mon Mar-Nov,

10.30am-5pm Wed-Mon Dec-Feb), Japan's oldest, dates back to 1853, and is an absolute delight for the young ones, who can clamber over rides, dress up in old Edo style and watch ninja and samurai shows. If you're having trouble finding the entrance, just listen for the delighted shrieking, as well as the rollercoaster creaking and whooshing along its ageing wooden tracks.

3 Asakusa Engei Hall (浅草演芸ホール) The centrepiece of Asakusa's old cinema district is this performance hall (p197), where *rakugo* (performances of stand-up comedy or long tales) are still held today. Unfortunately, the district itself is a little down-at-heel nowadays, and the few remaining cinemas don't screen much besides Japanese pornography. However, as you wander through this historic area, consider that this was once the liveliest of Tokyo's entertainment districts and the preferred haunt of everyone from prostitutes and gangsters to novelists and artisans.

4 Kaminarimon-dōri (雷門道り) The major street running through Asakusa is lined

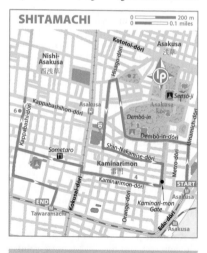

WALK FACTS

Start Asakusa Station (exit 6)
End Tawaramachi Station
Distance 1.5km
Time One hour, plus lunch
Fuel stop Sometarō

with traditional Japanese restaurants, any of which are perfect for a relaxing lunch break. Although there's no shortage of delicious spots in this stretch of town, our recommendation is Sometarō (p166), for cheap, quick and cheerful *okonmiyaki* (savoury pancakes grilled at your table) in a historic wooden house.

5 Higashi Hongan-ji (東本願寺) To escape the tourist crowds, take time out amid the gleaming gold-leaf columns and screen paintings of this little visited Buddhist temple (☎ 3843-9511; 10-5-5 Nishi-Asakusa, Taito-ku; admission free), headquarters of some 300 temples of the Higashi Hongan-ji sect of Jōdō (Pure Land) Buddhism. The present building dates from 1939 and was the first concrete temple in Japan – a great advantage against Tokyo's fires. It enshrines the Amida Buddha, and its roof was depicted in one of Hokusai's '36 Views of Mt Fuji'.

6 Kappabashi-dōri (合羽橋道り) Tokyo's wholesale restaurant supplies area, Kappabashi-dōri (p142) is shop upon shop selling plastic food models, bamboo cooking utensils, batik cushions and even the *aka-chōchin* (red lanterns) that light the back alleys of Tokyo by night. Go on – see if you can get a good deal on a plastic sushi model!

AOYAMA ARCHITECTURE

From the *cos-play* kids of Harajuku to the high-stepping fashionistas of Aoyama, Omote-Sandō stretches out in a veritable catwalk of style and architecture. Here you'll get to observe works by all of Japan's winners of the Pritzker Prize (like the Oscars of architecture), and others who are no doubt on their way. See Map p132.

1 Laforet Building (ラフォーレビル) Ascend the circular interior as if in a shopping-focused video game, and you'll soon discover the confusing half floors of the Laforet Building (p149), a popular shopping beacon in Aoyama. Of course, don't spend too much time here as you still need to explore the surrounding neighbourhood. Around the corner you'll find a number of experimental shop fronts, many of them belonging to cutting-edge fashion boutiques.

2 Design Festa (デザインフェスタ) One of the strangest buildings in Aoyama, the headquarters of Design Festa (☎ 3479-1433; 3-20-18 Jingūmae; ☾ 11am-8pm) looks like an industrial, spider-webbed diorama, though the space is actually home to a slew of galleries. It's also responsible for the enormous art and design festival, Design Festa (p19), that takes place biannually at the Tokyo Big Sight (p136).

3 Omotesandō Hills (表参道ヒルズ) The charms of this long, sleek and very chichi glass-fronted 2007 shopping complex on Omote-Sandō may not be immediately obvious, but give it some time. Pritzker Prize winner Andō Tadao designed this building to be a journey. For starters, it looks like three storeys from the street, when there are actually six storeys inside, around a trapezoidal spiral atrium. Our recommendation is to follow the walkways to the top and then look down. Its sister property is Roppongi Hills (p90).

4 Christian Dior Building (クリスチャンディオールビル) Cross the street from Omote-Sandō Hills, look right, and you'll see a five-storey glass building that looks as if it has a giant, undulating white dress suspended inside. The 2010 Pritzker Prize-winning Tokyo firm Sanaa (of Nishizawa Ryue and Sejima Kazuyo) was a bold choice for Paris design house Christian Dior (☎ 5464-6260; 5-9-11 Jingūmae; ☾ 11am-8pm). Inside, surfaces of white lacquer, glass and stainless steel are an austere backdrop for the couture and cosmetics.

5 Japan Nursing Association Building (日本看護協会) Take a look at the glass cone outside of this headquarters of the Japan Nursing Association (5-8-2 Jingūmae). If it looks familiar, maybe you've seen these cones, by Kurokawa Kishō, at the National Art Center, Tokyo (p93). This building was a precursor to that one, where he positioned a collection of cones even more adventurously. For a quick fuel-up on the fly, Heiroku Sushi (p174) lets you select sushi from a conveyor belt in front of you.

6 Louis Vuitton Building (ルイヴィトンビル) For several years running, the Japanese have had something of a love affair with Louis Vuitton (☎ 3478-2100; 5-7-5 Jingūmae; ☾ 11am-8pm), which is why this flagship store is usually packed wall-to-wall with shoppers. Meant to evoke a stack of clothes trunks, Aoki Jun's design features offset panels of tinted glass behind sheets of metal mesh of varying patterns.

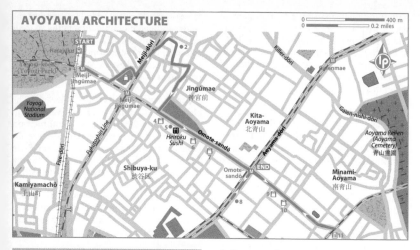

START

Hala juku

Meiji-dōri

●2

Killer-dōri

Jingūmae
神宮前

Kita-Aoyama
北青山

Omote-sandō

Aoyama-dōri

Galen-nishi-dōri

Aoyama Reien
(Aoyama
Cemetery)
青山霊園

Meiji-jingūmae

Meiji-jingūmae

Yoyogi National Stadium

Fukutoshin Line

Fire-dōri

Shibuya-ku
渋谷区

4 □ 5 □
Heiroku
Sushi

7

Omote-sandō M

END M

Minami-Aoyama
南青山

Kamiyamachō
上山町

●8

9 □

10

● 11

Start **Harajuku Station (Omote-Sandō exit)**

End **Omote-Station**

Distance **2.5km**

Time **One to two hours, plus stops**

Fuel stop **Heiroku Sushi**

7 Tod's (トッズ) Tokyo's home of Italian footwear designer Tod's (☎ 6419-2055; 5-1-15 Jingūmae), this shoe shop is one of the most distinguished buildings in Aoyama. Wrapped in glass and supporting beams whose shapes reflect the winter-bared branches of the Zelkova trees on Omote-Sandō, architect Itō Toyo's structure makes a statement while echoing the elements of its environment. A few doors to the left is the Hanae Mori building, an earlier work by another Pritzker winner, Tange Kenzō (closed for renovations at the time of research).

8 Spiral Building (スパイラルビル) Designed by Tokyo architectural luminary and Pritzker winner Maki Fumihiko, the 1st floor of this 1980s building is dramatically crowned by a semicylinder. Inside you'll find a listening station featuring Japanese and world music and an exhibition hall with displays of everything from fashion and accessories to sculpture and photography. If you have some time, it's worth ascending the whimsical spiral ramp to the museum-style gift shop located on the 2nd floor, or take coffee and cake in the ground-floor cafe.

9 Comme des Garçons Building (コムデギャルソン) The sloped windows of the flagship store of Kawakubo Rei's Comme des Garçons (p148) empire mildly prepare you for the architectural gems lying inside. Step through the entrance and admire the wares on display, which occupy minimalist, curvaceous spaces arranged in a disorienting maze of tilted walls.

10 Prada Aoyama Building (プラダ青山ビル) The dazzling Prada Aoyama building (☎ 6418-0400; 5-2-6 Minami-Aoyama) was designed by Swiss architects Jacques Herzog and Pierre de Meuron, also Pritzker Prize winners. The resulting building is a weirdly organic, bubble-surfaced crystal of a venue in which the goods almost play a secondary role. The exterior itself is stunning, with its panels of convex glass, but the design of the interior's six floors almost deceives the senses into seeing the space as a seamless whole.

11 Nezu Museum (根津美術館) The newest addition to the Aoyama architectural escapade (2009), Nezu Museum (p108) is by Kuma Kengō and has the feel of sort of a farmhouse in the big city. With one level below ground, two above and a formal noble garden out back, the building is meant to emphasise the harmony of architecture and nature, and of course, show off the museum's collection of priceless East Asian antiquities.

Once you've had your fill of architecture, turn back towards the Omote-Sandō intersection; it's just a few minutes' walk to the Omote-Sandō subway station.

WEST SHINJUKU

Looking up as you walk the streets of Nishi-Shinjuku may put a kink in your neck, while peering down from those skyscrapers will make your jaw drop (smog willing). Within these towering structures lie delights as unexpected as a plumbing gallery, the world's largest pendulum clock and Matisse originals.

1 Shinjuku L Tower (新宿Lタワー) The Shinjuku L Tower is home to the Toto Tokyo Center Showroom (☎ 3345-1010; 26th & 27th fl, 1-6-1 Nishi-Shinjuku; ☉ 10am-6pm, closed 1st & 3rd Mon of month), a high-tech kitchen, plumbing and bathroom showcase that gives you a great idea of what a contemporary Japanese home looks like, if you can't visit one yourself. There's lots of automation; the toilet lids that automatically lift when you approach are nifty.

2 Mode Gakuen Cocoon Tower (モード学園コクーンタワー) Nishi-Shinjuku's newest building (2008) is also its most exciting. The convex 50-storey tower (1-7-3 Nishi-Shinjuku), designed by the office of Tange Kenzō, is closed to the public except for a small cafe by the entrance. However, its exterior, wrapped in white strips as if by a silkworm, is really what you want to ogle anyway.

3 Pentax Square (ペンタックススクエア) Even nonphotography buffs will appreciate the photo exhibits at this diminutive gallery (☎ 3348-2941; 1-25-1 Nishi-Shinjuku; ☉ 10.30am-6.30pm), on the mezzanine of the courtyard behind the Shinjuku Center. For true camera buffs, however, the best part is the vast array of Pentax cameras, lenses and other optical equipment on display. It's completely hands-on – you can snap away with the cameras and spy into neighbouring buildings through the huge 1000mm lenses.

4 Sompo Japan Museum of Art (損保ジャパン東郷青児美術館) The Sompo Japan Museum of Art (p113), on the 42nd floor of the Sompo Building, is known mainly for its purchase of Van Gogh's *Sunflowers* for a whopping ¥5 billion. Although the famous painting is the undoubtable highlight, the museum focuses on the largely figurative work of Japanese artist Tōgō Seiji.

5 Shinjuku I-Land (新宿アイランド) This cluster of 1990s buildings (6-5 Nishi-Shinjuku) includes an office building and cylindrical, black granite event hall, but the reason to visit is the half-dozen or so outdoor sculptures, such as Robert Indiana's *Love* and two *Tokyo Brushstroke* sculptures by Roy Liechtenstein. They're interspersed with fountains and marble mosaics, which are works of art in themselves, and there are a number of inexpensive restaurants in the plaza below if you'd like to take a load off.

6 Shinjuku Sumitomo Building (新宿住友ビル) Although this hollowed-out vertical triangle is home to a large jewellery mall and a general shopping centre, the real attraction is the free observation platform on the 51st floor. Stop by for a quick bird's-eye view of the urban jungle that is Shinjuku.

7 Tokyo Metropolitan Government Offices (東京都庁) By now you've no doubt noticed the towering Tokyo Metropolitan Government Offices (p109) where some 13,000 government workers sweat over the administrative paperwork of running Tokyo in these buildings. The Citizen's Plaza features shops, restaurants, a passport section and, curiously, a blood donation room, though the views from the 45th-floor observation platform in Building No 1 are some of the best in the city.

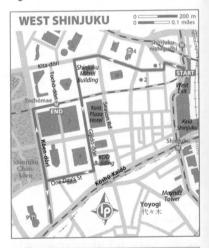

WALK FACTS

Start Shinjuku-nishiguchi Station (west exit)
End Tochōmae Station
Distance 3km
Time Two hours
Fuel stop Shinjuku NS Building

8 Shinjuku NS Building (新宿NSビル) If you're in the mood for a bit of eccentric high tech, the interior of this building is hollow, like the Sumitomo Building, and features a 1600-sq-metre area from which you can gaze upwards at the transparent roof. Overhead, at 110m, is a sky bridge. The square itself features a 29m pendulum clock, listed by the *Guinness Book of Records* as the largest in the world. You can take the glass lift to the restaurant level on the 29th floor.

9 Park Hyatt Tokyo (パークハイアット) To see where Bill Murray and Scarlett Johansson met Anna Faris in *Lost in Translation*, head up to the 40th-floor sky lobby of this fabled hotel. To stay for steak, dress up and head into the New York Grill (p175).

EAST SHINJUKU

This walking tour is best begun about an hour before dusk falls, when you'll observe the perceptible change of east Shinjuku's day life turn over to night. The neon burns brighter against the darkening sky, and the seedier side of Kabukichō likewise comes into sharper contrast.

1 Kinokuniya (紀伊國屋書店) This popular bookshop (see the boxed text, p58) is a great time-killer. You can pop in to browse its superb collection of foreign-language books and magazines on the 7th floor. And of course, this being Japan, no one will say anything to you if you decide to spend an hour or so reading something without buying it.

2 Isetan (伊勢丹ビル) Packed to the gills with fashionable boutiques and trendy shops, the shopping mecca of Isetan (p150) draws in crowds of fashionable Tokyoites ready to spend big. If you haven't yet visited a *depachika* (basement food floor), this is a great one to see.

3 Hanazono-jinja (花園神社) This shrine nestles so close to Tokyo's most infamous red-light district that its clientele can make for some interesting people-watching. Hanazono-Jinja (p114) has a reputation for bringing success to business ventures – both legit and less so.

4 Golden Gai (ゴールデン街) This intimate district is little more than a warren of alleyways devoted entirely to small, stand-up watering holes. Traditionally the haunt of bo-

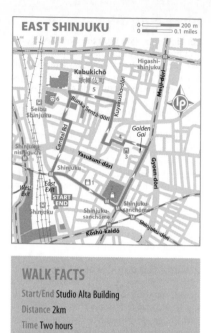

WALK FACTS

Start/End Studio Alta Building

Distance 2km

Time Two hours

Fuel stop *Depachika* of Isetan Department Store

hemian Tokyoites, Golden Gai (p114) is deserted by day, but can be great fun at night. It's said that the block is gradually being bought up by Seibu department store, but for now Golden Gai hangs tight.

5 Kabukichō (歌舞伎町) Despite its reputation as Tokyo's notorious red-light district, Kabukichō (p113) is a relatively safe area to stroll around. As it's aimed solely at Japanese clients, most of what goes on in these environs is pretty much off-limits to foreigners. Nevertheless, Kabukichō has everything from soaplands and peep shows to porn-video booths and strip shows that involve audience participation.

6 Milano-za Theatre Plaza (ミラノ座前) This complex contains a multiscreen cinema, bowling alley and restaurants, although these can all be had elsewhere at better quality. The square facing the theatre, however, is a popular busking spot at night, though *yakuza* are usually quick about moving anyone too popular along. Some locals refer to the square as Koma-za-mae (in front of the Koma theatre), although the theatre itself was recently torn down.

AN ISLAND STROLL

Pick and choose your stops on this walk. The entertainments of Odaiba are so humungous and sprawling that browsing one mall and one museum could easily take half a day. Shorten your journey by using the Yurikamome train (p126).

1 Decks Tokyo Beach (デックス東京ビーチ) There's no shortage of shopping on the island of Odaiba, though the 'day at the beach' theme at Decks Tokyo Beach (p151) is the perfect place for perking yourself up if the rain starts to fall. If you're planning to be on your feet all day, it's probably a good idea to eat your fill of conveyor-belt dim sum at Ten-Ten Tsune-Tsune Kaitenbō (p179), in Decks Tokyo Beach's Little Hong Kong food 'theme park'.

2 Fuji Television Japan Broadcast Center (フジテレビ日本放送センター) The headquarters of Fuji TV, an unmistakable lattice-shaped structure (by Tange Kenzō) suspending a giant orb, is straight out of the future and home to one of the city's best observatories. On a clear day you'll get picture-postcard views of Tokyo Bay, Rainbow Bridge and the towering skyline of Shinagawa. A ticket to the observatory (adult/child ¥500/300) also gets you a studio tour (in Japanese).

3 Miraikan (未来館) With a name like the National Museum of Emerging Science & Innovation (p126), you know it has to be good – especially if you're travelling with the little ones. With enough hands-on exhibits to occupy the attention spans of even the most finicky of children (or adults), it's easy to forget about your walking tour and lose an entire day here.

4 Ō-edo Onsen Monogatari (大江戸温泉物語) Just as dangerous to your itinerary as the Miraikan, this onsen resort is the perfect spot to soak your travel-worn bones. Of course, Ō-edo Onsen (p126 and p204) is so much more than a hot spring resort, especially since you can top off your bath with a delightful stroll through the shops and restaurants of 'Old Edo' while sporting your finest *yukata*.

5 Venus Fort (ビーナスフォート) A female-friendly shopping complex, Venus Fort (p151) stages faux sunrises and sunsets amid a kitschy Italian Renaissance theme, though none of this should detract from the real reason why you're here: to cash in on some retail therapy. There's Tokyo's first outlet mall on the 3rd floor.

WALK FACTS

Start Daiba Station (main exit)

End Kokusai-tenjijō Seimon Station

Distance 2.5km

Time 2½ hours, plus stops

Fuel stop Ten-Ten Tsune-Tsune Kaitenbō

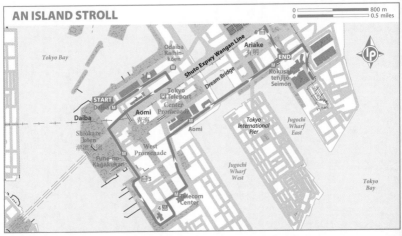

AN ISLAND STROLL

0 — 800 m
0 — 0.5 miles

Tokyo Bay

Odaiba Kaihin-kōen

Shuto Expwy Wangan Line

Ariake
有明

 END

Kokusai-tenjijō-Seimon

START
Daiba

Tokyo Teleport Center Promenade

Dream Bridge

Daiba

Aomi
青海

Aomi

Tokyo International Pier

Jugochi Wharf East

Shiokaze-kōen
潮風公園

West Promenade

Fune-no-Kagakukan

Jugochi Wharf West

Tokyo Bay

Miraikan Center

6 RiSūPia (リスーピア) Though on a smaller scale than Miraikan, RiSūPia (p128), a museum of maths and science, actually makes these ordinarily dry topics fun. Afterwards, drop in at the Panasonic Center (housed in the same building) to check out some of the latest innovations for the environment and design.

7 Tokyo Big Sight (東京ビッグサイト) The humorously named 'Big Sight' is an exhibition hall that looks like an Egyptian pyramid that fell to earth – upside down. If nothing else, it's one of Tokyo's architectural wonders, though the reason you're here is to snag a view of the bay from the roof of the hall, which is open any time a conference is not in session.

SHOPPING

top picks

SHOPPING

Tokyoites shop as they work – long and hard. Despite a challenging economy, Edokko (Tokyoites' nickname for themselves; literally 'children of Edo) continue to shop, for themselves and for gifts to grease the wheels of complex social and business relationships. Since the time of the Tokugawas, this city has craved the latest and greatest, so much so that there's a chain specialising in the most popular new goods (see p146).

A generation ago, if you asked a Tokyoite where to buy a…well, you name it, the answer would probably be a *depāto* (department store). The ones in Nihombashi and Ginza have the highest status, but *depāto* anchor sprawling retail clusters around town, particularly at rail hubs. That said, the last decade or two have seen an explosion of smaller designer and speciality boutiques – some very specialised indeed, from chopsticks to condoms. As a result, the city's shopping balance of power has shifted from east to west, with a preponderance of small shops in the backstreets of Harajuku, Omote-Sandō and Daikanyama. Young-and-trendies should hit Shibuya and Shimo-Kitazawa, while if it's old-school crafts you're after, try the alleys of Asakusa, and lovers of manga (Japanese comics) and electronics need look no further than Akihabara.

A word about bargaining: don't. It's simply not done in Japan, except at flea markets and the occasional electronics store. Just politely ask, '*Chotto, motto yasuku dekimasuka*?' (Can you make it a bit cheaper?)

IMPERIAL PALACE & MARUNOUCHI

Tokyo's epicentre boasts two of its oldest-line department stores in stately Nihombashi, and busy malls like Oazo and the Marunouchi Building by Tokyo Station, as well as in the station itself. International name-brand luxury shoppers and luxury gawkers will find plenty to enjoy along Marunouchi-Naka-dōri, between Tokyo Station and the Imperial Palace.

TOKYO CHARACTER STREET
Map p52   Character Goods

東京キャラクターストリート

☎ 3210-0077; First Avenue, Tokyo Station level B1; ⏱ 10am-8.30pm; ⓞ JR Yamanote Line to Tokyo (Yaesu exit), Marunouchi Line to Tokyo (Tokyo Station exit)

From Doraemon to Domo-kun, Hello Kitty to Ultraman, Japan knows *kawaii* (cute) and how to merchandise it. On the basement level of Tokyo Station, some 15 Japanese TV networks and toy manufacturers operate shop after shop selling official plush toys, sweets, accessories and the all-important miniature character to dangle from your mobile phone. Though the commerce is brisk, the characters are pretty innocent; fans of hard-core anime (Japanese animation) will be better off in Akihabara.

MITSUKOSHI Map p52   Department Store

三越

☎ 3241-3311; 1-4-1 Nihombashi-Muromachi, Chūō-ku; ⏱ 10am-8pm; ⓞ Ginza or Hanzōmon Line to Mitsukoshimae (exits A2, A3, A5, A7 & A8)

Though there are branches of this department store in Ginza (Map p57) and Ebisu (Map p96), the Nihombashi branch has the cachet as Japan's first department store – it even has a subway station named after it. Check out the floor dedicated to the art of the kimono or peruse the morsels in the depachika (department store food floor; p162). For the full effect, arrive at 10am for the bells and bows that accompany each day's opening.

TAKASHIMAYA Map p52   Department Store

高島屋

☎ 3211-4111; 2-4-1 Nihombashi, Chūō-ku; ⏱ 10am-8pm; ⓞ Ginza or Tōzai Line to Nihombashi (Takashimaya exit)

Takashimaya's branch on New York's Fifth Avenue is renowned for its cutting-edge Japanese-inspired interior, but the design of the Tokyo flagship store (1933) tips its pillbox hat to New York's Gilded Age. There is floor after floor of international luxury brands, a Japanese craft and kimono section on the 7th floor and uniformed female elevator operators – once commonplace in Tokyo – who still announce each floor in high-pitched sing-song voices.

GINZA

Ginza is the poshest shopping district in Tokyo. The quintessential Ginza experience is a department store; Mitsukoshi (松屋) (opposite) has pride of place, but Matsuya (松屋; ☎ 3567-1211; www.matsuya.com, in Japanese; 3-6-1 Ginza, Chūō-ku; 10am-8pm; Ginza, Hibiya or Marunouchi Line to Ginza, exits A12 & A13) and Matsuzakaya (松坂屋; ☎ 3572-1111; www.matsuzakaya.co.jp/ginza/index.html, in Japanese; 6-10-1 Ginza, Chūō-ku; 10am-8pm Thu-Sat, 10am-7.30pm Sun-Wed; Ginza, Hibiya or Marunouchi Line to Ginza, exit A3) are long-standing favourites, too. Tucked in between some of the more imposing facades are more simple pleasures such as fine papers and shelves stacked full of ingenious toys. Shopping options here really do reflect the breadth and depth of the city's consumer culture, equal parts high fashion glitz and down-to-earth dedication to craft.

ITŌYA Map p57   Art Supplies
伊東屋

☎ 3561-8311; 2-7-15 Ginza, Chūō-ku; 10.30am-8pm Mon-Sat, 10.30am-7pm Sun; Ginza or Hibiya Line to Ginza (exit A13)

Nine floors of stationery-shop love await visual-art professionals and seekers of office accessories from the everyday to luxury (fountain pens, Italian leather agendas). The 6th floor offers more traditional Japanese wares including *washi* (fine Japanese handmade paper), *tenugui* (beautifully hand-dyed thin cotton towels) and *furoshiki* (wrapping cloths).

NATSUNO Map p57   Chopsticks
夏野

☎ 3569-0952; 6-7-4 Ginza, Chūō-ku; 11am-8pm Mon-Sat, 11am-7pm Sun; Ginza or Hibiya Line to Ginza (exit B3)

Shelf after shelf of *ohashi* (chopsticks) in wood, lacquer, even gold leaf line the walls of this intimate shop on a Ginza side street, alongside plenty of *hashi-oki* (chopstick rests) to match. Prices run from a few hundred yen to ¥10,000. On the 6th floor, sister shop Konatsu sells adorable tableware for kids.

UNIQLO Map p57   Clothes
ユニクロ

☎ 3569-6781; www.uniqlo.com; 5-7-7 Ginza, Chūō-ku; 11am-9pm; Ginza or Hibiya Line to Ginza (exit A2)

Uniqlo has made its name by sticking to the basics and tweaking them with style – designer Jil Sander participated in a recent new launch. Offering inexpensive, quality clothing, this chain has taken Tokyo by typhoon and is expanding overseas, too. The Ginza store has recently refurbished and expanded to a whopping 2300 sq metres. Other locations are citywide.

MUJI Map p57   Clothes & Homewares
無印良品

☎ 5208-8241; www.mujiyurakucho.com, in Japanese; 3-8-3 Marunouchi, Chiyoda-ku; 10am-9pm; JR Yamanote to Yurakuchō (Kyōbashi exit), Yurakuchō Line to Yurakuchō (exit D9)

Tokyo's famously understated no-name brand is one of the hippest in Paris. But Muji

SHOPPING STREETS

Ameyoko Arcade (アメヤ横丁; Map p78) One of Tokyo's only old-fashioned, open-air pedestrian markets and a good place for bargains – from spices to shoes. See p81.

Hachiman-dōri (八幡通り; Map p96) Lined with shops purveying high and low fashion trends, this street is a delightful treasure hunt for local designs.

Kappabashi-dōri (合羽橋通り; p142) Food, food everywhere, and nary a rice grain to eat – because it's plastic.

Marunouchi Naka-dōri (丸の内仲通り; p145) A dignified assortment of tippy top international brands.

MISC (ミスク; p145) Meguro Interior Shops Community is an up-and-coming design district along Meguro-dōri.

Nakamise-dōri (仲見世通り; p142) Leading up to the grand gate that opens onto Sensō-ji, this is home to countless trinket, snack and knick-knack shops.

Nippori Nuno no Machi (日暮里布の街; p141) Where seamstresses, tailors and designers buy their fabrics.

Omote-Sandō (表参道; p147) Known as the centre of Tokyo's haute couture culture, Omote-Sandō is the place to take in Tokyo fashion on parade.

Takeshita-dōri (竹下通り; p148) Takeshita-dōri is to teenagers what Omote-Sandō is to dilettantes.

still sells simple, unadorned clothing and accessories for men and women. It also carries hard-to-find M and L sizes (though these, too, are small). This outlet in Yurakuchō also has a great cafeteria. There are branches in Harajuku (Map p106) and Roppongi (Map p92).

TAKUMI Map p57 — Crafts
たくみ

☎ 3571-2017; www.ginza-takumi.co.jp, in Japanese; 8-4-2 Ginza, Chūō-ku; ⏰ 11am-7pm Mon-Sat; ⊚ JR Yamanote Line to Shimbashi (Ginza exit), Ginza Line to Shimbashi (exit 5), Toei Asakusa Line to Shimbashi (exits 1 & 3)

Takumi has been around for more than 60 years and has acquired an elegant selection of toys, textiles, ceramics and other traditional folk crafts from around Japan. Ever thoughtful, the shop also encloses information detailing the origin and background of the pieces if you make a purchase.

KYŪKYODŌ Map p57 — Paper & Art
鳩居堂

☎ 3571-4429; 5-7-4 Ginza, Chūō-ku; ⏰ 11am-7.30pm Mon-Sat, 11am-7pm Sun; ⊚ Ginza or Hibiya Line to Ginza (exit A2)

Gorgeous traditional Japanese paper and note cards welcome you to the ground floor of this store in business since the early Edo Period (the current building is 20th century). Upstairs art is sold on *shikishi* (cardboard canvases), alongside hanging scrolls to display them. Should you want to try your own art, there are traditional brushes and ink stones, even incense for inspiration.

HAKUHINKAN Map p57 — Toys
博品館

☎ 3571-8008; www.hakuhinkan.co.jp; 8-8-11 Ginza, Chūō-ku; ⏰ 11am-8pm; ⊚ JR Yamanote Line to Shimbashi (Ginza exit), Toei Asakusa Line to Shimbashi (exits 1 & 3)

This layer cake of a 'toy park' is crammed with this year's models of character toys, the hottest squawking video games, seas of colourful plastic, the softest plush toys ever invented, even a model racetrack (¥200 per five minutes, plus ¥100 car rental) on the 4th floor. If you arrive after hours, a few dozen top-selling toys are available from vending machines outside the store.

IIDABASHI & AROUND

A few stops east of Shinjuku, the height of buildings descend to a more human scale. A stroll up the Kagurazaka slope from Iidabashi Station will turn up several shops selling *geta* (traditional wooden sandals) and drawstring purses made from lavish kimono fabric. Elsewhere in the area, wedged in unexpected places between pharmacies, groceries and *pachinko* (vertical pinball game) parlours, are shops carrying goods like Czech puppets and hand-painted kites.

BINGOYA Map p110 — Crafts
備後屋

☎ 3202-8778; www.quasar.nu/bingoya; 10-6 Wakamatsuchō, Shinjuku-ku; ⏰ 10am-7pm Tue-Sun; ⊚ Toei Ōedo Line to Wakamatsu-kawada (Kawada exit)

Richly dyed *washi*, batik textiles, ceramics and an assortment of folk crafts fill out the five floors of this wonderful shop. Find handmade glassware, cushions and Japanese tea cups for feathering your nest, or painted fans, *happi* (half-length coats) and *washi*-covered tea canisters.

PUPPET HOUSE Map p60 — Puppetry
パペットハウス

☎ 5229-6477; www.puppet-house.co.jp, in Japanese; 1-8 Shimomiyabi-chō, Shinjuku-ku; ⏰ 11am-7pm Tue-Sat; ⊚ JR Chūō or JR Sōbu Line to Iidabashi (east exit)

This is a wondrous workshop of functional international marionettes, run by a super-friendly couple who are happy to talk shop. Look for the sign of Punch in an alley near Mizuho Bank.

UENO

Although the Ueno Station area offers the usual assortment of department stores and clothing stores, the main reason for visitors to shop here is Ameyoko Arcade (p81), full of character and a step back in time. Two stations north, Nippori Nuno No Machi (Nippori Fabric Town) is where amateurs and pros alike source their textiles.

NIPPORI NUNO NO MACHI
(NIPPORI FABRIC TOWN) Map p78   Fabrics
日暮里布の街

Nippori Chūō-dōri, Arakawa-ku; ☽ **varied;** 🚇 **JR Yamanote Line to Nippori (south exit)**
If you've got a notion to sew, decorate or you like clothing on the cheap, this several-block stretch east of Nippori Station will hit you like a proverbial bolt. Dozens of shops purvey buttons to brocade, bathrobes and blankets, used kimono and contemporary wear. Many of the wares are off-price or remnants. If you're seeking something particular, shop around before leaving home; some of the fabrics are generic and you might find better deals where you come from.

AKIHABARA & KANDA

Akihabara, 'Akiba' to the legions of *otaku* (geeks) who call this a shopping mecca, was born out of a postwar black market for radio parts, matured into selling appliances and electronics and now also sells fantasy – manga, anime and merchandise such as plastic figurines and costumes. Kanda's Jimbōchō is the place to go for rare books, both Japanese and English (see p58).

AKIHABARA RADIO CENTER
Map p67   Electronics
秋葉原ラジオセンター

☎ **3253-1030; 1-14-2 Sotokanda, Chiyoda-ku;** ☽ **varied;** 🚇 **JR Yamanote or Sōbu Line to Akihabara (Electric Town exit)**

Strictly for old-school electronics *otaku*, this two-storey warren of several dozen electronics stalls under the elevated railway is the original, still-beating heart of Akihabara. By old-school, we mean connectors, jacks, switches, LEDs, semiconductors and other components. It's worth a peek as a cultural study.

TSUKUMO ROBOTTO Ō-KOKU
Map p67   Electronics
ツクモ ロボット王国

☎ **3251-0987; 4th fl, 1-9-7 Sotokanda, Chiyoda-ku;** ☽ **10.30am-8pm Mon-Sat, 10.30am-7.30pm Sun;** 🚇 **JR Yamanote or Sōbu Line to Akihabara (Electronic Town exit)**
Fancy a bipedal humanoid robot? Or would a talking Hello Kitty do the trick? Japan's first *robotto* (robot) shop (2000) is at the forefront of the home robot revolution; also sells DIY robot kits. It's one of several *ō-koku* (kingdoms) in the Tsukumo building, which also includes a *pasokon ō-koku* (personal computer kingdom), a *monitā-ō-koku* (monitor kingdom) etc. Did we mention *otaku* love Akihabara?

AKIHABARA RADIO KAIKAN
Map p67   Manga & Anime
秋葉原ラジオ会館

☎ **3253-1030; 1-15-6 Sotokanda, Chiyoda-ku;** ☽ **11am-8pm;** 🚇 **JR Yamanote or Sōbu Line to Akihabara (Electronic Town exit)**
Despite its name, Radio Kaikan has nothing to do with radios and everything to do with anime. There are more than a dozen shops over eight storeys, selling manga, anime, collectibles like models and figurines, fanzines, costumes and gear. Shops include Kotobukiya (寿や; ☎ 5298-6300; 1st & 2nd fl), K-Books (Kブックス; ☎ 3255-4866; 3rd fl) and Kayodo Hobby Lobby (海洋堂ホビーロビー; ☎ 3253-1951; 4th fl).

MANDARAKE COMPLEX
Map p67   Manga & Anime
まんだらけコンプレックス

☎ **3252-7007; www.mandarake.co.jp; 3-11-2 Sotokanda, Chiyoda-ku;** ☽ **noon-8pm;** 🚇 **JR Sōbu Line to Akihabara (Electric Town exit)**
When *otaku* dream of heaven, it probably looks a lot like this giant store. Mandarake has long been Tokyo's go-to store for manga and anime, and its new Akihabara location is the largest yet. Eight storeys are piled high with comic books and DVDs,

action figures and cel art just for starters. The 5th floor is devoted to women's comics in all its pink splendour, while the 4th floor is for men. Mandarake's original branch is in Nakano (Map pp48–9; ☎ 3228-0007; 5-52-15 Nakano, Nakano-ku; ♥ noon-8pm), and other branches include Shibuya (Map p102; ☎ 3477-0777; B2 fl, Shibuya Beam Bldg, 31-2 Udagawa-chō, Shibuya-ku; ♥ noon-8pm) and an entire Ikebukuro branch (Map p116; ☎ 5928-0771; B1 fl, Lions Mansion Ikebukuro, 3-15-2 Higashi-Ikebukuro, Tōshima-ku; ♥ noon-8pm) with manga for women.

ASAKUSA

Asakusa was once the heart of Edo's low city, home to numerous artisans and merchants. While Nakamise-dōri is a natural on any itinerary, many of the wares are meant for the thousands of tourists who flock there daily. Serious shoppers should head into the small surrounding lanes for high-quality works still made in the traditional manner, from venerable dolls to virtuosic drums. The long stretch of Kappabashi-dōri also yields uniquely Japanese curiosities in its little culinary-supply shops.

YOSHITOKU Map p122   Dolls
吉徳
☎ 3863-4419; www.yoshitoku.co.jp, in Japanese; 1-9-14 Asakusabashi, Taitō-ku; ♥ 9.30am-6pm; ◉ JR Sōbu Line to Asakusabashi (east exit), Toei Asakusa Line to Asakusabashi (exit A2)
Once known as doll maker to the emperor, Yoshitoku has been crafting and distributing dolls since 1711. The 1st floor is filled

with miniatures that depict kabuki actors, *hina* (princess dolls displayed for the Girl's Day holiday, 3 March) and samurai (for Boy's Day, 5 May), geisha and sumō wrestlers in minute detail and exquisite dress. Figures are designed with the serious collector in mind.

KAPPABASHI-DŌRI
Map p84   Kitchen & Restaurant Supplies
合羽橋通り
◉ Ginza Line to Tawaramachi (exit 3)
This street is most famous for its shops selling plastic food models, but Kappabashi-dōri supplies many a Tokyo restaurant in bulk, selling matching sets of chopsticks, uniforms, woven bamboo tempura trays and tiny ceramic *shōyu* (soy sauce) dishes. This makes it the perfect street for stocking up if you're setting up an apartment or seeking small, useful souvenirs.

NAKAMISE-DŌRI Map p84   Shopping Street
仲見世通り
◉ Ginza or Toei Asakusa Line to Asakusa
Nakamise-dōri, the long, crowded pedestrian lane running from Kaminarimon gate to Hōzōmon gate, has more than 80 stalls that for centuries have been helping the Japanese people fulfil their gift-giving obligations. The wide alley is chock-a-block with small shops selling temple paraphernalia as well as traditional items of varying beauty and quality. It's also the place to pick up locally made, salty *sembei* (rice crackers) and *age-manju* (deep-fried bean buns).

ASAKUSA TRADITIONAL PRODUCTS

The following shops specialise in Asakusa traditional products. If there are other crafts you're interested in, and there are dozens more, visit the Edo Shitamachi Dentō Kōgeikan (Shitamachi Traditional Crafts Museum, p83) or visit www.asakusa-e.com/dentokoge/dentokoge2.htm, in Japanese.

Bengara (べんがら; Map p84; ☎ 3841-6613; www.bengara.com, in Japanese; 1-35-6 Asakusa, Taitō-ku; ♥ 10am-6pm, closed 3rd Thu monthly; ◉ Ginza Line to Asakusa, exit 1, or Toei Asakusa Line to Asakusa, exit A5) Sells *noren*, the curtains that hang in front of shop doors. Some *noren* are very artful, with the spirit of the *mingei* movement (p36). It's one block east of Nakamise-dōri.

Kanesō (かね惣; Map p84; ☎ 3844-1379; www.kanesoh.com, in Japanese; 1-18-12 Asakusa, Taitō-ku; ♥ 11am-7pm; ◉ Ginza Line to Asakusa, exit 1, or Toei Asakusa Line to Asakusa, exit A5) This place has been selling knives since the early Meiji period. In a country where knives are a serious business, this shop is known as a favourite of the pros.

Miyamoto Unosuke Shoten (宮本卯之助商店; Map p84; ☎ 3844-2141; www.miyamoto-unosuke.co.jp; 2-1-1 Nishi Asakusa, Taitō-ku; ♥ 9am-6pm Thu-Tue; ◉ Ginza Line to Tawaramachi, exit 3) If it's festival products you're after, Miyamoto is one-stop shopping, from *mikoshi* (portable shrines) to drums, clappers and festival masks. It's on the ground floor of the building and downstairs from the drum museum (p86).

ROPPONGI

Though Roppongi is best known for wild bars, pick-up joints, increasingly high-end museums and hotels, it's also home to a few of the city's most interesting and idiosyncratic shops and showrooms and its megamalls, Roppongi Hills, both filled with finery from Japan and around the world and well worth a browse. Of special interest in Roppongi are the Axis Building with several floors of cutting-edge design shops, and Japan Sword, which displays and sells the exquisite weaponry of the samurai.

JAPAN SWORD Map p92   Antiques
日本刀剣
☎ 3434-4321; www.japansword.co.jp; 3-8-1 Toranomon, Minato-ku; ⏰ 9.30am-6pm Mon-Fri, 9.30am-5pm Sat; ⊖ Ginza Line to Toranomon (exit 2)
One of Tokyo's most-famous sellers of samurai swords and weaponry, it sells the genuine article – such as antique sword guards and samurai helmets dating from the Edo period – as well as convincing replicas crafted by hand. Make sure you enquire about export and transport restrictions.

TOLMAN COLLECTION Map p92   Art Gallery
トールマンコレクション
☎ 3434-1300; www.tolmantokyo.com; 2-2-18 Shiba-Daimon, Minato-ku; ⏰ 11am-7pm Wed-Mon; ⊖ Toei Ōedo Line to Daimon (exit 6)
American Norman Tolman has been collecting Japanese print art for 50 years and authored many books on the subject, and his gallery in a traditional building represents some 48 leading Japanese artists of printing, lithography, etchings, woodblocks and more. Prices aren't cheap – prints start at around ¥12,000 – but neither is quality.

BLUE & WHITE Map p92   Crafts
ブルー アンド ホワイト
☎ 3451-0537; 2-9-2 Azabu-jūban; ⏰ 11am-6pm Mon-Sat; ⊖ Namboku or Toei Ōedo Line to Azabu-jūban (exit 4)
Amy Katoh, the expat American behind this small crafts store, sells traditional and contemporary items such as tenugui, indigo-dyed yukata (light cotton kimono), bolts of nubby cloth, and painted chopsticks. Pick through tiny dishes of ceramic beads or

top picks

TRADITIONAL CRAFTS SHOPS

- Bingoya (p140)
- Japan Traditional Craft Center (p151)
- Yoshitoku (opposite)
- Takumi (p140)
- Oriental Bazaar (p148)

collect bundled-up swatches of fabric for your own crafty creations. Katoh's inspiration is the chubby, cherubic Japanese good-luck goddess Otafuku, who smiles from every corner of the shop.

AXIS Map p92   Design
アクシスビル
☎ 3587-2781; www.axisinc.co.jp, in Japanese; 5-17-1 Roppongi, Minato-ku; ⏰ 11am-7pm; ⊖ Hibiya or Toei Ōedo Line to Roppongi (exit 3)
Salivate over some of Japan's most innovative interior design at this high-end design complex. Of the 16-odd galleries and retail shops selling art books, cutting-edge furniture and other objets d'art, highlights include Nuno (布; ☎ 3582-7992; www.nuno.com; B1 fl; ⏰ closed Sun), whose innovative fabrics incorporating objects from feathers to washi appear in New York's Museum of Modern Art; Living Motif (リビング・モティーフ; ☎ 3587-2784), with three floors of soothing, contemporary design (both Japanese and international) from cushions to candle holders; and Le Garage (ル・ガラージュ; ☎ 3587-2875; 2nd fl), with gear and accessories for motor-racing enthusiasts.

DON QUIJOTE Map p92   Department Store
ドン・キホーテ
☎ 5786-0811; www.donki.com/index.php; 3-14-10 Roppongi, Minato-ku; ⏰ 24hr; ⊖ Hibiya or Toei Ōedo Line to Roppongi (exit 3)
The Roppongi branch of this jam-packed, bargain castle is where Japanese kids of all ages come to stock up for fun. Don Quijote sells everything from household goods and electronics to French-maid costumes, usually at cut-rate prices. You'll need to hack your way through cluttered aisles, but it's possible to find some really funky gifts here.

EBISU, DAIKANYAMA & MEGURO

Tokyo's southwestern corner has some of the most forward-thinking and interesting shopping in the city. Yebisu Garden Place, connected to JR Ebisu Station by moving walkways, has general mall and department store shopping, while up Hachiman-dōri, Daikanyama is the place to go for one-of-a-kind clothing by local designers. In Meguro, the MISC design district along Meguro-dōri can provide hours of happy browsing.

GDC Map p96 Clothing – Contemporary
☎ 5728-2947; www.gdcweb.jp, in Japanese; 19-8 A Sarugaku-chō, Shibuya-ku; ☷ noon-10pm; ⊜ Tōyoko Line to Daikanyama (main exit)
Tucked away on a Daikanyama backstreet, GDC is a popular casual-wear label under director Kumagai Takashi that focuses on cool T-shirts with provocative, seasonal signs.

KOROMON Map p96 Clothing – Contemporary
衣
☎ 5784-3711; 12-10 Sarugaku-chō, Shibuya-ku; ☷ noon-8pm Fri-Wed; ⊜ Tōkyū Tōyoko Line to Daikanyama (main exit)
In the back of a shopping building, this little store both blends and tweaks Japanese and Western sensibilities. Look for jeans masterfully painted with designs that you might be more used to seeing on kimono or scroll paintings, and kimono fabric used in ways you might never have dreamed.

HANJIRO Map p96 Clothing – Vintage
ハンジロー
☎ 5784-5627; B1 fl, 24-1 Sarugaku-chō; Shibuya-ku; ☷ noon-8pm; ⊜ Tōkyū Tōyoko Line to Daikanyama (main exit)

Even the used clothing stores in Daikanyama are chic. Amid Hanjiro's distressed floorboards, bath-tubs that double as koi ponds and a tiny garden out front, the western-style youthful duds are fashionable, fine and fun, with many bargain-priced selections. There's another branch (Map p106) in Harajuku.

KAMAWANU Map p96 Crafts
かまわぬ
☎ 3780-0182; www.kamawanu.co.jp, in Japanese; 23-1 Sarugaku-chō, Shibuya-ku; ☷ 11am-7pm; ⊜ Tōyoko Line to Daikanyama (west exit)
Looking for a unique, compact present from Japan? Kamawanu specialises in tenugui, dyed rectangular cloths of thin cotton, which are surprisingly versatile. These beautifully patterned kerchiefs – motifs take in everything from Mt Fuji to musical notes and skeletons – can be used as decorative art, bath towels, scarves or gift wrap. Turn down the little tower to the right of the post office; it's in a traditional building. Other locations include Omote-Sandō, beneath the Ukiyo-e Ōta Museum of Art (p107; ☎ 3401-7957; 1-10-10 Jingūmae, Shibuya-ku; ☷ 10.30am-7pm).

HACKNET Map p96 Design Books
ハックネット
☎ 5728-6611; www.hacknet.tv, in Japanese; 1-30-10 Ebisu-Nishi, Shibuya-ku; ☷ 11am-8pm; ⊜ Hibiya or JR Yamanote Line to Ebisu (exit 4 & west exit)
This is a bookshop for serious designers, or those who can get high on the fumes of elegant design. Hacknet specialises in cutting-edge design books from across disciplines and around the world. The small, well-lit space is excellent for browsing and the staff is incredibly, studiously unobtrusive.

GIFT BOX

Gift-giving in Japan is a complex art form, fraught with symbolism and design. While most Japanese will graciously forgive the faux pas of a foreigner, some basic etiquette is important.

If invited to someone's home, bring a small gift as a gesture of appreciation. Flowers are a good choice, as is a pretty package of sweets from a depachika (department store food floor). Bringing along some trinkets and speciality items from your home country will delight Japanese, but err on the side of modesty. Avoid anything in sets of unlucky four or nine, and don't wrap gifts in funereal white.

When offered a gift, the polite response is to initially refuse so as not to appear greedy. Conversely, when you offer a gift, expect to do a bit of gentle urging before it's accepted. In group situations, give a gift that can be shared (a box of biscuits, for example) but give individual gifts in private. It's good form to give and receive with both hands. And unless the giver insists, politely resist the temptation to tear into it – until later.

SHOPPING FOR KIMONO

So you've decided to take the plunge and buy a kimono – you can't imagine wearing anything more gorgeous and refined. Consider these tips before you buy.

First, think about where you might wear your kimono. If you aren't going to be attending formal functions with a lot of Japanese women, chances are it will sit at home. Japanese men wear kimono even less frequently. Of course, you can always buy a kimono to display on the wall. Generally, a long wooden dowel will do the trick.

The next question is how much. Prices are all over the map, from about ¥3000 for a used kimono with significant wear to ¥30,000 and upwards for something in better condition. New kimono can easily cost many times that as they are custom-made, starting with the bolt of cloth from speciality retailers.

Then there's the issue of size. Kimono are made to a standard size that's meant to fit Japanese frames and are too small on most western bodies.

Finally, learning to wear a kimono takes a lot of practice and usually at least one assistant. It's not just the outer robe. The full outfit involves *tabi* (socks with a separate space for your big toe so you can wear your...), *zori* (sandals), a slip, *eri* (collar), *obi* (sash around your waist) and *koshi-himo* (belt). One word about all these items: cha-*ching*! No wonder Japanese pass kimono from generation to generation.

If, after all that, you'd still like to buy a kimono, speciality shops for used/antique kimono include Gallery Kawano (ギャラリー川野; Map p106; ☎ 3470-3305, 4-4-9 Jingū-mae, Shibuya-ku; ⏰ 11am-6pm; ⓜ Ginza, Hanzōmon or Chiyoda Line to Omote-Sando, exit A2), Hayashi Kimono (林きもの; Map p57; ☎ 3501-4012; 2-1-5 Yūrakuchō, Chiyoda-ku; ⏰ 10am-7pm Mon-Sat, 10am-6pm Sun; ⓜ Hibiya, Ginza or Marunouchi Line to Ginza, exit C1), or Ooedo Kazuko (大江戸和子; Map p106; ☎ 5785-1045, 4-29-3 Jingū-mae, Shibuya-ku; ⏰ 11am-7pm; ⓜ Fukutoshin or Chiyoda Line to Meiji-jingu-mae, exit 5), beneath Lawson convenience store. Those with patience can also try flea markets (p150).

One popular alternative to kimono is *yukata*, light cotton bathrobes usually worn in summer. There is almost certainly one for you to try on in your hotel room (note: not to take away!), and department stores and souvenir stores like Oriental Bazaar (p148) have great selections for between about ¥2500 and ¥5000, in foreigner-friendly sizes.

MISC Map p96　　　　Design District
ミスク
Meguro-dōri

MISC (Meguro Interior Shops Community) lines Meguro-dōri west of Yamate-dōri, with some 60 design shops and dozens more cafes and restaurants. Look for vintage 1960s modern furniture, antiques from Japan and overseas, and stylish furnishings. Individual shop hours vary, but afternoons tend to be busiest and Wednesday is the most common closing day.

OKURA Map p96　　　　Indigo
オクラ

☎ 3461-8511; 20-11 Sarugakuchō, Shibuya-ku; ⏰ 11.30am-8pm Mon-Fri, 11.30am-8.30pm Sat & Sun; ⓜ Tōkyū Tōyoko Line to Daikanyama (main exit)

Japanese indigo is perhaps tops in the world, and this atmospheric shop of salvaged hardwood is a great place to find indigo-dyed organic T-shirts, shirts and jeans (many rather pricey). Note: there's no sign out the front, but look for the traditional building facing the perpendicular street. The cafe Bombay Bazaar (p171) is downstairs.

BEAMS Map p96　　　　T-Shirts
ビームズ

☎ 5428-5952; 19-6 Sarugakuchō, Shibuya-ku; ⏰ 11am-8pm; ⓜ Tōkyū Tōyoko Line to Daikanyama (main exit)

In this town that has made a cult of the humble decorated T-shirt, Beams must surely be one of its temples. There's a cluster of Beams shops in this Daikanyama shopping complex of glass boxes, including Mangart Beams T, with exclusive designs by manga artists, and Kodomo Beams for kids. Prices: sky high. There's another big Beams cluster off Omote-Sandō (Map p106).

SHIBUYA

Shibuya is the fount of teen trendiness in Japan. If you're over 30 you might feel way too old, but just cruise and amuse yourself in the madness. Music shops and cheap, outrageous apparel are everywhere, as are the hip kids who come to primp and pose. At weekends the street in front of the 109 Building closes to all but foot traffic. Detour to Shimo-Kitazawa for Shibuya-style shopping on a small town scale.

SHIBUYA 109 Map p102   Clothing
渋谷109

Ichimarukyū; ☎ 3477-5111; 2-29-1 Dōgenzaka, Shibuya-ku; ⏰ 10am-9pm; ⊙ Ginza, Hanzōmon or JR Yamanote Line to Shibuya (Hachikō exit)

Tokyo's fad-obsessed fashionistas come to the cylindrical tower of 109 (pronounced *ichi-maru-kyū*) for the season's freshest looks. Most of the clientele is girls under 20; the punk fabrics and wild designs reflect this – it's what kids are wearing on the street.

TSUTSUMU FACTORY Map p102   Crafts
包むファクトリー

☎ 5478-1330; www.tsutsumu.co.jp, in Japanese; 37-15 Udagawachō, Shibuya-ku; ⏰ 10am-7pm Mon-Sat; ⊙ Ginza, Hanzōmon or JR Yamanote Line to Shibuya (Hachikō exit)

It's the wrapping-paper centre of the packaging-excess capital: Tsutsumu, which translates into 'wrapping', carries hundreds of sorts of gorgeous *washi* as well as other kinds of paper, numerous greeting cards and boxes.

PARCO Map p102   Department Store
パルコ

☎ 3464-5111; www.parco-shibuya.com; 15-1 Udagawachō, Shibuya-ku; ⏰ 10am-9pm; ⊙ Shibuya (Hachikō exit)

Parco, divided into several stores located in the middle of Shibuya, carries contemporary designs for a very young crowd. In Parco I, you'll find a good magazine and bookstore on the 7th floor and edgy shops on floors three to six. There's another Parco (Map p116) in Ikebukuro.

TŌKYŪ HANDS Map p102   Department Store
東急ハンズ

☎ 5489-5111; www.tokyu-hands.co.jp/shibuya .htm, in Japanese; 12-18 Udagawachō, Shibuya-ku; ⏰ 10am-8.30pm; ⊙ Ginza, Hanzōmon or JR Yamanote Line to Shibuya (Hachikō exit)

This is Tokyo's favourite DIY store, with hardware and materials for home projects. What defines it is the sheer diversity of eccentric goodies: clocks that tick backwards, hand-blown glass pens and vibrating reflexology slippers. This is eight floors of oddball, functional stuff you never realised you needed. If you hit one store during your stay, let this be it. There's another huge store in Shinjuku's Takashimaya Times Square (Map p110).

LOFT Map p102   Department Store & Homewares
ロフト

☎ 3462-3807; www.loft.co.jp, in Japanese; 21-1 Udagawachō, Shibuya-ku; ⏰ 10am-9pm; ⊙ Ginza, Hanzōmon or JR Yamanote Line to Shibuya (Hachikō exit)

Loft's multiple levels of housewares, accessories, travel supplies and stationery are more compact than at Tōkyū Hands, aimed towards younger shoppers, the bias leans towards fun and oddities. Stylish bedding and blob-shaped vases distract the shopper from titanium jewellery and trendy make-up before the *kawaii* plastic toys and mobile-phone charms do 'em in. Another branch is in Ikebukuro (Map p116).

RANKING RANQUEEN
Map p102   Speciality Store
ランキンランキン

☎ 3770-5480; 2nd fl, Shibuya Station, Shibuya-ku; ⏰ 9am-11pm; ⊙ Ginza, Hanzōmon or JR Yamanote Line to Shibuya

Come here to find what young Japanese are nuts about – the hottest, quirkiest consumer products, ranked every month according to sales. The No 1 selling teeth whitener? They've got it. The best-selling bath salts, bottled tea, cellulite killers and tools to make your face look smaller are all here, too. Enjoy the madness.

SHIMO-KITAZAWA

IROHA-DŌ
Map p102   Accessories & Clothing – Casual
いろは堂

☎ 5481-7715; 2-14-18 Kitazawa, Setagaya-ku; ⏰ 11am-8pm; ⊙ Odakyū or Keiō Inokashira Lines to Shimokitazawa (south exit)

If you're on a mission to find the youth-oriented, the *kawaii* and the *oshare* (fashionable) in Shimo-Kita, this is a great place to start. Update your look with just the right hat, eyeglasses, belt or bag.

NICHŌME SANBANCHI Map p102   Toys
2丁目3番地

☎ 3419-7256; 5-30-3 Yazawa, Setagaya-ku; ⏰ noon-9pm Tue-Sun; ⊙ Odakyū or Keiō Inokashira Lines to Shimokitazawa (south exit)

Lovers of toy nostalgia should make a bee-line for this crammed little shop named after a classic TV show. Wares include snow globes, models, anime action figures and character goods inspired by Sesame Street to Barbapapa, Teletubbies to Disney. It's the essence of *kawaii*, though not always the essence of cheap pricing.

HARAJUKU & AOYAMA

Home to the famed Harajuku girls, Takeshita-dōri and the alleys packed with small, independent designers' shops and secondhand stores, Omote-Sandō is the most eclectic, experimental neighbourhood in Tokyo. High fashion rules the Aoyama end of Omote-Sandō, where 'fashionable' has an entirely different meaning than it has for the hipsters of Harajuku layering haute couture with secondhand finds. Creatively active but solidly established, Aoyama is grown-up, refined yet innovative. It's no wonder artistic designers and high-fashion flagship stores have made this section of Tokyo their creative home.

FUJI-TORII Map p106 Antiques
富士鳥居
☎ 3400-2777; www.fuji-torii.com; 6-1-10 Jingūmae, Shibuya-ku; ☽ 11am-6pm Wed-Mon, closed 3rd Mon of the month; ◉ JR Yamanote Line to Harajuku (Omote-Sandō exit), Fukutoshin or Chiyoda Line to Meiji-jingūmae (exit 4)
For more than half a century, this discriminating antique dealer has specialised in providing authentic lacquerware, ceramics, scrolls and *ukiyo-e* (wood-block prints) to interested buyers. Authenticity is guaranteed and there is also helpful English-speaking staff.

UT STORE HARAJUKU
Map p106 Clothing – Casual
ユーティーストア原宿
☎ 5468-7313; www.ut.uniqlo.com; 6-10-8 Jingūmae, Minato-ku; ☽ 11am-9pm; ◉ Fukutoshin or Chiyoda Line to Meiji-jingūmae (exit 4)
This spin-off of Uniqlo (p139) may be a triumph of marketing over substance, but who cares? Scrolling red LEDs announce the specials both outside and in. Designer T-shirts are sold in clear canisters that look like something tennis balls might come in, alongside hoodies, casual sweaters and other colourful goodies.

HYSTERIC GLAMOUR
Map p106 Clothing – Casual
ヒステリックグラマー
☎ 3409-7227; www.hystericglamour.jp, in Japanese; 6-23-2 Jingūmae, Shibuya-ku;

☽ 11am-8pm; ◉ JR Yamanote Line to Harajuku (Omote-Sandō exit), Chiyoda Line to Meiji-jingūmae (exits 1 & 4)
It's actually tongue-in-cheek rather than hysteric glamour, but whatever you want to call it, it's sexy and fun. These designer confections are a good place to start for hip fashion with a Tokyo twist. There's even a toddler line, the ultimate in designer punk for your little rocker.

A BATHING APE Map p106 Clothing – Designer
ア・ベイシング・エイプ
☎ 3407-2145; www.bape.com; 5-5-8 Minami-Aoyama, Minato-ku; ☽ 11am-7pm; ◉ Chiyoda, Ginza or Hanzōmon Line to Omote-Sandō (exit A4)
This A Bathing Ape Exclusive (Bape) outlet of the uberhip urban and hip-hop outfitter line is more like a museum than a shop, with fab sneakers on a rotating steel conveyor belt, mirrored surfaces and lots of sparkle. You can pick up Bape plastic models and some of the coolest bags in town.

CLOTHING SIZES

Women's clothing
Aus/UK	8	10	12	14	16	18
Europe	36	38	40	42	44	46
Japan	5	7	9	11	13	15
USA	6	8	10	12	14	16

Women's shoes
Aus/USA	5	6	7	8	9	10
Europe	35	36	37	38	39	40
France only	35	36	38	39	40	42
Japan	22	23	24	25	26	27
UK	3½	4½	5½	6½	7½	8½

Men's clothing
Aus	92	96	100	104	108	112
Europe	46	48	50	52	54	56
Japan	S		M	M		L
UK/USA	35	36	37	38	39	40

Men's shirts (collar sizes)
Aus/Japan	38	39	40	41	42	43
Europe	38	39	40	41	42	43
UK/USA	15	15½	16	16½	17	17½

Men's shoes
Aus/UK	7	8	9	10	11	12
Europe	41	42	43	44½	46	47
Japan	26	27	27½	28	29	30
USA	7½	8½	9½	10½	11½	12½

Measurements approximate only; try before you buy

¥100 SHOPS

Sign of trying financial times, or Japan waking up to the idea that high prices don't always mean the best value? Whatever the case, the popularity of these stores where everything costs ¥100 yen (well, ¥105 with consumption tax) has exploded in the last few years. It's not just made-in-China plastic ware, though that's there if you want it. Good bets include stationery and everyday food items, hats and houseplants, and you can outfit your entire kitchen with pots, pans, tableware and kitty-shaped sponges for under ¥3000. Because this is Japan, products tend to be cute, ingenious or both. Stocks are subject to change, but we dare you to walk out without buying something.

Daiso and Can Do are two big ¥100 shop (１００円ショップキャンドウ) chains, with locations everywhere, including Roppongi (Can Do; ☎ 3408-5991; 3-2-1 Nishi Azabu, Minato-ku; ☷ 11am-9pm), Takadanobaba (Can Do; Map p116; ☎ 3207-4551; Big Box, 1-35-3 Takadanobaba, Shinjuku-ku; ☷ 11am-9pm Mon-Sat, 11am-8pm Sun) and a multistorey Daiso (ザダイソ; Map p106; ☎ 5775-9641; 1-19-24 Jingumae, Shibuya-ku; ☷ 10am-9pm) in Harajuku.

COMME DES GARÇONS

Map p106   Clothing – Designer

コム・デ・ギャルソン

☎ 3406-3951; 5-2-1 Minami-Aoyama, Minato-ku; ☷ 11am-8pm; ⊕ Chiyoda, Ginza or Hanzōmon Line to Omote-Sandō (exit A5)

The architectural eccentricity of Kawakubo Rei's flagship store (see also p132) should come as no surprise – her radical designs have been refiguring the fashion landscape for more than 20 years. Both men's and women's fashions are on display. Most available sizes are quite small, but a quick circuit of the shop is interesting in itself.

ISSEY MIYAKE Map p106   Clothing – Designer

三宅一生

☎ 3423-1407; www.isseymiyake.com; 3-18-11 Minami-Aoyama, Minato-ku; ☷ 11am-8pm; ⊕ Chiyoda, Ginza or Hanzōmon Line to Omote-Sandō (exit A4)

Before Issey Miyake put Tokyo on the fashion map, Japanese designers were known to copy Western trends after they'd already hit the runway. Miyake's work has changed such conceptions. Check out the A-POC garments – each made from a single piece of fabric – and the signature Pleats collection.

YOHJI YAMAMOTO

Map p106   Clothing – Designer

山本耀司

☎ 3409-6006; www.yohjiyamamoto.co.jp; 5-3-6 Minami-Aoyama, Minato-ku; ☷ 11am-8pm; ⊕ Chiyoda, Ginza or Hanzōmon Line to Omote-Sandō (exit A5)

Wander down Omote-Sandō to check out Yohji Yamamoto's bold, timeless designs. Though there's no sign on it, his flagship store is recognisable by its distinctive bronze facade, which you'll want to get past for a look at the experimental interior.

CHICAGO THRIFT STORE

Map p106   Clothing – Vintage

シカゴ

☎ 3409-5017; www.chicago.co.jp, in Japanese; 6-31-21 Jingūmae, Shibuya-ku; ☷ 11am-8pm; ⊕ JR Yamanote Line to Harajuku (Omote-Sandō exit), Chiyoda Line to Meiji-jingūmae (exit 4)

Stuffed to the rafters with funky hats, ties and coats, Chicago is a treasure trove of vintage clothing and used duds stacked high and priced low. Of special note is the extensive collection of used kimono and yukata in the basement.

ORIENTAL BAZAAR

Map p106   Crafts & Souvenirs

オリエンタルバザール

☎ 3400-3933; 5-9-13 Jingūmae, Shibuya-ku; ☷ 10am-7pm Fri-Wed; ⊕ Fukutoshin or Chiyoda Line to Meiji-jingūmae (exit 4)

Carrying a wide selection at very reasonable prices, Oriental Bazaar is an excellent spot for easy one-stop shopping for souvenirs and a smattering of antiques. Good gifts to be found here include fans, folding screens, pottery, porcelain, kimono and, uh, T-shirts, some made in Japan, others not (read the labels). The branch at Narita Airport opens at 7.30am for last-chance purchases.

TAKESHITA-DŌRI Map p106   Market

竹下通り

⊕ JR Yamanote Line to Harajuku (Takeshita-dōri exit)

If you're struck with a sudden urge to fit into one of Tokyo's youth subcultures, passing through the flowered arches of Takeshita-dōri will reveal all you need. You'll find salons to puff your hair into a gigantic 'fro, white platform Mary Janes to go with your bloodied nurse's outfit and creative inspiration from the teen tribes.

SPIRAL RECORDS Map p106 Music
スパイラルレコード

☎ 3498-1224; www.spiral.co.jp, in Japanese;
🕙 11am-8pm; 5-6-23 Minami-Aoyama, Minato-ku;
Ⓜ Chiyoda, Ginza or Hanzōmon Line to Omote-Sandō (exit B1)
Located just inside the entrance of the Spiral building, Spiral Records is both a vendor and an experimental label. The listening stations feature avant-garde tunes both new and old. The staff spins records while you browse.

LAFORET BUILDING Map p106 Shopping Mall
ラフォーレ

☎ 3475-0411; 1-11-6 Jingūmae, Shibuya-ku;
🕙 11am-8pm; Ⓜ JR Yamanote Line to Harajuku (Omote-Sandō exit), Chiyoda Line to Meiji-jingūmae (exit 5)
This rounded 1970s edifice must be the teen shopping capital of the world. The mall's hundreds of shops sell the trendiest garb, meant to be worn for a fleeting season and then tossed into the trash. Sizes here fit tiny Tokyo teens, so unless you're very petite, this will be a window-shopping, people-watching venture.

CONDOMANIA Map p106 Speciality Shop
コンドマニア

☎ 3797-6131; http://condomania.jp; 6-30-1 Jingūmae, Shibuya-ku; 🕙 10.30am-10.30pm Mon-Thu, 10am-11pm Fri-Sun; Ⓜ Fukutoshin or Chiyoda Line to Meiji-jingūmae (exit 4)
Occupying a prime corner of the Omote-Sandō and Meiji-dōri intersection, the Condomania storefront just may be Tokyo's cheekiest rendezvous point. Inside are condoms of all colours, sizes and flavours.

MUSUBI Map p106 Speciality Shop
むす美

☎ 5414-5678; 2-31-8 Jingūmae, Shibuya-ku;
🕙 11am-8pm Mon-Fri, 11am-7pm Sat & Sun; Ⓜ JR Yamanote Line to Harajuku (Takeshita-dōri exit), Fukutoshin or Chiyoda Line to Meiji-jingūmae (exit 5)
Before shopping bags, Japanese carried their *bentō* (boxed lunch) and packages in elegant wrapping cloths called *furoshiki*, and this dainty shop and workshop both sells the cloths and gives lessons in how to use them (email info@kyoto-musubi.com for info about lessons). Modern-day uses for *furoshiki* include handbags and wine bottle carriers, and believe it or not they make nice table covers, too. The owner has even written a book about it in English.

KIDDYLAND Map p106 Toys
キデイランド

☎ 3409-3431; 6-1-9 Jingūmae, Shibuya-ku;
🕙 10am-9pm; Ⓜ Fukutoshin or Chiyoda Line to Meiji-jingūmae (exit 4)
Six floors of appealing products for your children to fall in lust with and which you may still be paying for next year. In fact, you yourself may be seduced by plastic-bobbled barrettes, Pokémon paraphernalia or nostalgia-inducers such as Hello Kitty or Ultraman and an entire Snoopy floor. Claustrophobes should avoid the store at weekends when it teems with teens.

SHINJUKU

Shopping in Shinjuku can be a little overwhelming. From the moment you step out of the train station (ringed by malls and department stores), the lights and noise make the whole place seem like the interior of a bus-

EVERYWHERE VENDORS

Japan has the largest number of vending machines in the world – 5.5 million and counting – and they suck in nearly $60 billion yearly. They are remarkable for both their ubiquity – they can be found everywhere from bullet trains to desolate rural villages to the slopes of Mt Fuji – and their variety. They dispense almost every consumer product conceivable: from cigarettes to sake, canned drinks (cold *or* hot!), rice, popcorn, hamburgers, hot noodles, pornography, sex toys, bouquets, kerosene, toys, toilet paper, fishing tackle, horseracing bets, travel insurance and underwear. Even, legends say, used underwear (for fetishists). Where do they all come from? Probably the best answer was from a newspaper cartoonist who drew a giant Japanese vending machine dispensing – you guessed it – vending machines.

Washizu Tsutomu, author of *Jidōhanbaiki no Bunkashi* (The Cultural History of Vending Machines) has suggested that the Japanese love of convenience and automation has fuelled their popularity – that's also why industrial robots are big in Japan. But do these quiet, fluorescent providers also address a deeper social need among a population constrained by rigid social hierarchies and protocols? Says Takashi Kurosaki, director-general of the Japan Vending Machine Manufacturers Association: 'People clearly want to purchase things without having to talk to others.'

tling casino. But there are some great shops amid all the chaos, and you can find just about anything your heart desires here. Two branches of the Kinokuniya bookstore (see p58 and p134) are here, as is stately Isetan, one of Tokyo's most revered department stores. It is also a great place to come to shop for electronics if you're not motivated to trek all the way to Akihabara, at places such as Yodobashi Camera (ヨドバシカメラ; ☎ 3346-1010; www.yodo bashi.com, in Japanese; 1-11-1 Nishi-Shinjuku, Shinjuku-ku; ⏰ 9.30am-10pm; ⦿ Shinjuku, west exit) and Sakuraya (さくらや; ☎ 3352-4711; www.sakuraya.co.jp, in Japanese; 3-26-10 Shinjuku, Shinjuku-ku; ⏰ 10am-10pm; ⦿ Shinjuku, central east exit).

ISETAN Map p110 Department Store
伊勢丹

☎ 3352-1111; www.isetan.co.jp; 3-14-1 Shinjuku, Shinjuku-ku; ⏰ 10am-8pm; ⦿ Marunouchi or Toei Shinjuku Line to Shinjuku-sanchōme (exits B3, B4 & B5)

In addition to its stunning food hall in the basement, Isetan boasts an entire separate building for men's fashions in addition to several floors of homewares and ladies' de-

signer goods. Check out the store's I-club, a free service that provides English-speaking staff for visiting shoppers. The membership desk for this service is located on the 6th floor near the entrance to the Isetan Men's building.

DISK UNION Map p110 Music
ディスクユニオン

☎ 3352-2691; www.diskunion.co.jp, in Japanese; 3-31-4 Shinjuku, Shinjuku-ku; ⏰ 11am-9pm; ⦿ Shinjuku (central east exit)

The stairwell at Disk Union is papered with posters of old glam and punk bands. The place is known by local audiophiles as Tokyo's best-used CD and vinyl store. Six storeys carry a variety of musical styles. There's a shop (Map p67) in the Jimbōchō area as well.

IKEBUKURO

Prices on everyday commodities such as eye-glasses may be slightly cheaper in Ikebukuro – come here to buy no-frills stuff, not Prada. Ikebukuro has two of Tokyo's biggest depart-

ANTIQUE FAIRS & FLEA MARKETS

After days of white-gloved attendants in Tokyo's perfectly ordered department stores, one longs for the colourful anarchy and dust of a good flea market. Tokyo has loads of flea markets and antique fairs, many held on temple or shrine grounds, where you can spend hours among the bric-a-brac. Don't get your hopes up about finding treasures, however, for gone are the days when astute buyers could cart off antique *tansu* (wooden chests) or virtuosic lacquer-ware worth thousands of dollars. Things to look for include old kimono, obi (belts used to fasten kimono), scrolls, pottery, old Japanese postcards, Chinese snuff bottles, antique toys and costume jewellery. Though bargaining is permitted, remember that it's considered bad form to drive too hard a bargain. If your Japanese is lacking, bring a pencil and paper.

The following are some of Tokyo's better flea markets and antique fairs. Check with Tourist Information Centers (TIC; p265) before going, as shrine and temple events sometimes interfere with the scheduling of markets. Because most of these are outdoors, weather may also interfere.

Hanazono-jinja Flea Market (花園神社青空骨董市; Map p110; ⏰ dawn-dusk Sun; ⦿ Marunouchi or Shinjuku Line to Shinjuku-sanchōme, exit B3 or B5) A good mix of old and new features at this market, ranging from antique ceramics to new junk jewellery and used *yukata* (light cotton summer kimono).

Nogi-jinja Flea Market (乃木神社古民具骨董市; Map p92; ⏰ 8am-3pm 2nd Sun of the month, except Nov; ⦿ Chiyoda Line to Nogizaka, main exit) The place to go for *ukiyo-e* (wood-block prints) and antiques from Asia and Europe.

Ōedo Antique Market (大江戸骨董市; Map p52; ☎ 6407-6011; Tokyo International Forum, 3-5-1 Marunouchi, Chiyoda-ku; ⏰ 9am-4pm 1st & 3rd Sun of the month; ⦿ JR Yamanote Line or Yūrakuchō Line to Yūrakuchō, exit D5) Some 250 licensed dealers populate Japan's largest outdoor antique market, in the courtyard of the Tokyo International Forum, with goods from furniture to pottery, sword guards to figurines. Phone ahead in case of inclement weather.

Tōgō-jinja Fine Arts Market (東郷の杜能美の市; Map p106; ⏰ 5am-3pm 1st Sun of the month; ⦿ JR Yamanote Line to Harajuku, Takeshita exit) Rummage through this trove of authentic antique wares and kimono, and odds and ends of various vintages.

ment stores – Seibu (西武; ☎ 3981-0111; www2
.seibu.co.jp, in Japanese; 1-28-1 Minami-Ikebukuro, Toshima-
ku; ◷ 10am-9pm Mon-Sat, 10am-8pm Sun) and Tōbu
(東武; ☎ 3981-2211; www.tobu-dept.jp; 1-1-25 Nishi-
Ikebukuro, Toshima-ku; ◷ 10am-8pm) – and no fewer
than four locations of Bic Camera (ビックカメ
ラ; ☎ 3988-0002; www.biccamera.com, in Japanese; 1-1-3
Higashi-Ikebukuro, Toshima-ku; ◷ 10am-9pm). If you're
an anime or manga fan, check out the shops
along Otome Rd by the Sunshine City complex (see also Mandarake, p141). All of these
are outside Ikebukuro Station's east exit

JAPAN TRADITIONAL CRAFT
CENTER Map p116   Crafts
伝統的工芸品館
　☎ 5954-6066; www.kougei.or.jp/english/center
.html; 1st & 2nd fl, Metropolitan Plaza Bldg, 1-11-1
Nishi-Ikebukuro, Toshima-ku; ◷ 11am-7pm;
Ⓜ Ikebukuro Line (Metropolitan exit)
Though this spot bills itself as a museum
(p115), it's primarily a shop that carries
traditional crafts in a variety of media.
Lacquerwork, ceramics, natural-bristle
paintbrushes and knives are on display and
for sale.

HMV Map p116   Music
エイチエムヴィー
　☎ 3983-5501; 6th fl, Metropolitan Plaza, 1-11-1
Nishi-Ikebukuro, Toshima-ku; ◷ 11am-9pm;
Ⓜ Ikebukuro Line (Metropolitan exit)
HMV has branches all over Tokyo, but this
one in the Metropolitan Plaza building
(next to Ikebukuro Station) focuses on
J-pop, contemporary Japanese music and a
well-regarded classical selection.

ODAIBA

Odaiba was designed as an entertainment and
shopping mecca, so it should come as no surprise that two of its main attractions are giant
malls. Decks Tokyo Beach has stunning bay
views. You'll find both big-name designers
and small shops here.

DECKS TOKYO BEACH
Map p127   Shopping Mall
デックス東京ビーチ
　☎ 3599-6500; www.odaiba-decks.com; 1-6-1
Daiba, Kōtō-ku; ◷ 11am-9pm; Ⓜ Yurikamome
Line to Odaiba Kaihin-kōen (main exit)
Decks is split into two malls, Island and
Seaside. Both house a rainy day's worth of
browsing, and if you're hungering for Chinese food, the Island Mall boasts Daiba Little
Hong Kong. There's also Tokyo Joypolis (p127), a
high-tech amusement park with virtual reality games and indoor roller-coasters.

VENUS FORT Map p127   Shopping Mall
ヴィーナスフォート
　☎ 3599-1735; www.venusfort.co.jp; 1 Aomi,
Kōtō-ku; ◷ 11am-9pm; Ⓜ Yurikamome Line to
Aomi (main exit), Rinkai Line to Tokyo Teleport
(main exit)
Outside, this giant mall in Palette Town looks
like a giant box. Inside, it's a faux Italian villa
with staged sunrises and sunsets and over
150 shops. The 1st floor is family themed,
the 2nd 'Venus Grand' floor is fancy stuff
particularly for ladies, while in a sign of the
times the 3rd floor is Tokyo's largest outlet
mall with brands from Japan and overseas
including Armani, Coach and United Arrows.

SHOPPING ODAIBA

EATING

top picks

What's your recommendation? www.lonelyplanet.com/tokyo

EATING

Who could ever weary of moonlit nights and well-cooked rice?

Traditional Japanese proverb

Tomes have been written about Japanese food, not least on the delights of noodles, the perils and pleasures of raw fish, and the health-inducing properties of everything from shiitake mushrooms and miso soup to pickled ginger and fresh wasabi. As visitors to Tokyo quickly discover, Japanese people are absolutely obsessed with food.

In Japan the simple act of eating permeates every walk of life, fills the airwaves and bookshelves, and figures large in most conversations. Indeed, an invitation to have a meal with a Japanese person is better seen as an opportunity to commune over food. Breaking bread (or sharing rice) is an act of mutual celebration, a way of reinforcing group identities and welcoming outsiders into the fold.

Needless to say, the Japanese are voracious gourmets, and a highlight of any trip to Tokyo is its vast culinary landscape. From traditional Japanese staples such as sashimi, soba and tempura to more modern incarnations such as *rāmen* (noodles) and *shabu-shabu* (beef hot-pot), Japanese cuisine is as varied as it is simply delicious. See the Language chapter (p272) for more information.

ETIQUETTE

If you're worried about putting your foot in it, relax – the Japanese don't expect you to know everything, and are unlikely to be offended as long as you follow the standards of politeness of your own country. Just follow the locals for things such as lifting soup bowls and slurping noodles.

Among the more important rules are those regarding chopsticks. Don't stick them upright in your rice – that's how rice is offered to the dead! Passing food from your chopsticks to someone else's is a similar no-no – that's how the bones of the dead are passed in Buddhist funeral rites.

When taking food from shared plates, avoid using the end of the chopsticks that's already been in your mouth – invert your chopsticks before reaching for that tasty morsel. When there are shared dishes, you will usually be given a *torizara* (small plate) to use as your own.

Before digging in, it's polite to say '*itadakimas[u]*' (literally 'I will receive'). At the end of the meal you should say '*gochisō-sama deshita*' (literally 'it was a feast'), a respectful way of saying that the meal was good.

Even if you're just enjoying a cup of coffee or sampling some snacks at a shop, it's polite to use these expressions.

If you're out drinking, remember that you're expected to keep the drinks of your companions topped up – beer bottles in Japan are typically large (at least 500mL) and the glasses small. Hold your glass with both hands while it's being filled, and don't fill your own glass; wait for someone to do this for you, and if you're done just leave your glass full. The Japanese equivalent of 'cheers' is *kampai!* Don't use the Mediterranean toast *chin chin* unless you want to induce peals of laughter. It translates to what boys have and girls don't!

The word for 'delicious' is *oishii* – if you only learn a handful of words in Japanese, make this one of them! If there's something you don't like, just leave it on your plate or in your bowl and don't make a big deal of it. If you're at a group dinner and have eaten enough, and the server brings more food, it's best just to accept it and leave it, rather than send it back.

If someone invites you to eat or drink with them, they will be paying. Generally, at the end of the meal something of a struggle ensues to see who gets the privilege of paying. If this happens, it is polite to at least make an effort to pay the bill, though it is extremely unlikely that your hosts will acquiesce. Exceptions are likely, for example, among younger people or coworkers out for lunch together; in these cases, Japanese cashiers are accustomed to splitting the bill.

JAPANESE FOOD GLOSSARY

See p273 for a glossary of foods and Japanese mealtime terms.

If you're arriving at someone's home, it is polite to bring a gift. See p144 for suggestions. And if you have been someone's guest, be sure to thank them upon leaving. Following up with a thank-you note is an excellent touch.

WHAT TO EAT & WHERE
Sushi & Sashimi

The tonnes of fish that pass through the fish market in Tsukiji (p63) are the tell-tale signs of what locals are eating. Almost every Japanese meal you eat will probably include something fishy, and at times the sheer variety of seafood available in Tokyo can be overwhelming.

That said, the first thing most visitors in Tokyo are intent on eating is either sushi (すし or 寿司) or sashimi (刺身). Sushi is raw fish served with sweetened, vinegared rice, while sashimi is slices of raw fish served with soy sauce for dipping.

There are two main types of sushi: *nigiri-zushi* (握りずし; a small slice of fish served on a small pillow of rice) and *maki-zushi* (巻き寿司; served in a seaweed roll). Lesser-known varieties include *chirashi-zushi* (ちらし寿司; a bowl of rice covered in strips of fish, vegetables and julienned egg), *oshi-zushi* (押し寿司; fish pressed in a mould over rice) and *inari-zushi* (いなり寿司; rice in a pocket of sweet fried tofu). *Nigiri-zushi* and *maki-zushi* usually contain a bit of wasabi (わさび). For tips on how to eat sushi, see the boxed text, below.

Sushi shops run the gamut from cheap and cheerful *kaiten-zushi* (回転寿司; conveyor-belt parlours) and stand-up eateries to more expensive and highly refined bars and restaurants. Generally speaking, quality is equated to price, though it's not necessary to eat at the best of the best to indulge in great sushi. With Tsukiji Fish Market right round the corner, chances are that everything you taste will be significantly fresher than the sushi you eat back home.

Noodles

It's hard to imagine how Tokyo could function without noodles. From traditional Japanese staples such as soba and udon to that much beloved Chinese import that is *rāmen*, Tokyoites slurp down an impressive amount of noodles in their daily lives.

Soba are thin, brownish buckwheat-based noodles, while udon are thick, white wheat noodles. Soba is more closely associated with the Kantō region, which includes Tokyo, while udon are more reminiscent of Kansai (around Osaka). With that said, the vast majority of restaurants throughout the country serve both. Here are a few serving styles you may find. We're using soba as an example, but these also apply to udon.

Kake-soba is served in a large bowl of light, bonito-flavoured broth. *Mori-soba* (aka *seiro-soba*) is served cold and piled on a bamboo mat; very refreshing in warm weather. Note that although it's highly rude in the West, it is customary to slurp your noodles, both to cool them (when hot) and to enhance the flavour.

The most popular type of cold noodles is *zaru soba*, topped with slivers of dried *nori* (海苔; seaweed). It comes with a cup of cool broth and small plate of wasabi and sliced spring onions – stir a bit of these at a time

---

SUSHI PRIMER

So, you've made it to the sushi restaurant, but now you're feeling a bit dumbfounded about what to do next. Here's a quick crash course to help you get started.

If you're seated at the sushi counter, you can simply point at what you want; most of the selections are visible in a refrigerated glass case between you and the *itamae* (sushi chef). One portion *(ichi-nin mae)* usually means two pieces of sushi. If ordering à la carte feels like a chore, you can order a *mori-awase* (assortment, generally six or seven pieces); prices vary according to the type of fish used.

Some sushi is served with a sauce already on it, while other kinds are meant to be dipped in soy sauce. If you're not sure, ask the server *'o-shōyu wa?'* ('Should I use soy sauce?'). Pour just a little soy sauce at a time from the bottle on the counter into the small saucer provided (don't fill the saucer), and if there is a side of wasabi, add a little at a time – it can be very hot! Remember, the soy sauce is used to flavour the fish and not the rice, so don't dip your sushi rice-side down (plus, the rice tends to fall apart in the soy sauce).

If you're not good at using chopsticks, don't worry; sushi is one of the few foods in Japan that it is perfectly acceptable to eat with your hands. Slices of *gari* (pickled ginger) are served to help refresh the palate. The beverage of choice with sushi is beer or sake, with a cup of cloudy green tea at the end of the meal.

into the cup of broth and eat the noodles by dipping them in this mixture. Do not pour the broth over the noodles – it creates a huge mess! At the end of your meal, the server may give you a container of *sobayu*, the hot water used for boiling the noodles, to mix with the leftover broth, which you drink like tea.

Rāmen originated in China, but its popularity in Japan is epic. Your basic *rāmen* is a big bowl of noodles in broth, served with toppings such as *chāshū* (sliced roast pork), *moyashi* (bean sprouts) and *negi* (leeks), though you can expect to see anything from Hokkaidō butter corn and fresh seafood to wontons and Chinese vegetables. Although you may be a loyal *rāmen* devotee in your own country, we can assure you that instant noodles in the West are a poor preparation for the deliciousness that is real *rāmen*.

Noodle shops run the gamut from *tachikui* (立ち食い; stand-and-eat) noodle bars in train stations and corner places where you purchase a ticket in advance for your meal (usually these places have picture menus) to highly refined restaurants with gorgeous pottery and gardens.

Izakaya

Izakaya (居酒屋) translates as 'drinking house' – the Japanese equivalent of a pub. They're great places for a casual meal, with a wide selection of food, hearty atmosphere and, of course, plenty of beer and sake. Traditionally, stand-alone *izakaya* can be identified by their rustic facades and the red lanterns outside their doors, but more and more *izakaya* are found on the restaurant floors of fancy office buildings.

Patrons typically order a few dishes at a time from a selection of Japanese foods such as *yakitori* (焼き鳥; skewers of grilled chicken), *kushiyaki* (串焼き; other grilled skewers, often vegetables), sashimi and grilled fish, as well as Japanese interpretations of Western foods such as French fries and beef stew. Say '*toriaezu*' ('that's all for now') when finished ordering each set of dishes.

Izakaya food is usually fairly inexpensive. Depending on how much you drink, you can expect to spend just ¥2000 to ¥5000 per person.

Tempura

Tempura (天ぷら) consists of portions of fish, prawns and vegetables cooked in fluffy, nongreasy batter. Typically, tempura is served with a small bowl of *ten-tsuyu* (天つゆ; a light brown sauce) and a plate of grated daikon (大根) to mix into the sauce ahead of time. Dip each piece of tempura into this sauce before eating it. Tempura is best when it's hot, so don't wait too long – use the sauce to cool each piece, and dig in.

Although there are speciality tempura restaurants in Tokyo, the dish is also commonly found elsewhere, such as at *izakaya*.

Sukiyaki, Shabu-Shabu & Yakiniku

Sukiyaki, *shabu-shabu* and *yakiniku* are favourites of most foreign visitors to Japan, perhaps because you get to cook them yourself at the table.

Sukiyaki (すき焼き) consists of thin slices of beef cooked in a broth of soy sauce, sugar

THE HOLY TRINITY OF JAPANESE FOOD

Although modern Japanese cuisine is highly refined, for millennia Japanese people survived on just three staple crops: rice, soya beans and pickled vegetables. Today these humble food items are often passed over in favour of fish and meats, though they continue to have a small but profound presence at virtually every meal.

Rice is more than just food in Japan; it's an essential component of Japanese culture. Throughout the majority of Japan's history, communities were founded on and maintained by rice farming. In fact, the food is so central to the Japanese idea of eating that the word for rice, *gohan* (ご飯), is also the word for a meal. Despite the influx of foreign cuisines, rice remains the centrepiece of a Japanese meal.

The humble soya bean has a revered place in the Japanese food pantheon, especially since it's versatile and monstrously good for you. You probably are familiar with soy sauce (しょうゆ; *shōyu*), but you may not know that miso (味噌) also comes from the soya bean. Tofu (豆腐) is another soya staple, as are edamame (枝豆), which are whole soya bean pods that have been quickly boiled.

Tsukemono (漬物; pickled vegetables) were essential to the diet of the Japanese, who until very recently had no way of procuring fresh vegetables for much of the year. In honour of this tradition, pickles are still eaten today, with the most common being made from daikon (大根), eggplant, cucumber and mixed greens.

JAPANESE BREAKFAST

A traditional Japanese breakfast consists of rice, miso soup and pickles, some kind of cooked egg, a piece of grilled fish and a cup of green tea. Tokyoites are also known to be fond of *nattō* (fermented soya beans) for breakfast, mixed into the rice with a dab of hot mustard.

That said, the breakfast of choice for more and more Japanese these days is a cup of coffee, a thick slab of white toast, an egg and a small green salad. You can enjoy this as a *mōningu setto* (モーニングセット; morning set) at small coffee houses for between ¥450 and ¥600. Many hotels serve both Western- and Japanese-style breakfasts, though at higher end hotels breakfast of any kind can be quite pricey if not included in your room rate.

and sake, together with a variety of vegetables and tofu. After cooking, dip the ingredients one by one in raw egg before eating. When made with high-quality beef, such as that from Kōbe, it is a sublime experience.

Shabu-shabu (しゃぶしゃぶ) consists of thin slices of beef and vegetables cooked by swirling the ingredients in a light broth ('*shabu-shabu*' is an onomatopoeia for the 'swish-swish' sound the beef makes in the pot), then dipping them in special *goma* (sesame-seed) and/or *ponzu* (citrus-based) sauce.

Yakiniku (焼肉) consists of thin slices of beef or pork that are grilled over hot coals, and then dipped in a variety of sauces. A variation on Korean barbecue, *yakiniku* is typically eaten with kimchi (キムチ; spicy pickled cabbage) and rice, and is currently one of the most popular types of cuisine in Tokyo.

All three of these dishes are prepared over a burner or grill at your table; your server will usually help you get started and keep a close watch on you. Take your time, add the ingredients little by little and savour the flavours as you go.

Okonomiyaki

The name means 'cook what you like', and *okonomiyaki* is an inexpensive opportunity to do just that. Sometimes described as Japanese pizza or pancake, the resemblance is in form only. At an *okonomiyaki* restaurant you sit around a *teppan* (iron hotplate), armed with a spatula and chopsticks, to cook your choice of meat, seafood and vegetables in a cabbage and vegetable batter.

Some restaurants will do most of the cooking and bring the nearly finished product to your hotplate for you to season with *katsuo bushi* (鰹節 or カツオ節; bonito flakes), soy sauce, *ao-nori* (青海苔; a sea green similar to parsley), Japanese Worcestershire-style sauce and mayonnaise. Cheaper places, however,

will simply hand you a bowl filled with the ingredients and expect you to cook it for yourself. If this happens, don't panic.

First, mix the batter and filling thoroughly, then pour it onto the hot grill, flattening it into a thick pancake. After five minutes or so, use the spatulas to flip it and cook for another five minutes. Then season and dig in.

Most *okonomiyaki* places also serve *yakisoba* (焼きそば; fried noodles) and *yasaiitame* (野菜炒め; stir-fried vegetables). All of this is washed down with mugs of draught beer. Also look for *okonomiyaki* at festivals and street fairs.

Shokudō

A shokudō (食堂) is the most common type of restaurant in Japan, and is found near train stations, tourist spots and just about any other place where people congregate. Easily distinguished by the presence of plastic food displays in the window, these inexpensive places usually serve a variety of *washoku* (和食; Japanese) and *yōshoku* (洋食; Western) dishes.

At lunch, and sometimes at dinner, the easiest meal to order at a shokudō is a *teishoku* (定食; set-course meal), which is sometimes also called *ranchi setto* (ランチセット; lunch set) or *kōsu* (コース; set meal). This usually includes a main dish of meat or fish, a bowl of rice, miso soup, a small salad and some *tsukemono* (漬物; pickled vegetables).

Kaiseki

Kaiseki (懐石; elegant ceremonial food) is the pinnacle of Japanese cuisine, where ingredients, preparation, setting and presentation come together to create a dining experience quite unlike any other. Born as an adjunct to the tea ceremony, *kaiseki* is a largely vegetarian affair (although fish is often served, meat never appears on the *kaiseki* menu).

One usually eats *kaiseki* in the private room of a *ryōtei* (料亭; an especially elegant style of traditional restaurant), often overlooking a tranquil garden. The meal is served in several small courses, giving the diner an opportunity to admire the plates and bowls, which are carefully chosen to complement the food and season. Rice is eaten last (usually with an assortment of pickles), and the drink of choice is sake or beer.

Tonkatsu

Tonkatsu (豚カツ) is a deep-fried, crumbed pork cutlet served with a savoury sauce. It's a staple of Japanese home-style cooking, though you'll have to head to the speciality shops for the good stuff. Different cuts of meat include *hire* (fillet) and *rōsu* (roast), and serving styles include on a plate with a mound of shredded cabbage or *katsu-don* (*donburi*; on a bowl of rice). For non-pork eaters, many *tonkatsu* restaurants make *tori-katsu* as well (with chicken instead of pork).

Unagi

Even if you can't stand the creature, you owe it to yourself to try *unagi* (うなぎ; freshwater eel) at least once while in Tokyo. It's cooked over hot coals and brushed with a rich sauce composed of soy sauce and sake. Often you can sprinkle it with powdered *sanshō* (山椒; Sichuan pepper), a pungent herb that has numbing properties in the mouth. Some *unagi* restaurants keep barrels of live eels to entice passers-by.

Fugu

The deadly *fugu* (globefish, aka pufferfish or blowfish) is eaten more for the thrill than the taste. The actual meat is rather bland, but acclaimed for its fine texture. Nonetheless, if you have the money to lay out for a *fugu* dinner (around ¥10,000), it makes a good 'been there, done that' story.

Since most of its internal organs (especially the liver) are highly poisonous, *fugu* can only be prepared by chefs who have a licence and have undergone extensive training. That said, the danger of *fugu* poisoning is negligible (there have been no deaths in Japan from *fugu* poisoning in decades), though Japanese joke that you should always let your dining companion try the first piece of *fugu*. If they are still talking after five minutes, you can consider the dish safe.

If you're eating *fugu* because you've been challenged by a Japanese friend, and you want to repay them with a cruel joke, hold your hand still and let your chopsticks drop onto the table (in case of poisoning, the extremities go first). On second thought, don't do this, as it will probably alarm everyone else in the restaurant.

For some liquid courage, try a glass of *hire-zake* (toasted *fugu* fin in hot sake), the traditional accompaniment to a *fugu* dinner.

Sweets

Although most Japanese-style restaurants don't serve dessert (plates of sliced fruit are sometimes served at the end of a meal), there is no lack of sweets in Japan. *Wagashi* (和菓子; traditional Japanese sweets) are sold in speciality shops for you to eat or to give as gifts at home. Many of the more-delicate-looking ones are made to balance the strong, bitter taste of the special *matcha* (抹茶; whisked green tea) served during the tea ceremony.

Even if you have the sweetest tooth in the world and have sampled every type of sweet that's come your way, you may find yourself surprised by Japanese confectionery. Many sweets contain the red adzuki-bean paste called *anko* (あんこ). This earthy, rich filling turns up in a variety of pastries, including those you pick up at the corner bakery shop. Legions of foreign visitors have been surprised – not altogether unpleasantly – expecting chocolate and finding *anko* instead.

With such a wide variety of sweets, it's impossible to list all the names. However, you'll probably find many variations on the *anko* with *mochi* (餅; glutinous rice) theme. Sweet shops are easy to spot – they usually have open fronts, with their wares attractively laid out in wooden trays to tempt hungry shoppers.

For Western-style sweets, try cafes, coffee shops and pastry shops for a variety of cakes, muffins and the like; these are also abundant in Tokyo. If all else fails duck into a convenience store for *aisukuriimu* (アイスクリーム; ice cream) or *chokorēto* (チョコレート; chocolate).

Drinks

Unlike the Western world, soft drinks (sodas) and other sweetened beverages rarely appear on the menu (with the exception, of course, being Western-style fast-food restaurants). Needless to say, the beverage of choice in Japan is *o-cha* (お茶; green tea), which is served hot or cold depending on the time of year. You can also expect to find subtle variations on this traditional brew.

Although the canned coffee you get from vending machines does resemble the watered-down brews you find in the US, European-style cafes serving the good stuff are found on virtually every corner in Tokyo. In addition to the standard cup of *kōhii* (コーヒー; coffee), you can also expect to find *esupuresso* (エスプレッソ; espresso), *kapuchīno* (カプチーノ; cappuccino) and even *matcha-ratte* (抹茶ラッテ; green-tea-flavoured latte).

When it comes to alcohol, the Japanese are avid consumers of *birru* (ビール; beer), which tend to be light and easy-drinking lagers. *Wain* (ワイン; wine) and *uisukī* (ウイスキー; whiskey) are also fairly common tipples, though their high status means that they're significantly more expensive than in the West.

Sake, aka Nihonshū (酒 or 日本酒; rice wine), is Japan's national beverage, and the variety of grades, flavours and regions of origin can be astounding. Although many visitors to Japan arrive assuming that sake should be drunk hot (and indeed this can be quite satisfying on a cold Tokyo night), purists would never dream of drinking a higher grade sake (such as *dai-ginjō*) any way but chilled. The website www.sake-world.com has a concise yet comprehensive guide to different types of sake.

Interestingly, sake is falling out of favour with the younger generation, while the potent *shōchū* (焼酎; liquor distilled from grains or sweet potato, for example) is becoming ever more popular. Taste testing *shōchū onzarokku* (on the rocks) is a great way to sample the different flavours.

VEGETARIANS & VEGANS

Japan can be a frustrating place for vegetarians and vegans, especially since *dashi* (だし; fish stock) is used as a base for most dishes, even ones that have no meat or fish in them. On the bright side, however, the more-cosmopolitan neighbourhoods in Tokyo boast vegetarian eateries, many of them serving vegan meals and exclusively organic produce. Look for the Ⓥ icon for vegetarian and veggie-friendly places throughout this book.

PRACTICALITIES

For first-timers (and some seasoned veterans) in Tokyo, deciphering Japanese menus is enough to make anyone lose their appetite. If you fall into this category, consider searching out restaurants where English menus are available. Throughout this chapter, we have added the symbol Ⓔ to listings where this is the case.

Many less-expensive restaurants boast windows with plastic models of their dishes. Others have *shashin menu* (写真メニュー; picture menus). Both of these make it easy to point and eat. If the prices are written in kanji (Chinese characters), refer to the language section of this book.

Opening Hours

Restaurants in hubs such as Shinjuku, Ikebukuro or Shibuya are usually open seven days a week from 11.30am or noon until 9pm or 10pm, with many offering set specials during lunch hours. In smaller eateries in less-central areas such as Ebisu or Asakusa, hours are often shorter, and it's not unusual to find some places shuttered on Sunday, Monday or Tuesday. Generally, the lunch hour goes from 11am or noon to 2.30pm or 3pm, while dinner is served from 6pm or 6.30pm to 9pm or 10pm. Last orders are usually taken an hour or half-hour before the kitchen actually closes.

How Much?

Yes, Tokyo has an expensive reputation, and from upmarket sushi to a chichi French dinner, haute cuisine fetches high prices here. At places like this, ¥20,000 per person is a baseline. Add even more for sake, significantly more for fine wine.

But take heart – the average Tokyoite cannot afford to eat this way regularly, and you don't have to either. It's possible to eat very well on a midrange or even modest budget without needing to raid the shelves of the convenience stores or eat curry rice twice a day. Good *teishoku* (定食) can be had for around ¥1000, and a tremendous bowl of noodle soup might set you back around ¥700. If you do want to try some of the high-end places, Tokyo's open secret, the bargain lunch set, can often allow you to put your foot in the door for a fraction of the dinner price. See p165 for a list of reasonably priced chain restaurants.

PRICE GUIDE

¥¥¥	over ¥5000 a meal
¥¥	¥2000-5000 a meal
¥	under ¥2000 a meal

Another cost-saving aspect of dining in Tokyo is that tips aren't expected. Some pricier restaurants add a 10% service fee, but if they do it is usually stated on the menu. If you do leave a tip on the table, you may get chased down the street by staff wanting to reunite you with your change.

Booking Tables

Reservations are essential at top-end spots. It usually helps if you can speak some Japanese when phoning for a reservation, but if you don't, your hotel can usually make the booking for you. As for midrange and budget spots, it's worth reserving if you've got your heart set on a place, although reservations are typically unnecessary except for larger groups. If you arrive without a reservation and no table is available, give your name and the number in your party to the host or hostess; typically there is seating while you wait until your table is ready.

IMPERIAL PALACE & MARUNOUCHI

There's no shortage of restaurants in the proximity of Tokyo Station and the Imperial Palace, though a good number of them cater to the dine-and-dash lunch crowd. Of course, even salarymen and government workers need a nice sit-down meal from time to time, which is why you can expect to find a number of trendy and upmarket eateries scattered among the avenues. Many of the best options are in Marubiru and Shin-Marubiru (see the boxed text, p175).

NUMAZU UOGASHI Map p52   Sushi ¥¥
沼津魚がし
☎ 5220-5550; 6th fl, Marunouchi Bldg, 2-4-1 Marunouchi, Chiyoda-ku; sets ¥980-3300; ☽ 11am-11pm Mon-Sat, 11am-10pm Sun; ⊕ Marunouchi Line to Tokyo (exit 4b), JR Yamanote Line to Tokyo (Marunouchi centre exit); Ⓔ
It may be in the lofty confines of Marubiru, but this friendly, workmanlike sushi shop

feels like Tsukiji. Single serves are pretty expensive, but portions are generous and set lunches are a great deal.

TORAJI Map p92   Yakiniku ¥¥
トラジ
☎ 5220-7071; 6th fl, Marunouchi Bldg, 2-4-1 Marunouchi, Chiyoda-ku; dishes ¥880-1600, sets ¥880-1880; ☽ 11am-11pm Mon-Sat, 11am-11pm Sun; ⊕ Marunouchi Line to Tokyo (exit 4b), JR Yamanote Line to Tokyo (Marunouchi centre exit); Ⓔ
Although it originates from the humble Korean dish known as *bulgogi, yakiniku* at this Marubiru establishment is anything but ordinary. Choose from a variety of immaculate cuts of meat, grill them over charcoals set into your table, and dip into a variety of sauces before popping into your mouth – delicious! Other branches around town include Roppongi (Map p92; ☎ 5786-1771; 3-24-22 Nishi-Azabu, Minato-ku; ⊕ Hibiya or Toei Ōedo Line to Roppongi, exit 1) and Shiodome (Map p64; ☎ 6215-8555; Caretta Bldg, Higashi-Shimbashi 1-8-2; ☽ 11am-3pm & 5-11.30pm Mon-Fri, 11am-11.30pm Sat, 11am-11pm Sun; ⊕ Toei Ōedo Line to Shiodome, exit A2).

MIMIU Map p52   Udon ¥¥
美々卯
☎ 3567-6571; 3-6-4 Kyōbashi, Chūō-ku; lunch ¥700-1400, side dishes ¥500-2200, dinner from ¥4800; ☽ 11.30am-9.30pm Mon-Sat, 11.30pm-9pm Sun; ⊕ Ginza Line to Kyobashi (exit 1 or 2); Ⓔ
Connoisseurs of udon say that Osaka-style broth is lighter in colour and more delicate in flavour than what Tokyoites favour. Try for yourself at this Osaka original that's said to have invented *udon-suki* (¥3700 per person), udon cooked sukiyaki-style in broth, with seafood, vegetables and meat. Look for the stately black building.

DIN TAI FUNG Map p52   Chinese ¥
鼎泰豐
☎ 3246-4768; B2fl, Takashimaya, 2-4-1 Nihombashi, Chūō-ku; dishes ¥630-1260; ☽ 11am-9.30pm; ⊕ Ginza or Tōzai Line to Nihombashi (Takashimaya exit); Ⓔ
One word is all you need at this branch of Taipei's most esteemed dumpling house: *shōronpō*. To enjoy these juicy pork 'soup' dumplings served in bamboo steamers, scoop one carefully into your spoon, sprinkle a drop of *sushōyu* (vinegar soy sauce) and a

few strands of grated ginger on top, poke a hole in it, slurp out the broth, then eat. Then move on to noodle soups and vegetable dishes from the picture menu. There's another branch in Shiodome (☎ 5537-2081; 2Bfl, Caretta Bldg, Higashi-Shimbashi 1-8-2; ☯ 10am-11pm; Ⓔ Toei Ōedo Line to Shiodome, exit A2).

GINZA

Ginza has always been a stronghold of the city's finest restaurants, with excellent sushi, marvellous French haute cuisine and ethereal surroundings. It can be challenging to find a modestly priced meal in the evenings, but poking around the *resutoran-gai* (restaurant floors) of department stores can turn up good lunch deals. If all else fails, try the clutch of inexpensive *yakitori* stalls under the tracks by Yūrakuchō Station, though watch that they aren't instead selling *horumon* (innard stew), which is, shall we say, an acquired taste.

L'OSIER Map p57   French ¥¥¥
レストランロオジェ
☎ 3571-6050; 7-5-5 Ginza, Chūō-ku; set meals lunch/dinner from ¥6800/19,000; ☯ noon-2pm & 6-9.30pm; Ⓔ Ginza, Hibiya or Marunouchi Line to Ginza (exit B6), JR Yamanote Line to Shimbashi (Ginza exit)

In Tokyo, French restaurants are at the top of the culinary ladder, which is why it's no small accolade that local gourmets consider L'Osier to be the best around. But if you wish to analyse the foie gras yourself, you'll need to book as far as possible in advance since a table at L'Osier is a highly coveted commodity. However, once the wine hits your head and the food hits your lips, you'll key into the art-deco-inspired surroundings and realise that Paris isn't that far away after all.

TEN-ICHI Map p57   Tempura ¥¥¥
天一
☎ 3571-1949; 6-6-5 Ginza, Chūō-ku; set meals lunch/dinner from ¥8400/10,500; ☯ 11.30am-9.30pm; Ⓔ Ginza, Hibiya or Marunouchi Line to Ginza (exits A1, B3 or B6); Ⓔ
Since 1930 Ten-Ichi has rightfully earned its reputation as Tokyo's go-to spot for tempura, which is supernaturally light and nongreasy here. The dignified dining area at the flagship Ginza restaurant has hosted royalty and corporate titans; if the set menus seem pricey, know that a single à la carte tempura prawn costs ¥1000. Book ahead. The entrance is on Namiki-dōri. Other locations include Akasaka (Map p88; ☎ 3581-2166; Akasaka Excel Tōkyū Hotel).

RESTAURANT PRIMER

When you enter a restaurant, often the entire staff will shout a hearty *'irasshaimase!'* (Welcome!). In all but the most casual places the waiter or waitress will next ask you, *'nan-mei sama?'* (How many people?). Indicate the answer with your fingers, which is what the Japanese do, or respond with the number (eg *san-nin* for 'three people'). You may also be asked if you would like to sit at a *zashiki* (low table on the tatami), at a *tēburu* (table) or *kauntā* (counter). More and more restaurants these days offer the fun compromise of *hori-kotatsu* seating: you sit on the tatami, but there's a well beneath the table for you to place your legs.

Once seated you will be given an *o-shibori* (hot towel), a cup of tea or water and a menu. The *o-shibori* is for wiping your hands and face. When you're finished with it, just roll it up and leave it next to your place. In many restaurants it will serve as your napkin later. You may also be asked at this point what you'd like to drink, especially in an *izakaya* (Japanese-style pub).

For ordering, if you don't read Japanese, ask for an English menu (*eigo-no-menyū*); use the romanised translations in this chapter or in the food glossary (p273) or direct the server's attention to the Japanese script. If this doesn't work, two helpful phrases are *'o-susume wa nan desuka?'* ('What would you recommend?') and *'o-makase shimasu'* ('I leave it to you'). If you're still having problems, try pointing at other diners' food or dragging the server outside to point at the plastic food displays in the window if the restaurant has them.

When you've finished eating, you can signal for the bill by crossing one index finger over the other to form an X. This is the standard sign for 'cheque please'. You can also say *'o-kanjō o kudasai'*. Remember, there is no tipping in Japan, and tea and tap water are free, though many high end restaurants charge a service fee of 10% above the menu prices. Usually you will be given a bill to take to the cashier at the front of the restaurant. At more upmarket places, the host of the party will discreetly ask to be excused and pay before the group leaves. Only the bigger and more-international places take credit cards.

When leaving, it is polite to say to the restaurant staff *'gochisō-sama deshita'* ('It was a real feast').

KYŪBEY Map p57   Sushi & Sashimi ¥¥¥
久兵衛

☎ 3571-6523; 8-7-6 Ginza, Chūō-ku; sushi sets lunch ¥4200-8400, dinner from ¥10,500; 🕙 11.30am-2pm & 5-10pm Mon-Sat; ⊕ Ginza Line to Shimbashi (exit 3), JR Yamanote Line to Shimbashi (Ginza exit); Ⓔ

If you can splurge on only one Tokyo sushi experience, make it this one. Established in 1936, Kyūbey's quality and presentation have attracted a moneyed and celebrity clientele ever since, seeking incomparable quality and presentation. Go for broke with kaiseki (course menu, lunch/dinner from ¥10,500/15,750), or have it served on pottery by famed artisan Kitaoji Rosanjin for ¥31,500. Otherwise just peruse the Rosanjin exhibition on the restaurant's 4th floor. Kyūbey continues to make headlines: in 2009, it bought at auction half of a single bluefin tuna that sold for a staggering ¥9.63 million (and sold single cuts of toro from it for ¥2000!).

BIRD LAND Map p57   Yakitori ¥¥
バードランド

☎ 5250-1081; 4-2-15 Ginza, Chūō-ku; dishes ¥150-1200, set meals ¥6000-8000; 🕙 5.30-10pm Tue-Sat; ⊕ Ginza, Hibiya or Marunouchi Line to Ginza (exit C6); Ⓔ

This kindly basement bar is a destination for gourmet grilled chicken. Chefs in whites behind a U-shaped counter dispense yakitori in all shapes, sizes, colours and organs – don't pass up the dainty serves of liver pâté or the tiny cup of chicken soup. Order a set menu for the most variety, and you can try sansho-yaki (like teriyaki) or oyako-don (chicken and egg on rice) as well. Enter beneath Suit Company.

NATARAJ Map p57   Vegetarian ¥¥
ナタラジ

☎ 5537-1515; 7th-9th fl, 6-9-4 Ginza, Chūō-ku; mains ¥1000-1450, sets ¥2100-3850; 🕙 11.30am-11pm; ⊕ Ginza, Hibiya or Marunouchi Line to Ginza (exit A2)

Herbivores don't have it easy in Tokyo, though thankfully there is reason to rejoice at this Indian-influenced vegetarian spot. Nataraj brings its warm colours, low-key elegance and animal-friendly cuisine to this enormous three-storey branch shop in the heart of Ginza. Sizeable set meals include appealing choices such as pumpkin curry and chickpea pakora, which go down well with an extensive wine and beer list of domestic and international favourites.

DEPACHIKA

Hungry for the next culinary novelty, OLs (office ladies) and o-bāsan (grandmotherly types) prowl the mazes of depachika, the cavernous food halls in department store basements. Depachika often take up several floors, housing a staggering array of foodstuffs of the highest order, freshly prepared and often gorgeously packaged for presentation as gifts. Depending on food trends, you could find black truffle oil or dessert vinegar just round the corner from the more-traditional 573 grades of the season's green tea and wagashi (delicate candies). Though samples are harder to come by these days, the sharp-eyed will find nibbles of sublime chocolate, sesame-seed sembei (crunchy rice crackers) and dried squid.

Large department stores are often attached to major train stations – uberconvenient for picking up museum-quality bentō (boxed lunches), picnic items for a sunny afternoon or a fancy gift of flower-shaped okashi (sweets).

If you can read Japanese, do as obsessive OLs do and monitor the day's specials on www.depachika.com. If not, descend into one of the following basements, among Tokyo's best depachika:

Isetan (Map p110; ☎ 3352-1111; 3-14-1 Shinjuku, Shinjuku-ku; 🕙 10am-8pm; ⊕ Marunouchi, Fukutoshin or Toei Shinjuku Line to Shinjuku-sanchōme, exits B3, B4 or B5) The grandmother of them all.

Matsuya (Map p57; ☎ 3567-1211; 3-6-1 Ginza, Chūō-ku; 🕙 10.30am-7.30pm; ⊕ Ginza, Hibiya or Marunouchi Line to Ginza, exits A12 or A13) An upmarket Ginza stalwart.

Mitsukoshi (Map p57; ☎ 3241-3311; 4-6-16 Ginza, Chūō-ku; 🕙 10am-7.30pm Mon-Sat, 10am-7pm Sun; ⊕ Ginza, Hibiya or Marunouchi Line to Ginza, exit A7) Classic style and status at this Ginza institution.

Seibu (Map p116; ☎ 3981-0111; 1-28-1 Minami-Ikebukuro, Toshima-ku; 🕙 10am-9pm Mon-Sat, 10am-8pm Sun; ⊕ JR Yamanote Line to Ikebukuro, east exit) Spanning several city blocks, this has a particularly comprehensive spice market.

Takashimaya Times Square (Map p110; ☎ 5361-1111; 5-24-2 Sendagaya, Shibuya-ku; 🕙 10am-8pm, closed occasional Wed; ⊕ JR Yamanote Line to Shinjuku, new south exit) Like the 15-storey department store above it, this depachika is enormous.

YABATON Map p57 Tonkatsu ¥¥
矢場とん

☎ 3546-8810; 4-10-14 Ginza, Chūō-ku; mains ¥1050-1890; ⏰ 11am-10pm Tue-Sun; ⊕ Hibiya or Toei-Asakusa Line to Higashi-Ginza (exit A2); Ⓔ
Not everything in Ginza has to be chic and sleek. Yabaton sells *miso-katsu,* a very workmanlike take on *tonkatsu* that's slathered in miso sauce. *Waraji-tonkatsu* is a big-as-your-head flattened cutlet, or try *kani-korokke* (crab croquettes). *Yabaton-salada* (boiled pork with miso sesame sauce over vegetables) is kinda sorta good for you. Look for the pig wearing a sumō wrestler's apron, one block west of Shōwa-dōri.

IIDABASHI & AROUND

More a geographic area than a contiguous neighbourhood, the Iidabashi area has a variety of offerings ranging from Italian eateries overlooking the canal to spots off the intimate side streets of Kagurazaka. Kagurazaka-dōri, the main drag heading uphill from Iidabashi Station, is lined with reasonably priced chain restaurants, and there are some gems tucked away near Kagurazaka Station as well.

IIDABASHI
CANAL CAFÉ Map p60 Italian ¥¥
カナルカフェ

☎ 3260-8068; 1-9 Kagurazaka, Shinjuku-ku; mains ¥700-1900; ⏰ 5.30-11.30pm Tue-Sun; ⊕ Namboku, Tōzai, Yūrakuchō or Toei Ōedo Line to Iidabashi (exit B3); Ⓔ
When summer evenings in the capital hang heavy with humidity, this is one of the rare spots in the city centre with breathing room, allowing you to enjoy a cold glass of white wine and a light meal by the water. The specialities are wood-fired thin-crust pizza, and Italian pasta such as scallop dishes and prawns in a light cream sauce, though the real reason you're here is to savour a cocktail while soaking up the European atmosphere.

LE BRETAGNE Map p60 French ¥
ル ブルターニュ

☎ 3478-7855; 4-2 Kagurazaka, Shinjuku-ku; crêpes ¥550-1680; ⏰ 11.30am-11.30pm Tue-Sat, 11.30am-10pm Sun; ⊕ Namboku, Tōzai, Yūrakuchō or Toei Ōedo Line to Iidabashi (exit B3); Ⓔ Ⓥ
This French-owned Kagurazaka cafe is credited with starting the Japanese rage for crêpes. Its stucco walls, beamed ceilings and front terrace make for a rustic setting to sample savoury crêpes with ingredients like ham, gruyère, artichokes and tomato, or sweet crêpes like Quimpéroise with caramelised butter, apple compote and vanilla ice cream.

KAGURAZAKA
KADO Map p60 Traditional ¥¥
カド

☎ 3268-2410; 1-32 Akagi-Motomachi, Shinjuku-ku; lunch sets ¥800-1000, dinner sets ¥3150; ⏰ 11.30am-4pm & 5-11pm; ⊕ Tōzai Line to Kagurazaka (exit 1)
Set in a house built in 1950 in a residential neighbourhood, Kado reveals a rare glimpse of Tokyo prior to the late-20th-century economic miracle. Lunch is simple, such as curry rice or *om-rice* (seasoned rice in an omelette), while five-course dinners emphasise traditional Japanese recipes and seasonal produce, enhanced by the familial ambience. There is no English menu, though the staff do their best to accommodate. From Kagurazaka Station, turn left and left again into the jagged street across from Copain Copine; Kado is at the first four-way corner.

SEIGETSU Map p60 Izakaya ¥¥
霽月

☎ 3269-4320; 2nd fl, 6-77 Kagurazaka, Shinjuku-ku; dishes ¥680-880; ⏰ 5-11.30pm Mon-Thu & Sat, 5pm-2am Fri, 5-11pm Sun; ⊕ Tōzai Line to Kagurazaka (exit 1)
Located in a district increasingly becoming dominated by chain pubs, this traditional *izakaya* is perfect for all of your dining and drinking needs, especially since there are on-call *shōchū* consultants to help you match your meal to your booze. Although there isn't an English menu, the speciality here is charcoal-grilled meats and seasonal vegetables…not so difficult. It's across the street from Café de Crie.

TSUKIJI & SHIODOME

Right on the waterfront of Tokyo Bay, the Tsukiji neighbourhood encircles the busiest fish market on earth. It is here that any hardworking, tough-talking fisherman will be proud to tell you that you'll find the best sushi breakfast in Japan and the freshest sashimi in the world. In Shiodome, the landscape is distinguished by skyscrapers with food floors like Caretta (see the boxed text, p175).

DAIWA SUSHI Map p64
Sushi & Sashimi ¥¥
大和寿司

☎ 3547-6807; Bldg 6, 5-2-1 Tsukiji, Chūō-ku; sushi set ¥3500; ⏰ 5am-1.30pm Mon-Sat, closed occasional Wed; ⓜ Toei Ōedo Line to Tsukijishijō (exit A2)

Waits of over one hour are commonplace at Tsukiji's most famous sushi bar, but it's all worth it once you're past the *noren* (curtains) and your first piece of sushi hits the counter. Unless you're comfortable ordering in Japanese, the standard set (seven *nigiri*, plus *maki* and miso soup) is a good bet; there's a picture menu. Though the staff may be too polite to say so, you're expected to eat and run so others can partake in this quintessential Tsukiji experience.

EDOGIN Map p64
Sushi & Sashimi ¥
江戸銀

☎ 3543-4401; 4-5-1 Tsukiji, Chūō-ku; sushi sets ¥1000-4300; ⏰ 11am-9.30pm Mon-Sat, 11am-8pm Sun; ⓜ Hibiya Line to Tsukiji (exit 2)

Fat pieces of superfresh sashimi and sushi draw the crowds at this little hole-in-the-wall spot just up the way from Tsukiji Central Fish Market. The lunchtime *teishoku* (定食) is a steal at ¥1000, especially since the fish comes from up the street. Though there's nothing in the way of atmosphere, the locals who come here to eat provide the colour you need.

AKIHABARA & KANDA

Kanda has a large concentration of historic eateries, some specialising in dishes as simple as soba, others prewar favourites on traditional tatami. In stark contrast, Akihabara is home to cheap chain restaurants, few of which really stand out, but it does have maid cafes.

KANDA

BOTAN Map p67
Sukiyaki ¥¥¥
ぼたん

☎ 3251-0577; 1-15 Kanda-Sudachō, Chiyoda-ku; set meals around ¥7000; ⏰ 11.30am-9pm Mon-Sat; ⓜ Marunouchi Line to Awajichō (exit A3), Toei Shinjuku Line to Ogawamachi (exit A3); Ⓔ

Botan has been making a single, perfect dish in the same button-maker's house since the 1890s. Sit cross-legged on rattan mats as chicken *nabe* (鍋; meat cooked in broth with vegetables) simmers over a charcoal brazier next to you, allowing you

to take in the scent of prewar Tokyo. Try to get a seat in the handsome upstairs dining room.

ISEGEN Map p67
Traditional ¥¥
いせ源

☎ 3251-1229; 1-11-1 Kanda-Sudachō, Chiyoda-ku; set meals from ¥3465; ⏰ 11.30am-2pm & 5-9pm Mon-Sat, closed Sat Jun-Aug; ⓜ Marunouchi Line to Awajichō (exit A3) or Toei Shinjuku Line to Ogawamachi (exit A3)

From early autumn to mid-spring, this old Edo-style restaurant dishes up monkfish stew in a splendid communal tatami room. The rest of the year, when monkfish is out of season, expect the same traditional surroundings and a menu offering fresh river fish. There is no English menu, but the communal surroundings mean that it shouldn't be too hard to point to what you want.

KANDA YABU SOBA Map p67
Soba ¥
神田やぶそば

☎ 3251-0287; 2-10 Kanda-Awajichō, Chiyoda-ku; noodles ¥700-2000; ⏰ 11.30am-8pm; ⓜ Marunouchi Line to Awajichō (exit A3) or Toei Shinjuku Line to Ogawamachi (exit A3); Ⓔ

A wooden wall and a small garden enclose this venerable buckwheat-noodle shop. When you walk in, staff singing out the orders is one of the first signs that you've arrived in a singular, ageless place. Raised tatami platforms and a darkly wooded dining room set the stage for show-stopping soba. There's a sister branch in Asakusa: Namiki Yabu Soba (並木やぶそば; ☎ 3841-1340; 2-11-9 Kaminarimon, Taitō-ku; ⏰ 11am-10pm Fri-Wed; ⓜ Ginza or Toei Asakusa Line to Asakusa, exit A4).

AKIHABARA

@HOME CAFÉ Map p67
Cafe ¥
@ほぉ～むカフェ

☎ 5294-7704; www.cafe-athome.com; 7F Mitsuwa Bldg, 1-11-4 Soto-kanda, Chiyoda-ku; mains ¥1100-1200, drinks & desserts ¥400-800, plus per person ¥700; ⏰ 12.30-10pm Mon-Fri, 11.30am-10pm Sat, 10.30am-10pm Sun; ⓜ JR Sōbu Line to Akihabara (Electric Town exit)

Wanna walk on the wild side of Tokyo's fetish for *kawaii* (cuteness)? Try being served coffee by girls dressed as French maids! You'll be welcomed as *go-shujinsama* (master) the minute you enter this cafe. It's titillating, perhaps, but it's no sex joint – just (more or less) innocent fun for Akihabara's

CHAINS WORTH KNOWING

Tokyo has plenty of fine restaurants, and not all of them are stand-alones. Here are some worthwhile chain restaurants with citywide locations. Visiting these can also help reduce your eating budget. All have English menus, except as noted.

- **Fuji Soba** (富士そば; mains ¥290-690) These counter service soba and *donburi* (rice dish) restaurants are pretty low on the food chain, but they're cheap, quick and ubiquitous, and many Japanese secretly admire them. Choose your poison from the plastic food models in the window, purchase a ticket with the same number from the vending machine, hand it to the staff, and presto! Locations throughout town, particularly near train stations.

- **Kohmen** (光麺; www.kohmen.com; rāmen ¥680-990; **E**) At this cheerful rāmen specialist, noodles come in everything from docile salt, soy sauce or pork broth to 'painful rāmen of sesami flavour', served in rustic pottery. Add-ons might include bamboo shoots, *chāshū* (roast pork), bamboo shoots and garlic. Locations include Ueno, Omote-Sandō and Takadanobaba.

- **Mos Burger** (モスバーガー; www.mos.jp; burgers ¥320-470; **E**) Even if you don't go for fast food, these diminutive delights have a cult following. The namesake Mos Burger is a beef patty topped with chopped sweet onion, mayonnaise, mild chilli sauce and a thick slice of tomato. Mos Rice Burgers have 'buns' made of cooked rice; the veggie *kinpira* version comes with marinated *gobo*, a long, brown root vegetable. Locations throughout Tokyo include Roppongi, Ikebukuro and Iidabashi.

- **Sekai no Yamachan** (世界の山ちゃん; dishes ¥310-520; **E**) Even if chicken wings are a staple of yours at home, chances are you've never had anything like *maboroshino tebasaki* (Nagoya-style wings) in five levels of spice. Other pub dishes include *miso-kushikatsu* (deep-fried pork skewers in miso sauce) and giant salads. Instead of miso soup try *cōchin dango* (free-range chicken meatball in broth). Locations include Shinjuku, near Hanazono Shrine.

- **Tofūro** (土風炉; mains ¥650-1980; **E**) Typically found in business districts, these dimly lit, old Edo-style *izakaya* (Japanese-style pub) have tasty and reasonably priced humble noodles to splashy *gozen* set meals and great lunch *teishoku* (set meals). Locations include Ginza and Shinjuku.

- **Za Watami** (坐・和民; dishes ¥313-628; **E**) The Watami group lets you enjoy your *izakaya* faves such as giant salads of organic vegetables, tender chicken with green onions, and lotus root chips or sashimi (from fish to horsemeat), all in a variety of stylish seating options from hardwood counter to small private booths. Look for the signs in English in busy restaurant districts such as Akasaka and Shibuya.

otaku. Dishes such as curried rice are even topped with smiley faces. And business is expanding: @Home Café now occupies four floors, with themes from pop princess to old Japan, with varying opening days. From Chūō-dōri, turn left where you see Sofmap.

UENO

Holding on to its Shitamachi (low city) style and atmosphere, Ueno's culinary landscape pales in comparison to the bigger players inside the Yamanote (high city). Of course, after a long day of meandering the halls of Ueno-kōen's many museums, you may want to stick around for dinner. While the local restaurants aren't doing anything cutting edge, they are satisfyingly down to earth and modestly priced.

SASA-NO-YUKI Map p78　　　　　Tofu ¥¥
笹乃雪
☎ 3873-1145; 2-15-10 Negishi, Taitō-ku; dishes ¥350-1000, set meals ¥2600-4500; ⏲ 11.30am-9pm Tue-Sun; ⓙ JR Yamanote Line to Uguisudani (north exit); **E**

Sasa-no-Yuki opened its doors in the thriving Edo period, and continues to serve tofu in elegant arrangements and traditional surroundings; the best seats overlook a tiny garden with a koi pond. Set meals allow you to sample a broad range of tofu delicacies, like *hiryuzu* (tofu dumpling with vegetables), *gomadofu* (sesame tofu), *ankake* (in savoury gravy) and even *aisu kuriimu* (ice cream). Vegetarians take note: many dishes include chicken and fish stock, if not the meat itself.

HANTEI Map p78　　　　　Traditional ¥¥
はん亭
☎ 3828-1440; 2-12-15 Nezu, Bunkyō-ku; set meals lunch ¥3500, set meals dinner from ¥2835; ⏲ noon-3pm & 5-10pm Tue-Sun; ⓜ Chiyoda Line to Nezu (exit 2)
In an updated Meiji-era house, delectable set menus of skewers of *kushiage* (fried meat, fish and vegetables) are counterbalanced by small, refreshing side dishes. Lunch courses are eight sticks, and dinner courses start with six, with add-on courses available (from ¥1365). All you really need to decide is whether to drink sake or beer.

IZU-EI Map p78   Unagi ¥¥
伊豆栄

☎ 3831-0954; 2-12-22 Ueno, Taitō-ku; set meals ¥1785-4410; ⏰ 11am-2pm & 5-11pm; ◉ JR Yamanote Line to Ueno (Hirokō-ji exit); Ⓔ

Izu-ei specialises in *unagi*, which you can take in two ways: in a *bentō* that includes tempura and pickled vegetables; or charcoal-grilled, sauced and laid on a bed of steamed rice, as *unagi* purists might insist. Try to get seated near an upstairs window for the best views of the large lily pads of nearby Shinobazu-ike.

COCA Map p78   Thai ¥
コカ

☎ 5826-5825; 2nd fl, Retro-kan, Atré Ueno, 7-1-1 Ueno, Taito-ku; mains ¥650-1050, set meals ¥1300-1900; ⏰ 11am-11pm; ◉ Ueno (Ueno Hirokō-ji exit); Ⓔ

Appreciate the prewar architecture of Ueno's station building along with authentic Thai curries, fried rice, omelettes and noodle soups. If Thai's not your thing, there are many other restaurants in the station's 'Retro-kan' (Retro Hall), but Coca is one of the few where you can see the original details: curved walls, hardware and such.

CHALET SWISS MINI Map p78   Swiss ¥
シャレースイスミニ

☎ 3822-6034; 3-3-12 Nishi-Nippori, Arakawa-ku; dishes ¥350-600, fondues ¥3675-5040; ⏰ 10am-7pm Tue, Wed & Sun, 10am-9pm Thu-Sat; ◉ JR Yamanote Line to Nishi-Nippori (south exit); Ⓔ

Somehow this odd little school and cafe works. Nestled among the temples and shrines on a hill, this log house serves fondue (cheese or meat), and pasta or sandwich lunch sets (¥900 to ¥1260), or coffee, herbal tea and pastries, often to children who have left class upstairs. If you want chocolate fondue (¥1800 per person, minimum of two), order it a couple of days in advance.

ASAKUSA

Despite the fact that Sensō-ji is Tokyo's most-frequented tourist attraction, the neighbourhood itself retains its own working-class, laugh-out-loud character. Delightfully, almost none of the restaurants cater to tourists, and so, here you are, just another person in the neighbourhood to be fed and then sent gently on your way. There's also a branch of Kanda Yabu Soba (p164) here.

ASAKUSA IMAHAN
Map p84   Shabu-Shabu ¥¥¥
浅草今半

☎ 3841-1114; 3-1-12 Nishi-Asakusa, Taitō-ku; lunch courses ¥2100-5250, dinner courses from ¥6300; ⏰ 11.30am-9.30pm; ◉ Ginza Line to Tawaramachi (exit 3); Ⓔ

It's fitting that the original branch of Imahan, the city's most famous chain of *shabu-shabu* restaurants, is located at the edge of Shitamachi. While sitting at low tables on the tatami mats, get happy on sake as your meat and seasonal vegetables simmer. Although it's certainly an expensive affair (prices rise with the quality of the meat ordered), a meal at Imahan is the most dignified way to enjoy this revered culinary treat.

KOMAGATA DOJŌ Map p84   Traditional ¥
駒形どぜう

☎ 3842-4001; 1-7-12 Komagata, Taitō-ku; set meals ¥1500-1700; ⏰ 11am-9pm; ◉ Ginza or Toei Asakusa Line to Asakusa (exits A2 or A4)

The sixth-generation chef running this marvellous restaurant is continuing the tradition of transforming the humble river fish called *dojō* (aka *dozeu*, Japanese loach, which look something like miniature eels) into various incarnations: from grilled to miso-simmered, to stewed on your own private hibachi. The open seating around wide, wooden planks heightens the traditional flavour.

SOMETARŌ Map p84   Okonomiyaki ¥
染太郎

☎ 3844-9502; 2-2-2 Nishi-Asakusa, Taitō-ku; mains ¥390-880; ⏰ noon-10pm; ◉ Ginza Line to Tawaramachi (exit 3); Ⓔ

Sometarō is a fun and funky place to try *okonomiyaki*, savoury Japanese-style pancakes filled with meat, seafood and vegetables that you cook yourself. This historic, vine-covered house is a friendly spot where the menu includes a how-to guide for even the most culinary-challenged.

DAIKOKUYA Map p84   Tempura ¥
大黒家

☎ 3844-1111; 1-38-10 Asakusa, Taitō-ku; mains ¥1500-1950; ⏰ 11am-8.30pm Mon-Fri, 11am-9pm Sat; ◉ Ginza or Toei Asakusa Line to Asakusa (exit 6); Ⓔ

The long line around the building should tell you something about this much-loved tempura place even before you catch the unmistakable fragrance of it. Sneak off to the other branch around the corner if the line seems to put too much distance between you and your *ebi tendon* (tempura prawns over rice).

AKASAKA

This is where both fiscal and governmental business gets done. Good portions of the neighbourhood empty at night as limousines take officials and luminaries elsewhere for secret suppers behind thick doors. But since low-key, nonpower lunches need to happen and movers and shakers often work late, Akasaka has a few real finds in comfortable quarters.

NINJA AKASAKA
Map p88   Contemporary ¥¥¥

忍者赤坂

☎ 5157-3936; www.ninjaakasaka.com; Akasaka Tōkyū Plaza, 2-14-3 Nagata-cho, Chiyoda-ku; set meals from ¥7777; ⏰ 5pm-1am Mon-Sat, 5-11pm Sun; Ⓜ Ginza or Marunouchi Line to Akasaka-mitsuke (Belle Vie exit); Ⓔ

Staff dressed like ninja escort you via trapdoors to your table, take your order and might even perform special ninja magic tricks. Sure it's campy and even touristy, but dude, they're ninjas! Kids will love it, and grown-ups don't have to suffer through bad food. À la carte dishes with ninjafied names ('transformation of tuna and *negi* leek sashimi') are creative but dainty for the price; go for the 10-dish set menus.

HAYASHI
Map p88   Izakaya ¥

林

☎ 3582-4078; 4th fl, 2-14-1 Akasaka, Minato-ku; dishes ¥200-800, yakitori sets ¥1100-1200; ⏰ 5pm-2am Mon-Sat, 5-11pm Sun; Ⓜ Ginza or Marunouchi Line to Akasaka-mitsuke (Belle Vie exit); Ⓔ

Ensconce yourself in your *hori-kotatsu* or on a log bench, drape a napkin made of kimono fabric over your lap, and pretend you're somewhere in the Japan Alps. Kindly staff grill *yakitori* over *irori* (hearths) set into your table and serve it on rustic pottery while you swig *shōchū* from Kyūshū. It's a great place to observe local salarymen and the occasional actor from the theatre down the street. It's upstairs from Lotus Palace.

LOTUS PALACE
Map p88   Vietnamese ¥

ロータスパレス

☎ 5114-0747; 2-14-1 Akasaka, Minato-ku; dishes ¥950-1600; ⏰ 11am-11pm; Ⓜ Ginza or Marunouchi Line to Akasaka-mitsuke (Belle Vie exit); Ⓔ

Lunch and dinner are an absolute steal at this foreigner-friendly Vietnamese noodle shop, which serves up set meals that are centred on huge bowls of *pho* (rice-noodle soup) and rounded out with prawn spring rolls and mung-bean pudding. If you need to put an extra spring in your step, the syrupy Vietnamese coffee with condensed milk will no doubt get you where you want to be.

ROPPONGI

At any given hour, the population of Roppongi probably maintains the highest saturation of ethnic diversity (and perhaps also the highest saturation, drinkwise) in Tokyo. Long the district favoured by randy foreigners and Tokyo party people, it's also adjacent to nearby embassies and upmarket hotels. So while some Roppongi restaurants serve indifferent sustenance to those merely fuelling up for a long night, some of Tokyo's more refined culinary experiences exist amid the madness. Roppongi Hills is a dream for restaurant seekers in a range of budgets (see the boxed text, p175), while the offerings at Tokyo Midtown (p91) are more high end, particularly in its Garden Side building.

INAKAYA
Map p92   zakaya ¥¥

田舎屋

☎ 3408-5040; 5-3-4 Roppongi, Minato-ku; small dishes ¥650-1050, fish & seafood ¥1750-3600; ⏰ 5pm-11pm; Ⓜ Hibiya or Toei Ōedo Line to Roppongi (exit 3)

You're bombarded with greetings at the door, and the action doesn't stop at this old-guard *robatayaki* (a place that grills vegetables, fish and meat to go beautifully with booze). It's a party, it's joyous, it's boisterous – and that goes for the profusion of toothsome dishes as well as the attitude one must have when the bill arrives. Live large!

FUKUZUSHI
Map p92   Sushi & Sashimi ¥¥¥

福寿司

☎ 3402-4116; 5-7-8 Roppongi, Minato-ku; lunch sets ¥2656-4725, dinner sets from ¥6300; ⏰ 11am-2pm & 5-11pm Mon-Sat; Ⓜ Hibiya or Toei Ōedo Line to Roppongi (exit 3)

Arguably some of Tokyo's best sushi is served at Fukuzushi's lovely wooden counter, where the chefs can satisfy your palate with conventional favourites, but can just

BEAM ME TO THE KONBINI

Konbini (コンビニ; convenience stores) are a way of life for many Tokyoites, and even if you had never set foot in one at home you may find yourself visiting them daily here. Indeed, there seems to be a Sunkus, AM-PM, Lawson, 7-Eleven or Family Mart on just about every corner. Here's the difference: Japanese convenience-store food tends to be both fresh and of decent quality, and whether you're going home after a late night or heading out on a hike, it's hard to do better than their basic *bentos*, drinks and chocolates. Here are some other *konbini* staples:

Inari-sushi (いなり寿司) Sushi rice in a tofu pouch. If you find it a little sweet, cut it with soy sauce.

Niku-man (肉まん) Steamed buns filled with pork, pizza flavourings, curry sauce and more.

Oden (おでん) Fish cakes, hard-boiled egg, vegetables and more, stewed in a *dashi* (fish-stock) broth. Enjoy with hot mustard. It's not winter without it.

Onigiri (おにぎり) King of them all. A triangle of rice with a dollop of some treasure inside (salmon, tuna salad, marinated kelp etc), wrapped in a plastic sheath together with a sheet of *nori* (seaweed).

as easily piece together something more innovative if you wish. Reservations aren't taken at this popular spot, so plan on a few minutes' wait – it's a small inconvenience for great sushi. Dress code for gents: no sleeveless shirts.

SHABU-ZEN ROPPONGI
Map p92   Shabu-Shabu ¥¥¥

しゃぶ禅六本木

☎ 3585-5600; Aoba Roppongi Bldg B1, 3-16-33 Roppongi, Minato-ku; meals from ¥3600; 🕙 11am-11.30pm Mon-Sat, 11am-11pm Sun; 🚇 Hibiya or Toei Ōedo Line to Roppongi (exit 5); Ⓔ
This nationwide group of some 20 *shabu-shabu* speciality restaurants started right here in Roppongi. Single-order set menus start at ¥3600, but most guests plonk down an extra ¥600 for *tabe-hōdai* (all you can eat). Prices continue to rise further with the grade of beef and if you add extras, including the fearsome *fugu* (blowfish; course from ¥6100). Superclean rooms offer a choice of table or *zashiki* (tatami mat) seating and a bonafide non-smoking section. Shabu-Zen is downstairs from the Hobgoblin bar.

NIRVANA NEW YORK
Map p92   Indian ¥¥

ニルヴァーナニューヨーク

☎ 5647-8305; Tokyo Midtown, Minato-ku; dishes ¥1200-2400, dinner courses ¥3000-8000; 🕙 11am-midnight Mon-Sat, 11am-11pm Sun; 🚇 Hibiya or Toei Ōedo Line to Roppongi (exit 8); Ⓔ
Upmarket Tokyo Midtown's signature Indian eatery is shiny and sceney. Nirvana's butter-chicken curry has fans all over town. If dinner's a bit pricey, the lunch buffet (¥2000) is practically a steal; the half-dozen desserts alone would cost that

much elsewhere. In warm weather, order a beer and preen like a pasha on the terrace overlooking the little people on Midtown Garden.

MOTI
Map p92   Indian ¥¥

モティ

☎ 3479-1939; 6-2-35 Roppongi, Minato-ku; mains ¥1350-2310, set lunches ¥1000-1450; 🕙 11.30am-10pm; 🚇 Hibiya or Toei Ōedo Line to Roppongi (exits 1C or 3)
Loved by local expats, Moti maintains a loyal base of foodies who come for the set lunches and well-seasoned curries. Settle into one of the comfortable booths and watch as first one embassy staffer and then another comes and goes. Moti can fill to the rafters around noon.

SUJI'S
Map p92   American ¥¥

スジズ

☎ 3505-4490; 3-1-5 Azabudai, Minato-ku; sandwiches & brunches ¥900-1500, mains ¥1200-2500; 🕙 11am-11pm Mon-Fri, 9am-11pm Sat & Sun; 🚇 Hibiya or Toei Ōedo Line to Roppongi (exit 5); Ⓔ
Suji's is a landmark for homesick Yanks and Japanese craving a bite of the Big Apple. Weekend brunch is always busy thanks to eggs Benedict, pancakes, smoked-salmon bagels, and breakfast burritos. Suji's house-cured meats (pastrami, corned beef, honey-cured ham etc) are a rarity in Tokyo.

HU TONG SAN LA JU
Map p92   Chinese ¥¥

胡同三辣居
フートンサンラーキョ

☎ 5770-2280; 5-10-19 Roppongi, Minato-ku; dishes ¥880-1980; 🕙 11.30am-2.30pm daily, 5.30-10pm Sun-Thu, 5.30-11pm Fri & Sat; 🚇 Hibiya

or Toei Ōedo Line to Roppongi (exit 3), Namboku or Toei Ōedo Line to Azabu-Jūban (exit 7); **E**
Walking into this two-storey spot on a corner near Roppongi Hills is like walking across the Sea of Japan. There are white-washed walls reminiscent of Shanghai, plus Peking duck, Sichuan-style dishes, renowned dumplings and service more typical of Beijing than snooty Edo. Dishes are typically meant for sharing.

HONMURA-AN Map p92 — Soba ¥
本むら庵
☎ 5772-6657; 7-14-18 Roppongi, Minato-ku; dishes ¥980-2625; ⏰ noon-3pm & 5.30-10pm Tue-Fri, noon-9.30pm Sat & Sun, closed 1st & 3rd Tue of each month; Ⓜ Hibiya or Toei Ōedo Line to Roppongi (exit 4b); **E**
The soba is made right here at this mini-malist noodle shop on a Roppongi side street; try these delicately flavoured noodles on a bamboo mat, with tempura or with dainty slices of *kamo* (duck). Hon-mura-An had legions of fans from when it was a famed and fashionable shop in Lower Manhattan; the owner has since returned home and created legions of fans here, too.

HAINAN JEEFAN SHOKUDŌ
Map p92 — Singaporean ¥
海南鶏飯食堂
☎ 5474-3200; 6-11-16 Roppongi, Minato-ku; mains ¥850-1300; ⏰ 11.30am-3pm & 6-11pm; Ⓜ Hibiya or Toei Ōedo Line to Roppongi (exits 1C & 3); **E**
This cosy, white-walled 'hawker-style Asian canteen' is a small slice of Singapore near Roppongi Hills. Hainan-style chicken rice, Singapore's national dish, is the special-ity; the steamed chicken and rice spring to life with the addition of accompanying sauces (detailed eating instructions of-fered), alongside other sprightly dishes. It's located in the alley behind the market 'Foo:d magazine'.

ICHIRAN Map p92 — Rāmen ¥
一蘭
☎ 3796-7281; 2nd fl, 4-11-11 Roppongi, Minato-ku; rāmen ¥790; ⏰ 11am-6pm; Ⓜ Hibiya or Toei Ōedo Line to Roppongi (exits 4a or 7); **E**
Steps from Tokyo Midtown and a world away in attitude, purchase a ticket from a vending machine and cram yourself into a one-person booth. Check off your choice on a little paper menu (broth, richness,

SELF-CATERING

Serious foodies will want to hit the elegant department store basement food halls (*depachika*; see p162), while casual visitors will do well enough with convenience stores (*konbini*; see opposite). In between, family-owned grocers dot the city, selling seasonal produce and daily basics. Then there are international supermarkets catering to Western palates. Although they charge import prices, fussy expats would starve without them.

- **Kinokuniya International Supermarket** (Map p106; ☎ 3409-1236; 3-11-7 Kita-Aoyama, Minato-ku; ⏰ 9.30am-8pm; Ⓜ Chiyoda, Ginza or Hanzōmon Line to Omote-sandō, exit B2) Kinokuniya carries expat lifesavers such as Marmite and peanut butter, Belgian chocolate and herbal tea. Foreign imports such as cheese, salami and Finnish bread generally fetch high prices, much like the flawless produce.
- **Meidi-ya** (Map p92; ☎ 3401-8511; 7-15-14 Roppongi, Minato-ku; ⏰ 10am-9pm; Ⓜ Hibiya Line to Roppongi, exit 2) Established in the 19th century, not too long after strangers in black ships started arriving on Japan's shores, Meidi-ya specialises in higher-end groceries for foreign predilections. It's a midsized store with a corre-sponding selection of goods. There are other locations throughout the city.
- **National Azabu** (Map p92; ☎ 3442-3181; 4-5-2 Minami-Azabu, Minato-ku; ⏰ 9.30am-7pm; Ⓜ Hibiya Line to Hiro-o, exit 2) Deep in the '*gaijin* ghetto', National Azabu carries an impressive array of expat staples such as imported cheeses, wines, Vegemite and natural foods, as well as hard-to-find produce. Also notable is the pharmacy with English-speaking staff and the small bookshop upstairs.
- **Natural House** (Map p106; ☎ 3498-2277; 3-6-18 Kita-Aoyama, Minato-ku; ⏰ 10am-10pm; Ⓜ Chiyoda, Ginza or Hanzōmon Line to Omote-sandō, exit B4) Natural House serves the ecoconscious trendsters around Aoyama, meeting a growing demand for wholefood and organic produce. Along with bricks of rye loaves and pricey but nutritious *bentō* (boxed lunch), Natural House also peddles natural beauty products and health supplements.
- **Yamaya** (Map p88; ☎ 3583-5657; 2-14-33 Akasaka, Minato-ku; ⏰ 10am-9pm; Ⓜ Chiyoda Line to Akasaka, exit 2) Yamaya's shelves are stuffed primarily with European wines, though there's also a representative selection of American and Australian wines as well. Most branches are discount retailers and offer some imported packaged foods in addition to wine and liquor.

garlic, tenderness etc), push a button, and a curtain levitates to where your *rāmen* is delivered through a curtain. It's either the ultimate Zen experience or the ultimate in dislocation.

NISHI-AZABU

GONPACHI Map p92   Izakaya, Soba, Sushi ¥¥
権八
☎ 5771-0170; 1-13-11 Nishi-Azabu, Minato-ku; dishes ¥290-1280, lunch sets ¥900-1050; ⏰ 11.30am-5am; ◉ Hibiya or Toei Ōedo Line to Roppongi (exit 1); Ⓔ

Old Japan hands deride this foreigner-friendly institution on the busy Nishi-Azabu crossing, but many of them probably had their first meal in Japan here. The first two storeys are a cavernous glam space where Quentin Tarantino shot *Kill Bill*, and now soba and *kushiyaki* (skewers) are served here. A separate 3rd floor specialises in sushi. Another location in Odaiba (Map p127; ☎ 3599-4807; 4th fl, Aqua City Odaiba, 1-7-1 Daiba, Minato-ku; ⏰ 11am-11pm) features *kushiyaki* and soba only, enjoyed with sweeping views.

TOKYO TOWER AREA

TOFUYA-UKAI Map p92   Tofu ¥¥¥
とうふ屋うかい
☎ 3436-1028; www.ukai.co.jp; 4-4-13 Shiba Kōen, Minato-ku; lunch courses ¥5500-6500, dinner courses ¥8400-12,600; ⏰ 11am-10pm; ◉ Toei Ōedo Line to Akabanebashi (exit 8); Ⓔ

Make your reservations when you book your flights. You'll be glad you did, for this is perhaps Tokyo's most gracious restau-rant, in a former sake brewery moved from northern Japan and an exquisite garden in shadow of Tokyo Tower. Seasonal preparations of the namesake tofu and accompanying dishes are served in more ways than you may have thought possible, in *kaiseki* style.

EBISU & DAIKANYAMA

Ebisu and Daikanyama, though not on most short-term visitors' radar, are home to a grown-up creative community of 30- and 40-something designers, artists and architects. As such, the neighbourhoods are full of independent boutiques and European-style cafes, and the area's sophisticated aesthetics and flavours reflect a hip and worldly population.

EBISU

RICO'S KITCHEN Map p96   International ¥¥
リコスキッチン
☎ 5791-4649; 2nd fl, 4-23-7 Ebisu, Shibuya-ku; dinner course ¥5775, brunch course ¥2940; ⏰ 6-11pm Tue-Sun & 11.30am-3pm Sat & Sun; ◉ JR Yamanote Line to Ebisu (east exit)

From light and fruity California wines to juicy New Zealand rack of lamb, this international bistro brings together the best flavours from around the globe to create some truly innovative meals. With vaulted wooden ceilings and a wall of fanciful line-drawing portraits, the setting at Rico's Kitchen is personal and relaxed, which makes this the perfect spot for slowing down and enjoying the art of fine cuisine.

AISUKURIIMU, YŪSUKURIIMU...

Although most Japanese had never tried dairy products until the Meiji Period, Japan has taken a big licking to *aisukuriimu* (ice cream), from a delicate scoop of green-tea flavour after a *kaiseki* dinner to Dippin' Dots at the playgrounds of Odaiba.

A deliciously convenient landmark/meeting place at Nishi-Azabu Crossing, Hobson's (Map p92; ☎ 3406-0962; 4-1-1 Nishi-Azabu, Minato-ku; ice cream ¥230-460; ⏰ 11am-3am Sun-Thu, 11am-4am Fri & Sat; ◉ Hibiya or Toei Ōedo Line to Roppongi, exit 1C; Ⓔ) is originally from Santa Barbara, California, but has been here since 1985. Familiar ice-cream and frozen-yoghurt flavours still tempt, alongside Japanese tastes like *yuzu* (citron), sweet potato and *mikan* (mandarin orange). Try a 'blend-in', where fruit, cookies and such (¥50 each) are added using what looks like a giant drill.

Ouca (Map p96; ☎ 5449-0037; 1-6-6 Ebisu, Shibuya-ku; ice cream from ¥380; ⏰ 11am-11.30pm or until sold out; ◉ JR Yamanote Line to Ebisu, east exit, or Hibiya Line to Ebisu, exit 1) in Ebisu takes it even further, with fresh-made flavours and toppings including black sesame, *shio konbu* (salted kelp), pumpkin and *karinto* (crunchy brown sugar snacks).

THE OCTOPUS & THE SEA BREAM

Riding a nostalgia wave, two old-school street snacks are back, and there are two stands in Meguro's MISC (p145) design district selling them – with 21st-century twists.

Ganko Dako (Map p96; ☎ 5725-6696; 3-11-6 Meguro, Meguro-ku; takoyaki ¥500; ⏰ 11am-1am; ⊕ JR Yamanote Line, Namboku Line or Mita Line to Meguro, west exit) dispenses *takoyaki*: spherical dumplings with a morsel of *tako* (octopus) inside. Toppings include green onion, kimchi and the traditional Worcestershire sauce. Taiyaki Fujiya (Map p96; ☎ 3716-8187; 3-11-9 Meguro, Meguro-ku; taiyaki ¥150; ⏰ 11am-10pm; ⊕ JR Yamanote Line, Namboku Line or Mita Line to Meguro, west exit) sells *taiyaki*: sweet dumplings shaped like the festive *tai* (sea bream). In addition to the traditional *anko* (bean paste) filling, *taiyaki* here come filled with chocolate, custard, *kurogoma* (black sesame) or *matcha* (green tea) flavours. Elsewhere, look for *taiyaki* and *takoyaki* in traditional flavours at street fairs.

KIMUKATSU Map p96   Tonkatsu ¥
キムカツ

☎ 5420-2929; 4-9-5 Ebisu, Shibuya-ku; lunch sets $1260, mains ¥1480, set menus from ¥2460; ⏰ 11.30am-11pm Mon-Thu, 11.30am-11.30pm Fri & Sat; ⊕ Hibiya Line to Ebisu (exit 1), JR Yamanote Line to Ebisu (east exit)

You can find *tonkatsu* throughout Tokyo, but this rustically contemporary shop serves it millefeuille style, with the pork sliced and stacked before breading and frying, which makes it unusually light and juicy. Expect a line out the door at lunchtime. From JR Ebisu Station east exit, bear diagonally to the right, and the restaurant is past the stop light, down the block from FedEx.

ZEST CANTINA EBISU Map p96   Mexican ¥
ゼストキャンティーナ恵比寿

☎ 5475-6291; 1-22-19 Ebisu, Shibuya-ku; dishes ¥760-2600; ⏰ 11.30am-3.30am Mon-Sat; ⊕ JR Yamanote Line to Ebisu (east exit); Ⓔ

You'd be forgiven for thinking you were eating Tex-Mex somewhere in America after walking into this cavernous Ebisu institution. Although the jumbo margaritas, enormous bowls of nachos and sizzling hotplates of fajitas are reason enough to stop by, there's something endearing about Japanese waiting staff in cowboy boots and hats.

DAIKANYAMA

BOMBAY BAZAAR Map p96   International ¥¥
ボンベイバザー

☎ 5489-1346; 20-11 Sarugaku-cho, Shibuya-ku; mains ¥650-1200; ⏰ noon-8pm; ⊕ Tōkyū Tōyoko Line to Daikanyama (main exit); Ⓔ

This basement cafe, beneath Okura (p145) clothing shop, is funky (but not junky), artsy, antique-y and woodsy…in short, supercool. There's a spin-the-globe menu of light fare (pizza, pasta, curries, tempura), as well as baked goods all made in house. A real find.

EATALY Map p96   Italian ¥
イータリー

☎ 5784-2736; 2nd fl, 20-23 Daikanyama-cho, Shibuya-ku; mains ¥980-2500; ⏰ 10am-9.30pm; ⊕ Tōkyū Tōyoko Line to Daikanyama (main exit)

In this neighbourhood – in this city – that worships all things Italian, airy, rambling Eataly is one-stop shopping: trattoria, bakery, espresso bar, *salumeria*, cheese shop, wine shop and outdoor cafe. Even the shopping carts are so cute that you'll want to pinch their little shopping-cart cheeks.

SIGN Map p96   French ¥
サイン

☎ 3780-9570; Daikanyama Station Bldg, 19-4 Daikanyama-chō, Shibuya-ku; mains ¥980-1680; ⏰ 11am-11pm; ⊕ Tōkyū Tōyoko Line to Daikanyama (main exit)

Situate yourself on the terrace or inside the glass jewel box of a room at this stylish cafe, right at the exit to Daikanyama station, for some of the neighbourhood's best people-watching, while poppy music plays in the background. You *could* snack on galettes, *poulet basque* or fruit tarts, but the shop is really famous for curry rice.

SHIBUYA

After seeing the teenagers cruising Shibuya Crossing and clusters of young fashionistas awaiting their cohorts at Hachikō Plaza, your attention span might only allow you a quick bite at a greasy spoon near the station before darting back into the melee. But for those nights when you need a bigger gastronomic thrill, stray outwards onto the streets spoking away from Shibuya Station and discover the neighbourhood's more-sophisticated delights.

COUCAGNO Map p102   French ¥¥¥
クーカーニョ

☎ 3476-3000; 40th fl, Cerulean Tower, 26-1 Sakuragaokachō, Shibuya-ku; lunch courses ¥4100-5600, dinner courses from ¥6500; ⏰ 11.30am-2pm & 5.30-10pm; Ⓜ JR Yamanote, Ginza or Hanzōmon Line to Shibuya (Hachikō exit); Ⓔ

Few restaurants in Tokyo can claim more-stunning views than the highly praised Coucagno, which occupies the 40th floor of the Cerulean Tower, one of the most dramatic buildings in both Shibuya and Tokyo. From such lofty heights, the Shibuya street scene looks as if it's populated by tiny ants, though attention quickly shifts to the food once the chef gets going. As you'd expect, everything from the delicate sauces drizzled across your roast duck to the perfect crust atop your crème brûlée is indeed a class act.

OKINAWA Map p102   Izakaya, Okinawan ¥¥
沖縄

☎ 3464-2576; 1Bfl, Shibuya Deli Tower, 2-23-13 Dōgenzaka, Shibuya-ku; dishes ¥650-1100; ⏰ noon-2pm Mon-Fri, 5.30pm-midnight Mon-Thu, 5.30pm-1am Fri, noon-1am Sat, noon-11pm Sun; Ⓜ JR Yamanote, Ginza or Hanzōmon Line to Shibuya (Hachikō exit)

If you've never been to the far-flung tropical islands of Okinawa, then this speciality izakaya will have you racing to the travel agent. Start things off with a cold Orion beer or a potent glass of awamori (Okinawan-style shōchū), and then jump right into Okinawan staples such as gōya chanpū (sautéed bitter melon and egg), mimiga (pig ears), sōki-soba (Okinawan-style soba) and rafutē (stewed pork belly with brown sugar).

TUCANO'S Map p102   Brazilian ¥
トゥッカーノ

☎ 5784-2661; B1 fl, Phontis Bldg, 2-23-12 Dōgenzaka, Shibuya-ku; lunch ¥880-2980, all you can eat dinner 1½/2hr ¥3300/4000; ⏰ noon-2pm daily, 5.30-11.30pm Mon-Fri, 5-11pm Sat & Sun; Ⓜ JR Yamanote, Ginza or Hanzōmon Line to Shibuya (Hachikō exit); Ⓔ Ⓥ

In this basement bar, waiters rove with churrascaria (Brazilian-style grills) – cuts of beef, pork and chicken, served by the slice off giant skewers. It attracts plenty of Brazilians, particularly on weekends, and Japanese who are curious about samba and other musical performances. Vegetarians, if they can get past the sight of all that meat, will be reasonably satisfied with the buffet that accompanies every churrascaria meal.

SONOMA Map p102   American ¥
ソノマ

☎ 3462-7766; www.moderndining.com/sonoma/index.shtml; 2-25-17 Dōgenzaka, Shibuya-ku; mains ¥900-1200; ⏰ 6-11.30pm Mon-Thu, 6pm-midnight Fri & Sat; Ⓜ JR Yamanote, Ginza or Hanzōmon Line to Shibuya (Hachikō exit); Ⓔ

Favourites such as crispy-skinned salmon with lime aioli, and porterhouse steak with truffle butter form the mainstay of this unpretentiously inspired and priced Californian fusion menu. The interior resembles a Sonoma Wine Country restaurant and the menu is complemented by a strong selection of Californian wines.

CHRISTON CAFÉ Map p102   International ¥
クリストンカフェ

☎ 5728-2225; B2 fl, 2-10-7, Shibuya-ku; mains ¥900-1600; ⏰ 5-11.30pm Sun-Thu, 5pm-4am Fri & Sat; Ⓜ JR Yamanote, Ginza or Hanzōmon Line to Shibuya (Hachikō exit); Ⓔ

Irreverent in the most orthodox sense of the word, this cathedral-like spot fetishises the Catholic aesthetic and turns the dining experience into something your inner goth will love. From its (sort of) English menu, order Italian-inspired selections (think grills, pasta, gorgonzola-and-apple pizza, asparagus rolled in pancetta etc) to share with your brethren and sistren under gigantic altars and doleful images of the Pietà.

EL CASTELLANO Map p102   Spanish ¥
エルカステリャーノ

☎ 3407-7197; 2nd fl, 2-9-12 Shibuya, Shibuya-ku; dishes ¥500-2000; ⏰ 6-11pm Mon-Sat; Ⓜ JR Yamanote, Ginza or Hanzōmon Line to Shibuya (east exit); Ⓔ

El Castellano's longevity (30-plus years!) could be attributed to the warmth of its owner, who casts a friendly eye over the evening's progress and affectionately greets his regulars with sunny Spanish hospitality. But that would discount the definite draw of his home-style cooking, which includes a scrumptiously mean paella and the sangria that goes so well with it.

GYŪBEI Map p102 Yakiniku ¥
牛兵衛
☎ 3770-6060; B1fl, 2-25-5 Dōgenzaka, Shibuya-ku; dishes ¥390-1300; ⏰ 11.30am-3.30pm & 5pm-midnight Mon-Fri, 11.30am-midnight Sat & Sun; ⊜ JR Yamanote, Ginza or Hanzōmon Line to Shibuya (Hachikō exit); Ⓔ
This brick-walled basement workhorse of a Korean barbecue joint is a fine place to grill *kalbi* (short ribs) or chicken in any of four exotic marinades over hot coals set into your table. For an extra treat, order a dish of *namuru* (marinated Korean vegetables) and generous pours of Korean *soju* (what Japan calls *shōchū*). It's across the three-way intersection from both H&M and Tōkyū department store.

NODAIWA off Map pp48-9 Unagi ¥¥
野田岩
☎ 3413-0105; 2-19-15 Kitazawa, Setagaya-ku; mains ¥2100-4730; ⏰ 5-8.30pm Thu-Tue, also noon-2pm Sun; ⊜ Odakyū or Keio Inokashira Line to Shimo-Kitazawa (south exit)
This fifth-generation shop has been serving melt-in-your-mouth *unagi* in this location since the 1960s. There's usually a line out the door, but once you take a seat beneath the country-style beams and tuck into your *ojū* (*unagi* over rice in a classic lacquer box) or *shirayaki-don* (grilled *unagi*) set lunch, you'll understand.

NANBANTEI off Map pp48-9 Okonomiyaki ¥
なんばん亭
☎ 3419-6938; 2nd fl, 2-12-3 Kitazawa, Setagaya-ku; okonomiyaki ¥900-1100; ⏰ 5pm-11pm daily, noon-2pm Sat & Sun; ⊜ Odakyū or Keio Inokashira Line to Shimo-Kitazawa (south exit); Ⓔ
In this studenty pub at the heart of Shimo-kita, knock back a *shōchū* and groove out to the rock'n'roll while a skilled young chef prepares *okonomiyaki* so you don't have to. Recommended combos: *negi-pokkake* (piled high with green onion and beef) and *mikkusu* (a mix of everything). Turn left where you see Softbank, and it's upstairs, next to Cowboy restaurant.

HARAJUKU & AOYAMA

Like the boutiques and galleries that flank Omote-sandō, and the winding lanes that diverge from it, the cafes and eateries in this area are eclectic, running from inexpensive-but-tasty eats to savvy young shoppers to long-standing institutions and good-for-you organic spots.

FONDA DE LA MADRUGADA
Map p106 Mexican ¥¥¥
フォンダデラマドゥルガーダ
☎ 5410-6288; 2Bfl, 2-33-12 Jingūmae, Shibuya-ku; small dishes ¥840-1575, mains ¥1785-3045; ⏰ 5.30pm-2am Sun-Thu, 5.30pm-5am Fri & Sat; ⊜ Fukutoshin Line to Kita-sando (exit 2), JR Yamanote Line to Harajuku (Takeshita exit); Ⓔ
We tend not to trust Mexican cooking outside of Mexico and the border regions, but we make an exception for this rambling restaurant in a sub-basement. Mariachis stroll through the florid, Spanish-style 'courtyard' as you tuck into *enchiladas tricolores* (chicken enchiladas with three colours of mole sauce), surprisingly gourmet fish and meat dishes, and potent margaritas (pay ¥150 extra for the good tequila). The downside: it may be the most expensive Mexican meal we've ever eaten. Still, it's less than a plane ticket to Guadalajara.

MAISEN Map p106 Tonkatsu ¥
まい泉
☎ 3470-0071; 4-8-5 Jingūmae, Shibuya-ku; mains ¥1470-2995; ⏰ 11am-10pm; ⊜ Chiyoda, Ginza or Hanzōmon Line to Omote-sandō (exit A2); Ⓔ
Set in a converted public bathhouse, Maisen is rightfully famous for its *tonkatsu*. In addition to regular pork, other fries include prawns and *korokke* (croquettes), all served with heaps of shredded cabbage and sweet or spicy sauces. There's also a takeaway window for picking up *tonkatsu bentō*.

NABI Map p106 Korean ¥
ナビ
☎ 5771-0071; 2-31-20 Jingūmae, Shibuya-ku; mains ¥1050-1260; ⏰ 11.30am-4pm & 6-11.30pm; ⊜ JR Yamanote Line to Harajuku (Takeshita exit), Chiyoda or Fukutoshin Line to Meiji-jingūmae (exit 5); Ⓔ
There seems to be *yakiniku* on every corner in Tokyo these days, but this contemporary spot concentrates on home-style Korean

cooking: *dak-hanmali* (whole chicken in broth; ¥4200), *bibimbap* (rice and marinated vegetables), *sundubu jiggae* (spicy tofu stew) and *samgyeupsal* (pork belly), which you can wrap in *ssam* (leaves of sesame and lettuce). Bonus: it's organic. The biggest problem is finding it. From Meiji-dori, head into the alley left of the Diesel shop.

MOMINOKI HOUSE Map p106   Organic ¥
モミノキハウス

☎ 3405-9144; 2-18-5 Jingūmae, Shibuya-ku; dishes ¥980-2480; ◷ 11am-11pm; ◉ JR Yamanote Line to Harajuku (Takeshita exit), Chiyoda or Fukutoshin Line to Meiji-jingūmae (exit 5); Ⓔ Ⓥ
Since 1976 boho Tokyoites and personages such as Paul McCartney and Stevie Wonder have descended into Mominoki House's multilevel rabbit warren of a dining room. Chef Yamada's menu is heavily vegetarian – with an emphasis on *seitan* (gluten) and tofu – but also includes free-range chicken and *Ezo shika* (Hokkaidō venison; ¥4800). Food here is lovingly prepared, and enriching to both body and soul.

LAS CHICAS Map p106   International, Cafe ¥
ラスチカス

☎ 3407-6865; 5-47-6 Jingūmae, Shibuya-ku; dishes around ¥1500; ◷ 11.30am-11pm Mon-Thu, 11.30am-11.30pm Fri, 11am-11.30pm Sat, 11am-11pm Sun; ◉ Chiyoda, Ginza or Hanzōmon Line to Omote-sandō (exit A2); Ⓔ
Urbane and relaxed, Las Chicas draws an international crowd with its artsy location, unfussy cuisine and friendly foreign staff. Its inviting terrace being a rarity in Tokyo, you might have to – sigh – settle for a place at the bar. An English menu details comfort food with fun twists, like the Caligula, its version of the Caesar salad. From Aoyama-dōri, turn down the side street with Muji (無印良品) on the corner.

YAKI-IMO...

You hear it before you see it, and you smell it before you taste it. The 'it' is *yaki-imo* (roasted whole sweet potatoes), sold from October to March from carts roving the city, much as ice-cream trucks do elsewhere. On a cold day, these stone-roasted treats warm your hands and your insides. Bull horns on the carts croon recordings of a male voice chanting '*yaki-imohhhhh...!*' (the first notes sound like a sombre 'Here Comes the Bride'). Figure on about ¥300/500 for a small/large *yaki-imo*.

KYŪSYŪ JANGARA Map p106   Ramen ¥
九州じゃんがら

☎ 3404-5572; 1-13-21 Jingūmae, Shibuya-ku; dishes ¥600-1050; ◷ 10.45am-2am Mon-Thu, 10.45am-3am Fri, 10am-3am Sat, 10am-2am Sun; ◉ JR Yamanote Line to Harajuku (Omote-sandō exit), Chiyoda or Fukutoshin Line to Meiji-jingūmae (exit 3); Ⓔ
There always seems to be a line for seats outside this Kyūshū-style *rāmen* shop near Harajuku Station, and with good reason: elegantly thin noodles, your choice of a half-dozen broths, silky *chashu* (roast pork), righteous *karashi takana* (hot pickled greens) and energetic staff. Even the background music is cool, like *Riverdance* played on electric *shamisen* (three-stringed instrument). Look for it above Indio clothing shop.

HEIROKU SUSHI Map p106   Sushi & Sashimi ¥
平禄寿司

☎ 3498-3968; 5-8-5 Jingūmae, Shibuya-ku; dishes ¥130-480; ◷ 11am-9.30pm Mon-Sat, 11am-9pm Sun; ◉ Chiyoda or Fukutoshin Line to Meiji-jingūmae (exit 4), Chiyoda, Ginza or Hanzōmon Line to Omote-sandō (exit A1)
Kaiten (conveyor belt) sushi was long looked down on, but it's gained new popularity in Japan's recession age; this neat but utilitarian shop in the heart of chic Omote-Sandō is living proof. *Itamae* (sushi chefs) plonk cuts of sushi on plates colour-coded to their prices. Sit at the counter, choose what you like, and total up the plates for what works out to be a pretty good deal. We've seen nonsushi dishes come around, too: edamame, orange slices, even strawberries and cream.

SHINJUKU

At the end of the work day, a few million sturdy pairs of shoes carry Shinjuku's workforce out of office doors towards the train stations. To avoid the worst of rush hour, most stop along the way for *yakitori* or *rāmen*, or a more convivial sit-down affair with colleagues. Once you're inside most eateries on the eastern side of the station, the pace slows and the light show outside disappears. On the western side, restaurants within the towers of the luxury hotels and shopping malls are designed for the view hungry, including the restaurant floors of Takashimaya Times Square and Shinjuku NS Tower (see the boxed text, p162).

SPOILT FOR CHOICE

Can't decide between sukiyaki or spaghetti, *tonkatsu* or teacakes, or maybe you just like to peek inside a restaurant before you commit? Many Tokyo office and shopping complexes have entire restaurant floors where you can stroll the corridors and peek at menus or plastic food models for a DIY dinner. Hours vary by establishment, but if you go between about 11.30am and 9.30pm you'll most certainly find something worthwhile. Here are some standouts to go walkabout:

- Caretta (Map p64; www.caretta.jp; Higashi-Shimbashi 1-8-2; ⓢ Ginza Line, exit 4; Toei Asakusa or JR Yamanote Line to Shimbashi, Shiodome Shio-site exit; Toei Ōedo Line to Shiodome, exit for Shimbashi Station) Staying in Shiodome? This office building has restaurants upstairs (46th and 47th floors) and down (basement levels), including branches of Din Tai Fung (p160) and Toraji (p160).
- Marunouchi Building (Map p52; www.marunouchi.com/marubiru; 2-4-1 Marunouchi, Chiyoda-ku; ⓜ Marunouchi Line to Tokyo, exit 4b, JR Yamanote Line to Tokyo, Marunouchi exit) Out the Marunouchi exit of Tokyo Station, 'Marubiru' overflows with over 75 options for all budgets and tastes, including soaring, pricey Italian, *kaiseki* and Chinese on the 35th and 36th floors, Hawaiian hamburgers to Fukuoka *rāmen* on the 5th and 6th, and casual and takeaway in the basement.
- Shin-Marunouchi Building (Map p52; www.marunouchi.com/shinmaru; 2-5-1 Marunouchi, Chiyoda-ku; ⓜ Marunouchi Line to Tokyo, exit 4b, JR Yamanote Line to Tokyo, Marunouchi exit) North of Marubiru, the 5th through 7th floors of (you guessed it) 'Shin-Marubiru' are gorgeously decked out like a ramble through old Edo.
- Roppongi Hills (p90) Like the mall around it, the restaurant options at Roppongi Hills are head spinning. It makes more sense if you concentrate on one building: Metro Hat options are more budget-friendly, Hillside gets fancier with spots like L'Atelier de Joël Robuchon, while the Grand Hyatt's French Kitchen and Shunbou are splurgeworthy.
- Shinjuku NS Building (新宿NSビル; Map p110; 2-4-1 Marunouchi, Chiyoda-ku; ⓢ Toei Ōedo Line to Tochōmae, exits A7 or C4) Take the glass lift to the 29th floor for one of Shinjuku's largest restaurant extravaganzas, and stroll the catwalk across the atrium!
- Takashimaya Times Square (Map p110; 5-24-2 Sendagaya, Shibuya-ku; ⓜ JR Yamanote Line to Shinjuku, new south exit) The 12th to 14th floors of this upmarket department store are foodie heaven. Sandaya Honten (below) and Ningyōchō Imahan (below) are among the dozens of choices.

NEW YORK GRILL
Map p110   Steak House ¥¥¥
ニューヨークグリル
☎ 5323-3458; 52nd fl, Park Hyatt Tokyo, 3-7-1-2 Nishi-Shinjuku, Shinjuku-ku; dinner mains ¥4600-11,000, set meals lunch/dinner from ¥5200/11,000; ⏱ 11.30am-2.30pm & 5.30-10.30pm; ⓜ Toei Ōedo Line to Tochōmae (exit A4); Ⓔ
You may not be staying at the Park Hyatt, but don't let that stop you from ascending to the 52nd floor to swoon over the stunning views of the city below. Prices may be as high as the altitude, but where else can you splurge on a romantic, sumptuous supper enhanced by sparkling night-time lights and live jazz? And in case everything looks familiar, the adjacent New York Grill & Bar (p183) was where Bill Murray drank glass upon glass of Suntory whiskey in Sofia Coppola's *Lost in Translation*. Reservations are advised, especially on weekends and for brunch.

SANDAYA HONTEN Map p110 Steak House ¥¥¥
三田屋本店
☎ 5361-1870; 14th fl, Takashimaya Times Square, 5-24-2 Sendagaya, Shibuya-ku; set meals lunch ¥1995-2940, dinner ¥4935-5985; ⏱ 11am-10pm; ⓜ JR Shinjuku, new south exit; Ⓔ
If the New York Grill is glitzy and Western, Sandaya delivers *wagyū* (Japanese beef) in a humbler Japanese style, though you still get both the steak and the sizzle. Slices of beef arrive on a *teppan* (hot steel plate) piled high with onions and other veggies that cook while your steak does. Eat it with chopsticks while a live *koto* or piano player entertains. Meals come with soup, salad, rice, dessert and coffee. Our only disappointment: the limited wine selection.

NINGYŌCHŌ IMAHAN
Map p110   Sukiyaki & Shabu-Shabu ¥¥
人形町今半
☎ 5361-1871; 14th fl, Takashimaya Times Square, 5-24-2 Sendagaya, Shibuya-ku; lunch sets ¥1575-3990, dinner sets ¥4515-10,605; ⏱ 11am-11pm; ⓜ JR Yamanote Line to Shinjuku (new south exit); Ⓔ
Down the hall from Sandaya, elegant Imahan is also all about beef, served as sukiyaki and *shabu-shabu;* there's even a board showing (in Japanese) where the meats

of the day come from. Also look for such delicacies as *fugu*, marbled beef sashimi and scaled-down *kaiseki* dinners. Come with comrades, as this cookery is meant to be shared for maximum merriment.

KUSHIYA MONOGATARI
Map p110   Traditional ¥¥

串家物語

☎ 5321-6166; 5th fl, Sunflower Bldg, 1-3-1 Nishi-Shinjuku, Shinjuku-ku; set menu ¥2625; ☺ 4-11pm daily, 11.30-3pm Sat & Sun; ◎ Toei Ōedo Line to Shinjuku Nishi-Guchi (exit D4), JR Yamanote Line to Shinjuku (west exit)

The Tokyo branch of this popular Osaka chain specialises in *kushiage*, which are deep-fried skewers of grilled meats, fish and vegetables. For the bargain price of only ¥2625, you have up to 90 minutes to fry up at your tabletop as many skewers as you'd like. Since this is one of the few Japanese foods where it's probably best to go easy and consider your waistline, there are also salads and rice.

OMOIDE-YOKOCHŌ
Map p110   Yakitori ¥

思い出横丁

Nishi-Shinjuku 1-chōme, Shinjuku-ku; skewers from ¥100; ◎ JR Yamanote Line to Shinjuku (west exit), Marunouchi or Toei-Ōedo Line to Shinjuku Nishiguchi (exit D3)

Since the postwar days, smoke has been billowing nightly from the little shacks lining this alley by the train tracks, purveying *yakitori* and cold beers to long-time regulars. Literally translated as 'Memory Lane' (and less politely known as Shoben-yokochō, 'Piss Alley') Omoide-yokochō may actually be just a memory someday; there's been on-again, off-again talk of razing it to make way for new development. Stop by at around 7pm to indulge in a few skewers and some pre-emptive nostalgia.

IKEBUKURO & TAKADANOBABA

East of Ikebukuro station, eateries tend to be cheap, uninspired and jammed with young salarymen and commuters. There are better pickings west of the station, including the block-long Gurume-michi (Gourmet Street; グルメ道), which boasts some good choices, even if its name is overblown.

Takadanobaba, at the crossroads of several universities, has its artsy cafes and international restaurants (Thai, Cambodian, Indian and of course Japanese) catering to students with big appetites and small budgets. Waseda-dōri and its neighbouring streets offer particularly good grazing.

IKEBUKURO

MALAYCHAN
Map p116   Malaysian ¥

マレーチャン

☎ 5391-7638; 3-22-6 Nishi-Ikebukuro, Toshima-ku; mains ¥740-1680, dinner ¥2100-2400; ☺ 5am-11pm Mon, 11am-11pm Sun & Tue-Thu, 11am-midnight Fri & Sat; ◎ JR Yamanote Line to Ikebukuro (west exit), Yurakucho, Fukutoshin or Marunouchi Line to Ikebukuro (exit 1a)

If you've never tried Malaysian cooking, it's like a mix of Thai and Indonesian with a bit of Indian thrown in, redolent with chilli, lemon grass, garlic and dried prawns. At this cosy, corner, halal eatery at the end of Ikebukuro's Gourmet Street, start off with spring rolls, chicken satay and *murtabak* (ground chicken crêpes) then move on to savoury curries and *nasi goreng* (fried rice).

AKIYOSHI
Map p116   Yakitori ¥

秋吉

☎ 3982-0601; 3-30-4 Nishi-Ikebukuro, Toshima-ku; dishes around ¥500; ☺ 5-11pm; ◎ JR Yamanote Line to Ikebukuro (west exit), Yurakucho, Fukutoshin or Marunouchi Line to Ikebukuro (exit 1a)

If you're in the mood for *yakitori*, Akiyoshi is an approachable, ebullient place to partake. The open grill at centre stage ignites a festive, sociable space. The chefs work quickly to help move traffic along, but that doesn't mean you can't sit comfortably through several small courses and at least one conversation.

ANPUKU
Map p116   Udon ¥

あんぷく

☎ 6915-2646; 1-37-8 Nishi-Ikebukuro, Toshima-ku; mains ¥680-1380; ☺ 11am-3pm & 5pm-midnight Mon-Thu, 11am-5am Fri & Sat, 11am-midnight Sun; ◎ JR Yamanote Line to Ikebukuro (west exit), Yurakucho, Fukutoshin or Marunouchi Line to Ikebukuro (exit C9); Ⓔ

Udon goes international at this new spiffy little white-walled cafe. Creative young chefs make the noodles right there and put them in *so* not Japanese dishes: carbonara, chicken with mushrooms in cream sauce or spicy Sichuan eggplant. It's eaten with chopsticks, so staff supply you with a paper bib. There's also stellar traditional udon for purists, and side dishes including grills.

TAKADANOBABA AREA

TAVERNA Map p116 — Italian ¥
タベルナ

☎ 3232-1997; 2-5-10 Takadanobaba, 2nd fl, Shinjuku-ku; dishes around ¥1000, set meals ¥1980-3880; ☽ 5-11pm Mon-Sat; ⊚ JR Yamanote Line to Takadanobaba (main exit), Tōzai Line to Takadanobaba (exit 4); Ⓔ
Here are some reasons this cosy, Roman-inspired spot has been here forever: spaghetti *all'amatriciana* (with bacon and tomato sauce) or *vongole* (clams, olive oil and garlic), and pizza *mista* (with anchovy, tuna and prosciutto). Some people eat here every night, inspired by the authentic cuisine, the charm of the owner and reasonable prices.

MUCHA-AN Map pp48-9 — Soba ¥
無茶庵

☎ 3943-5481; 2-10-8 Sekiguchi, Bunkyō-ku; mains ¥1100-1890; ☽ 5pm-9pm daily, plus 11.30am-3.30pm Mon-Fri; ⊚ JR Yūrakuchō Line to Edogawabashi (exit 1a), Toden Arakawa Line to Waseda
Perched on a hill inside Chinzan-sō garden, this shop in a wood-built former ryokan (transported from across town) makes its own noodles and serves them simply: on a *seiro* (bamboo mat on a wooden box), or with *kamo* (duck), hot or cold. Grab a seat by the window for the best views. When you're done, there are bamboo toothpicks.

KAO TAI Map p116 — Thai ¥
カオタイ

☎ 3204-5806; 2-14-6 Takadanobaba, Shinjuku-ku; mains ¥840-1200; ☽ 11.30am-2pm & 5-10.30pm; ⊚ JR Yamanote Line to Takadanobaba (main exit), Tōzai Line to Takadanobaba (exit 6); Ⓔ
From the bamboo-framed doorway to its snug dining room, Kao Tai feels like a warm slice of Southeast Asia. Most dishes are small-plate affairs, allowing you to sample and share while swigging on a Singha. While it's not the most complicated Thai food around, the feel more than makes up for it.

BEN'S CAFE Map p116 — Cafe ¥
ベンズカフェ

☎ 3202-2445; 1-29-21 Takadanobaba, Shinjuku-ku; dishes ¥500-980; ☽ 11.30am-11.30pm Sun-Thu, 11.30am-12.30am Fri & Sat; ⊚ JR Yamanote Line to Takadanobaba (main exit), Tozai Line to Takadanobaba (exit 5); Ⓔ
Local Waseda students and expats come to Ben's to quell cravings for quiche, cappuccino or Belgian beer – or just to chill. There's no smoking indoors, and the patio out front is a good place to sip wine and watch life amble by on warm evenings. Ben's also hosts poetry readings and exhibitions by local artists, and it has wi-fi access. Head uphill to the left of Big Box, turn left at the corner where you see New Yorkers Café and right at the next corner.

SHINAGAWA

Restaurants around Shinagawa Station tend to cater to salarymen and office ladies populating the office towers nearby, as well as commuters, leading to some fun and unique casual options. There's also a lovely brewery restaurant by the harbour, or it's a short hop to the upmarket residential neighbourhoods of southern Tokyo.

T Y HARBOR BREWERY Map p119 — Eclectic ¥¥
ティーワイ ハーバーブルワリー

☎ 5479-4555; 2-1-3 Higashi-Shinagawa, Minato-ku; mains ¥1700-3800; ☽ 11.30am-2pm & 5.30-10pm Mon-Fri, 5.30-10pm Sat, 11.30am-3pm & 5.30-9pm Sun; ⊚ JR Yamanote Line to Shinagawa (Kōnan east exit); Ⓔ
A waterside location, Louisiana crab cakes, a cold brew and thou. This American-style brew pub boasts an eclectic menu (pan-roasted scallops with curry and couscous anyone?), beer tanks on the premises and a huge, loyal following. It's a gathering place for Tokyo's moneyed expat community, especially for weekend brunch.

DAVID'S DELI Off Map p119 — Israeli ¥
デビッドデリ

☎ 5441-1211; 5-13-13 Mita, Minato-ku; sandwiches & small dishes ¥520-1080, mains ¥1680-3280; ☽ 7.30am-11pm Mon-Fri, 10am-11pm Sat, 10am-10pm Sun; ⊚ Nanboku Line to Shirokane-Takanawa (exit 3); Ⓔ Ⓥ
If you hanker for hummus, fawn for falafel or *kvell* for kebabs, this cafe is like the Holy Land on the Pacific, right down the

miniature Chagall stained-glass windows in the upstairs dining room. Ingredients are imported from Israel, and the pita, rye and other breads are baked fresh in house. Traditional Jewish specialties like gefilte fish and matzo-ball soup are also available, plus lots of veggie options.

USHIO Map p119   Sushi ¥
潮

☎ 6717-0934; 2nd fl, Atré Shinagawa, 2-18-1 Shinagawa, Minato-ku; sushi per piece ¥90-350, sushi sets ¥900-1200; ⏰ 11am-11pm; ⦿ JR Yamanote Line to Shinagawa (Kōnan east exit); Ⓔ
Tachikui (stand-and-eat) noodles are a longstanding (forgive the pun) Tokyo tradition, but *tachikui* sushi…well, that's new. So is the way you order. Take a little plastic coin, each with the name of the fish in Japanese and English, from a rack on the counter, plunk it onto a small plate in front of you, and the *itamae* makes it. Genius. The atmosphere: utilitarian and immaculate. It's in the corridor as you exit Shinagawa Station.

SHINATATSU Map p119   Donburi & Rāmen ¥
品達

☎ 5475-7020; 3-26-20 Takanawa, Shingawa-ku; mains ¥650-1000; ⏰ 11am-11pm; ⦿ JR Yamanote Line to Shinagawa (Takanawa exit)
A bit of a ramble, a bit of a gamble (if you don't speak Japanese), Shinatatsu is a collection of seven *rāmen* shops and five *donburi* shops lining the trackside arcade beside Shinagawa Station. Shops don't have English menus, so you may want to pick up Shinatatsu's picture booklet or ask for explanations of the different varieties before you purchase your meal ticket from the vending machines. Among them, Tetsu serves *tsukemen* – plain noodles that you dip in soup, which is all the rage right now. *Donburi* toppings (beef, tempura, sashimi etc) are a little more easily decipherable.

SUMIDA RIVER – EAST

Primarily a suburban residential area, the neighbourhoods east of Sumida-gawa are home to few noteworthy restaurants that are worth seeking out. However, if you have any interest in trying *chankonabe* (ちゃんこ鍋), the sumō wrestler's staple, it's worth heading to Ryōgoku for lunch or dinner.

TOMOEGATA Map p116   Chankonabe ¥¥
巴潟

☎ 3632-5600; 2-17-6 Ryōgoku, Sumida-ku; lunch courses ¥2100-3150, chankonabe ¥2940; ⏰ 11am-11pm; ⦿ JR Sōbu Line to Ryōgoku (west exit)
Given the preponderance of sumō stables in Ryōgoku, it's only natural that you'll find restaurants serving the calorie-rich *chankonabe*. Recipes vary for this hearty stew, but count on beef, chicken, pork, fish and/or seasonal vegetables. Tomoegata has been serving it for generations – go with a group, or eat it all by yourself if you want to become big like a sumō wrestler.

ODAIBA

The majority of eating and drinking options on Odaiba are in the giant malls, with options for every taste and budget. Yet it's not your standard mall food – there are many unique choices where cooking doesn't suffer for the scene. Some of the best also offer gripping bay views.

Odaiba is particularly known for themed restaurant malls that are fun for a ramble: Daiba Ichōme Shōtengai (築地玉寿司) on the 4th floor of Decks Tokyo Beach (Seaside building) rides the nostalgia wave with restaurants made to look like postwar Tokyo. On the 7th floor of Decks Island Side is Little Hong Kong (小香港), with a half-dozen Chinese places. Italian restaurants dominate the Italian-themed Venus Fort.

Gonpachi (p170) also has a location here.

TSUKIJI TAMA SUSHI
Map p127   Sushi & Sashimi ¥¥
築地玉寿司

☎ 3599-6556; 5th fl, Decks Tokyo Beach, 1-6-1 Daiba, Minato-ku; lunch sets ¥945-1260, all-you-can-eat dinner women/men ¥3045/3675; ⏰ 11am-11pm; ⦿ Yurikamome Line to Odaiba Kaihin-kōen (main exit); Ⓔ
Settle yourself near the windows and sip from a huge, earthy cup of green tea while you wait for your sushi, which will come immaculately presented and perfectly fresh. The menu also includes set meals and udon if you prefer; either way, this is a pleasant corner from which to take in good Japanese food and bay views. Dinner is *tabe-hōdai* (all you can eat) for 90 minutes, though we're guessing they probably take a loss on some diners from overseas.

TAKE…TAKE ME HOME…

Because you've read this book so carefully, you already know that it's good manners to take a gift when you're invited to someone's home. (Haven't read that part yet? See p144.) But *o-miyage* (souvenirs) can also enthral, endear and impress friends and family back home. Here are some foods (from most traditional to least) that make excellent gifts and where you can find them. Just be sure to note whether there's an expiration date.

Sembei (せんべい) Roasted rice crackers, usually basted with soy sauce and sometimes studded with *goma* (sesame) or wrapped in *nori* (seaweed). Available everywhere from street markets to convenience stores.

Manjū (饅頭 or まんじゅう) Steamed sweet dumplings, traditionally filled with *kuro-an* (sweet red-bean paste). Best purchased at a traditional stop like on Nakamise-dori in Asakusa.

Yoku-Moku (ヨックモック) This confectioner's shop has been around for ages, making it a very old-line Tokyo take-away indeed. Best-sellers include the *cigare* (rolled wafer cookies) and *bateau de macadamia* (oblong cookies coated with chocolate and crushed macadamia nuts). Old Japan hands will love them. Locations include Omote-sandō and airports.

Kit-Kat (キットカット) Yes, we know you have these at home, but in wasabi and green-tea flavours? Available everywhere.

Tokyo Banana (東京ばな奈) Miniature sponge cakes filled with banana cream. Fab, fab, fab. Sold only at *shinkansen* stations and airports.

Ginza no Ichigo Keiki (銀座のいちごケーキ) These little cakes do for strawberries what Tokyo Banana does for bananas and are usually sold near Tokyo Banana.

HIBIKI Map p127   Japanese Pub ¥
響

☎ 3599-5500; 6th fl, Aqua City Odaiba, 1-7-1 Daiba, Minato-ku; dishes ¥700-1700; ⏰ 11am-11pm; ◉ Yurikamome Line to Daiba (south exit); Ⓔ

The inventive menu at this Japanese pub-style restaurant emphasises quality meats and hearty side dishes, all of which perfectly accompany the extensive selection of booze. However, don't let all this fine food and drink distract you from the incredible views of the Rainbow Bridge across Tokyo Bay.

SEIRYŪMON Map p127   Chinese ¥
青龍門

☎ 3599-2255; 1040, Venus Fort, 1-7-1 Aomi, Kōtō-ku; dishes ¥400-1300; ⏰ 11am-11pm; ◉ Yurikamome Line to Aomi (south exit); Ⓔ

Take a break from Italian-mad Venus Fort and head upstairs to this spot that looks like a night market in Beijing. It serves dozens of small dishes (stir-fried water spinach, Taiwanese soup noodles) and some larger ones too (hotpot of braised seafood). And at what other Chinese restaurant in the world do you get to peer through Corinthian columns as the sun 'rises' and 'sets' in an artificial sky?

TEN-TEN TSUNE-TSUNE
KAITENBŌ Map p127   Chinese ¥
点点常常回転坊

☎ 3599-6705; 7th fl, Decks Tokyo Beach, 1-6-1 Daiba, Minato-ku; dishes ¥150-380, all-you-can-eat lunches ¥1260; ⏰ 11am-11pm; ◉ Yurikamome Line to Odaiba Kaihin-kōen (main exit); Ⓔ

There is no shortage of great Chinese restaurants in 'Little Hong Kong', though we've never seen anything quite like this novelty dim sum spot. Drawing inspiration from *kaiten-sushi* (conveyor-belt sushi) restaurants, Ten-Ten Tsune-Tsune Kaitenbō (try saying that with your mouth full!) offers conveyor-belt dim sum feasts to hungry shoppers in need of a dumpling-fuelled boost. Although there is a limited English menu available, it is not hard to simply grab what looks good!

LES DEUX BLEUE Map pp48-9   Cafe ¥
レドゥブルー

☎ 3536-8326; 1st fl, LaLaPort Toyusu, 2-4-9 Toyosu, Kōtō-ku; dishes ¥1000-1560, lunch specials ¥880-1180; ⏰ 11am-11pm; ◉ Yurakucho Line to Toyosu (exit 2), Yurikamome Line to Toyosu (main exit); Ⓔ

As you gaze out over Tokyo Bay on a sunny day or a sparkly night, this glassed-in cafe at the far corner of the LaLaPort shopping centre might become the favourite place of you and your loved one – assuming your loved one has a waggly tail and cold nose. While humans can fill up on burgers, pizzas and pastas, there's an entire menu for the four-legged ones, from organic chicken liver to doggy birthday cake. After your meal, you can both burn off the calories at the fenced-in dog run.

DRINKING & NIGHTLIFE

top picks

What's your recommendation? www.lonelyplanet.com/tokyo

DRINKING & NIGHTLIFE

Slicing into a pumpkin-sized, ice cream–topped loaf of toasted bread while swilling draught Kirin and belting out your fave Queen tunes in a room the size of a broom closet. Or quaffing thimble after thimble of sake with an unknown and increasingly rosy salaryman, who then insists you join him at a bar down a dark lane in Shinjuku.

That's fun, Tokyo-style. The city will rock you 'til you drop in its live houses, and drink you under the table in its *izakaya* (Japanese pubs). Entertainment-wise, Tokyo is a microcosm of the best of Japan and the world. What Dr Johnson said of London also applies to this city on speed – if you're bored in Tokyo, you might as well be dead.

BARS

Alcohol is very much a social lubricant in Japan, and a lot of heavy drinking goes on in Tokyo, something you will realise if you happen to hop on any train after 10pm; violence, though, is quite rare. Roppongi, long the *gaijin* (foreigners; literally 'outside people') bar capital of Tokyo, has the lion's share of bars per square metre, though Shinjuku is no slouch.

SHINJUKU

The streets and lanes radiating from the world's busiest train station hide enough watering holes to souse an army. The largest red-light district in East Asia, Kabukichō, is northwest of the station and abuts the storied old drinking alleys of Golden Gai. Next door is Shinjuku Ni-chōme, Japan's gay mecca, home to about 300 gay and lesbian bars.

ADVOCATES CAFÉ Map p110   Gay & Lesbian
アドヴォケッツカフェ

☎ 3358-8638; B1 fl, 2-18-1 Shinjuku, Shinjuku-ku; 🕑 8pm-4am; 🚇 Marunouchi or Toei Shinjuku Line to Shinjuku-sanchōme (exits C7 & C8)
This corner bar is so small that as the crowd magically expands during the course of an evening, it becomes more like a block party and takes to the streets. Advocates welcomes people of all genders, identities and nationalities. It's a great place to start off the night.

ALBATROSS Map p110   Arty/Stylish
アルバトロス

☎ 3342-5758; www.alba-s.com; 1-2-11 Nishi-Shinjuku, Shinjuku-ku; 🕑 5pm-2am; 🚇 Shinjuku (west exit)
Tucked away in aromatic Omoide-yokocho (Memory Lane), Albatross and the surrounding *yakitori* (charcoal-broiled chicken and other meats or vegetables, cooked on skewers) joints would have been knocked down long ago if owners had let developers have their way.

ARTY FARTY Map p110   Gay & Lesbian
アーティファーティ

☎ 5362-9720; www.arty-farty.net; 2nd fl, 2-11-7 Shinjuku, Shinjuku-ku; 🕑 5pm-5am Mon-Sat, 4pm-5am Sun; 🚇 Marunouchi or Toei Shinjuku Line to Shinjuku-sanchōme (exits C7 & C8)
This bar for boys and gals has been the gateway to Tokyo's gay neighbourhood, Ni-chōme, for many a moon. A cavernous place with a dance floor and intimate booths, Arty Farty is open to all in the community.

AURORA LOUNGE Map p110   Cocktail Lounge
オーロララウンジ

☎ 3344-0111; 45th fl, 2-2-1 Nishi-Shinjuku, Shinjuku-ku; 🕑 11.30am-11.30pm; 🚇 Toei Ōedo Line to Tochōmae (exit B1)
Perched 150m up in the Keiō Plaza Hotel (p224), this bar has great views and drinks. On the same floor, the crisp, elegant Sky Bar Polestar (🕑 5-11.30pm) is built for gazing out over the city, with each seat facing the windows. Drinks start at ¥1050.

DRINKS WITH A VIEW

To decompress from pounding the pavement all day, rise to a different atmosphere. Savour spectacular views while sipping a vodka martini at these bars with views.

New York Grill & Bar (opposite) Get the *Lost in Translation* experience with floor-to-ceiling vistas.

Sky Bar (p186) Drink in the panorama or chew the scenery in a revolving dining space.

Aurora Lounge & Sky Bar Polestar (above) Both have fine views from the Keiō Plaza Hotel in Shinjuku.

GAY & LESBIAN TOKYO

Though issues like gay marriage are not on the public radar in Japan, media is rife with *tarento* (media celebrities) who are gay or who pretend. The Tokyo Pride Festival is sometimes held around Yoyogi-kōen in May, though in some years it has been called the Tokyo Pride Parade and held in August. Entertainment-wise, the Tokyo scene is concentrated in Shinjuku Ni-chōme, a few blocks east of Shinjuku Station that house around 300 G&L establishments (not all welcome foreigners).

For detailed maps and information about Ni-chōme, drop into the friendly Akta Community Center (☎ 3226-8998; www.rainbowring.org/akta, in Japanese; 3rd fl, Nakae Bldg, 2-15-13 Shinjuku, Shinjuku-ku; ◷ 4-10pm Tue-Sun). Look for the blue-white pavement sign. Other resources on Tokyo's gay and lesbian scene are www.utopia-asia.com and www.japanvisitor.com.

BAR PLASTIC MODEL Map p110   Arty/Stylish
バープラスチックモデル
☎ 5273-8441; 1-1-10 Kabukichō, Shinjuku-ku; ◷ 8pm-5am Mon-Sat, 6pm-midnight Sun; Ⓜ Marunouchi or Toei Shinjuku Line to Shinjuku-sanchōme (exit B5)
Bar Plastic Model is one of the new joints run by a younger generation in venerable Golden Gai, with an '80s soundtrack and decorated with retro knick-knacks.

DRAGON MEN Map p110   Gay & Lesbian
ドラゴン
☎ 3341-0606; 2-11-4 Shinjuku, Shinjuku-ku; ◷ 6pm-3am Sun-Thu, 6pm-5am Fri-Sun; Ⓜ Marunouchi or Toei Shinjuku Line to Shinjuku-sanchōme (exits C7 & C8)
One of the largest bars in the gay village, Dragon has sleek modern decor, an easy-going vibe and a great mix of Japanese and foreigners. Women are welcome, too. Happy hour from 6pm to 9pm.

DUBLINERS Map p110   Pub
ダブリナーズ
☎ 3352-6606; www.dubliners.jp; 2nd fl, Lion Beer Hall Bldg, 3-28-9 Shinjuku, Shinjuku-ku; ◷ noon-1am Mon-Sat, noon-11pm Sun; Ⓜ Shinjuku (east exit)
Live music and good beer have made this one of the city's most frequented international watering holes. Pub grub includes a few Irish standards in portions that are larger than normal for Tokyo.

GARAM Map p110   Speciality
ガラム
☎ 3205-8668; www17.big.or.jp/~kamal; 7th fl, Dai-roku Polestar Bldg, 1-16-6 Kabukichō, Shinjuku-ku; admission incl 1 drink from ¥1000; ◷ 8pm-5am; Ⓜ Shinjuku (east exit)
Garam is a cool little reggae club with a friendly owner and no Rasta poseurs. The house DJ spins a mix of dub, hip-hop and roots reggae, and guest DJs also appear.

GB Map p110   Gay & lesbian
☎ 3352-8972; 2-12-13 Shinjuku, Shinjuku-ku ◷ 8pm-3am; Ⓜ Marunouchi or Toei Shinjuku Line to Shinjuku-sanchōme (exit C8)
A welcoming, dimly lit bar with 1980s videos on the tube and a cruisy vibe. GB has friendly staff and generous drinks and makes for a great spot to begin the night.

KINSWOMYN Map p110   Gay & Lesbian
キンズウィミン
☎ 3354-8720; 3rd fl, Dai-ichi Tenka Bldg, 2-15-10 Shinjuku, Shinjuku-ku; ◷ 8pm-4am Wed-Mon; Ⓜ Marunouchi or Toei Shinjuku Line to Shinjuku-sanchōme (exit C8)
This established girls-only spot is welcoming and comfortable, and is run by a lesbian activist. English is spoken here, making it a perfect stop for visitors, but it's more a spot for drinking and chatting than for dancing. Drinks start at ¥700.

LA JETÉE Map p110   Arty/Stylish
ラジェッテイ
☎ 3208-9645; 1-1-8 Kabukichō, Shinjuku-ku; ◷ 7pm-late Mon-Sat; Ⓜ Marunouchi or Toei Shinjuku Line to Shinjuku-sanchōme (exit B5)
Kawai-san, the proprietor of this Golden Gai bar, knows more about film (especially that of Chris Marker) than most of us ever will. No English is spoken here, though you're welcome to practise your rusty Français.

NEW YORK GRILL & BAR Map p110   Bar
ニューヨークグリル
☎ 5322-1234; 52nd fl, 3-7-1-2 Nishi-Shinjuku, Shinjuku-ku; ◷ 5pm-midnight Sun-Wed, 5pm-1am Thu-Sat; Ⓜ Toei Ōedo Line to Tochōmae (exit A4)
You may not be lodging at the Park Hyatt, but that doesn't mean you can't ascend to the 52nd floor to swoon over stunning views of Mt Fuji and the city. There's a cover charge of ¥2000 after 8pm (7pm Sunday).

SHIBUYA & HARAJUKU

Shibuya mainly caters to teens and 20-some-things, but more adult-oriented pubs and lounges abound. For Golden Gai–style old-timey watering holes not reviewed here, check out Nonbei Yokocho alley northeast of the station by the JR Yamanote Line tracks; most bars there only seat a handful.

BELLO VISTO Map p102   Bar
ベロビスト

☎ 3476-3000; 40th fl, 26-1 Sakuragaokachō, Shibuya-ku; ☉ 4pm-midnight Mon-Fri, 3pm-midnight Sat & Sun; ⊚ Shibuya (south exit)

This 40th-floor eyrie on the Cerulean Tower keeps the interior dim so that you can see the lights on the far horizon. The 95-seat capacity ensures the atmosphere is always intimate. Cocktails and wine start at ¥1270.

CHESTNUT & SQUIRREL Map p102   Bar
☎ 090-9834-4842; www.chestnutandsquirrel .com; 3rd fl, 3-7-5 Shibuya, Shibuya-ku; ☉ 8pm-midnight Wed; ⊚ Shibuya (south exit)

This cafe has international lesbian nights on Wednesdays; Halloween and Christmas events; and guest DJs. It's in the Oishi Building behind the Shibuya police station.

DEN AQUAROOM Map p106   Speciality
デンアクアルーム

☎ 5778-2090; B1 fl, FIK Aoyama Bldg, 5-13-3 Minami-Aoyama, Minato-ku; admission ¥500-1000; ☉ 6pm-2am Mon-Sat, 6-11pm Sun; ⊚ Chiyoda, Ginza or Hanzōmon Line to Omote-sandō (exit B1)

Darting fish within the walls of immaculate blue aquariums make a visual counterpoint to the bop of jazz bass lines. But even prettier than the dark decor is the chic clientele hanging out here for the evening. Chill with a fruity cocktail in this velvety lounge and enjoy the view.

INSOMNIA LOUNGE Map p102   Arty/Stylish
インソムニアラウンジ

☎ 3476-2735; Ikushin Bldg, B1 fl, 26-5 Udagawachō, Shibuya-ku; ☉ 6pm-5am; ⊚ JR Shibuya (Hachikō exit)

Insomnia Lounge is that rare Shibuya find: a bar for grown-ups. Good food, low music and a cosy, mirrored red interior make it the kind of place to come when you're in the mood for conversation.

PINK COW Map p102   Arty/Stylish
ピンクカウ

☎ 3406-5597; www.thepinkcow.com; B1 fl, 1-3-18 Shibuya, Shibuya-ku; ☉ 5pm-late Tue-Sun; ⊚ Chiyoda, Ginza or Hanzōmon Line to Omote-sandō (exit B2)

With its animal-print decor, rotating display of local artwork and terrific all-you-can-eat buffet (¥2625) every Friday and Saturday, the Pink Cow is a funky, friendly place to hang out. Also host to stitch-and-bitch evenings, writers' salons and indie film screenings, it's a good bet if you seek some artistic stimulation.

ROPPONGI

With the opening of posh megacomplexes Roppongi Hills and Tokyo Midtown, Roppongi's downhill slide into a jungle of pushy foreign touts luring drinkers to rip-off joints has slowed somewhat, but you should still use caution (p94). Roppongi remains one of the best places to drink in Tokyo, though it may not feel especially Japanese. There's a great mix of cheap shot-bars and upscale spots here.

A971 Map p92   Arty/Stylish
☎ 5413-3210; www.a971.com, in Japanese; 9-7-1 Akasaka, Minato-ku; ☉ 10am-2am Mon-Thu, 10am-5am Fri & Sat, 10am-midnight Sun; ⊚ Hibiya or Toei Ōedo Line to Roppongi (Tokyo Midtown exit)

Tucked into an outside corner of the recently built Tokyo Midtown complex, this hip restaurant-bar pulsates with friendly drinkers on Friday and Saturday nights. The crowd, a good mix of gaijin and locals, spills out onto the surrounding pavement and the vibe is very laid-back and conversational.

AGAVE Map p92   Speciality
アガヴェ

☎ 3497-0229; www.agave.jp; B1 fl, 7-15-10 Roppongi, Minato-ku; ☉ 6.30pm-2am Mon-Thu, 6.30pm-4am Fri & Sat; ⊚ Hibiya or Toei Ōedo Line to Roppongi (exit 2)

Rawhide chairs, cruzas de rosas (crosses decorated with roses) and tequila shots for the willing make Agave a good place for a long night in search of the sacred worm. Luckily, this gem in the jungle that is Roppongi is more about savouring the subtleties of its 400-plus varieties of tequila rather than tossing back shots of Cuervo.

BUL-LET'S Map p92 — Speciality
ブレッツ

☎ 3401-4844; www.bul-lets.com; B1 fl, Kasumi Bldg, 1-7-11 Nishi-Azabu, Minato-ku; admission ¥2000; ⏰ from around 6pm; Ⓜ Hibiya or Toei Ōedo Line to Roppongi (exit 2)

This mellow basement space plays worldwide trance and ambient sounds for barefoot patrons. Mattresses in the middle of the floor provide refuge from the madding crowd, but don't get the wrong idea – it's not always tranquillity and deadbeats.

HEARTLAND Map p92 — Arty/Stylish
ハートランド

☎ 5772-7600; www.heartland.jp, in Japanese; 6-10-1 Roppongi, Minato-ku; ⏰ 11am-5am; Ⓜ Hibiya or Toei Ōedo Line to Roppongi (exit 3)

Named for the house beer from Kirin, Heartland is a chic, easygoing watering hole at the base of Roppongi Hills' West Tower that caters to professional expats and Japanese.

MISTRAL BLUE Map p92 — Shots
ミストラルブルー

☎ 3423-0082; www.trainbar.com; 5-5-1 Roppongi, Minato-ku; ⏰ 6pm-3am Mon-Sat; Ⓜ Hibiya or Toei Ōedo Line to Roppongi (exit 3)

This lovable hole in the wall also known as Train Bar is about as unpretentious as it gets in Roppongi. The many foreign customers who have drained cheap beers here have left their mark – every surface, even the light bulbs, is covered with signatures.

MOTOWN HOUSE 1 & 2 Map p92 — Shots
モータウンハウス

☎ 5474-4605; www.motownhouse.com; 2nd fl, 3-11-5 Roppongi, Minato-ku; ⏰ 6pm-5am; Ⓜ Hibiya or Toei Ōedo Line to Roppongi (exit 3)

The crass may call it 'ho town', but on the pick-up front it's no worse (or better?) than its neighbours, and since it expanded to two venues, it can actually be quite relaxed. Drinks start at ¥800. Funk, soul, R&B and hip-hop dominate here, of course.

PROPAGANDA Map p92 — Shots
プロパガンダ

☎ 3423-0988; www.propaganda-tokyo.com; 2nd fl, 3-14-9 Roppongi, Minato-ku; ⏰ 6pm-dawn Mon-Sat; Ⓜ Hibiya or Toei Ōedo Line to Roppongi (exit 3)

A shot bar calling itself Propaganda couldn't possibly take itself too seriously,

and it doesn't specials cost pick-up scen

TOKYO SP
東京スポー

☎ 5411 8939 Roppongi, Mi Ⓜ Hibiya or With Kilken a talking co friendly spo cheering on your favourite

near Iidabashi Station European-style bars more relaxed, slow

BEER BAR B
ビア・バー
☎ 5261-3
ku; ⏰
Yūra
(B

lonelyplanet.com

wise, it's more Rotherham United than Chicago Bulls, and many events here are broadcast live.

GINZA

Ginza is a pricier drinking destination than Roppongi unless you stick to the *yakitori* joints under the *shinkansen* tracks. There are plenty of upscale *izakaya* and European-style bars to clink glasses in here.

AUX AMIS DES VINS Map p57 — Speciality
オザミデヴァン

☎ 3567-4120; 2-5-6 Ginza, Chūō-ku; ⏰ 5.30pm-2am Mon-Fri, noon-midnight Sat; Ⓜ Yūrakuchō Line to Ginza-itchōme (exits 5 & 8)

Even when it rains, the plastic tarp comes down and good wine is drunk alleyside. The enclosed upstairs seating area is warm and informal, and you can order snacks to go with your wine or full *prix-fixe* dinners. A solid selection of wine comes by the glass (¥800) or by the bottle.

ICEBAR TOKYO Map p57 — Speciality
アイスバー東京

☎ 6228-5021; www.icebartokyo.com; 8-5-15 Ginza, Chūō-ku; ⏰ 3-11pm Sat-Tue, 3pm-4am Wed-Fri; Ⓜ Ginza Line to Shimbashi (exit 5)

The relocated Tokyo branch of this frosty international franchise imports ice from Lapland for the counters, walls and glasses. The ¥3500 door charge includes rental parka, gloves and one drink. Perfect for those sweltering summer nights.

AKASAKA & IIDABASHI

The salaryman's paradise of Akasaka is full of rosy-cheeked businessmen letting loose at night. It offers a good mix of pricey *izakaya*, karaoke joints and the odd pub. Kagurazaka

...3) is home to many ...d bistros, and has a ...be.

...TTER Map p60   Speciality
ビター

...087; 2nd fl, 1-14 Tsukudochō, Shinjuku-...pm-late Mon-Fri; ◎ Namboku, Tōzai, ...uchō, Toei Ōedo or JR Sōbu Line to Iidabashi ...5 or west exit)

This mellow Euro-bar in Kagurazaka has a super selection of Belgian beers from around ¥900, as well as snacks such as Iberico ham (¥1300). Going up Kagurazaka hill, look for the fourth lane on your right, called Honda-yokochō (本多横町). Go down it until you see a pale, three-story building on your right with a red *yakitori* lantern hanging outside. Take the stairs on the right.

HOBGOBLIN Map p88   Pub
ホブゴブリン

☎ 6229-2636; www.hobgoblin.jp; B1 fl, Tamondo Bldg, 2-13-19 Akasaka, Minato-ku; ☿ 11am-3pm & 5pm-late Mon-Fri, 5pm-late Sat; ◎ Chiyoda Line to Akasaka (exit 2), Ginza or Namboku Lines to Tameike-sannō (exit 9)

Far better than your average Brit-pub replica, Akasaka's Hobgoblin is supported by an Oxfordshire brewery. It serves good pub fare with excellent microbrews such as Hobgoblin Dark. Two huge plasma screens show rugby and football.

SAKE PLAZA Map p88   Speciality
日本酒造会館

☎ 3519-2091; 1-1-21 Nishi-Shimbashi, Minato-ku; ☿ 10am-5.30pm Mon-Fri; ◎ Ginza Line to Toranomon (exit 9)

Sake Plaza isn't a bar, but who cares when you can get five thimbles of regionally brewed sake for only ¥525. This showroom and tasting space is a perfect way to start the night while learning about the national drink. It's on the ground floor of the Japan Sake Brewers Association Building (日本酒造会館).

SKY BAR Map p88   Cocktail Lounge
スカイ バー

☎ 3238-0028; 17th fl, Hotel New Otani, 4-1 Kioi-chō, Chiyoda-ku; ☿ 5-11pm; ◎ Ginza or Maru-nouchi Line to Akasaka-mitsuke (BelleVie exit)

Sip cocktails from ¥1300 on vine-print seats while diners revolve around you

above a sublime cityscape. The rotating rim is a buffet restaurant with exquisite sushi, teppanyaki, Chinese and Western fare from ¥9240.

EBISU & NAKA-MEGURO

Ebisu is packed with small bars, *izakaya* and noodle shops. Down Komazawa-dōri around Nakameguro Station you'll find artsy bars run by DJs, skateboarders and culture vultures.

BAJA off Map p96   Shots
バハ

☎ 3715-2929; 1-16-12 Kami-Meguro, Meguro-ku; ☿ 5pm-5am Mon-Fri, noon-5am Sat & Sun; ◎ Hibiya Line to Nakameguro

Roll up to this tiny white taco shack off Yamate-dōri and knock back beers for ¥500, tacos for ¥330 and tequila for ¥300. It's operated by a friendly skateboarder, who's happy to dispense tips on hip local hang-outs.

BURI Map p96   Standing Bar
ぶり

☎ 3496-7744; www.buri-group.com; 1-14-1 Ebisu-Nishi, Shibuya-ku; ☿ 5pm-3am; ◎ Ebisu (west exit)

The name means 'super' in Hiroshima dialect, and this bar does not disappoint, with its colourful wall-mounted sake cups to the 'magical' ice sake served semi-solid. The many kinds of sake start at ¥750, *shōchū* from ¥550. Snacks include prosciutto, escargot and *tsukune* meatballs.

FOOTNIK Map p96   Sports
フットニック

☎ 5795-0144; www.footnik.net; 1-11-2 Ebisu, Shibuya-ku; ☿ 5pm-1am Mon-Fri, 3pm-1am Sat & Sun; ◎ Ebisu (east exit)

Cold pints cost only ¥700, and the big-screen TVs broadcast – what else? – footy (er, soccer) for the footniks.

KINFOLK LOUNGE Map p96   Lounge
キンフォーク

☎ 5489-8683; wegotways.com/kinfolk; 2nd fl, 1-11-1 Kami-Meguro, Meguro-ku; ☿ 6pm-midnight Tue-Sun; ◎ Hibiya Line to Nakameguro

Sip mint mojitos under racing bike frames hanging from the wooden rafters in this hipster lounge run by cycling nuts. From

Nakameguro Station, take the footbridge over Yamate-dōri, then the first right and continue until you hit a T-junction. Turn left, go about two blocks and it's on the left above a restaurant.

TABLEAUX LOUNGE Map p96 Lounge
タブローズ ラウンジ

☎ 5489-2202; www.lounge.tableaux.jp; B1F, Sunroser Daikanyama, 11-6 Sarugakucho, Shibuya-ku; admission ¥1050; ⏰ 9pm-4am; Ⓜ Tōkyū Tōyoko Line to Daikanyama

If you love jazz, wine and cigars, Tableaux is the perfect spot to mix all three under chandeliers and stuffed bookshelves. Drinks start at ¥1000 and the band from 9.30pm. Oysters and Cohiba cigars are also on offer. It's next door to the Tableaux restaurant.

WHAT THE DICKENS Map p96 Pub
ザ ディッケンズ

☎ 3780-2099; www.whatthedickens.jp; 4th fl, 1-13-3 Ebisu-Nishi, Shibuya-ku; ⏰ 5pm-1am Tue-Sat, 5pm-midnight Sun; Ⓜ Ebisu (west exit)

What the Dickens occupies the 4th floor of the Roob building, whose outstanding facade looks as if it's finished with a layer of mud and adorned with the mirrored replica of a hummingbird. The beer and pub grub are up to snuff, and good live music and the occasional poetry reading keep things rolling.

CAFES

Tokyo has some uniquely atmospheric cafes that range from homey old mom-and-pop shops to uberdesigned hipster hang-outs. They may not have the smoke-free, vanilla-latte-dispensing convenience of global chains, but they make for a great spot to rest your dogs while sightseeing.

ATTIC ROOM Map p102 Cafe-Bar
アティックルーム

☎ 5489-5228; 4th fl, 31-1 Udagawachō, Shibuya-ku; ⏰ noon-midnight Tue-Sun, 5pm-midnight Mon; Ⓜ Shibuya (Hachikō exit)

Take the stairs up to the 4th floor of this old corner building near Tōkyū Hands and you'll find a very chilled space of burnished wood and old leather recliners. Coffee and soy-milk lattes cost ¥450, while simple but tasty pizzas and pastas are around ¥1000.

CAFÉ MEURSAULT Map p84 Cafe-Bar
カフェムルソー

☎ 3843-8008; http://cafe-meursault.com; 2-1-5 Kaminarimon, Taitō-ku; ⏰ 11am-10pm; Ⓜ Toei Asakusa Line to Asakusa (exit A3)

With a large window open to Sumida-gawa, this panoramic cake shop serves lunches such as lemon herb chicken sandwiches from ¥1100. You can sip beers (¥630) here at night and watch the ferry boats rolling by.

LAS CHICAS Map p106 Cafe-Bar
ラスチカス

☎ 3407-6865; 5-47-6 Jingūmae, Shibuya-ku; ⏰ 11am-11pm; Ⓜ Chiyoda, Ginza or Hanzōmon Line to Omote-sandō (exit B2)

Las Chicas is a stylish alfresco cafe-restaurant (see p174) and one of Harajuku's core art spaces. But that doesn't mean you can't come here just to hang out in the bar area, which is the kind of place where you will want to sit and sip for hours.

MILONGA NUEVA Map p67 Cafe
ミロンガヌオーバ

☎ 3295-1716; 1-3 Kanda Jimbōchō, Chiyoda-ku; ⏰ 10.30am-10.30pm Mon-Fri, 11.30am-7pm Sat & Sun; Ⓜ Toei Shinjuku Line to Jimbōchō (exit A7)

Off an alley parallel to Yasukuni-dōri, this wonderfully retro Euro cafe plays old tango tunes on the sound system and serves up blends like Kilimanjaro coffee for ¥650.

ROYAL GARDEN CAFÉ Map p88 Cafe
ローヤルガーデンカフェ

☎ 5414-6170; www.royal-gardencafe.com, in Japanese; 2-1-19 Kita-Aoyama, Minato-ku; ⏰ 11am-11pm; Ⓜ Ginza Line to Gaienmae (exit 4A)

This large airy bakery along the gingko-lined path to Jingū Gaien park has year-round outdoor seating, wi-fi and lunch sets from ¥950. To support sustainable lifestyles, it also hosts the occasional farmers market.

TOKYO APARTMENT CAFÉ
Map p106 Cafe-Bar
東京アパートメントカフェ

☎ 3401-4101; 1-11-11 Jingūmae, Shibuya-ku; ⏰ 11am-3am; Ⓜ Chiyoda Line to Meiji-jingūmae (exit 1)

This subterranean room with a view doubles as a cool daytime coffee house and eatery. At night the atmosphere goes a shade hipper and cocktails are served until closing. This is a good place to hole up for the evening if you're out for the night on Omote-sandō.

KARAOKE

You can't avoid it! Karaoke is a national pastime in Japan, an ice-breaker and welcome tonic for the strictures of the daily grind. Luckily, most group singing is not open-mic bar-room style – it takes place in private rooms rented by the hour, usually for around ¥600 per person. Parlours are ubiquitous but the big ones are in hubs such as Shinjuku and Shibuya.

KARAOKE-KAN Map p102
カラオケ館

☎ 3462-0785; 30-8 Udagawachō, Shibuya-ku; per hr Fri-Sun ¥1200, Mon-Thu ¥1000; ⏲ 11am-6am; ◉ Shibuya (Hachikō exit)

This branch of a generic national karaoke chain has rooms on the 6th floor that were used as a location in the film *Lost in Translation*. Excellent discounts are available to customers during weekday mornings and afternoons.

LOVE NET Map p92
ラブネット

☎ 5771-5511; www.lovenet-jp.com; 3rd fl, Hotel Ibis, 7-14-4 Roppongi, Minato-ku; suites per hr from ¥4000; ⏲ 6pm-5am; ◉ Hibiya or Toei Ōedo Line to Roppongi (exit 4A)

Love Net has 25 themed suites with a dizzying range of decor. There's an Arabian Suite, a Heaven Suite, and an Aqua Suite, complete with large jacuzzi for getting wet while yodelling. Just watch the microphones!

PASELA Map p92
パセラ

☎ 0120-759-880; www.pasela.co.jp, in Japanese; 5-16-3 Roppongi, Minato-ku; per hr per person Sun-Thu ¥525, Fri & Sat ¥630; ⏲ 5pm-8am Mon-Fri, 2pm-10am Sat & Sun; ◉ Hibiya or Toei Ōedo Line to Roppongi (exit 3)

Pasela boasts decor that is a cut above the other yodelling parlours, as well as six floors of karaoke rooms including swanky VIP suites. There's an extensive selection of Western songs, wine, champagne and sweets on the menu, and a decent Mexican bar-restaurant in the basement. From 5pm to 7pm it's karaoke happy hour – ¥400, including one drink.

SHIDAX VILLAGE Map p102
シダックスビレッジ

☎ 3461-9356; www.shidax.co.jp/sc, in Japanese; 1-12-13 Jinnan, Shibuya-ku; per hr Fri-Sun ¥1030, Mon-Thu ¥950, 2hr all you can drink ¥4200; ⏲ 11am-5am; ◉ Shibuya (Hachikō exit)

Topped by a massive red neon sign, Shidax Shibuya has about 90 private karaoke rooms, some of which are barrier-free. Others are specially designed for groups of up to 40 people, children (with playroom slides), and even dogs.

CLUBBING

You'll find tons of techno, disco and house in the city. Most of the music starts when doors open, usually around 8pm – but you won't want to arrive until 10pm or so, when the volume increases and the floor fills. At most places, you can dance until dawn. The biggest concern is when the trains stop and start.

AGEHA Map pp48-9
アゲハ

☎ 5534-1515; www.ageha.com; 2-2-10 Shin-Kiba, Kōtō-ku; admission ¥4000; ⏲ 11pm-5am Thu-Sat; ◉ Yūrakuchō Line to Shin-Kiba (main exit)

This gigantic waterside club rivals any you'd find in LA or Ibiza. Mostly international DJs appear here, with Japanese DJs filling out the mix. Counterbalancing the thumping dance floors are lounge spaces and a little pool area. Free buses run to the club every half-hour from the east side of Shibuya Station on Roppongi-dōri; bring photo ID.

CLUB 3.2.8 Map p92
クラブサンニイハチ

☎ 3401-4968; www.3-2-8.jp, in Japanese; B1 fl, 3-24-20 Nishi-Azabu, Minato-ku; admission incl 2 drinks ¥2000-2500; ⏲ 8pm-5am; ◉ Hibiya or Toei Ōedo Line to Roppongi (exit 1)

DJs at San-ni-pa (aka San-ni-hachi) spin a quality mix, from funk to reggae to R&B. With its refreshing un-Roppongi feel and a cool crowd of Japanese and *gaijin*, 3.2.8 is a fabulous place to boogie 'till dawn.

CLUB ASIA Map p102
クラブエイジア

☎ 5458-2551; www.clubasia.co.jp, in Japanese; 1-8 Maruyamachō, Shibuya-ku; admission around ¥2500; ⏲ 11pm-5am; ◉ Shibuya (Hachikō exit)

This massive club is worth a visit if you're on the younger end of 20-something.

Events here are usually jam-packed every night. Occasionally the club hosts some of Tokyo's bigger DJ events and hip-hop acts.

MUSE Map p92
ミューズ

☎ 5467-1188; www.muse-web.com, in Japanese; B1 fl, 4-1-1 Nishi-Azabu, Minato-ku; admission Sat men/women incl 2 drinks ¥2000/free; ⏰ 7pm-midnight Mon-Fri, 9pm-midnight Sat; ⊖ Hibiya or Toei Ōedo Line to Roppongi (exit 3)

Muse, a catacomblike underground space with intimate booths, dance floors and billiards, has an excellent mix of locals and foreigners. There's something for everyone here, whether you want to dance up a storm or just feel like playing darts or table tennis.

NEW LEX TOKYO Map p92
ニューレックストウキョウ

☎ 3479-7488; B1 fl, 3-13-14 Roppongi, Minato-ku; admission men/women from ¥4000/3000; ⏰ 8pm-5am; ⊖ Hibiya or Toei Ōedo Line to Roppongi (exit 3)

The Lex was one of Roppongi's first discos and is still the place where every visiting celebrity ends up. The cover here starts at around ¥3000 unless you've had your visage on the front of *Vogue* or *Rolling Stone*. But even noncelebrities get a free drink with admission.

RUBY ROOM Map p102
ルビールーム

☎ 3780-3022; www.rubyroomtokyo.com; 2nd fl, Kasumi Bldg, 2-25-17 Dōgenzaka, Shibuya-ku; admission varies; ⏰ 9pm-late; ⊖ Shibuya (Hachikō exit)

This cool, sparkly gem of a cocktail lounge is on a hill behind the Shibuya 109 building. With both DJ'd and live music, the Ruby Room is an appealing spot for older kids hanging in Shibuya. The cover includes one drink, but if you dine downstairs at Sonoma (p172), admission is free.

SALSA SUDADA Map p92
サルサスダーダ

☎ 5474-8806; www.salsasudada.org; 3rd fl, Fusion Bldg, 7-13-8 Roppongi, Minato-ku; admission Fri & Sat ¥1500; ⏰ 6pm-6am; ⊖ Hibiya or Toei Ōedo Line to Roppongi (exit 4)

Tokyo's sizable population of Peruvian and Colombian workers, many of whom grind away at factories in Kawasaki and Yoko-

top picks

CLUBS

Ageha (opposite)
Club 3.2.8 (opposite)
Ruby Room (left)
Muse (left)

hama, come here to salsa and merengue, as do many salsa-mad locals. If you don't know how to dance, they'll teach you (lessons held nightly).

SUPERDELUXE Map p92
スーパー・デラックス

☎ 5412-0515; www.super-deluxe.com; B1 fl, 3-1-25 Nishi-Azabu, Minato-ku; admission varies; ⏰ 6pm-late Mon-Sat; ⊖ Hibiya or Toei Ōedo Line to Roppongi (exits 1B & 3)

This groovy basement performance space, also a cocktail lounge and club of sorts, is very eclectic in its offerings, staging everything from hula-hoop gatherings to literary evenings. It's all fun. Check the website for event details.

WOMB Map p102
ウーム

☎ 5459-0039; www.womb.co.jp; 2-16 Maruyamachō, Shibuya-ku; admission ¥1500-4000; ⏰ 8pm-late; ⊖ JR Yamanote Line to Shibuya (Hachikō exit)

Womb is all about house, techno and drum 'n' bass. All four floors get jammed at weekends. Bring a flyer and they'll knock ¥500 to ¥1000 off the cover – check around Shibuya music shops beforehand, or print one from Womb's website. Picture ID required at the door.

LIVE MUSIC

Though the live-music scene keeps geriatric hours (shows often end around 9pm), rock, house, blues, jazz and electronica are thriving in Tokyo. Big international acts often appear at large venues such as the National Stadium (p209) in Yoyogi or Budōkan (Map pp48–9). But Tokyo has many good small live houses. Shibuya is particularly ripe with them, and exceptional, idiosyncratic venues are also scattered throughout the city.

BILLBOARD LIVE Map p92
ビルボードライブ東京

☎ 3405-1133; www.billboard-live.com; 4th fl, Tokyo Midtown, 9-7-4 Akasaka, Minato-ku; admission varies; ⏰ 5.30-9.30pm Mon-Fri, 5-9pm Sat & Sun; ◉ Hibiya or Toei Ōedo Line to Roppongi (Tokyo Midtown exit)

This glitzy amphitheatre-like space in Tokyo Midtown plays host to major foreign talent such as Steely Dan, The Beach Boys and Arrested Development. Japanese jazz, soul and rock groups also shake the rafters. The service is excellent and the drinks are reasonably priced.

CAVERN CLUB Map p92
カバーンクラブ

☎ 3405-5207; www.cavernclub.jp, in Japanese; 5-3-2 Roppongi, Minato-ku; admission ¥1500; ⏰ from 6pm; ◉ Hibiya or Toei Ōedo Line to Roppongi (exit 3)

The heartfelt, adeptly executed covers performed at Cavern Club continue to shine after all these years. The name of the spot, as any good John, Paul, George or Ringo fan would know, is the same as that of the Liverpool club that first featured the fabulous four flopheads.

CLUB QUATTRO Map p102
クラブクアトロ

☎ 3477-8750; www.club-quattro.com; 32-13 Udagawachō, Shibuya-ku; admission ¥3000-4000; ◉ Shibuya (Hachikō exit)

This venue feels like a concert hall, but it's actually more along the lines of a slick club. It books local and international bands of generally high quality. Though there's no explicit musical focus, emphasis is on rock and roll with leanings towards world music.

EGGMAN Map p102
エッグマン

☎ 3496-1561; www.eggman.jp, in Japanese; 1-6-8 Jinnan, Shibuya-ku; admission ¥1000-3000; ◉ JR Yamanote Line to Shibuya (Hachikō exit)

Follow the spiral staircase to the basement to hear blues, rock or light jazz musicians get down low. Most acts are local and of the lighter, sweeter variety. Show up to see whether tickets aren't completely sold out on a given night, and be sure to take a quick listen at the door to sample before committing. Most shows commence at around 7pm.

LA.MAMA Map p102
ラママ

☎ 3464-0801; www.lamama.net, in Japanese; B1 fl, 1-15-3 Dōgenzaka, Shibuya-ku; admission ¥2000; ⏰ 6.30pm-12.30am; ◉ Shibuya (Hachikō exit)

Just about every Japanese band from Buck-Tick to Melt-Banana has passed through here. The room is fairly spacious, but even when the place gets crowded you'll never be far from the stage. Shows usually begin around 7pm.

LIQUID ROOM Map p96
リキッドルーム

☎ 5464-0800; www.liquidroom.net; 3-16-6 Higashi, Shibuya-ku; admission varies; ⏰ 7pm-late; ◉ Ebisu (east exit)

Some of the world's greatest performers have graced the stage of the Liquid Room, from the Flaming Lips to Linton Kwesi Johnson. This is an excellent place to see an old favourite or find a new one, but you'll have to buy tickets as soon as they go on sale.

LOFT Map p110
ロフト

☎ 5272-0382; www.loft-prj.co.jp, in Japanese; B2 fl, 1-12-9 Kabukichō, Shinjuku-ku; admission ¥1500-3000; ⏰ 5pm-late; ◉ Shinjuku (east exit)

This well-respected, quarter-century-old Tokyo live house, whose chequerboard stage has hosted the feedback and reverb of many a Tokyo punk, is often grungy and smoky – with just the right level of sweaty intimacy. The music is always loud and usually good.

SHIBUYA-AX Map p102
渋谷アックス

☎ 5738-2020; www.shibuya-ax.com, in Japanese; 2-1-1 Jinnan, Shibuya-ku; admission varies; ◉ JR Shibuya (Hachikō exit)

Shibuya-Ax has hosted big international names such as Stereophonics, the Pogues and Cyndi Lauper as well as Japanese acts such as Triceratops. It's a large, slick venue with its own line of proprietary merchandise. Look for the logo evoking the nuclear hazard symbol.

SHIBUYA O-EAST Map p102
渋谷オーイースト

☎ 5458-4681; www.shibuya-o.com; 2-14-8 Dōgenzaka, Shibuya-ku; admission varies; ◉ JR Shibuya (Hachikō exit)

Shibuya O-East is the big mama of several related venues forming a compound of clubs up Love Hotel Hill. With its sheer size, this house draws bigger-name international and domestic acts.

CINEMAS

Tokyo cinemas show blockbuster movies in small spaces, while charging you an average ¥1800. Some Hollywood flicks take a while to open here. Most independent films in English are not dampened by dubbing and some of the more avant-garde theatres show films you might not see anywhere else. Take a look at www.japantimes.co.jp to check for listings.

EUROSPACE Map p102
ユーロスペース

☎ 3461-0211; www.eurospace.co.jp; Q-Ax Bldg, 1-5 Maruyamachō, Shibuya-ku; Ⓢ Shibuya (Hachikō exit)
The focus at this fine theatre remains unwaveringly on small European and Asian films. Eurospace also occasionally hosts documentary or feature-film festivals, which will be listed in the major English-language weeklies, and sometimes screens late shows.

TOHO CINEMAS ROPPONGI HILLS
Map p92

TOHO シネマズ六本木ヒルズ

☎ 5775-6090; www.tohotheater.jp; 6-10-2 Roppongi, Minato-ku; adult ¥1800-3000, child ¥1000, 1st day of month & women on Wed ¥1000; ⏲ 10am-midnight Sun-Wed, 10am-5am Thu-Sat; Ⓢ Hibiya or Toei Ōedo Line to Roppongi (Roppongi Hills exit)
Virgin's nine-screen multiplex has the biggest screen in Japan, as well as luxurious reclining seats and internet booking up to two days in advance for reserved seats. This state-of-the-art theatre also holds all-night screenings on nights before holidays.

YEBISU GARDEN CINEMA Map p96
恵比寿ガーデンシネマ

☎ 5420-6161; www.kadokawa-gardencinema .jp/yebisu, in Japanese; Yebisu Garden Pl, 4-20-2 Ebisu, Shibuya-ku; adult/child ¥1800/1000, 1st day of month ¥1000; ⏲ 10am-11pm; Ⓢ Ebisu (east exit, then Skywalk)
This small, comfortable movie house is at the far end of Yebisu Garden Place and screens foreign independent films, many in English. Tickets are numbered as they are sold and theatre-goers are called to screenings as their numbers come up, preventing competition for seats.

THE ARTS

top picks

What's your recommendation? www.lonelyplanet.com/tokyo

THE ARTS

PERFORMING ARTS

Tokyo has a stunningly vibrant performing-arts scene, offering top-notch classical music and jazz to traditional and contemporary dance and drama. If you've never seen a shower of artificial snow falling on kabuki actors who have just dispatched their samurai foes with feats of swordsmanship and acrobatics in *The Tale of the Forty-Seven Rōnin*, a beloved Japanese epic of revenge, then you're in for a treat. While many performing arts shows require Japanese language comprehension, their visual spectacle alone makes them very worthwhile.

TRADITIONAL THEATRE

Tokyo has one of the best traditional-theatre scenes in Japan. Watching a kabuki performance (see p37) at the Kabuki-za is usually a must-do, but while the theatre is being rebuilt 2013 (until spring) try the Shimbashi Embujō Theatre. You've probably already been warned, but keep in mind that *nō* (stylised Japanese dance-drama) performances can feel like they're crawling at a snail's pace (see p36). Believe it or not, it's even considered acceptable to doze (though not to snore). Outdoor *takigi* (torch-lit) *nō* performances, usually held from April to October on the grounds of a Buddhist temple or Shintō shrine, are more rousing because of the fires.

Happily, if you want to see kabuki, bunraku or *nō*, the Kabuki-za, Kokuritsu Gekijō and Kokuritsu Nō-gakudō have earphones or subtitles with English translation of the dramatic dialogue.

SHIMBASHI EMBUJŌ THEATRE Map p64
新橋演舞場

☎ 3541-2600; www.shochiku.co.jp/play/enbujyo, in Japanese; 6-18-2 Ginza, Chūō-ku; tickets ¥2500-17,000; Ⓜ Hibiya or Toei Asakusa Line to Higashi-Ginza (exit 6)

While Ginza's storied Kabuki-za Theatre is being rebuilt until 2013, corporate owner Shōchiku will mainly stage the plays at its Embujō Theatre, which also puts on super kabuki, a rocking subgenre that incorporates modern stagecraft. A full performance of traditional kabuki (see

p37) comprises three or four acts (usually from different plays) over an afternoon or an evening (typically 11am to 3.30pm or 4.30pm to 9pm), with long intervals between the acts. If four-plus hours sounds too long, you can usually purchase last-minute tickets for a single act. Since some acts tend to be more popular than others, enquire ahead as to which to catch, and arrive well in advance.

KOKURITSU GEKIJŌ Map p52
国立劇場

National Theatre; ☎ 3230-3000; www.ntj.jac .go.jp/english/; 4-1 Hayabusachō; tickets for kabuki/bunraku from ¥1500/4500; Ⓜ Hanzōmon Line to Hanzōmon Station (exit 1)

The prestigious National Theatre is Japan's premier venue for its traditional performing arts. Performances include kabuki, *gagaku* court music and *bunraku* puppetry (see p37). Earphones with English translation are available for rent (¥650 plus ¥1000 deposit). Check the website for performance schedules.

KOKURITSU NŌ-GAKUDŌ Map p106
国立能楽堂

National Nō Theatre; ☎ 3423-1331; www.ntj .jac.go.jp/english/; 4-18-1 Sendagaya, Shibuya-ku; tickets ¥2800-5600; Ⓜ JR Chūō Line to Sendagaya (main exit)

This theatre stages the traditional music, poetry and dances that *nō* is famous for, as well as the interludes of *kyōgen* (short, lively comic farces) that serve as cathartic comic relief. The stark legends and historical dramas unfold on an elegant cypress stage. Each seat has a small screen that can display an English translation of the dialogue.

CERULEAN TOWER NŌ THEATRE
Map p102
セルリアンタワー能楽堂

☎ 3477-6412; www.ceruleantower-hotel.com; B2 fl, 26-1 Sakuragaokachō, Shibuya-ku; admission varies; Ⓜ Shibuya (south exit)

Performances in Japanese are held in this traditional theatre (you can also pop by just to admire it between 2.30pm and 5.30pm daily) in the Cerulean Tower Tōkyū Hotel (p222).

THE ARTS PERFORMING ARTS

194

KANZE NŌ-GAKUDŌ Map p102
観世能楽堂

Kanze Nō Theatre; ☎ 3469-5241; www.kanze.net, in Japanese; 1-16-4 Shōtō, Shibuya-ku; tickets from ¥3150; ⊕ Shibuya (Hachikō exit)

Kanze Nō-gakudō is the main theatre for one of Tokyo's most highly regarded *nō* troupes. It houses a typical nō cypress stage, but there is no English translation.

TAKARAZUKA GEKIJŌ Map p57
宝塚歌劇

☎ 5251-2001; http://kageki.hankyu.co.jp/english/ index.html; 1-1-3 Yūrakuchō, Chiyoda-ku; tickets ¥3500-11,000; ⊕ Chiyoda, Hibiya or Toei Mita Line to Hibiya (exits A5 & A13)

While not really traditional theatre, the all-female Takarazuka Gekijō revue, going back to 1914, exposes Tokyo's knack for complexity. These musicals are in Japanese, but English synopses are available. A mostly female audience swoons over actresses in drag. If you love camp, this is for you.

CONTEMPORARY THEATRE

Tokyo has a lively contemporary theatre scene. Language can be a barrier, as most of the productions taking place in these alternative performance venues are in Japanese. Again, the visual spectacle can more than make up for gaps in understanding.

In addition to the listings here, Roppongi's SuperDeluxe (p189) often stages unique performance art pieces created by or involving foreign talent. The venerable Tokyo International Players troupe (www.tokyoplayers.org) also puts on English-language shows, such as *Little Shop of Horrors*, at different venues; they also welcome volunteer actors and production staff. Meanwhile, Festival/Tokyo (http://festival-tokyo.jp) is a newly established festival for avant-garde performing arts held in October to December and centred in Ikebukuro. The 2009 edition featured 16 international performances, including a Swiss-German production in which audience members were driven around Tokyo in a cargo truck.

DIE PRATZE Map pp48-9
ディプラッツ

☎ 3235-7990; www.geocities.jp/kagurara2000, in Japanese; 2-12 Nishi-Gokenchō, Shinjuku-ku; admission varies; ⊕ Tōzai Line to Kagurazaka (exit 1)

Home to experimental theatre group OM-2, this small space features a variety of genres, from ballet to *butō* (contemporary dance style; p32) to experimental performance pieces. Die Pratze is northwest of the Imperial Palace, near Kagurazaka Station.

GLOBE TOKYO THEATRE Map pp48-9
東京グローブ座

☎ 3366-4020; www.tglobe.net, in Japanese; 3-1-2 Hyakuninchō, Shinjuku-ku; admission varies; ⊕ JR Yamanote Line to Shin-Ōkubo

This modern replica of the famed Globe Theatre in London mainly stages plays by Shakespeare from Japanese troupes as well as foreign companies. From the station, go north along the railway to the Globe.

DENTSŪ SHIKI THEATRE UMI Map p64
電通四季劇場[海]

☎ 120-489-444; www.shiki.gr.jp; 1F Caretta Bldg, 1-8-2 Higashi-shimbashi, Minato-ku; admission varies; ⊕ Toei Ōedo Line to Shiodome (Caretta Shiodome exit)

Located in the Shio-Site complex beside the headquarters of the Dentsū advertising group, Shiki Theatre Sea stages Japanese versions of hit Western works such as *Mamma Mia!* and *Aida*. Other Shiki theatres near Takeshiba station on the Yurikamome monorail stage shows such as *The Lion King*. See the website for details.

KINGYO Map p92
金魚

☎ 3478-3000; www.kingyo.co.jp; 3-14-17 Roppongi, Minato-ku; admission from ¥3500; ☾ shows 7.30pm & 10pm daily, 1.30am Fri & Sat; ⊕ Hibiya or Toei Ōedo Line to Roppongi (exit 3)

By a cemetery off Roppongi's main drag, cheeky Kingyo puts on a glitzy, colourful cabaret of transsexual ('new half' in Japanese) and drag queen performers who revel in social critique. Look for the yellow sign showing a goldfish *(kingyo)* kissing a penis.

MUSCLE THEATRE Map p102
マッスルシアター

☎ 3465-9903; www.musclemusical.com; 2-1-1 Jinnan, Shibuya-ku; admission ¥5800-9800; ⊕ Shibuya (Hachikō exit)

Opened in 2007, the popular Muscle Theatre shows campy but exciting performances of acrobatics, dance, juggling acts and gravity-defying jumps and BMX stunts that are part of the Muscle Musical experience.

SUZUNARI THEATRE off Map pp48-9
ザ・スズナリ

☎ 3469-0511; www.honda-geki.com/suzunari .html, in Japanese; 1-45-15 Kitazawa, Setagaya-ku; admission varies; ◉ Odakyū or Keiō Inokashira Line to Shimokitazawa (south exit)

A good bit of Japanese would be helpful in getting the gist of these underground theatre pieces. Like most avant-garde theatre, plays here tend towards experimental explorations of contemporary issues.

ZA KŌENJI off Map pp48-9
座・高円寺

☎ 3223-7300; http://za-koenji.jp; 2-1-2 Kōenji-Kita, Suginami-ku; admission varies; ◉ JR Chūō Line to Kōenji (north exit)

Za Kōenji stages Japanese and foreign contemporary plays, dance, music and storytelling events. Designed by Itō Toyō, this architecturally splendid venue in western Tokyo opened in May 2009. It houses three theatres, a literature archive and the very sleek cafe Henri Fabre. A rehearsal hall here is set aside for the neighbourhood's summer Awa Ōdori dance parade.

SETAGAYA PUBLIC THEATRE
off Map pp48-9
世田谷パブリックシアター

☎ 5432-1526; http://setagaya-pt.jp/en/; 4-1-1 Taishiodo, Setagaya-ku; admission varies; ◉ Tōkyū Den-en-toshi Line to Sangenjaya (Carrot Tower exit)

The two spaces in this excellent venue, the Public Theatre and Theatre Tram, can seat more than 800. It has achieved popular success based on performances including Shakespeare, Oscar Wilde, *nō, kyōgen,* and a mixture of jazz and comedy shows, some directed at children. It also offers a good mix of foreign contemporary drama.

DANCE

Tokyo's dance scene is a mixture of both international and indigenous styles. At venues around the city you will find all the usual Western dance forms – ballet, modern, jazz and experimental – in abundance. You may also be able to see *butō* in its home environment, if your trip happens to coincide with a performance here.

AOYAMA ENKEI GEKIJŌ Map p106
青山円形劇場

Aoyama Round Theatre; ☎ 3797-5678; www .aoyama.org; 5-53-1 Jingūmae, Shibuya-ku; admission varies; ◉ Chiyoda, Ginza or Hanzōmon Line to Omote-sandō (exit B2)

Found within Kodomo-no-Shiro (National Children's Castle; p81) this midsized round theatre stages musicals, ballet and modern dance. The theatre is lovely; performances tend towards the conservative. Because of the venue's location, many programs are ideal for kids.

BUNKAMURA THEATRE COCOON
Map p102
文化村シアターコクーン

☎ 3477-9999; www.bunkamura.co.jp/english; 2-24-1 Dōgenzaka, Shibuya-ku; admission varies; ◉ Shibuya (Hachikō exit)

This dance space in one of Tokyo's largest arts complexes (p102) shows occasional experimental works by international dance troupes. It has also been known to stage musical dramas, though these take place less frequently than dance programs.

SESSION HOUSE Map p60
セッションハウス

☎ 3266-0461; www.session-house.net, in Japanese; 158 Yaraichō, Shinjuku-ku; admission varies; ◉ Tōzai Line to Kagurazaka (exit 1)

Most dance aficionados consider Session House one of the best traditional-, folk- and modern-dance spaces in the city. The small theatre seats only 100 people, which means that all performances have an intimate feel to them. Exit right from the station, make a right into the first narrow alley, and turn left where it becomes a dead-end. Session House will be a few metres on your right. Performances start around 7pm.

SPACE ZERO Map p110
スペースゼロ

☎ 3375-8741; www.spacezero.co.jp, in Japanese; B1 fl, 2-12-10 Yoyogi, Shinjuku-ku; admission varies; ◉ Toei Ōedo or Shinjuku Line to Shinjuku (exit 6)

This is a 550-seat fine-art performance venue that happens to be located centrally in Shinjuku. Space Zero is host to contemporary dance performances and experimental theatre productions. You'll find it in the basement of the Zenrōsai Kaikan building.

COMEDY

Japanese comedy relies more on silly puns and slapstick than irony as in the West, but laughs both modern and traditional, home-grown and foreign are on offer in Tokyo. Tokyo Comedy Store, a collective of foreign-language comics, puts on shows at venues such as Crocodile (below). See www.tokyocomedy.com for details.

CROCODILE Map p106
クロコダイル
☎ 3499-5205; www.crocodile-live.jp; B1 fl, New Sekiguchi Bldg, 6-18-8 Jingūmae, Shibuya-ku; admission ¥2000; 8-10.30pm; Chiyoda Line to Meiji-jingūmae (exit 1)
The Crocodile, which hosts all sorts of music acts on any given week, has live English stand-up, sketch and improv comedy on the last Friday of every month, sponsored by Tokyo Comedy Store.

ASAKUSA ENGEI HALL Map p84
浅草演芸ホール
☎ 3841-6545; 1-43-12 Asakusa, Taitō-ku; adult/student/child ¥2500/2000/1100; Ginza Line to Tawaramachi (exit 3)
Asakusa Engei Hall hosts traditional *rakugo*, with all performances conducted in Japanese. The linguistic confusion is mitigated by lively facial expressions and traditional props (performers use only a hand towel and a folding fan), which help translate comic takes on universal human experiences.

JAZZ

Tokyo has long loved jazz, and affections don't seem to be on the wane. Major international artists invariably stop in the city, particularly at the Blue Note, and Japan's emerging improvisers most often get their start here at one of the smaller clubs.

B-FLAT Map p88
ビーフラット
☎ 5563-2563; B1 fl, 6-6-4 Akasaka, Minato-ku; admission from ¥2500; 6.30-11pm; Chiyoda Line to Akasaka (exits 5A & 5B)
Located in a part of Akasaka that empties and grows quiet at night, this hip jazz club often features local and European talent, as well as healthy doses of Latin jazz.

BLUE NOTE TOKYO Map p92
ブルーノート東京
☎ 5485-0088; www.bluenote.co.jp; 6-3-16 Minami-Aoyama, Minato-ku; admission ¥6000-15,000; 5.30pm-1am Mon-Sat, 5pm-12.30am Sun; Chiyoda, Ginza or Hanzōmon Line to Omote-sandō (exit B3)
Serious cognoscenti roll up to Tokyo's prime jazz spot in Aoyama to take in the likes of Maceo Parker, Herbie Hancock and Doctor John. Like its sister acts in New York and Milan, the digs here are classily decorated with dark wood and deep velvet, making this a good spot for a slow night of cool sounds.

BUSKER HEAVEN Tim Hornyak

Going to my weekend news job at NHK TV, I would get off the Yamanote Line at JR Harajuku Station and proceed through three distinct Japanese subcultures until I reached, what I called, Busker Heaven. First there are the *gosurori* (gothic Lolita) teens who sport black neo-Victorian fashions – lace, frills and Little Bo Peep frocks. They congregate on Jingū-bashi between JR Harajuku Station and the entrance to Meiji-jingū. Next, just inside Yoyogi-kōen, are the twisting rockabillies with their pompadours, leather jackets and sound systems pumping out Chubby Checker. Finally there are the BMX kids doing freestyle tricks on their bikes, plus a few skateboarders. Each group keeps to its own turf, and each attracts foreign gawkers.

But travellers who keep going towards NHK Hall (Map p102) will meet an amazing parade of rockers, rappers, folk singers, acrobats and unclassifiable misfits who are out to show off their skills. They can be found on the pavement lining Yoyogi-kōen and in the pedestrian lane between the park and Kōen-dōri leading to Shibuya Station (the lane also hosts ethnic and organic food fairs as well as flea markets). These performers are a throwback to the days of the *takenoko-zoku* (bamboo-shoot tribe), youth who thronged here in the 1970s and 1980s in colourful, exotic costumes to dance and sing. The weekend scene got so popular and crowded that authorities shut it down in the early 1990s, but these vestiges are still highly entertaining – you'll find everything from *manzai* stand-up comics to inscrutable men in white body stockings. Most are out to promote themselves and have fun, not make money. This cornucopia of independent talent is the flipside of Tokyo's conformity, homogeneity and corporatism. It's also the best free spectacle in town.

NEW DUG Map p110
ニューダグ

☎ 3354-7776; www.dug.co.jp, in Japanese; 3-15-12 Shinjuku, Shinjuku-ku; admission varies; ◷ noon-2am Mon-Sat, noon-11.30pm Sun; ◉ Shinjuku (east exit)

The old Dug was a legend of the Tokyo jazz scene, hosting foreign and Japanese jazz greats and appearing in Murakami Haruki's novel *Norwegian Wood*. The new Dug is basically a jazz cafe offering more than 100 cocktails and Belgian beer, but the odd live performance has been held here. The owner is an avid photographer and has lined the walls with pics of Miles, Coltrane and others.

JAZZ SPOT INTRO Map p116
イントロ

☎ 3200-4396; www.intro.co.jp; B1 fl, NT Bldg, 2-14-8 Takadanobaba, Shinjuku-ku; admission ¥1000; ◷ from noon; ◉ JR Yamanote Line to Takadanobaba (main exit)

It's a good sign when a little club allows a quarter of its floor space to be monopolised by a sexy grand piano. It also bodes well when the place is staffed by musicians who love to talk shop all night. At Jazz Spot Intro, all the omens are favourable.

JZ BRAT Map p102
ジェイゼットブラット

☎ 5728-0168; 2nd fl, 26-1 Sakuragaokachō, Shibuya-ku; admission ¥3000-5000; ◷ 6-11pm Mon-Sat; ◉ Shibuya (south exit)

This lovely, airy venue in the Cerulean Tower Tōkyū Hotel books consistently solid acts from Tokyo and abroad. The space seats just over 100, who are always treated to an intimate ambience.

SHINJUKU PIT INN Map p110
新宿ピットイン

☎ 3354-2024; www.pit-inn.com; B1 fl, 2-12-4 Shinjuku, Shinjuku-ku; admission ¥3000-10,000; ◷ from 7.30pm Mon-Fri, from 2pm Sat & Sun; ◉ Marunouchi Line to Shinjuku-sanchōme (exit C5)

Shinjuku Pit Inn, which has been around for more than 35 years, is not the kind of place you come to talk over the music. Aficionados come here to listen in silence to Japan's best jazz performers. Weekend matinees are half the price of evening performances.

STB 139 Map p92
スイートバジル139

☎ 5474-1395; http://stb139.co.jp; 6-7-11 Roppongi, Minato-ku; admission ¥3000-7000; ◷ 6-11pm Mon-Sat; ◉ Hibiya or Toei Ōedo Line to Roppongi (exit 3)

STB has a large, lovely space that draws big-name domestic and international jazz acts. Performances run the gamut of the genre; check the calendar on the website for the current line-up. This classy joint is a good place to have an Italian dinner before a show; call for reservations between 11am and 8pm Monday to Saturday.

HOT HOUSE Map pp48-9
ホットハウス

☎ 3367-1233; 3-23-5 Takadanobaba, Shinjuku-ku; admission varies; ◷ 8.30pm-2am; ◉ JR Yamanote Line to Takadanobaba (main exit)

This must be the smallest jazz dive in the world. Musicians play in twos and threes (there's no room for more). Audiences are usually about 10; get here early if you're set on sitting in for the evening.

OPERA

World-class opera can regularly be seen in Tokyo at venues such as the New National Theatre, next to Tokyo Opera City (p111) in Shinjuku. The Japan Opera Foundation, managing the renowned Fujiwara Opera troupe, stages French and Italian operas.

NEW NATIONAL THEATRE Map p110
新国立劇場

Shin Kokuritsu Gekijō; ☎ 5351-3011; www.nntt .jac.go.jp/english/index.html; 1-1-1 Honmachi, Shibuya-ku; admission varies; ◉ Toei Shinjuku Line to Hatsudai (Theatre exit)

This is a main venue for opera in Tokyo, with Fujiwara Opera, Nihon Opera Kyokai and Nikkai Opera performing here. Part of the New National Theatre's arts complex, the Playhouse and the Pit are performance venues for modern dance, with the latter hosting just about every international dance luminary who passes through.

CLASSICAL MUSIC

Many of the world's top classical musicians are trained in Japan and much of the nation's talent makes its home in Tokyo. A thumb through one of the English dailies or a quick navigation through their websites will tell you what's on.

TOKYO PHILHARMONIC ORCHESTRA
www.tpo.or.jp/english/index.html

Founded in Nagoya in 1911, the Tokyo Philharmonic is Japan's oldest and largest orchestra with 166 members. Featuring distinguished foreign soloists and conductors and a perennial presence on the NHK TV New Year's special, the Philharmonic is based at Tokyo Opera City (p111) in Shinjuku but also performs at Suntory Hall in the Ark Hills complex in Akasaka (Map p88) and at Bunkamura Orchard Hall (p102) in Shibuya.

TOKYO SYMPHONY ORCHESTRA
www.tokyosymphony.com

One of Tokyo's best, established in 1946, this orchestra premieres works by contemporary Japanese composers, such as Dan Ikuma and Yoshiro Irino. It also performs traditional works by Western masters, such as Berlioz, Mahler and Schoenberg. Check its website for performance times and venues.

NHK SYMPHONY ORCHESTRA
www.nhkso.or.jp

Closely associated with luminaries such as Charles Dutoit, Vladimir Ashkenazy and André Previn, the NHK has worked with top-flight conductors and musicians over its 80-year history. It usually performs at Suntory Hall in the Ark Hills complex in Akasaka (Map p88) and NHK Hall at the NHK Broadcast Centre in Shibuya (Map p102).

SPORTS & ACTIVITIES

top picks

- Aqua Garden Mitsukoshi-yū (p204)
- Ryōgoku Kokugikan (p208)
- Jingū-gaien Cycling Centre (p205)
- Jingū Baseball Stadium (p209)
- Aqua Field Shiba Park (p207)
- Tokyo Dome (p209)

SPORTS & ACTIVITIES

Everyone needs to let off some steam once in a while, and though you may be working up a sweat navigating the streets, you may crave a more intense workout than the subway station stairs can offer. From martial-arts training and pumping iron to a vigorous swim and a series of transcendental asanas, there is no shortage of sports on offer in the Japanese capital.

Even if you're not the athletic type, Tokyo brims with activities catering to both the casual dabbler and the devout practitioner. Try your hand at flower arranging, take a few Japanese classes, catch a few innings of baseball or, better yet, a few bouts of sumō.

Also open to the public are Tokyo's many public baths and hot springs. If you've had a long day of sightseeing and are starting to feel a bit travel worn, a blissful soak in a steaming bath is indeed the perfect antidote.

HEALTH & FITNESS

Most Tokyoites join private gyms or clubs to participate in recreational sports, which is why most facilities in the city are closed to non-members. However, you'll find that visitors do have access to some of the city's excellent, and heavily subsidised, public sports facilities.

MARTIAL ARTS

Martial arts in Japan are not as popular as foreigners might imagine, but they are practised widely. Small dōjō (places of practice) of disciplines exist in neighbourhoods all over Tokyo, but most instruction and practice is conducted in Japanese. The following organisations can point you to dōjō where you may be able to take lessons or attend a training session.

AIKIKAI FOUNDATION Map p110
財団法人 合気会
☎ 3203-9236; www.aikikai.or.jp; 17-18 Wakamatsuchō, Shinjuku-ku; ☻ 6am-7.30pm Mon-Sat, 8.30-11.30am Sun; ◉ Toei Ōedo Line to Wakamatsu-Kawada (main exit)
Practicing aikidō at the Aikikai Foundation requires filling out an application form and paying a registration fee in addition to a monthly course fee. Shorter-term visitors should check the website for details about training at the headquarters.

JAPAN KARATE ASSOCIATION Map p60
日本空手協会
☎ 5800-3091; www.jka.or.jp; 2-23-15 Kōraku, Bunkyō-ku; ◉ JR Sōbu Line or Nambuku, Yūrakuchō, or Tōzai Lines to Iidabashi (east or A1 exits)

The Tokyo headquarters of the JKA teaches Shōtokan-style karate under the tradition of Master Funakoshi Gichin, born in the Ryūkyū Kingdom in 1868. About 100 Japanese and foreign karateka (karate practitioners) train at this dōjō, which welcomes visitors. Email sohonbu@jka.or.jp if you're interested.

KŌDŌKAN JUDŌ INSTITUTE Map p78
講道館
☎ 3818-4172; www.kodokan.org; 1-16-30 Kasuga, Bunkyō-ku; ☻ 3.30-8pm Mon-Fri, 4-7.30pm Sat; ◉ Toei Mita or Toei Ōedo Line to Kasuga (exits A1 & A2)
Students of judō who are looking to keep up their practice while in Tokyo are welcome to stop by Kōdōkan Judō Institute in the afternoons for open practice. Lessons are also available here on a long-term basis, and visitors are welcome to observe training during practice hours.

KYŪMEIKAN off Map pp48-9
久明館
☎ 3930-4636; www.kyumeikan.info; 2-1-7 Akatsuka-Shinmachi, Itabashi-ku; ◉ Yūrakuchō Line to Chikatetsu-Narimasu (main exit)
Kyūmeikan dōjō welcomes foreign observers as well as practitioners of kendō (meaning 'way of the sword'), a discipline of wooden sword fighting that evolved from actual sword techniques used by samurai in battle. There's a fee of around ¥5000 for a lesson lasting one hour or more; those seeking to practice here can usually reach an English speaker on the phone at the dōjō.

PUBLIC BATHS & ONSEN

Before modern housing, everyone in Tokyo bathed at sentō (public baths) and onsen (hot springs). While the latter remain popular vacation spots outside the capital, *sentō* have seen customers dwindle. Still, for only around ¥500, you can get the perfect soak alongside locals at neighbourhood baths. If you're craving a detour off the beaten tourist path, this is it.

Though typically associated with mountain resorts and small country inns, several onsen are found in Tokyo. Most of these onsen draw their mineral water from deep underneath Tokyo Bay – what sets an onsen apart from a *sentō* is that onsen water issues from a natural hot spring. For more on onsen, see p228.

ASAKUSA KANNON ONSEN Map p84
浅草観音温泉

☎ 3844-4141; 2-7-26 Asakusa, Taitō-ku; admission ¥700; ⏰ 6.30am-6pm Fri-Wed; ⓣ Tsukuba

Express Line to Asakusa (exit 2), Ginza Line to Asakusa (exit 1)
Near Sensō-ji, the brownish water at this traditional bathhouse is a steamy 40ºC. Asakusa's historic ambience makes this a great place for a soul-soothing soak.

JAKOTSU-YU Map p84
蛇骨湯

☎ 3841-8645; 1-11-11 Asakusa, Taitō-ku; admission ¥450; 1pm-midnight Wed-Mon; ⓣ Tsukuba Express to Asakusa (exit 5), Ginza Line to Tawara-machi (exit 3)
This recently renovated Edo-era bath is one of our favourite *sentō* in Tokyo. Once you're cooked in the hot indoor bath, you're ready for the real treat: the lovely,

SENTŌ PRIMER

Prior to Japan's miraculous postwar economic revolution, most private homes in Japan did not have baths, so every evening people gathered their toiletries into a bowl and headed off to the local neighbourhood *sentō* (public bath). More than just a place to wash oneself, the *sentō* served as a kind of community meeting hall, where news and gossip were traded and social ties strengthened.

Unfortunately, the number of *sentō* in Japan is rapidly declining, but there are still enough left in Tokyo for you to sample this most traditional aspect of Japanese life. More than just a cultural experience, however, a soak in a *sentō* is the ideal way to cure the sore muscles born of a day of sightseeing.

Sentō can be identified by their distinctive *noren* (half-length curtains over the doorway). *Sentō noren* usually bear the hiragana (ゆ, *yu*) for hot water (occasionally, it may be written in kanji: 湯). At the bottom of the *noren*, look for the kanji for men (男) and for women (女).

Once you've located a *sentō*, determine the men's or women's side, take off your shoes, place them in a locker in the entryway and slide open the door to the changing room. As you enter, you'll see the attendant, who sits midway between the men's and women's changing rooms, collecting the entry fee. *Sentō* usually cost between ¥300 and ¥500, which generally includes the rental of a modesty towel. If you've forgotten any of your toiletries, you can buy them here for a small price. Most *sentō* are open from around 3pm to midnight.

In the changing room, you'll see a bank of lockers and stacks of wicker or plastic baskets. Grab a basket and drop your clothes into it. Next, find one of the common *senmenki* (washbowls) and place your toiletries in it, then place your basket in a locker (these have keys on elastic bands). Now, use your modesty towel to cover up your sensitive bits, but don't be alarmed if others around you haven't – public nudity doesn't have the same negative connotation here as it does in the West.

Before you jump head first into the bath and immediately horrify all of your fellow bathers, you will first need to rigorously wash your entire body. This is done at the banks of low showers and taps that line the walls of the place. Grab a low stool and a bucket, and plant yourself at an open spot. First, fill the bucket with hot water and soap, work up a lather, and start scrubbing everywhere (and we do mean everywhere!). As a foreigner, your scrub-down process might be scrutinised by your fellow bathers, so it does pay to be thorough.

Once you've washed thoroughly and removed all the soap, you are ready for a relaxing soak in the tubs. At a good *sentō*, you'll have a choice of several tubs, which usually include a scalding tub, a cold tub and a whirlpool bath, as well as a sauna. At a great *sentō*, you may also find a variety of mineral-water tubs and possibly even an electric bath, which, believe it or not, is meant to simulate swimming with electric eels!

While soaking in the tub, it's good form to adhere to the following etiquette: try not to enter the tub with your modesty towel, keep your head above the water, minimise your splashing and never wash yourself with the bath water. Otherwise, feel free to spread out, chit-chat with your fellow bathers and even take a snooze.

After soaking away the strains of the day, if you've done everything correctly, you will have achieved a state called *yude-dako* (boiled octopus). This is the point when you're going to want to rehydrate with a sports drink, or go for broke by downing a beer or two. Regardless of which route you choose, however, you're going to want to stagger home quickly and collapse onto your futon. Trust us – after a day at the *sentō*, you'll sleep like the dead.

FEELING TONGUE-TIED?

Don't know your *sayonara* from your *sumimasen*? The following language schools can help you start speaking the Japanese language in no time:

Academy of Language Arts (日本語学校; ALA; Map p60; ☎ 3235-0071; www.ala-japan.com; 5th fl, No 2 Tōbundō Bldg, 2-16-2 Agebachō, Shinjuku-ku; ⊛ Namboku, Tōzai, Yūrakuchō or Toei Ōedo Line to Idabashi, exit B1)

East West Japanese Language Institute (イーストウエスト日本語学校; off Map pp48–9; ☎ 3366-4717; www.eastwest.ac.jp; 2-36-9 Chūō, Nakano-ku; ⊛ Marunouchi Line to Nakano-sakaue)

Sendagaya Japanese Institute (千駄ヶ谷日本語教育研究所; Map p116; ☎ 3232-6181; www.jp-sji .org; 7th fl, Takadanobaba Centre Bldg, 1-31-18 Takadanobaba, Shinjuku-ku; ⊛ JR Yamanote Line to Takadanobaba, Waseda exit)

lantern-lit, rock-framed *rotemburo* (outdoor bath) that's just outside. You could sit here for hours, perhaps wandering occasionally to the cold bath a few steps away, just to keep yourself awake. Keep in mind that the sauna is off limits unless you pay an extra ¥200.

KOMPARU-YU ONSEN Map p57
金春湯

☎ 3571-5469; 8-7-5 Ginza, Chūō-ku; admission ¥450; ⏰ 2-11pm Mon-Sat; ⊛ Ginza or JR Yaman-ote Line to Shimbashi (exit 1)

The Meiji-era Komparu-yu is a refreshing slice of Shitamachi (low city) in the midst of posh Ginza. This is a simple bathhouse without a sauna or stand-up showers. Tile art includes old-school koi motifs. The matriarch here keeps a watchful eye over everyone from her perch on the old wooden *bandai* (counter).

AQUA GARDEN MITSUKOSHI-YŪ
Map pp48-9
アクアガーデン三越湯

☎ 3473-4126; 5-12-16 Shirokane, Minato-ku; admission from ¥420; ⏰ 3.30-11.30pm Sat-Thu; ⊛ Hibiya Line to Hirō (exit 4)

This charming *sentō* has an outdoor bath that fits five to 10 comfortably (it rotates sexes each week). Other aquatic attractions include saunas, jacuzzis and a hammam-style marble slab that drips water down your back. For ¥1220 you get access to the *sentō* and sauna, plus towel rental and a large locker.

LA QUA SPA Map p60
スパラクーア

☎ 5800-9999; www.tokyo-dome.co.jp/e/laqua/ spa.htm; 1-3-61 Kōraku, Bunkyō-ku; admission ¥2565, Healing Baden extra ¥525, late-night bath-ing extra ¥1890; ⏰ 11am-9am; ⊛ Marunouchi Line to Kōrakuen, JR Chūō or JR Sōbu Line to Suidōbashi (west exit)

One of the city's few true *onsen*, this unbelievably chic and sophisticated spa complex is where serious bathing aficionados go to indulge in a bit of class and luxury. With multiple floors boasting an incredible variety of baths, massage parlours, restaurants and relaxation areas, achieving beauty as well as peace of mind has never been easier.

Ō-EDO ONSEN MONOGATARI Map p127
大江戸温泉物語

☎ 5500-1126; http://www.ooedoonsen.jp /higaeri/english/index.html; 2-57 Aomi, Kōtō-ku; adult/child from ¥2900/1600, from 6pm-2am ¥2000/1600; ⏰ 11am-9am; ⊛ Yurikamome Line to Telecom Center (main exit), Rinkai Line to Tokyo Teleport; free shuttle buses from Shinagawa, Tokyo, other stations

Ō-edo Onsen Monogatari does bill itself as an old Edo 'theme park', so come here for kitsch rather than authenticity. It's a good place to socialise in mixed groups, as there's an outdoor footbath area for relaxing in your *yukata* (light cotton robe). You wouldn't come here for a simple scrub, but if you'd like to make a day of it in Odaiba with some chums, this is a good place for an evening soak. See p126 for more information.

ROKURYU KŌSEN Map p78
六龍鉱泉

☎ 3821-3826; 3-4-20 Ikenohata, Taitō-ku; admission ¥450; ⏰ 3.30-11pm Tue-Sun; ⊛ Chiyoda Line to Nezu (exit 2)

The bubbling amber water here contains minerals that the many old timers who come here in the afternoon claim can cure a number of ailments. These same folk tell stories about the occasional ancient leaf that's worked its way up the pipes and into the tub. These leaves are in high demand and are reputed to be excellent for your skin. The bath is located down a small lane on the right; look for the traditional Japanese building with the blue curtains.

RUNNING

While Tokyo's city streets are generally much too crowded for jogging – though they do make an excellent obstacle course in that respect – there are parks aplenty for runners. Some of the best places to run, with lots of greenery and long paths, include Yoyogi-kōen (p107), Meiji-jingū (p105) and Higashi-gyōen (p51). If you prefer not to jog solo, and instead like it to be a social event, try 'hashing' with the Tokyo members of that famous drinking organisation with a running problem.

HASH HOUSE HARRIERS
http://tokyohash.org
Formed in 1938, this worldwide club's activities are a mix of mad dashing and serious drinking done by cheeky joggers with sobriquets such as 'Sakura Sucker'. Several planned runs meander through a variety of routes each week. Bring your best drinking shoes.

CYCLING

Tooling around Tokyo on a bike can lead you onto some wonderful unexpected alleys and backstreets, but you will have to sharpen your senses to avoid taxi doors opening and pedestrians suddenly veering into your path. Some ryokan (traditional Japanese inns) rent or loan bicycles to their guests, and there are a few mellow cycling courses in the city parks. Be sure to always lock up your bike as theft does happen.

IMPERIAL PALACE CYCLING COURSE
Map p52
パレスサイクリングコース
☎ 3211-5020; ☷ 10am-3pm Sun; ⊜ Chiyoda Line to Nijūbashimae (exit 2)
Every Sunday, 500 free bicycles are lent for use along the 3.3km Imperial Palace cycling course. Bikes are given on a first-come, first-served basis and can be picked up next to

the Babasakimon police box just outside the station exit.

JINGŪ-GAIEN CYCLING CENTRE
Map p106
神宮外苑サイクリングセンター
☎ 3405-8753; 10-2 Kasumigaoka, Shinjuku-ku; ☷ 9am-3.30pm Sun & holidays; ⊜ Toei Ōedo Line to Kokuritsu-Kyōgijō (exit A2)
On Sundays and holidays, 400 bicycles are lent to ride the circular road at Meiji-jingū's outer gardens. Pick up these free bikes outside Jingū-Gaien Cycling Centre near the National Stadium (Map p106).

TOKYO RENT A BIKE Map p96
東京レンタル自転車
☎ 080-3209-9996; www.tokyorentabike.com; 8th fl, 3-5-11 Nakameguro, Meguro-ku; per day from ¥600; ☷ 10am-1pm; ⊜ Hibiya Line to Nakameguro
This shop up Yamate-dōri from Nakameguro Station rents out multi- and single-gear city bicycles for touring around Tokyo. Check it out on its YouTube channel for details.

top picks

ACTIVITIES

- Sumō wrestling (p207) Watch the big guys take each other on at this traditional Japanese outing.
- Baseball (p208) It may be as American as apple pie, but it's also as Japanese as raw tuna.
- Sento (p203) Nothing treats those travel-worn bones like a good soak in a communal tub.
- Ikebana (p207) It takes a lifetime to learn, but only a few classes to get the basics of flower arranging.
- Learn Japanese (opposite) Nihongo wo wakarimasu ka? If not, then it might be time to learn the lingo.
- Martial Arts (p202) Tokyo may be one of the world's safest cities, but it's still good to know how to defend yourself.
- Cycle (left) One of the best ways to learn the lay of the land is to travel on two wheels.
- Conversation cafes (p208) Make new friends while helping a few Japanese people brush up on their English.
- Golf (p206) Sure enough, 18 holes might break the bank, but it's a quintessential Japanese experience.
- Horse racing (p209) See if you can win some extra yen.

GOLF

Golfers who live in Tokyo claim that it's cheaper to tee off in Hawaii because the entire trip costs less than booking a space at one of the 500 local courses. Sadly, they're probably right, though Tokyo does have around 20 public golf courses that are somewhat reasonable (assuming you can get a spot). For detailed info on golfing in and outside Tokyo, make sure you log on to www.golf -in-japan.com.

TOKYO TOMIN GOLF COURSE
off Map pp48-9
東京都民ゴルフ場
☎ 3919-0111; 1-15-1 Shinden, Adachi-ku; admission weekdays/holidays from ¥6000/7000; ☺ JR Keihin-Tohoku Line or Namboku Line to Ōji, then taxi (10 min)

If you dream of sand traps and short puts, you'll want to consider giving this 18-hole, 63-par course a go. Some ability to speak Japanese will be useful when making a reservation, though most hotel staff can easily help you past this obstacle. One thing to keep in mind is that spring and autumn tend to be when the weather is fine and the course is often booked out many weeks in advance. It's the most conveniently located of all the public golf courses.

SKATING

What could be better on a sweltering summer afternoon than gliding around an icy, indoor skating rink? If you'd rather mentally score the double axels than execute them, the rinks sell 'observer' tickets (¥300 to ¥400) for those not taking to the ice.

CITIZEN PLAZA Map pp48-9
シチズンプラザ
☎ 3371-0910; 4-29-27 Takadanobaba, Shinjuku-ku; adult/child ¥1300/800; ☺ noon-7.45pm Mon-Sat, 10am-6.30pm Sun; ☺ JR Yamanote Line to Takadanobaba (Waseda exit)

This 30m by 60m slab of ice is used for lessons, ice hockey, speed skating and general-purpose fun. Skate rental will set you back ¥500; discounts are taken off admission if you show up after 5pm. Head west out of Takadanobaba Station and walk about five minutes along Waseda-dōri; look for the big white building to your left.

MEIJI-JINGŪ GAIEN ICE SKATING RINK Map p106
明治神宮アイススケート場
☎ 3403-3458; 11-1 Kasumigaoka, Shinjuku-ku; adult/child ¥1300/900; ☺ noon-6pm Mon-Fri, 10am-6pm Sat & Sun; ☺ Toei Ōedo Line to Koko-ritsu-Kyōgijō (exit A2), JR Sōbu Line to Sendagaya (main exit)

Open year-round, Meiji-jingū Ice Skating Rink is there for a good twirl and glide around the rink. When you arrive you'll be given a choice between three types of skates – ice hockey, speed skating and figure skating (rentals cost ¥500). Choose whichever will help you move across the NHL-sized rink. Discounts on admission are offered after 3pm (adult ¥1000).

GYMS & POOLS

In general, joining a Japanese gym is a cumbersome, expensive process best undertaken only by those who will be living in Tokyo. With that said, if you're here for the long run, we recommend it – most gyms have very good facilities and superb bathing areas that are especially tempting in winter. However, if you're just in the mood for a good swim or functional workout, the following spots should help you work up a good sweat. Most swimming pools require that swimmers wear bathing caps.

CHIYODA SOGO TAIKUKAN POOL
Map p67
千代田区立総合体育館プール
☎ 3256-8444; www.city.chiyoda.tokyo.jp/english/ e-guide/sports.html; 2-1-8 Uchi-Kanda, Chiyoda-ku; pool/gym ¥600/350; ☺ 9am-9.30pm, closed 3rd Mon; ☺ JR Yamanote Line to Kanda (west exit)

A public pool and weight room are available for reasonable fees. The pool is open to the public from 5pm to 9pm on most days, but hours vary. Keep in mind that certain times during the day are reserved for those residing in Chiyoda. The website lists details in English.

CHŪŌ-KU SŌGŌ SPORTS CENTRE
Map p122
中央区総合スポーツセンター
☎ 3666-1501; 2-59-1 Nihombashi-Hamachō, Chūō-ku; pool/gym ¥500/400; ☺ 7am-9.30pm; ☺ Toei Shinjuku Line to Hamachō

Another of Tokyo's public gyms, this one in Chūō-ku has gym facilities and a swimming pool. Kyūdo (Japanese archery) prac-

THE GENTLE ART OF IKEBANA

Fancy a hand at ikebana, the traditional Japanese art of flower arranging? Schools to get you started:

Ohara School of Ikebana (小原流いけばな; International Division; Map p106; ☎ 5774-5097; www.ohararyu.or.jp; 5-7-17 Minami-Aoyama, Minato-ku; ◉ Chiyoda, Ginza or Hanzōmon Line to Omote-sandō, exits B1 & B3) Ohara specialises in flower-arranging classes for students of all levels. One-timers and short-term visitors are welcome, as are those who'd just like to watch (observation fee ¥800). English classes are Wednesdays and Thursdays; trial lesson ¥4000.

Sōgetsu Kaikan (草月会館; Map p88; ☎ 3408-1151; www.sogetsu.or.jp/english/index.html; Sōgetsu Kaikan Bldg, 7-2-21 Akasaka, Minato-ku; ◷ 9.30am-8.30pm Mon-Thu, 10am-8pm Fri; ◉ Ginza, Hanzōmon or Toei Ōedo Line to Aoyama-itchōme, exit 4) An avant-garde ikebana school, with ikebana displays, a bookshop and coffee shop. English classes are held on Mondays from 10am to noon, and cost ¥3800. See p89 for more information.

tice also takes place at the sports centre; though no lessons are given, spectators are welcome to watch this graceful discipline if anyone is practising here.

TOKYO METROPOLITAN GYMNASIUM INDOOR POOL Map p106
東京体育館

☎ 5474-2111; 1-17-1 Sendagaya, Shibuya-ku; admission up to 2 hr ¥600; ◷ 9am-10pm Mon-Sat, 9am-8pm Sun; ◉ JR Sōbu Line to Sendagaya (main exit)

If all that movement on land has made you crave a few laps, head here. In addition to a pool there's a weights room, although its use requires an extra fee. The gymnasium and pool are located to the northwest of the National Stadium in Harajuku, a few minutes' walk from the Sendagaya JR station.

AQUA FIELD SHIBA PARK Map p92
アクアフィールド芝公園

☎ 5733-0575; 2-7-2 Shibakōen, Minato-ku; admission up to 2hr adult/child ¥400/150; ◷ 9am-8pm Jul & Aug, 9am-5pm Sept; ◉ Mita Line to Shibakōen (exit A3)

Open from the beginning of July through till mid-September, this outdoor 50m x 18m pool near Tokyo Tower is a great spot to beat the heat (it's a sports field the rest of the year). There's also a kids' pool with a slide and a sauna.

YOGA & PILATES

Although yoga is not as popular as it was a few years back, loyal devotees are still twisting and contorting themselves in the pursuit of peace of mind and strength of body. If you're looking to take part in yoga or Pilates classes, try the following.

INTERNATIONAL YOGA CENTER
off Map pp48-9
インターナショナルヨガセンター

☎ 5397-2741; www.iyc.jp/en; 4th fl, 5-30-6 Ogikubo, Suginami-ku; sessions ¥3000; ◉ JR Chūō Line or Marunouchi Line to Ogikubo (south exit)

Drop in to do the downward dog at the International Yoga Center, which has branches across Tokyo. Ninety-minute classes in Ashtanga and Iyengar yoga are given in Japanese, but you can check the website for a list of English-speaking instructors and where and when they'll be teaching.

BODY ARTS & SCIENCE INTERNATIONAL Map p92

☎ 6425-7054; www.basipilates.jp; 7th fl, Fleg Roppongi Quarto, 7-19-9 Roppongi, Minato-ku; trial lessons from ¥3000; ◉ Toei Ōedo Line or Hibiya Line to Roppongi (exits 4B or 2)

This Pilates studio near the Roppongi Hills complex is one of several BASI branches in the capital offering machine and mat sessions. Check the website for discounts on lesson fees.

SPECTATOR SPORT

From sumō and baseball to soccer and horse racing, the Tokyo's sports calendar is jam-packed full of exciting events year-round.

SUMŌ

Sumō is a fascinating, highly ritualised activity steeped in Shintō tradition. Perhaps sumō's continuing claim on the national imagination lies in its ancient origins and elaborate rites; it's the only traditional Japanese sport that still has enough clout to draw big crowds and dominate primetime TV.

ENGLISH CONVERSATION CAFES

An excellent way to meet Japanese people is to stop by an English conversation cafe, where you can chat with students looking to brush up their language skills. The following list should get you started:

Com 'Inn (コムイン; Map p96; ☎ 3794-7366; www.cominn-jp.com; admission ¥1000; 5th fl, Arai Bldg, 1-3-9 Minami-Ebisu, Shibuya-ku; ⊚ Ebisu, west exit) The longest-running and most established conversation cafe in Tokyo, Com 'Inn holds international parties on the first Saturday and third Friday of every month; admission costs ¥1500.

Leafcup (リーフカップ; Map p60; ☎ 5856-7587; www.leafcup.com; party admission men/women ¥3000/2000; 4-2-6 Iidabashi, Chiyoda-ku; ⊚ Namboku, Yūrakuchō or Toei-Ōedo lines to Iidabashi, exit A4) A comfortable, attractive conversation cafe, Leafcup holds biweekly international parties on Saturday nights that highlight different fun-filled themes.

Mickey House (英会話喫茶ミッキハウス; Map p116; ☎ 3209-9686; www.mickeyhouse.jp; foreigner admission incl 1 drink ¥500; 4th fl, Yashiro Bldg, 2-14-4 Takadanobaba, Shinjuku-ku; ⊚ JR Yamanote Line to Takadanobaba, Waseda exit) An excellent place for a beer and light conversation most nights of the week, Mickey House really picks up on Friday and Saturday nights during international parties of their own.

When a tournament isn't in session, you can enjoy the Sumō Museum (p121), next door to the stadium. Displays include humungous wrestler hand-prints and the referees' ceremonial clothing. Unfortunately, there are no English explanations, and during tournaments the museum is open only to attending ticket holders. Another option is visiting a sumō stable to see the wrestlers at morning practice.

RYŌGOKU KOKUGIKAN Map p122
両国国技館

☎ 3623-5111; www.sumo.or.jp/eng/index.html; 1-3-28 Yokoami, Sumida-ku; admission ¥2100-14,300; ⊗ main bouts, ceremonies from 3.40pm; ticket office for same-day/advance sales 8am-5pm/10am-4pm; ⊚ JR Sōbu or Toei Ōedo Lines to Ryōgoku Tokyo's *bashō* (sumō wrestling tournaments) take place at this stadium in January, May and September. Unless you're aiming for a big match at a weekend you should be able to secure a ticket: *bashō* take place over 15 days. Upstairs seats are usually available and cost from ¥2100 to ¥8200. Tickets can be purchased up to a month prior to the tournament at http://sumo-ticket.jp or at FamilyMart and Lawson store ticket machines (all in Japanese), or you can simply turn up on the day of the match, but it's advisable to get there early. Note that only one ticket is sold per person, a clever device used to foil scalpers. The stadium is adjacent to JR Ryōgoku Station, on the north side of the railway tracks. If you can't go in person, NHK televises sumō from 3.30pm daily during tournaments.

TOMOZUNA STABLE Map pp48-9
友綱部屋

☎ 3624-0242; www.tomozuna-beya-fansite.biz; 3-1-9 Narihira Sumida-ku; ⊗ 8-10.30am; ⊚ Toei Asakusa or Hanzōmon Lines to Oshiage (exit A2) Established in 1757, the Tomozuna *heya* (sumō training house) is home to about 10 wrestlers including Ozeki Kaiō under the tutelage of former grappler Kaiki. You can watch them butting heads at morning practice when possible; send an email in advance to overseas_visitor@tomozuna-beya.jp. Be sure to follow the conduct rules and never set foot in the ring!

BASEBALL

Baseball is Japan's most popular sport and five of Japan's 12 pro-baseball teams are based in or near Tokyo. A trip to one of the local ballparks is truly a cultural (or perhaps a religious?) experience – the crowd behaviour is completely unlike what you're probably used to at home. The home team's fans often turn up in matching *happi* (half-length coats) and perform intricate cheering rituals in perfect unison led by special cheerleaders, one for each section, who make a job out of whipping fans into a well-ordered frenzy. Sitting in the cheap seats will put you right in the middle of it.

Baseball season starts at the end of March or the first week of April and runs until October. Tokyo Dome is probably the most exciting place to take in a game, though Jingū Stadium can make for a fun afternoon out when the weather is fair.

See also the Japanese Baseball Hall of Fame (p61) for some history of the sport in Japan.

JINGŪ BASEBALL STADIUM Map p106
神宮球場

Jingū Kyūjo; ☎ 3404-8999; www.jingu-stadium
.com; 13 Kasumigaoka, Shinjuku-ku; tickets adult/
child from ¥1500/500; ⏰ games 6pm; ⊙ Ginza
Line to Gaienmae (north exit)

Home to the Yakult Swallows, Tokyo's
number two team, Jingū Baseball Stadium
was originally built in 1926. When not hosting Yakult Swallows games, the baseball
stadium is sometimes used for high-profile
Little League and intercollegiate championships. You can buy tickets from the booth
in front of the stadium; outfield tickets can
cost as little as ¥1500.

TOKYO DOME Map p60
東京ドーム

Big Egg; ☎ 5800-9999; www.tokyo-dome.co.jp/e;
1-3-61 Kōraku, Bunkyō-ku; seats from ¥1700, standing room ¥1000; ⊙ JR Chūō or Sōbu Line or Mita
Line to Suidōbashi (west exit)

The 'Big Egg', as it's affectionately known,
is the best place to catch a baseball game
in the city, as it's the home turf of Japan's
most popular baseball team, the Yomiuri
Giants. Night games tend to be well-
attended and can be especially exciting.
There are ticket booths on three sides of
the Big Egg; after purchasing your ticket,
navigate to the gate you want.

J-LEAGUE SOCCER

Japan was already football crazy when the
World Cup came to Saitama and Yokohama
in 2002. Now it's a chronic madness, and five
minutes of conversation with any 10-year-
old in Tokyo about why they wanna grow
up to be like David Beckham should clear up
any doubts you might have to the contrary.
J-League games are generally played outside
the city. If you'd like to catch an international
match, try the National Stadium.

NATIONAL STADIUM Map p106
国立競技場

Kokuritsu Kyōgijō; ☎ 3403-1151; 3-1 Kasumi-
gaokamachi, Shinjuku-ku; admission from ¥2000;
⊙ JR Chūō Line to Sendagaya (east exit), Ōedo Line
to Kokuritsu Kyōgijō (exit A2)

Completed in 1958 and used as one of
the primary venues for the 1964 Olympics,
National Stadium now hosts the annual
Toyota Cup (November or December) and
other international soccer events.

HORSE RACING

There are two big racing tracks in the Tokyo
area, offering weekend gamblers a good
chance to wager (and lose) some money. Gam-
bling is illegal in Japan except in sanctioned
contexts – horse racing being one of them. If
you're itching to take your chances, look up
the Japan Racing Association's English guide
online at http://japanracing.jp. Races are generally held at weekends from 11am to 4pm
and are a hot destination for young couples
on dates.

ŌI KEIBAJŌ Map pp48-9
大井競馬場

☎ 3763-2151; www.tokyocitykeiba.com; 2-1-2
Katsushima, Shinagawa-ku; general admission ¥100,
reserved seats ¥500-4000; ⊙ Tokyo Monorail to
Ōi-Keibajōmae

Each year from late March to November,
Ōi Keibajō, also known as Tokyo City
Keibajō, offers night-time 'Twinkle Races'.
The races are lit by mercury lamps, whose
diffused light draws young couples out
on hot dates. Kids can try the pony rides
here, too.

TOKYO KEIBAJŌ off Map pp48-9
東京競馬場

Fuchū Racecourse; ☎ 0423-633-141; 1-1
Hiyoshichō, Fuchū-shi; admission ¥200; ⊙ Keiō Line
to Fuchūkeiba-Seimonmae (pedestrian overpass)

More popularly known as Fuchū Racecourse, Tokyo Keibajō's 525m-long turf
home stretch is the longest in the country
and can make for exciting, win-by-a-nose
finishes. This track is where most major and
international races take place. Admission is
generally ¥200 but varies depending on the
popularity of the event.

SLEEPING

top picks

- **Westin Hotel Tokyo** (p222)
- **Park Hyatt Tokyo** (p223)
- **Ryokan Shigetsu** (p219)
- **Sukeroku No Yado Sadachiyo** (p219)
- **Kimi Ryokan** (p225)

SLEEPING

Tokyo has thousands of places to sleep, and not all of them will cost you an arm and a leg. But if you've come here on a budget, expect some noise, less space and a longer walk from the train station. If expense is not so much of an issue, you can choose from myriad decadent rooms – many boast incredible city views. Central neighbourhoods like Ginza, Shinjuku and Akasaka are ideal, with loads of high-end options.

Though most of the accommodation in Tokyo is Western style, there are a few traditional inns and hotels. For full definitions of each type of lodging, see below. Note that most Tokyo ryokan (traditional Japanese inns) don't exactly fit the mould found elsewhere in Japan.

Most hotels in Japan supply amenities such as disposable toothbrushes and toothpaste, razors, slippers and *yukata* (light cotton robes for sleeping or lounging). The symbol '🖳' denotes wi-fi, LAN or computer terminals in lobbies or business centres.

Rack rates are quoted in this chapter, but prices can vary drastically. Most business and high-end hotels offer discounts, often significant ones, for reservations made in advance via phone or internet; check their websites for seasonal deals. Rates at budget places usually remain as quoted. Keep in mind that during Golden Week (29 April to 5 May) and other national holidays (p259), rooms may be booked out or, if available, very expensive.

ACCOMMODATION STYLES

Business Hotels

A common form of midrange accommodation is the so-called 'business hotel' – usually as functional and economical as the name would suggest. Geared to the lone traveller on business, the typical Tokyo business-hotel room will have pay TV (often used with pre-paid cards available from machines in the hotel) and a tiny bathroom, and cost between ¥7000 and ¥12,000. Most accept credit cards, but you should always ask when you check in. Some of the nicer business hotels have large shared baths and saunas.

Boutique Hotels

As accommodation in Tokyo becomes increasingly international, high-end chains are opening branches here, and boutique hotels are cropping up, too. These emphasise architecture and unique design, and usually have fewer than 100 rooms.

Capsule Hotels

Of course they're small, but they're roomy enough to recline in, and each capsule is fitted with a bed, reading light, TV and alarm clock. Most are men-only, while others are segregated. Despite the room's size, prices still range from ¥3500 to ¥5000; capsules are also cash only. Most of their business comes from drunken office workers who have missed the last train home, but their novelty value attracts the odd foreigner. Many capsule hotels have a well-appointed bath area similar to a good local *sentō* (public bath).

Gaijin Houses

If you're a budget traveller planning on settling in Tokyo, you might consider landing first at a *gaijin* (foreigner) house while getting your bearings. These are private dwellings that have been partitioned into rooms or apartments and rented out to *gaijin*. See opposite for reputable agencies.

Luxury Hotels

In the top-end bracket, you can expect to find the amenities of deluxe hotels anywhere in the world: satellite TV beaming in CNN and the BBC, high-speed internet access and enough space to properly unwind. The staff speak English, the rooms are spotless and the service is impeccable. In addition, most of Tokyo's luxury hotels have several good restaurants and bars, many of which offer outstanding city views.

PRICE GUIDE

¥¥¥	over ¥16,000 a night
¥¥	¥6500 to ¥16,000 a night
¥	under ¥6500 a night

Ryokan

For those travellers who crave a really traditional Japanese experience with tatami (woven-mat floor) rooms and futon instead of beds, the ryokan (traditional Japanese inns) certainly have it. Although the more exclusive establishments can charge upwards of ¥25,000, there are a number of relatively inexpensive ryokan in Tokyo. These places are generally more accustomed to catering for foreigners than their counterparts in the more remote parts of the country, and the rules tend to be a bit more relaxed as a result. The trade-off is that you don't usually get the strictly traditional experience, with Japanese meals and the diurnal stowing away of your futon.

Some ryokan offer rooms with private baths, but the communal ones are often designed with 'natural' pools or a window looking onto a garden. Bathing is communal, but sexes are segregated. Make sure you can differentiate between the bathroom signs for men and women (although ryokan will often have signs in English).

At traditional ryokan, dinner is usually laid out in the guest rooms. Along with rice, the meal usually includes standard dishes such as miso soup, *tsukemono* (pickles), *sunomono* (vegetables in vinegar), *zensai* (hors d'oeuvres), sashimi (fish either grilled or raw), and perhaps tempura and a stew. Meals at a ryokan can become flamboyant displays of local cuisine or refined arrangements of *kaiseki* (p157). After dinner, the dishes are cleared and your bedding is prepared – a futon is placed on the tatami floor and a quilt put on top.

Although some ryokan will allow you to pay by credit card, you should always inquire at check-in if you hope to do so. The ryokan listed in this book are generally at the budget and midrange level; those wishing to stay in top-end ryokan should inquire at the Japan National Tourism Organization (JNTO; p265).

Hostels

The good news for foreign budget travellers is that more and more hostels are opening in Asakusa and elsewhere along the Sumida River. They are usually very clean and well managed, and have a mixture of dorms and private rooms. Expect to pay about ¥3200; check their websites for amenities, location and other details.

top picks

RYOKAN

- Sukeroku no Yado Sadachiyo (p219)
- Sawanoya Ryokan (p218)
- Kimi Ryokan (p225)

Other Options

The JNTO can give you information about several other lodging options in and around Tokyo, including *shukubō* (staying on the grounds of a temple), *onsen* (hot-spring resorts) and converted farmhouses or *kokuminshukusha* (people's lodges). It also has information for travellers with special needs, such as seniors and travellers with disabilities, and those with children.

TAX

A 5% consumption tax applies to room rates across all accommodation categories, with the exception of *gaijin* houses (see opposite) and some of the other budget options. At high-end places (generally rooms costing over ¥16,000), a 3% local tax is also added to the 10% to 15% service charge. Ask your hotel whether tax is included in the price they give you. Finally, the Tokyo Metropolitan Government now tacks on a small per-person accommodation tax on all rooms costing more than ¥10,000: ¥100 for rooms costing up to ¥14,999 and ¥200 for rooms costing ¥15,000 or more.

LONGER-TERM RENTALS

Renting an apartment in Tokyo can be a real challenge – expect a big deposit (often five months' rent) and an unwillingness to rent to foreign tenants. The deposit usually consists of a one-month finder's fee for the real-estate agency, the landlord's *reikin* (key money – a 'gift' that is usually two months' rent) and a deposit for the last month as well as the first month's rent. Rooms with no *reikin* can be found, but check their age and distance from the closest station.

There are plenty of Japanese apartment agencies online, such as www.tokyoapartments.jp, www.oakhouse.jp and www.japt.co.jp. The following are some English-speaking real estate agents in Tokyo that specialise in helping foreigners find rentals in *gaijin* houses. Rents may be a bit higher through these agencies because you're receiving the apartment without the hefty deposit. If you plan on staying in Japan for more than a year, it's worth paying the larger deposit to get a bigger place with lower rent.

Kimi Information Center (Map p116; ☎ 3986-1604; www.kimiwillbe.com; 8th fl, 2-42-3 Ikebukuro, Toshima-ku; ⊚ Yūrakuchō, Fukutoshin or Marunouchi Line to Ikebukuro, exit C9, JR Yamanote Line to Ikebukuro, west exit) Run by the family owning Kimi Ryokan (p225), Kimi Information Center can help you to find an affordable apartment. Kimi charges an agency fee equal to one month's deposit. Locations tend to be around working-class Ikebukuro.

Sakura House (Map p110; ☎ 5330-5250; www.sakurahouse.com; 2nd fl, 7-2-6 Nishi-Shinjuku, Shinjuku-ku; ⊚ Toei Ōedo Line to Shinjuku-nishiguchi, exit D5, JR Yamanote Line to Shinjuku, west exit) Sakura House has extensive listings of apartments that welcome foreigners. They have staff members who are fluent in English, Korean and Chinese, and they'll escort you to visit apartments or shared housing. The minimum occupancy is one month.

Serviced Apartments

If you're in Tokyo for more than a week or a month, serviced apartments can be more comfortable and affordable than a hotel. Look in the *Japan Times* or *Metropolis*. No key money is required, but you generally pay a one-month deposit. For nice digs in prime neighbourhoods, rent may be ¥100,000 to ¥180,000 per week.

The following offer serviced apartments:

Mori Building (☎ 6406-6687; www.moriliving.com) Mori Building runs a number of landmark structures catering to longer-term visitors, including the exclusive Roppongi Hills Residences.

Oakwood Worldwide (☎ 5412-3131; www.oakwood.com) Oakwood Worldwide has eight serviced apartments of varying classes in central Tokyo, mostly Minato-ku, that are ideal if you're looking for a stylish place for at least a month. Rates including utilities and maid service start at ¥530,000 for studio apartments.

IMPERIAL PALACE & MARUNOUCHI

At the doorstep of the Imperial Palace and the heart of the Marunouchi business district, the Tokyo Station area has a few fine hotels and some good midrange places designed for short-term business travellers. Having undergone a major facelift with new shops and restaurants, Marunouchi has finally out-poshed neighbouring Ginza. The area provides quick access to the rest of the city via the JR Yamanote Line, as well as Kyoto and other destinations via *shinkansen* (bullet train).

PENINSULA HOTEL   Map p52   Luxury Hotel ¥¥¥
ザ・ペニンシュラ東京
☎ 6270-2288; http://tokyo.peninsula.com; 1-8-1 Yurakuchō, Chiyoda-ku; r from ¥60,000; ⊚ JR Yamanote Line to Yurakuchō (Hibiya exit), Chiyoda, Hibiya or Toei Mita Line to Hibiya (exits A6 & A7); 💻 ⚐
One almost gets a feeling of guilty extravagance when sprawling out in the Peninsula's vast rooms (starting at 51 sq metres), which overlook the Imperial Palace and Hibiya Moat and have floor-to-ceiling windows. Latticed caramel woodwork, sumptuous marble bathrooms and a dark central atrium filled with luminous art unite in a delicious symphony of modern design.

SHANGRI-LA HOTEL
Map p52   Luxury Hotel ¥¥¥
シャングリ・ラ ホテル東京
☎ 6739-7888; www.shangri-la.com; 1-8-3 Marunouchi, Chiyoda-ku; r from ¥53,330; ⊚ JR Yamanote Line to Tokyo (Yaesu exit); 💻 ⚐
Nestled in the Marunouchi Trust Tower beside Tokyo Station, the Shangri-La's 202 rooms offer superb views of the Nihombashi district, a range of pillow options, rain showers and deep, luxurious bedding. Decor is understated but luxurious. The delightful CHI spa is themed on a Tibetan oasis in the sky.

MANDARIN ORIENTAL TOKYO
Map p52   Luxury Hotel ¥¥¥
マンダリン オリエンタル 東京
☎ 3270-8800; www.mandarinoriental.com/tokyo; 2-1-1 Nihonbashi-muromachi, Chūō-ku; r/ste from ¥39,000/79,000; ⊚ Ginza Line to Mitsukoshimae (exit A7); 💻 ♿
The Mandarin boasts cavernous, exquisitely decorated suites, three Michelin-starred

restaurants and a lofty spa from which you can sometimes poke Mt Fuji with your toes. Rooms incorporate kimono weaving designs and glass-walled baths. The highlight here is the atrium lobby and breathtaking views.

MARUNOUCHI HOTEL

Map p52   Luxury Hotel ¥¥¥

丸の内ホテル

☎ 3215-2151; www.marunouchi-hotel.co.jp; Oazo Bldg, 1-6-3 Marunouchi, Chiyoda-ku; s/d from ¥23,300/31,385; ⊙ JR Yamanote Line to Tokyo (Marunouchi north exit)

Located in the Oazo Building, this swanky business hotel deftly synthesises modern conveniences with Japanese style. Rooms have vaulted ceilings and views of Tokyo Station. Look for the two canaries that keep watch over the lobby.

YAESU TERMINAL HOTEL

Map p52   Business Hotel ¥¥

八重洲ターミナルホテル

☎ 3281-3771; www.yth.jp; 1-5-14 Yaesu, Chūō-ku; s/d ¥11,340/16,590; ⊙ JR Yamanote Line to Tokyo (Yaesu north exit)

This sleek little business hotel on cherry-tree-lined Sakura-dōri has contemporary lines and a minimalist look. Though room sizes are most definitely on the microscopic side, they're decently priced for this neighbourhood and very modern.

GINZA

Ginza and the nearby revitalised Shiodome offer some of Tokyo's poshest accommodation, all with easy transport access. Along with the ultraluxurious, however, are some sleek midrange hotels. Expect rates to be higher than in the rest of the city – Ginza real estate is some of the priciest on the planet.

HOTEL SEIYŌ GINZA

Map p57   Luxury Hotel ¥¥¥

ホテル西洋 銀座

☎ 3535-1111; www.seiyo-ginza.com; 1-11-2 Ginza, Chūō-ku; r ¥63,525-219,450; ⊙ Yūrakuchō Line to Ginza-itchōme (exit 7), Ginza Line to Kyōbashi (exit 2)

The Hotel Seiyō Ginza, part of the luxury Rosewood group, resembles a rambling but homey mansion. Each of the rooms here has a personal butler (with 20 on staff altogether). The rooms are cavernous, though

the decor could use an update. For those requiring rarefied isolation, the Seiyō can be a secret hideaway.

IMPERIAL HOTEL Map p57   Luxury Hotel ¥¥¥

帝国ホテル

☎ 3504-1111; www.imperialhotel.co.jp; 1-1-1 Uchisaiwaichō, Chiyoda-ku; s/d from ¥32,000/37,000; ⊙ Chiyoda, Hibiya or Toei Mita Line to Hibiya (exit A13); ▣

The legendary Imperial Hotel's present building is the successor to Frank Lloyd Wright's 1923 masterpiece, and small tributes to Wright can be found in the lobby and elsewhere. Large rooms on the newest Imperial floor have been updated with features such as large-screen plasma TVs and high-speed internet. Service at the Imperial is virtually peerless.

GINZA NIKKŌ HOTEL

Map p57   Business Hotel ¥¥¥

銀座日航ホテル

☎ 3571-4911; www.ginza-nikko-hotel.com; 8-4-21 Ginza, Chūō-ku; s/d from ¥21,000/31,000; ⊙ JR Yamanote Line to Shimbashi (Ginza exit), Ginza or Toei Asakusa Line to Shimbashi (exit 5); ▣

Though this Ginza hotel has been around for some 50 years, it's looking fine and bright after a thorough renovation. The decor is a cut above business hotel generic, with commodious beds and full bathtubs.

MERCURE HOTEL GINZA TOKYO

Map p57   Luxury Hotel ¥¥¥

メルキュールホテル銀座

☎ 4335-1111; www.mercure.com; 2-9-4 Ginza, Chūō-ku; s/d from ¥18,375/24,150; ⊙ Yūrakuchō Line to Ginza-itchōme (exit 11); ▣

This refreshingly designed little boutique hotel has chinoiserie prints, floral decor, snazzy red doors and leather chairs. A short walk from the department stores, it's popular with women from out of town who come for Ginza shopping trips, but is equally suited to business travellers and tourists.

HOTEL COM'S GINZA

Map p57   Business Hotel ¥¥

ホテルコムズ銀座

☎ 3572-4131; www.granvista.co.jp; 8-6-15 Ginza, Chūō-ku; s/d from ¥14,500/25,000; ⊙ JR Yamanote Line to Shimbashi (Ginza exit), Ginza or Toei Asakusa Line to Shimbashi (exit 3); ▣

Recently relaunched, the Hotel Com's rooms are presented in mahogany and caramel tones, with special 'Audrey' rooms featuring amenities for women. Restaurants here serve udon noodles, Chinese fare and healthy breakfasts.

YOSHIMIZU   Map p57   Ryokan ¥¥
吉水

☎ 3248-4432; www.yoshimizu.com; 3-11-3 Ginza, Chūō-ku; s/d without bathroom incl breakfast from ¥10,600/21,200; ◉ Hibiya or Toei Asakusa Line to Higashi-ginza (exit 3); 🖳

This traditional inn has been designed with minimumal artificial materials. Simple rooms feature bamboo flooring, mud walls and organically grown tatami reed mats. There are no TVs, but there is a large, relaxing bath. Organic dinners from ¥3150 are available on request. Look for the small bamboo trees outside.

IIDABASHI & AROUND

This quiet area along the old castle moat is especially worthwhile in spring when there are myriad cherry trees in bloom. Nightlife isn't far away, with the old geisha district of Kagurazaka near Iidabashi Station.

TOKYO INTERNATIONAL HOSTEL
Map p60   Hostel ¥
東京国際ホステル

☎ 3235-1107; www.tokyo-ih.jp; 1-1 Kagurakashi, Shinjuku-ku; dm adult/student ¥3860/3360; ◉ JR Sōbu Line to Iidabashi (west exit), or Namboku or Toei Oedo Line to Iidabashi (B2b exit); 🖳

These clean, well-managed dorm rooms have some of the best sunset and night views in all of Tokyo, looking west over the old outer moat of Edo Castle. The design is rather institutional (there's even a conference room), but this is a superbly run hostel outfitted with a cafeteria (serving breakfast and dinner), laundry and internet access. Be aware of the 11pm curfew.

SHIODOME

Revitalised Shiodome, a sliver of slick development between Shimbashi and Hama Rikyū Onshi-teien (Detached Palace Garden; p65), provides an upmarket, high-rise accommodation alternative to the smaller hotels of Ginza, and it's quieter in the evenings. Some rooms have great night-time views of Tokyo Bay and Rainbow Bridge.

CONRAD HOTEL   Map p64   Luxury Hotel ¥¥¥
コンラッド東京ホテル

☎ 6388-8000; www.conradtokyo.co.jp; 1-9-1 Higashi-Shimbashi, Minato-ku; s/d from ¥71,000/76,000; ◉ JR Yamanote, Ginza or Toei Asakusa Line to Shimbashi (Shiodome exit), Toei Ōedo Line to Shiodome

One of the gigantic, glittery gems of the Shiodome development adjacent to Hama Rikyū Onshi-teien, the Conrad Hotel is definitely a new contender for the attention of upmarket travellers looking for that central, super-sophisticated base in Tokyo. The garden or city views are equally spectacular, as are the varnished hardwood interiors and floor-to-ceiling glassed bathrooms.

HOTEL VILLA FONTAINE SHIODOME
Map p64   Business Hotel ¥¥
ホテルヴィラフォンテーヌ汐留

☎ 3569-2220; www.hvf.jp/eng; 1-9-2 Higashi-Shimbashi, Minato-ku; s/d from ¥10,000/14,000; ◉ JR Yamanote, Ginza or Toei Asakusa Line to Shimbashi (Shiodome exit), Toei Ōedo Line to Shiodome; 🖳

Cone-shaped lanterns light the high-ceilinged black marble lobby. Sculptural red blobs and flame-themed art on the walls lead to upmarket rooms with internet, TV and partial views of Hama Rikyū Onshi-teien. This is an excellent deal in one of Tokyo's newest neighbourhoods.

AKIHABARA & KANDA

Kanda is Tokyo at its most drab, but it does have some good midrange bargains because of the many salarymen who throng here. It's also a stone's throw from the electronics and pop culture mecca of Akihabara. Nearby are some of Tokyo's finest traditional restaurants (see p164 for listings) and Jimbōchō's millions of antique manuscripts (see p58 for more information).

YAMA-NO-UE (HILLTOP) HOTEL
Map p67   Luxury Hotel ¥¥¥
山の上ホテル

☎ 3293-2311; www.yamanoue-hotel.co.jp; 1-1 Kanda-Surugadai, Chiyoda-ku; s/d from ¥17,850/25,200; ◉ JR Chūō or JR Sōbu Line to Ochanomizu (Ochanomizu exit), Toei Mita, Hanzōmon or Toei Shinjuku Line to Jimbōchō (A5 exit)

This grand old place from the 1930s exudes personality and charm, with antique wooden furniture and a wood-panelled lounge. Mishima Yukio (p34) wrote his last

WORTH THE TRIP

Though the bulk of Tokyo's accommodation is located in the central neighbourhoods we've listed, those looking to get a bit further afield might seek out these two options.

Andon Ryokan (行燈旅館; Map pp48–9; ☎ 3873-8611; www.andon.co.jp; 2-34-10 Nihonzutsumi, Taitō-ku; r per person ¥8190; ◉ Hibiya Line to Minowa, exit 3; 🖥) Fabulously designed in form and function, the minimalist and modern Andon Ryokan has tiny but immaculate tatami rooms. Pluses include free internet access, DVD players, cheap breakfast and laundry facilities.

Claska (クラスカ; Map pp48–9; ☎ 3719-8121; www.claska.com/en/hotel; 1-3-18 Chūō-chō, Meguro-ku; s/d from ¥12,600/19,950, weekly s ¥7875; ◉ Tōkyū Toyoko Line to Gakugei-daigaku, east exit, JR Yamanote Line to Meguro, west exit). The Claska is a dream of contemporary design. This boutique hotel's gorgeous tatami rooms were created by different designers and have touches such as form-fitting wall cubby holes for hairdryers (room 603) and some have vast terraces. With neat shops and a hip lobby cafe, the Claska is in a line of design and interior stores on Meguro-dōri.

few novels here. The older rooms in the main building come with antique writing desks and overstuffed chairs.

HOTEL MY STAYS OCHANOMIZU

Map p67   Business Hotel ¥¥

ホテルマイステイズ御茶ノ水

☎ 5289-3939; www.mystays.jp/ochanomizu, in Japanese; 2-10-6 Kanda Awajichō, Chiyoda-ku; s/d from ¥10,000/14,000; ◉ JR Chūō or JR Sōbu Line to Ochanomizu (Hijiribashi exit), Chiyoda Line to Shin-Ochanomizu (B2 exit)

Reopened in 2007, this stylish business hotel stands out for its bold brown-and-white colour scheme, good prices and extras such as large Simmons beds. The Family Mart and modern European cafe OAKS on the ground floor are additional conveniences.

PRESSO INN KANDA

Map p67   Business Hotel ¥¥

プレッソイン神田

☎ 3252-0202; www.presso-inn.com; 2-8 Kanda-Tachō, Chiyoda-ku; s/d ¥7770/13,650; ◉ JR Yamanote Line or Chūō Line to Kanda (west exit), Ginza Line to Kanda (exit 4), Marunouchi Line to Awajichō (exit A1); 🖥

The Presso Inn chain is very much a businessperson's hotel, with purely functional decor and few frills – rooms are cramped and institutional but fine for crashing. There is a complimentary breakfast of croissants baked on site.

NEW CENTRAL HOTEL

Map p67   Business Hotel ¥¥

ニューセントラルホテル

☎ 3256-2171; www.pelican.co.jp/newcentralhotel, in Japanese; 2-7-2 Kanda-Tachō, Chiyoda-ku; s/d ¥7350/7875; ◉ JR Yamanote Line or Chūō Line to Kanda (west exit), Ginza Line to Kanda (exit 4), Toei Shinjuku or Marunouchi Line to Awajichō (exit A2)

The New Central may be as generic as its salaryman clientele, but the homey shared bath facilities (separate for men and women) make it stand out. The location, on a quiet side street, makes this a worthwhile base.

SAKURA HOTEL JIMBOCHŌ

Map p67   Hostel ¥

サクラホテル神保町

☎ 3261-3939; www.sakura-hotel.co.jp; 2-21-4 Kanda-Jimbōchō, Chiyoda-ku; dm/s/d from ¥3150/6090/8200; ◉ Marunouchi, Toei Mita or Toei Shinjuku Line to Jimbōchō (exit A6); 🖥

The Sakura Hotel is a great budget option with a sociable atmosphere. Staff are bilingual and helpful, and the rooms, though basic, are comfortable and clean. There's a 24-hour cafe, a laundry and internet access.

UENO

Though it may be lacking the full visual phantasmagoria and throbbing nightlife of Shinjuku and Shibuya, Ueno is a good base because of the Keisei Skyliner express trains running to Narita airport and the presence of Ueno Zoo, Ueno-kōen, an expansive smorgasbord of top-class museums, abundant cherry trees and a pond with paddleboats. Yanaka, which is perfect for temple walks, beckons to the north.

HŌMEIKAN   Map p78   Ryokan ¥¥

鳳明館

☎ 3811-1181; www.homeikan.com; 5-10-5 Hongō, Bunkyō-ku; r from ¥11,600; ◉ Toei Ōedo or Toei Mita Line to Kasuga (exit A6)

The venerable Hōmeikan is a beautifully crafted wooden ryokan, with its main

Honkan wing from the Meiji era registered as an important cultural property. The Daimachi Bekkan wing is equally inviting, with 31 tatami rooms and a large downstairs communal bath. This oasis in the middle of Tokyo is a real treasure.

HOTEL PARKSIDE Map p78 Business Hotel ¥¥
上野 ホテル パークサイド
☎ 3836-5711; www.parkside.co.jp; 2-11-18 Ueno, Taitō-ku; s/d from ¥9200/14,000, Japanese-style r from ¥18,000; ☺ JR Ueno (Shinobazu exit)
This hotel offers some of the best midrange accommodation in Ueno, as well as views of the gigantic lily pads on Shinobazu Pond. Choose either a Western or Japanese room, but make sure it's above the 4th floor for the best views.

SUIGETSU HOTEL ŌGAISŌ
Map p78 Business Hotel ¥¥
水月 ホテル鴎外荘
☎ 3822-4611; www.ohgai.co.jp; 3-3-21 Ikenohata, Taitō-ku; s/d ¥7980/11,550, Japanese-style r from ¥18,000; ☺ Chiyoda Line to Nezu (exit 2); ⌨
Japanese literary great Mori Ōgai lived here in the late 1880s, and part of his lovely tiled wooden home still fronts the peaceful interior garden. Skip the cramped standard singles and go for the deluxe version instead, or sprawl out on tatami. The cypress baths are open to visitors for ¥1500.

SUTTON PLACE HOTEL UENO
Map p78 Boutique Hotel ¥¥
上野サットンプレイスホテル
☎ 3842-2411; www.thehotel.co.jp; 7-8-23 Ueno, Taitō-ku; s/d from ¥7800/11,000; ☺ Ueno (Iriya exit); ⌨
This snazzy little joint by Ueno Station hits all the right notes, with chocolate-coloured wood and black leather setting the tone in designer rooms. There are large tiled bathrooms, rare four-person rooms for families, and complimentary light breakfasts.

RYOKAN KATSUTARŌ ANNEX
Map p78 Ryokan ¥
アネックス勝太郎旅館
☎ 3828-2500; www.katsutaro.com; 3-8-4 Yanaka, Taitō-ku; s/d ¥6300/10,500; ☺ Chiyoda Line to Sendagi (exit 2); ⌨
Opened in 2001, this spotless, efficient establishment seems more modern hotel than traditional ryokan. Though far from

Ueno Station, it's ideal for exploring the old Yanaka district. The 17 tatami rooms, while rather small, have attached Western bathrooms.

RYOKAN KATSUTARŌ Map p78 Ryokan ¥
旅館勝太郎
☎ 3821-9808; www.katsutaro.com; 4-16-8 Ikenohata, Taitō-ku; s/d ¥5200/8400; ☺ Chiyoda Line to Nezu (exit 2); ⌨
This older, more homey sister inn to Ryokan Katsutarō Annex has a quiet and more family-like atmosphere, with very affable managers. Though the building may be aged, the seven tatami rooms here have been renovated without ruining the inn's character.

SAWANOYA RYOKAN Map p78 Ryokan ¥
旅館澤の屋
☎ 3822-2251; www.sawanoya.com; 2-3-11 Yanaka, Taitō-ku; s/d from ¥5040/10,080; ☺ Chiyoda Line to Nezu (exit 1); ⌨
The Sawanoya is a budget gem in quiet Yanaka, with very friendly staff and all the traditional hospitality you would expect of a ryokan – even origami paper cranes perched on your futon pillow. The shared cypress and earthenware bathrooms are the perfect balm after a long day of walking.

ASAKUSA

If you are in Tokyo only for a short visit or if you want a glimpse of old Japan, Asakusa is a charming, laid-back anachronism with some good budget options. Though not the geographical centre of Tokyo, it is the heart of the old Shitamachi downtown quarter, which was depicted in the millions of *ukiyo-e* (woodblock prints) that were pressed here. You will also find two wonderful, classic ryokan near Sensō-ji.

ASAKUSA VIEW HOTEL
Map p84 Luxury Hotel ¥¥
浅草ビューホテル
☎ 3847-1111; www.viewhotels.co.jp/asakusa/english; 3-17-1 Nishi-Asakusa, Taitō-ku; s/d from ¥15,000/23,100; ☺ Tsukuba Express Line to Asakusa (hotel exit), Ginza Line to Tawaramachi (exit 3); ⌨ ▣
If you're not into ryokan, the Asakusa View is the ritziest Western-style hotel around. From the lacquer-patterned elevator walls

CHEAP SLEEPS IN SANYA

Sanya is an old neighbourhood north of Asakusa notorious for its down-and-out day labourers. But the 2002 Japan–Korea World Cup saw many budget travellers seeking accommodation here, and now there's a wealth of cheap places to bunk. However, most 'rooms' are barely large enough to stretch out in.

Hotel Accela (ホテルアクセラ; Map pp48–9; ☎ 3871-5568; www.accela.co.jp, in Japanese; 1-40-12 Nihonzutsumi, Taitō-ku; r ¥3350-4800; ⓜ Hibiya Line to Minami-senju, south exit) This hotel is a tad institutional, but friendly and bright with three-tatami-mat rooms, coin-operated showers and laundry, and a spacious shared bath. It's just past Namidabashi Crossing on the right.

Hotel New Azuma (ホテルニューあづま; Map pp48–9; ☎ 6802-0716; www.gcc-web.net/azuma; 2-38-3 Kiyokawa, Taitō-ku; r ¥2900-3100; ⓜ Hibiya Line to Minami-senju, south exit) Warm and quieter than other budget spots, the New Azuma has small tatami rooms, free internet access, laundry facilities and a shared bath and kitchen.

Hotel New Kōyō (ホテルニュー紅陽; Map pp48–9; ☎ 3873-0343; www.newkoyo.com; 2-26-13 Nihonzutsumi, Taitō-ku; r ¥2500-4800; ⓜ Hibiya Line to Minowa, exit 3) Very friendly, and featuring some of Tokyo's cheapest rooms, the New Koyo has rooms such as the golden, minute Samurai Suite, about the size of two tatami mats, and a large shared bathroom.

Juyoh Hotel (ホテル寿陽; Map pp48–9; ☎ 3875-5362; www.juyoh.co.jp; 2-15-3 Kiyokawa, Taitō-ku; s/d ¥3200/6400; ⓜ Hibiya Line to Minami-senju, south exit) The three tiny doubles and numerous three-tatami-mat singles fill up fast at this hospitable little spot. For reservations and directions, check the excellent website.

Tokyo Backpackers (東京バックパッカーズ; Map pp48–9; ☎ 3871-2789; www.tokyo-backpackers.jp; 2-2-2 Nihonzutsumi, Taitō-ku; d ¥2100; ⓜ Hibiya Line to Minami-senju, south exit) Even though it was built in 2006, Tokyo Backpackers is still dirt-cheap. Modern, clean dorm rooms have six wooden bunk beds, and there is free internet and a women-only floor. The entire place shuts from 11am to 4pm daily for cleaning.

to the cypress and granite baths, the hotel is lavishly designed. While the spacious rooms aren't striking, large windows overlook Sensō-ji.

SUKEROKU NO YADO SADACHIYO
Map p84   Ryokan ¥¥
助六の宿 貞千代
☎ 3842-6431; www.sadachiyo.co.jp; 2-20-1 Asakusa, Taitō-ku; s/d ¥14,000/19,000; ⓜ Tsukuba Express Line to Asakusa (exit A3), Ginza or Toei Asakusa Line to Asakusa (exit 1)
This stunning ryokan virtually transports its guests to old Edo. Gorgeously maintained tatami rooms are spacious for two people, and all come with modern, Western-style bathrooms. Splurge on an exquisite meal here, and make time for the o-furo (traditional baths), one made of fragrant Japanese cypress and the other of black granite. Look for the rickshaw parked outside.

RYOKAN SHIGETSU   Map p84   Ryokan ¥¥
旅館指月
☎ 3843-2345; www.shigetsu.com; 1-31-11 Asakusa, Taitō-ku; Western-style r ¥7665-14,700; Japanese-style s/d ¥9450/16,800; ⓜ Toei Asakusa

or Ginza Line to Asakusa (exit 1), Tsukuba Express to Asakusa (exit 4)
South of Sensō-ji, this spotless and atmospheric ryokan has mostly Japanese-style rooms. The entire inn is immaculate, with carpeted entrance halls and shōji-screened doors and windows. It's absolutely a requirement to take at least one bath here.

CAPSULE HOTEL RIVERSIDE
Map p84   Capsule Hotel ¥
カプセルホテルあさくさリバーサイド
☎ 3844-5117; www.asakusa-capsule.jp; 2-20-4 Kaminarimon, Taitō-ku; capsules ¥3000; ⓜ Ginza or Toei Asakusa Line to Asakusa (exit 4)
The very clean Riverside sells an encapsulated night's sleep right by the river. Unlike most capsule hotels, it accepts both women and men, with the 8th floor reserved for female guests only.

TOKYO RYOKAN   Map p84   Ryokan ¥
東京旅館
☎ 090-8879-3599; www.tokyoryokan.com; 2-4-8 Nishi-Asakusa, Taitō-ku; per person ¥3000; ⓜ Ginza Line to Tawaramachi (exit 3); ▫
This tidy little inn has only three tatami rooms and no en-suite bathrooms but

tonnes of charm. There are touches of calligraphy, attractive woodwork and sliding screens. This is an authentic ryokan experience on the cheap.

SAKURA HOSTEL Map p84   Hostel ¥
サクラホステル

☎ 3847-8111; www.sakura-hostel.co.jp; 2-24-2 Asakusa, Taitō-ku; dm/tw ¥2940/8295; Ⓔ Tsukuba Express Line to Asakusa (exit A1); ▯
Billed as the largest in Tokyo, this new hostel in a modern, comfortable building has helpful staff and a great location near Sensō-ji. Rooms with wooden bunks overlook the aged Hanayashiki amusement park. There's no curfew, breakfast is only ¥315 and major credit cards are accepted. Check out the old-time shopping arcade behind it.

K'S HOUSE Map p84   Hostel ¥
ケイズハウス

☎ 5833-0555; http://kshouse.jp; 3-20-10 Kuramae, Taitō-ku; dm/d ¥2800/3200; Ⓔ Toei Ōedo or Tōei Asakusa Line to Kuramae (exits A2 & A6); ▯
This homey, modern hostel is quickly becoming a backpacker favourite. Just steps from the Sumida-gawa and Sensō-ji, K's feels more like someone's apartment, with comfy sofas in the living room and a tatami common space. Another branch – the family-oriented K's House Tokyo Oasis – recently opened closer to Sensō-ji; see the website for details.

KHAOSAN TOKYO GUESTHOUSE
Map p84   Hostel ¥
カオサン東京ゲストハウス

☎ 3842-8286; www.khaosan-tokyo.com; 2-1-5 Kaminarimon, Taitō-ku; dm/tw ¥2200/5000; Ⓔ Ginza or Toei Asakusa Line to Asakusa (exits 4 & A2b); ▯
If you're visiting during the summer fireworks season in late July, this comfy hostel's rooftop terrace is a front-row seat for the popular river spectacle. But you'll get a warm welcome at all times of the year here, which is one of the cheapest spots in central Tokyo.

AKASAKA

Who knows how many behind-the-scenes political deals have been made in the hushed rooms of Akasaka's luxury hotels. This neighbourhood is pretty exclusive and geared to salarymen, though you'll see a few functional (but not outstanding) midrange options here.

HOTEL ŌKURA Map p88   Luxury Hotel ¥¥¥
ホテルオークラ東京

☎ 3582-0111; www.okura.com/tokyo; 2-10-4 Toranomon, Minato-ku; s/d from ¥36,750/42,000; Ⓔ Ginza Line to Toranomon (exit 3), Hibiya Line to Kamiyachō (exit 4b); ▯
The Ōkura is an old-fashioned, elegant standby and the meeting place of Japan's political and business elite. Lovely and lived-in, the 1960s decor and low-lying architecture are matched by personable staff. The beautiful Japanese garden and top-notch restaurants complete the picture.

HOTEL NEW ŌTANI Map p88   Luxury Hotel ¥¥¥
ホテルニューオータニ

☎ 3265-1111; www.newotani.co.jp; 4-1 Kioi-chō, Chiyoda-ku; s/d from ¥31,500/37,800; Ⓔ Ginza or Marunouchi Line to Akasaka-mitsuke (exit D); ▯ ▨
There's a whiff of pretension about the New Ōtani, but it's justified, loaded as it is with large, luxurious rooms, upmarket restaurants, boutiques and gift shops. This landmark has its own art museum and an immaculate 400-year-old garden (p89).

ANA INTERCONTINENTAL TOKYO
Map p88   Luxury Hotel ¥¥¥
ANAインターコンチネンタルホテル東京

☎ 3505-1111; www.anaintercontinental-tokyo .jp/e; 1-12-33 Akasaka, Minato-ku; s/d from ¥26,200/36,750; Ⓔ Ginza Line to Tameike-sannō, (exit 13), Namboku Line to Roppongi-itchōme (exit 3); ▯ ▨ ▨
A short walk from Roppongi, the plush 37-storey ANA Intercontinental has large, gorgeously designed rooms with LCD screens and fantastic night views. With an outdoor pool, a small gym and an excellent business centre, this remains a sleek and sophisticated choice. Renovated club floors feature bathroom windows and evening cocktails.

HOTEL AVANSHELL AKASAKA
Map p88   Business Hotel ¥¥
ホテル アバンシェル赤坂

☎ 3568-3456; www.avanshell.com, in Japanese; 2-14-14 Akasaka, Minato-ku; s/d ¥15,750/19,950; Ⓔ Chiyoda Line to Akasaka (exit 2)
The rooms in this beautifully designed 2004 high-rise are laid out under themes such as 'primo', and have zippy decor ranging from black leather couches and puffy white

bedspreads to cool green tatami spaces. It's a visually appealing cut above most business hotels.

ASIA CENTER OF JAPAN
Map p88   Business Hotel ¥¥
ホテル アジア会館
☎ 3402-6111; www.asiacenter.or.jp; 8-10-32 Akasaka, Minato-ku; s/d from ¥7980/11,130; Ⓜ Ginza, Hanzōmon or Toei Ōedo Line to Aoyama-itchōme (exit 4); 🖥
The Asia Center covers the basics of a business hotel – the decor is generic and forgettable but the rooms are decently sized and staff are old hands at helping foreign visitors.

ROPPONGI
With its high concentration of foreigners and party people of all stripes, Roppongi is hardly typical of Tokyo. It's great for clubbing and bar hopping, but the area is a bit of a human zoo and accommodation is relatively pricey. There are a few excellent midrange hotels conveniently placed close to Roppongi Crossing, in addition to the upmarket choices nearby.

RITZ-CARLTON TOKYO
Map p92   Luxury Hotel ¥¥¥
ザ・リッツ・カールトン東京
☎ 3423-8000; www.ritzcarlton.com; Tokyo Midtown, 9-7-1 Akasaka, Minato-ku; s/ste from ¥77,000/126,500; Ⓜ Hibiya or Toei Ōedo Line to Roppongi (exits 4A & 8); 🖥
Crowning Tokyo Midtown, the Ritz-Carlton literally begins where other hotels leave off. The lobby – with giant paintings by Sam Francis and views clear to the Imperial Palace – is on the 45th floor, and capacious rooms go up from there. Concierges can do just about anything, blackout curtains open at the touch of a button, and if you send your shoes for a complimentary shine they return in a lovely wooden box.

GRAND HYATT TOKYO
Map p92   Luxury Hotel ¥¥¥
グランド ハイアット 東京
☎ 4333-1234; www.grandhyatttokyo.com; 6-10-3 Roppongi, Minato-ku; s/d from ¥57,750/63,525; Ⓜ Hibiya or Toei Ōedo Line to Roppongi (exits 1C & 3); 🖥 📺
Architecturally open and bright despite its somewhat labyrinthine layout, the Grand Hyatt is warmly and gorgeously chic. Smooth mahogany and natural fabrics

give an organic flavour to the rooms, while its Roppongi Hills location imbues it with vibrant energy. Even the bathrooms feature rainshower fixtures and rough-cut stone, continuing a nature-in-architecture motif.

THE B ROPPONGI Map p92   Business Hotel ¥¥¥
ザ・ビー六本木
☎ 5412-0451; www.ishinhotels.com/theb -roppongi/en; 3-9-8 Roppongi, Minato-ku; s/d from ¥18,000/22,000; Ⓜ Hibiya or Toei Ōedo Line to Roppongi (exit 5)
The b roppongi has slick, white-brown rooms ranging in size from 10 to 31 sq metres, albeit with small, prefab unit bathrooms. Atmosphere is business-casual and the location is perfect for Roppongi's nocturnal attractions. A light breakfast is included.

HOTEL IBIS Map p92   Business Hotel ¥¥
ホテルアイビス六本木
☎ 3403-4411; www.ibis-hotel.com; 7-14-4 Roppongi, Minato-ku; s/d from ¥13,382/19,026; Ⓜ Hibiya or Toei Ōedo Line to Roppongi (exit 4A); 🖥
The decor here is uninspiring and purely utilitarian, but the Ibis has a great location steps from Roppongi's bars and restaurants. The singles are somewhat cramped, so go for the semidoubles. Light sleepers should request a quiet room not facing the back.

VILLA FONTAINE ROPPONGI ANNEX
Map p92   Business Hotel ¥¥
ホテルヴィラフォンテーヌ六本木アネックス
☎ 3560-5550; www.hvf.jp/eng/roppongi_annex .php; 3-2-7 Roppongi, Minato-ku; s/d from ¥9500/11,000; Ⓜ Namboku Line to Roppongi-itchōme (exit 1), Hibiya or Toei Ōedo Line to Roppongi (exit 5)
Stylish, modern and reasonably priced, the new Roppongi Annex offers 140cm-wide beds, a complimentary buffet breakfast, and free LAN access if you're lugging a PC. It's close enough to Roppongi's centre to experience its madness, but far enough away for a quiet sleep.

EBISU
Just up the JR Yamanote Line from Shibuya, Ebisu is a quieter neighbourhood that lacks the flair of the larger, neon-fringed hubs, but it still draws crowds for its pubs, restaurants and the Yebisu Garden Place shopping complex.

WESTIN HOTEL TOKYO

Map p96   Luxury Hotel ¥¥¥

ウェスティンホテル東京

☎ 5423-7000; www.westin-tokyo.co.jp; 1-4-1 Mita, Meguro-ku; r from ¥41,000; ⓔ JR Yamanote Line to Ebisu (east exit); 🖳

The Westin plays host to royals, celebs and business moguls from around the world. Rooms are opulent but tasteful, with a laid-back European panache. The Spa Parisien is a large, sumptuous sanctuary that can quickly melt all your stress. From the station, take the Skywalk to Yebisu Garden Place and head towards the road around the back.

SHIBUYA

Clustered around heavily crowded Shibuya Station and the streets spoking away from it are a variety of great midrange and high-end hotels. Naturally enough, it's still the neighbourhood where visiting rock stars set up camp after a big show at NHK Hall or a smaller gig at one of Shibuya's myriad live-music houses.

CERULEAN TOWER TŌKYŪ HOTEL

Map p102   Luxury Hotel ¥¥¥

セルリアンタワー東急ホテル

☎ 3476-3000; www.ceruleantower-hotel.com/en; 26-1 Sakuragaokachō, Shibuya-ku; s/d from ¥33,000/43,500, Japanese-style s/d ¥75,500/78,000; ⓔ JR Yamanote, Saikyo or Keiō Inokashira Line to Shibuya (south exit); 🖳

Sprawl out on the huge beds and drink deeply of the big views, because there's room to breathe in these enormous rooms. The sleek lobby looks out on a charming rock garden, an organic complement to the sleek modern aesthetic. Quality nō (stylised Japanese dance drama) occasionally takes place at the in-house Nō Theatre (p194), while jazz club JZ Brat (p198) has lots of live shows.

EXCEL TOKYU HOTEL

Map p102   Luxury Hotel ¥¥¥

エクセルホテル東急

☎ 5457-0109; www.tokyuhotelsjapan.com/en; 1-12-2 Dōgenzaka, Shibuya-ku; s/d from ¥25,000/35,000; ⓔ JR Yamanote, Saikyo or Keiō Inokashira Line to Shibuya (Shibuya Mark City exit); 🖳

This tower, right beside Shibuya Station, boasts excellent night views of Tokyo. Singles are spacious if bland, but at least

you're right on top of the action. There's a very comfortable high-ceilinged lounge here, as well as 25th-floor restaurants with terrific skyline panoramas.

SHIBUYA TŌKYŪ INN

Map p102   Business Hotel ¥¥

渋谷東急イン

☎ 3498-0109; www.tokyuhotels.co.jp/en; 1-24-10 Shibuya, Shibuya-ku; s/d from ¥15,600/24,500; ⓔ JR Yamanote, Saikyo or Keiō Inokashira Line to Shibuya (east exit); 🖳

This chain hotel has some style thanks to a recent renovation, with clean lines and sliding window screens in primary shades. Spacious singles are a superb deal, and come with a modern work desk and a flat-screen TV.

SHIBUYA GRANBELL HOTEL

Map p102   Boutique Hotel ¥¥

渋谷グランベルホテル

☎ 5457-2681; www.granbellhotel.jp; 15-17 Sakuragaokachō, Shibuya-ku; s/d from ¥13,000/21,000; ⓔ JR Yamanote, Saikyo or Keiō Inokashira Line to Shibuya (south exit); 🖳

There's a breezy, tropical atmosphere in these modestly sized, but hip, rooms, which contain funky cartoonish curtains, Simmons beds and glass-walled bathrooms. Some suites have two floors, terraces and spiral staircases. Try to book early.

HOTEL METS SHIBUYA

Map p102   Business Hotel ¥¥

ホテルメッツ渋谷

☎ 3409-0011; www.hotelmets.jp/shibuya; 3-29-17 Shibuya, Shibuya-ku; s/d from ¥11,000/18,000, wheelchair-accessible r ¥19,000; ⓔ JR Yamanote, Saikyo or Keiō Inokashira Line to Shibuya (new south exit); 🖳

Super convenient and squarely comfortable, the Hotel Mets is inside Shibuya Station's quiet new south exit. It's worth laying out the extra ¥500 for a roomier deluxe single. Rates include free broadband internet and the rarity of a free buffet breakfast.

SHIBUYA CITY HOTEL

Map p102   Business Hotel ¥¥

渋谷シティホテル

☎ 5489-1010; www.shibuya-city-hotel.com, in Japanese; 1-1 Maruyamachō, Shibuya-ku; s/d from ¥9800/17,900, wheelchair-accessible r ¥14,800; ⓔ JR Yamanote, Saikyo or Keiō Inokashira Line to Shibuya (Hachikō exit); 🖳

This place is in the Love Hotel district, where couples seek intimacy, but it's not seedy. It's a short downhill roll from loads of good live-music venues and clubs. It has spacious but simple rooms, a superb location and even a tricked-out wheelchair-friendly room.

NATIONAL CHILDREN'S CASTLE
HOTEL Map p106   Business Hotel ¥¥
こどもの城ホテル

☎ 3797-5677; www.kodomono-shiro.or.jp
/english/hotel; 5-53-1 Jingūmae, Shibuya-ku; s/d
¥7455/11,340, Japanese-style r per person ¥7875;
Ⓔ JR Yamanote, Saikyo or Keiō Inokashira Line to
Shibuya (east exit), Ginza Line to Omote-Sandō (exit
B2); 🖳 🖳
Though you may be disappointed to learn that it's not actually a castle, this small, uber child-friendly hotel is perfect for families. Rooms are spiffy and clean, with fine views. The National Children's Castle (p81) is a paradise of play, with art projects, a swimming pool, puppet shows and endless amusements.

CAPSULE LAND SHIBUYA
Map p102   Capsule Hotel ¥
カプセルランド渋谷

☎ 3464-1777; www.capsule-land.com/shibuya/
sinfo.html, in Japanese; 1-19-14 Dōgenzaka,
Shibuya-ku; capsules from ¥3700; Ⓔ JR Yamanote,
Saikyo or Keiō Inokashira Line to Shibuya (Hachikō
exit)
This is a standard men only capsule hotel perched atop Dōgenzaka hill. Extras include large shared bathrooms, massage chairs, laundry machines and coin lockers. It's a clean, well-run place, and major credit cards are accepted.

SHINJUKU

If you have only a day in Tokyo and want the full-bore hyper-Japan experience, stay in this nonstop whirlwind of neon, crowds, pachinko parlours and hostess clubs. East and west Shinjuku are different worlds when it comes to accommodation. The west has the lion's share of luxury hotels, while the east generally offers better deals and a more central location. Capsule hotels and manga cafes (below) provide alternative accommodation.

PARK HYATT TOKYO
Map p110   Luxury Hotel ¥¥¥
パークハイアット東京

☎ 5322-1234; http://tokyo.park.hyatt.com;
3-7-1-2 Nishi-Shinjuku, Shinjuku-ku; r/ste from
¥55,650/68,250; Ⓔ Toei Ōedo Line to Tochōmae
(exit A4); 🖳
Views are stunning and appear to be part of another world from these serene heights. Dignified but relaxed, the stylishly under-stated rooms are done in naturally finished wood, fabric and marble. Staff are gracefully and discreetly attentive and the restaurants are some of Tokyo's best – check the panorama from the top-level New York Grill (p175).

HYATT REGENCY TOKYO
Map p110   Luxury Hotel ¥¥¥
ハイアットリージェンシー東京

☎ 3348-1234; www.hyattregencytokyo.com;
2-7-2 Nishi-Shinjuku, Shinjuku-ku; s/d from
¥26,670/29,820; Ⓔ Toei Ōedo Line to Tochōmae
(exits A7 & C4); 🖳 🖳
This marble behemoth holds its own as one of Shinjuku's best high-end options. Always housing a healthy population of international businesspeople, the Hyatt Regency

ALTERNATIVES TO SLEEPING

If you've missed the last train back to your hotel, that ¥3000 in your pocket might be better spent staying out all night than on a taxi ride home. Happily, nocturnal Tokyo has options for insomniacs. There's often a nearby manga (comic book) cafe. For around ¥1500 for a 'night pack', you can while away the wee hours watching DVDs, reading manga, surfing the internet and having a bite to eat (including free drinks) – or napping in your lounge chair.

Gera Gera (まんが喫茶＆インターネットカフェ　ゲラゲラ; Map p110; ☎ 3204-8532; www
.geragera.co.jp; Chūdai Bldg, 3rd fl, 1-27-9 Kabukichō, Shinjuku-ku; 🕐 24hr; Ⓔ JR Yamanote Line to Shinjuku,
east exit)

Gran Cyber Cafe Bagus (バグースグラン・サイバーカフェ; Map p92; ☎ 5786-2280; www.gcc
-bagus.jp; Roi Bldg, 12th fl, 5-5-1 Roppongi, Minato-ku; 🕐 24hr; Ⓔ Hibiya or Toei Ōedo Line to Roppongi, exit 3)

Manga Hiroba (まんが広場渋谷店; Map p102; ☎ 3463-0261; www.mangahiroba.com; World Udagawachō
Bldg, B1 fl, 36-6 Udagawachō, Shibuya-ku; 🕐 24hr; Ⓔ JR Yamanote Line to Shibuya, Hachikō exit)

has swanky new Regency Club rooms and lounges. Other rooms are being renovated, but all offer excellent views of Shinjuku and (if you're lucky) Mt Fuji.

KEIŌ PLAZA HOTEL Map p110 Luxury Hotel ¥¥¥
京王プラザホテル

☎ 3344-0111; www.keioplaza.com; 2-2-1 Nishi-Shinjuku, Shinjuku-ku; s/d from ¥25,000/28,000, Japanese-style ste from ¥80,000; ⊕ Toei Ōedo Line to Tochōmae (exit B1); 💻 🏊

The 47-storey Keiō Plaza has a whopping 1440 rooms, and while all have excellent city views, be sure to ask for one that has been renovated. The Plaza Premier suites (from ¥43,000) have soothing olive tones, rounded lines and king-sized beds.

HILTON TOKYO Map p110 Luxury Hotel ¥¥¥
ヒルトン東京

☎ 3344-5111; www.hilton.com; 6-6-2 Nishi-Shinjuku, Shinjuku-ku; r from ¥19,000; ⊕ Marunouchi Line to Nishi-shinjuku (exit C8), Toei Ōedo Line to Tochōmae (exit C8); 💻 🏊

The Hilton covers all the bases. Comforts like firm mattresses and full-sized bathtubs are complemented by aesthetically pleasing elements such as *shōji* over the windows. A warren of shops, restaurants and bars lies downstairs, and stressed-out professionals can work it off in the indoor heated pool, tennis courts or gym.

SHINJUKU PRINCE HOTEL
Map p110 Luxury Hotel ¥¥¥
新宿プリンスホテル

☎ 3205-1111; www.princehotels.co.jp/shinjuku-e; 1-30-1 Kabukichō, Shinjuku-ku; s/d from ¥18,500/32,400; ⊕ Toei Ōedo Line to Shinjuku-nishiguchi (exit B14), JR Yamanote Line to Shinjuku (west exit); 💻

Beside Shinjuku Station and the Kabukichō nightlife, this towering wedge has a location that can't be beaten and snazzy rooms in mahogany and white that were renovated in 2006. Don't let the faded lobby throw you – ask for an upper-floor room and enjoy some of the best views in town.

HOTEL CENTURY SOUTHERN TOWER
Map p110 Luxury Hotel ¥¥¥
ホテルセンチュリーサザンタワー

☎ 5354-0111; www.southerntower.co.jp/english; 2-2-1 Yoyogi, Shibuya-ku; s/d from ¥16,000/24,000; ⊕ JR Yamanote Line to Shinjuku (south & southern terrace exits); 💻

This is one of the best deals for accommodation in Shinjuku. With winter views of Mt Fuji possible from one side and the green space of Shinjuku-gyōen on the other, this monolith is very reasonably priced for its central location.

KADOYA HOTEL Map p110 Business Hotel ¥¥
かどやホテル

☎ 3346-2561; www.kadoya-hotel.co.jp; 1-23-1 Nishi-Shinjuku, Shinjuku-ku; s/d from ¥7560/13,650; ⊕ JR Yamanote Line to Shinjuku (west exit); 💻

A steal for its Nishi-Shinjuku address, the Kadoya has simple, clean rooms with flat-screen TVs, unit bathrooms and free LAN access (¥16,800 'double comfort' rooms have the best decor). For southern Japan fare, try *izakaya* Hatago downstairs.

CITY HOTEL LONESTAR
Map p110 Business Hotel ¥¥
シティホテルロンスター

☎ 3356-6511; www.thehotel.co.jp/en/lornstar; 2-12-12 Shinjuku, Shinjuku-ku; s/d from ¥7350/9450; ⊕ Marunouchi or Toei Shinjuku Line to Shinjuku-sanchōme (exit C8); 💻

The City Hotel Lonestar is a friendly, updated place to bunk with rooms that are small but cheery. In the heart of Tokyo's gay district, it caters to all sorts of clients. A basic continental breakfast is laid out free of charge.

TOKYO BUSINESS HOTEL
Map p110 Business Hotel ¥
東京ビジネスホテル

☎ 3356-4605; 6-3-2 Shinjuku, Shinjuku-ku; s/d from ¥4900/9800; ⊕ Marunouchi Line to Shinjuku-gyōenmae (exit 1)

This no-frills hotel off Meiji-dōri is an older building and very simple in terms of decor and amenities, but you get a fairly large shared bathroom and some eye-popping night views of the skyscrapers in west Shinjuku. Go for the larger Type A singles (¥6000).

GREEN PLAZA SHINJUKU
Map p110 Capsule Hotel ¥
グリーンプラザ新宿

☎ 3207-5411; www.hgpshinjuku.jp/hotel, in Japanese; 1-29-2 Kabukichō, Shinjuku-ku; capsules from ¥4300; ⊕ JR Yamanote Line to Shinjuku (east exit); 💻

Smack in the middle of sleazy Kabukichō, Green Plaza Shinjuku offers 630 standard and 'upgrade' capsules for men only. However, the ladies' sauna on the 9th floor allows women to check in for the night (¥3400).

IKEBUKURO

Ikebukuro lacks the charm of other busy neighbourhoods in Tokyo and often seems like a poor cousin to Shinjuku. There are many cheap hotels here, but the trick is to avoid the flea pits in favour of spots near the station for quick access to more happening 'hoods. Takadanobaba is a student zone to the south with lots of great ethnic restaurants.

HOTEL METROPOLITAN
Map p116   Luxury Hotel ¥¥¥
ホテルメトロポリタン
☎ 3980-1111; www.metropolitan.jp; 1-6-1 Nishi-Ikebukuro, Toshima-ku; s/d from ¥18,000/24,000; ⊚ JR Yamanote Line to Ikebukuro (west exit); 🖵 ☐

The commodious rooms here have been updated with boutique patterns, flatscreen TVs and deluxe wooden panelling. Mt Fuji is sometimes visible, and some superior rooms have unique round beds.

HOTEL STRIX TOKYO
Map p116   Business Hotel ¥¥
ホテルストリックス東京
☎ 5396-0111; www.strix.jp, in Japanese; 2-3-1 Ikebukuro, Toshima-ku; s/d from ¥15,000/20,000; ⊚ JR Yamanote Line to Ikebukuro (west exit), Yūrakuchō, Fukutoshin or Marunouchi Line to Ikebukuro (exit C6); 🖵 ☐

The renovated Strix has some very appealing, modern rooms with wide beds, cosy couches and spacious bathrooms. High-speed internet is available in all rooms. Navigate towards its teal-coloured roof; it's just steps from the C6 subway station exit of Ikebukuro Station.

KIMI RYOKAN   Map p116   Ryokan ¥
貴美旅館
☎ 3971-3766; www.kimi-ryokan.jp; 2-36-8 Ikebukuro, Toshima-ku; s ¥4500, d ¥6500-7500; ⊚ JR Yamanote Line to Ikebukuro (west exit), Yūrakuchō, Fukutoshin or Marunouchi Line to Ikebukuro (exit C6); 🖵 ☐

Easily one of the best budget ryokan in Tokyo, this convivial inn provides a welcoming base for travellers discovering the city. Fragrant tatami rooms are small but

not cramped, and the large, wood-floored lounge area is a comfortable place to meet fellow travellers over green tea. Clean showers and toilets are shared, and there's a lovely Japanese cypress bath. Book well in advance.

HOUSE IKEBUKURO   Map p116   Hostel ¥
池袋之家
☎ 3984-3399; www.housejp.com.tw; 2-20-1 Ikebukuro, Toshima-ku; r ¥6000-12,000; ⊚ JR Yamanote Line to Ikebukuro (west exit), Yūrakuchō, Fukutoshin or Marunouchi Line to Ikebukuro (exit C1); 🖵

Spotless tatami rooms are the rule at House Ikebukuro, a rather institutional, but very clean, place run by Taiwanese and catering mainly to Asian backpackers. It's a busy, well-run establishment that's often fully booked. All singles share bathrooms, but some doubles have private ones.

SAKURA HOTEL IKEBUKURO
Map p116   Hostel ¥
サクラホテル池袋
☎ 3971-2237; www.sakura-hotel-ikebukuro.com; 2-40-7 Ikebukuro, Toshima-ku; dm ¥3200, s/d from ¥6800/9000; ⊚ JR Yamanote Line to Ikebukuro (west exit), Yūrakuchō, Fukutoshin or Marunouchi Line to Ikebukuro (exit C6); 🖵

The Sakura Hotel is divided into two buildings, both a six-minute walk from the station. This large facility also has family and Japanese-style rooms, several shared kitchens and a 24-hour terrace cafe-restaurant. Check the website for deals.

TAKADANOBABA

Takadanobaba is a busy, funky college neighbourhood, with Waseda University next door. It has loads of cheap restaurants serving international cuisine, as well as several good jazz bars (p198).

FOUR SEASONS HOTEL CHINZAN-SŌ
off Map pp48-9   Luxury Hotel ¥¥¥
フォーシーズンズホテル　椿山荘
☎ 3943-2222; www.fourseasons.com/tokyo/; 2-10-8 Sekiguchi, Bunkyō-ku; r from ¥43,000; ⊚ Yūrakuchō Line to Edogawabashi (exit 1a)

Ridiculously opulent with Japanese antiques and a European feel, the Four Seasons Chinzan-sō is about 2km east of Takadanobaba Station on the grounds of a Meiji-era ornamental garden. It abuts the Kanda-gawa canal, which is very pleasant during cherry-blossom season.

TAMA RYOKAN Map p116   Ryokan ¥
多摩旅館

☎ 3209-8062; www.tamaryokan.com; 1-25-33 Takadanobaba, Shinjuku-ku; s/d ¥4500/8000; ◉ JR Yamanote Line to Takadanobaba (Waseda-dōri exit), Tōzai Line to Takadanobaba (exit 7)

Four traditional tatami rooms fill out the 2nd floor of this private home, kept by a sweet couple. The ryokan is up a small alley – look for the Starbucks to the right of it on the road. While it lacks a traditional bath, there's a local *sentō* located nearby.

SHINAGAWA

This emerging transport and business hub at the southern end of the JR Yamanote train loop has less hustle and bustle than other major stations and fewer eating options. But it makes for a quick getaway to Kyoto and elsewhere thanks to the local *shinkansen* station.

STRINGS HOTEL TOKYO
Map p119   Luxury Hotel ¥¥¥
ストリングズホテル東京

☎ 5783-1111; www.intercontinental-strings.jp; 2-16-1 Kōnan, Minato-ku; r from ¥48,000; ◉ JR Yamanote Line to Shinagawa (Kōnan exit); 🖳

Take in the views of Tokyo Tower and the Rainbow Bridge in this serene, lofty space designed by award-winning architect Terry McGinnity. The 'premier' corner rooms offer the most spectacular panoramas, visible also from the gym on the 26th floor. Deluxe bath view rooms have tubs right by the windows.

PRINCE HOTEL SHINAGAWA
Map p119   Luxury Hotel ¥¥
品川プリンスホテル

☎ 3440-1111; www.princehotels.co.jp/shina gawa; 4-10-30 Takanawa, Minato-ku; s/d from ¥9300/16,300; ◉ JR Yamanote Line to Shinagawa (Takanawa exit); 🖳 📶

Set in a large entertainment complex in front of Shinagawa Station, the Prince has thousands of rooms housed in several towers, though singles are cramped. Go for the Annex Tower, which has the most-renovated rooms and fresh air piped from outside.

TŌYOKO INN Map p119   Business Hotel ¥¥
東横イン

☎ 3280-1045; www.toyoko-inn.com; 4-23-2 Takanawa, Minato-ku; s/d ¥7140/9240; ◉ JR Yamanote Line to Shinagawa (Takanawa exit); 🖳

The full name is Tōyoko Inn Shinagawa-eki Takanawaguchi, and this branch of the popular business hotel chain contains small, well-kept rooms, free internet access and a light complimentary continental breakfast.

RYOKAN SANSUISŌ Map p119   Ryokan ¥
旅館山水荘

☎ 3441-7475; www.sansuiso.net; 2-9-5 Higashi-Gotanda, Shinagawa-ku; s/d ¥4900/8600; ◉ JR Yamanote Line to Gotanda (east exit); 🖳

This sweet, 10-room ryokan gets a bit of rail noise from the JR tracks nearby, but the trade off is the experience of staying in a real Japanese home.

SUMIDA RIVER

New hostels are opening all the time in older, relatively cheap neighbourhoods along the Sumida River, making Tokyo more affordable than ever for travellers. These areas are still home to a mixture of companies, distributors and wholesalers, but the east bank of the river has a good boardwalk for jogging.

KHAOSAN TOKYO NINJA Map p122   Hostel ¥
カオサン東京忍者

☎ 6905-9205; www.khaosan-tokyo.com; 2-5-1 Nihonbashi-Bakurochō, Chūō-ku; dm/tw from ¥2200/3000; ◉ JR Sōbu or Tōei Asakusa Line to Asakusabashi (east or A2 exit); 🖳

There's no mistaking the black-and-white pattern of flying stars on the exterior of this hip, young hostel, which features capsule-like wooden sleeping berths and a funky living room that plays host to DJ events and performances of traditional culture.

ANNE HOSTEL Map p122   Hostel ¥
浅草橋旅荘 庵

☎ 5829-9090; http://j-hostel.com; 2-21-14 Yana-gibashi, Taitō-ku; dm/tw from ¥2400/6400; ◉ JR Sōbu or Tōei Asakusa Line to Asakusabashi (east or A6 exit); 🖳

Located in a former corporate space, laid-back Anne has standard wooden bunk beds, modern toilets and showers, and a homey, cosy atmosphere. To help find it, look for the traditional wooden lantern on the street outside.

EXCURSIONS

EXCURSIONS

Step outside Tokyo for a breath of fresh air, and you will encounter a whole different world from the nonstop super bustle of the capital. Located just an hour or two by train are soothing onsen (hot springs) in natural settings, refreshing mountain hikes and walks, and a few decent beaches on the Pacific. If you have got the time and a yen for careful planning, you will be able do all three in one trip. Plus, there are the must-see tourist destinations of Nikkō and Kamakura, as well as the hot springs of Hakone, and Izu-hantō (Izu peninsula) near breathtaking Mt Fuji. The first two, rich in gorgeous temples and shrines, are particularly worth seeing if you don't have time to jump on a *shinkansen* (bullet train) to see the splendid architecture of Kyoto and Nara near Osaka. Thanks to Japan's unsurpassed public transport infrastructure, sightseeing in the Kantō area around Tokyo is easy, quick and very much worth the time.

Places listed in this chapter can be visited as day trips, although if you're planning on being in Tokyo for a week or more, an overnight stay can make these excursions infinitely more relaxing, especially if it's at a ryokan (traditional Japanese inn).

ONSEN

Hot springs heaven, here we come! Getting naked with total strangers is not, for most of us, the cultural norm, and those not from Japan often feel self-conscious at first. But shy *gaijin* (foreigners) should know that the Japanese perceive bathing as a great social leveller; all revel in the anonymity that nudity allows.

The baths themselves come in as many different shapes and sizes as the customers, varying from the deluxe to the primitive. Essentially, you will either visit solely for an *o-furo* (traditional Japanese bath, which translates literally as the 'honourable bath') or stay at an *onsen ryokan* (traditional hot-spring inn) to enjoy good food, copious amounts of alcohol, karaoke and a soak in the establishment's private baths, which may be located either indoors or outside. Ryokan will often allow you to have a soak even if you aren't staying there (ask for *ofuronomi* or *higaeri-onsen*), although late-night privileges are often reserved for guests. This is an excellent and affordable way to experience some beautiful, traditional baths. Unfortunately, bathing is also big business and rampant commercialism has marred many once-lovely onsen.

There are two excellent books devoted to onsen: *A Guide to Japanese Hot Springs* by Anne Hotta and Yoko Ishiguro, and *Japan's Hidden Hot Springs* by Robert Neff. Both are worth seeking out for anyone looking to onsen-hop their way through Tokyo's outlying onsen resorts. Holders of the Japan Rail (JR) Pass can use JR lines to hop to hot springs far afield from Tokyo, utilising the *shinkansen* to get out of the city as swiftly as possible.

In most of the destinations that follow, there are onsen listings, so if you're off to Nikkō (p235) or Hakone (p238) for a day or two, you can certainly get your feet (and more) wet. But the star in the Kantō area hot-spring firmament is Gunma-ken, where water bubbles out of the ground wherever you poke a stick into it.

Get to Gunma from Ueno Station in Tokyo via Takasaki (*shinkansen* ¥4600, one hour; *tokkyū* ¥3700, 80 minutes; *futsū* ¥1890, 110 minutes) and Jōmō-Kōgen Stations (*shinkansen* ¥5550, 1¼ hours) on the Jōetsu *shinkansen* line, or via Maebashi (*tokkyū* ¥3190, 100 minutes; *futsū* ¥1890, two hours) on the Ryōmō Line, and Shibukawa (*tokkyū* ¥3510, 105 minutes; *futsū* ¥2210, 2¼ hours) on the Agatsuma Line.

The following Gunma onsen are highly recommended and within a day's journey of Tokyo via *shinkansen*.

Chōjūkan Inn (法師温泉長寿館; Map p229; ☎ 0278-66-0005; www.houshi-onsen.jp, in Japanese; Minakami-machi, Tone-gun) To get to the gorgeous, wood-walled inn at Hōshi Onsen, take the Jōetsu *shinkansen* from Tokyo Station to Jōmō-Kōgen Station (¥5240, 1¼ hours). From there, take the bus for Sarugakyō Onsen (30 minutes). At the last stop, take another bus for Hoshi Onsen (25 minutes). Try to arrive around noon to sample the inn's mountain-vegetable steamed rice. The highlight here is the all-wooden indoor mixed bath, a masterpiece of onsen architecture. There are also segregated open-air baths.

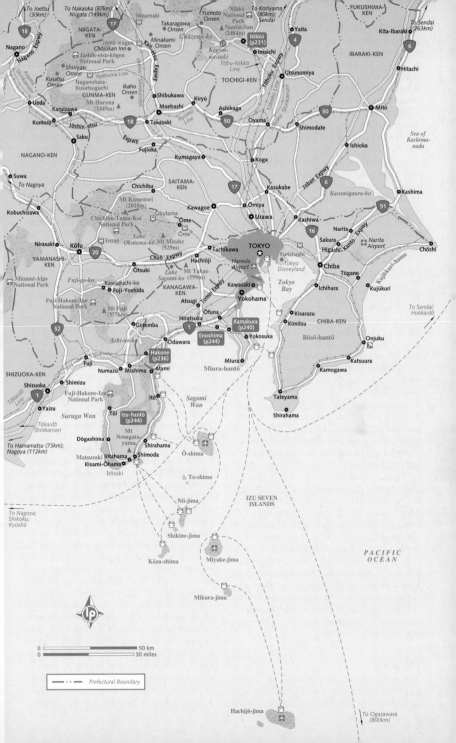

Ikaho Onsen (伊香保温泉; Map p229; www.ho tels-ikaho.or.jp, in Japanese) is a great public bath with views of Mt Haruna. To get there, take the Jōetsu Line from Takasaki to Shibukawa Station (*futsū* ¥400, 25 minutes), and then a local bus to the onsen (¥550, 20 minutes). There's also a shuttle bus from the east exit of Takasaki Station to Ikaho Onsen Bus Terminal (¥1000, 55 minutes, three daily), and buses from Shinjuku (¥2300, 2½ hours, nine daily).

Kusatsu Onsen (草津温泉; Map p229; www.kusatsu -onsen.ne.jp) is a quintessential old-time onsen town. Take the Agatsuma Line from Takasaki to Naganohara-Kusatsuguchi Station (*futsū* ¥1110, 87 minutes), then a local bus to the onsen (¥670, 30 minutes). There is an express bus from Shinjuku Station New South Exit Bus Terminal (¥3200, 4¼ hours, nine daily).

Minakami Onsen (水上温泉; Map p229; www .minakami-onsen.com) is a thriving onsen town that frequented by couples. If you're not interested in a romantic rendezvous, you can white-water raft in the summer. To get there, take the Jōetsu Line from Takasaki to Minakami Station (*tokkyū/futsū* ¥2360/950, 54/64 minutes). From the station, the onsen is a pleasant 15-minute walk. Or take the Jōetsu *shinkansen* from Tokyo Station to Jōmō-Kōgen Station (¥5240, 1¼ hours), then a 15-minute shuttle bus (¥600).

Shiriyaki Onsen (尻焼温泉; Map p229), an 'arse-burning' hot spring, was a favourite of haem-orrhoid sufferers of the Heike clan. At this onsen, you strip and climb into the river – though not during spring, when the river is high and the water quite cold. Bring a *bentō* (boxed lunch) as there are no food options in the area, and start out early. To get there, take the Agatsuma Line from Takasaki to Nagano-hara-Kusatsuguchi Station (*futsū* ¥1110, 87 minutes) where you can catch a local bus to Hanashiki Onsen (¥800, 30 minutes). From the bus stop, it's a 10-minute walk.

Complete with river bathing, Takaragawa Onsen (宝川温泉; Map p229; www.takaragawa.com) has oft been voted the nation's best. To get there, take the Jōetsu Line from Takasaki to Minakami Station (*tokkyū/futsū* ¥2360/950, 54/64 minutes), where you will be able to catch a local bus to the onsen (¥1100, 35 minutes).

HIKING

The mountains surrounding Tokyo offer exquisite hiking and walking trails through quiet forests of lofty Japanese cedars, around waterfalls and lakes. Such activities can often be planned with a soak in the local onsen with a cool *nama-biiru* (draught beer) after-wards. The region includes some of Japan's most famous peaks including majestic Mt Fuji (p239), but far easier and flatter walking paths abound. Trails can be reached by a train journey of one to two hours from hubs such as Shinjuku, Ueno and Tokyo. One of the best English guidebooks is Lonely Planet's *Hiking in Japan*; Tokyo's foreigner-friendly International Adventure Club (www.iac-tokyo.org) organises regular hikes for hikers of all abilities as well as more challenging outings like ice climbing and snow camping.

Be sure to bring enough water and to stock up on snacks at a convenience store or super-market, as some rural train stations may have very little in terms of local shops and restau-rants. Other items you should consider bring-ing include maps, sturdy footwear, a torch (flashlight), a first-aid kit and rain gear. It's a good idea to drop by the tourist information office near the trailhead – if there is one – to get the latest information on routes, times, and weather and trail conditions.

Ōme (青梅) is a quiet town along the Tama-gawa (Tama River) in western Tokyo, just outside Chichibu-Tama-Kai National Park. There's a lovely, relaxing and quite flat trail through the hills behind Ōme Station (*futsū* from Shinjuku on the Chūō and Ōme Lines ¥780, one hour) that runs parallel to the JR Ōme Line. To reach it, turn left once you exit the station and continue for a few blocks until you come to a road that crosses the railway over a small bridge to your left. Take another left here, follow the road around some tennis courts up to a park, where you'll find a trailhead leading up on your right. This leads to the main westward trail, which you can continue on until signs for Futamatao Station (二俣尾駅, about two hours), a few stops down the Ōme Line.

Okutama (奥多摩) is at the terminus of the JR Ōme Line and is a gateway to the trails in the Chichibu-Tama-Kai National Park. Regular trains from Shinjuku run here daily with changes at Tachikawa and Ōme (¥1050, 110 minutes) but on weekends and holidays there are faster Okutama Holiday Express services in the morning (¥1050, 1½ hours). A great hike with an inspiring Shintō shrine at the end is from Okutama to Mitake-san (御岳山; 929m). From Okutama Station, take a left past the tourist information centre (奥多摩観光案内所; ☎ 0428-83-2152; 210 Hikawa, Okutama-machi; ⏰ 8.30am-5pm), a good source for

English maps and local information, and cross a bridge over the Tama River just before the trailhead going to Nokogiri-yama (鋸山; 1109m). This moderate climb continues to Ōdake-san (大岳山; 1267m), which has superb vistas, and then down to Mitake-san (929m), whose charming mountaintop village is home to the impressive Mitake-jinja and quaint *minshuku* (B&Bs). The hike takes three to five hours and there is a funicular (¥570, five minutes) leading down from Mitake to Takimoto, where buses run to Mitake Station on the Ōme Line. Otherwise it's a pleasant 30-minute walk.

Takao-san (高尾山; 599m) is a family-friendly sacred mountain south of Ōme that is an easy climb (or funicular ride; ¥470, six minutes) with a picturesque temple, shrine and a monkey park atop it. It is easily reached from Shinjuku on the Keiō Line to Takaosan-guchi (*jun-tokkyū* ¥370, 53 minutes), but JR Rail Pass Holders can ride the JR Chūō Line for free to Takao Station (47 minutes) and then get on the Keiō Line to Takaosan-guchi (¥120, two minutes). From Takaosan-guchi Station, turn right and continue straight through the village to the funicular station (where English maps are available), passing it on the left and climbing to the top via the forested Inari-yama trail (稲荷山コース; 1½ hours). From the summit, you can try to spy Mt Fuji to the southwest and then pause for a snack at the noodle shops. If you have the time and energy, keep hiking westward following the signs to Shiro-yama (城山; 670m), a 45-minute trek away. There are refreshment facilities here, and then the trail dips down to Lake Sagami-ko (相模湖; one to 1½ hours). Nearby JR Sagami-ko Station on the Chūō Line will bring you back to Shinjuku (¥950, one hour).

BEACHES

If you're seeking sun but shunning crowds, don't head for the beach on weekends and holidays when there's a predictable inflow of city dwellers (with a sometimes appalling penchant for littering). When school's out for summer (mid-July through August), students will also be flocking to the shoreline. Surfers can find respectable waves along the Pacific coast of the Bōsō peninsula, in Chiba prefecture, and sunbathers will find decent beaches on both Bōsō-hantō and Izu-hantō. Be warned that many beaches have very strong rip currents.

South of Tokyo

Kamakura has its own beach at Zaimokuza; nearby is Enoshima Island (p244). Both are is best visited on a weekday when it's less crowded.

There are some lovely beaches near Shimoda (p244) on Izu-hantō. Ten minutes north of town by bus, Shirahama (白浜) can see good surf, but if the tides are uncooperative the expansive, beautiful beach awaits your towel. Buses from Shimoda leave hourly (¥320). Ten minutes south of Shimoda are a string of lovely beaches, of which Iritahama (入田浜) and Kisami-Ōhama (吉佐美大浜) are favourites with surfers and sunbathers. Further around to the western side of the peninsula, Dōgashima (堂ヶ島; p245) is another charming town.

East of Tokyo

Underrated and untainted by overdevelopment, Bōsō-hantō (Bōsō Peninsula) boasts some of the best, mellow beaches near Tokyo. Onjuku (御宿) is the nicest of those most easily accessed from Tokyo, with beachfront cafes, a laid-back coastal vibe and lots of white sand and decent waves. South of Onjuku, Katsuura (勝浦) and Kamogawa (鴨川) also get good swells. Wakashio trains to Onjuku Station (*tokkyū*, ¥3700, 80 minutes) depart from the southeast end of Tokyo Station on the JR Keiyō Line. About half the cost, but much slower, are the regular trains on the JR Sotobō Line.

North of Onjuku, Kujūkuri-hama (九十九里浜) has more than 60km of smooth, sandy, sparsely populated beaches. To access them, take the JR Sotobō Line to Oami Station, transfer to the Tōgane Line, and disembark at Kujūkuri town. Frequent buses ply Kujūkuri-hama's coastal towns, and you can hop off when you see a spot that appeals to you.

NIKKŌ 日光

An excellent day trip from Tokyo, Nikkō is one of Japan's major tourist attractions due to the splendour of its shrines and temples, and the surrounding natural beauty. Nikkō can become extremely crowded, especially during spring and autumn foliage seasons. If it's at all possible, it's certainly best to visit early on a weekday to avoid the worst of the crowds. Before you head to the shrine area either by bus or on foot, you may want to stop by the Tōbu Nikkō Station Information Centre (p235) or the Kyōdo Center Tourist Information office (p235) to give yourself the lay of the land.

NIKKŌ

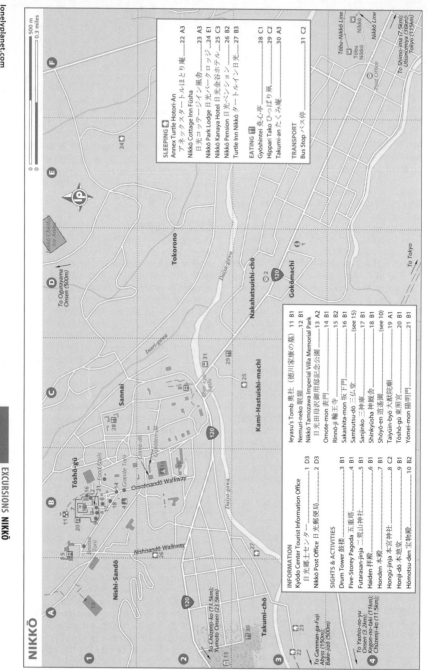

EXCURSIONS NIKKŌ

INFORMATION
Kyodo Center Tourist Information Office
日光郷土センター 1 D3
Nikko Post Office 日光郵便局 2 D3

SIGHTS & ACTIVITIES
Drum Tower 鼓楼 3 B1
Five-Storey Pagoda 五重塔 4 B1
Futarasan-jinja 二荒山神社 5 B1
Haiden 拝殿 6 B1
Honden 本殿 7 B1
Hongū-jinja 本宮神社 8 C2
Honji-dō 本地堂 9 B1
Homotsu-den 宝物殿 10 B2
Ieyasu's Tomb 奥社 (徳川家康の墓) 11 B1
Nemuri-neko 眠猫 12 B1
Nikko Tamozawa Imperial Villa Memorial Park
日光田母沢御用邸記念公園 13 A2
Omote-mon 表門 14 B1
Rinnō-ji 輪王寺 15 B2
Sakashita-mon 坂下門 .... (see 15)
Sambutsu-dō 三仏堂 16 B1
Sanjinko 三神庫 17 B1
Shinkyūsha 神厩舎 18 B1
Shōyō-en 逍遥園 .... (see 10)
Taiyūin-byō 大猷院廟 19 A1
Tōshō-gū 東照宮 20 B1
Yōmei-mon 陽明門 21 B1

NIKKŌ COMBINATION TICKET

Although you can buy separate tickets to each of Nikkō's attractions, it makes sense to buy a combination ticket (¥1000), which is valid for two days. The ticket covers entry to Rinnō-ji and to Tōshō-gū and Futarasan-jinja. Most sights are open 8am to 5pm (to 4pm November to March). Note that there are few signs in English in the complex.

Nikkō's history as a sacred site stretches back to the middle of the 8th century when the Buddhist priest Shōdō Shōnin established a hermitage here in 782. For many years it was known as a famous training centre for Buddhist monks, although after a time it declined into obscurity. Nikkō remained forgotten until it was chosen as the site for the mausoleum of Tokugawa Ieyasu (p234), the warlord who took control of all Japan and established the shōgunate that ruled for 250 years until Commodore Perry and his American ships arrived in Tokyo Bay, just in time to usher in the Meiji Restoration and the end of the feudal era.

Tokugawa Ieyasu was laid to rest among Nikkō's towering cedars in 1617, but it was his grandson Tokugawa Iemitsu who, in 1634, commenced work on the imposing shrine that can be seen today. The original shrine, Tōshō-gū, was completely rebuilt using an army of 15,000 artisans from all over Japan. The work on the shrine and mausoleum took two years to complete, and the results continue to receive mixed reviews.

Tōshō-gū was constructed as a memorial to a warlord who devoted his life to conquering Japan. Tokugawa Ieyasu was a man of considerable determination and was not above sacrificing a few scruples, or a few people, in order to achieve his aims. He is attributed with having had his wife and eldest son executed because it was politically expedient for him to do so. Interestingly, Tokugawa's final resting place manages to reflect the imperiousness and the austerity of the powerful leader.

RINNŌ-JI 輪王寺

You can approach this ancient temple via Shin-kyō-bashi, a sacred bridge, leading to the Toshogu area. Shōdō Shōnin was reputedly carried across the river at this point on the backs of two huge serpents. Tourists not toted by reptiles can cross the bridge on foot. The next stop is 1200-year-old Rinnō-ji, also founded by Shōdō Shōnin of the Buddhist Tendai sect. On its grounds is Sambutsu-dō (Three Buddha Hall), which houses a trio of huge, remarkable gold-lacquered images: a senjū (1000-armed Kannon, the Buddhist goddess of mercy); the central image of Amida Nyorai (Buddha of the Western Paradise); and Batō, a horse-headed goddess of mercy. Hōmotsu-den (Treasure Hall; Rinnō-ji; admission ¥300; 8am-4pm), also in the temple grounds, has a splendid collection of temple artefacts, sculptures and scrolls. Admission to Hōmotsu-den includes entry to the lovely Edo-period garden Shōyō-en.

TŌSHŌ-GŪ 東照宮

A huge stone torii (gate) marks the entrance to Tōshō-gū, while to the left is a five-storey pagoda. The pagoda dates from 1650 but, like so many structures destroyed by natural disasters, was reconstructed in 1818. The pagoda is remarkable for its lack of foundations – the interior contains a long suspended pole that apparently swings like a pendulum in order to maintain equilibrium during an earthquake.

The true entrance to Tōshō-gū is through the torii at Omote-mon, which is protected on either side by deva kings. Through the entrance to the temple to the right is Sanjinko (Three Sacred Storehouses). The upper storey of this building is renowned for the imaginative relief carvings of elephants by an artist who had apparently never seen the real thing. To the left of the entrance is the Shinkyūsha (Sacred Stable), a suitably plain building housing a carved white horse. The stable's only adornment is an allegorical series of relief carvings depicting the lifecycle of the monkey. They include the famous 'hear no evil, see no evil, speak no evil' trio that is now emblematic of Nikkō and a favourite subject for shutterbugs.

Once you're finished taking in the stable, pass through another torii and climb another flight of stairs, and on the left and right you will see a drum tower and a belfry. To the left of the drum tower is Honji-dō, with its huge ceiling painting of a dragon in flight known as the Roaring Dragon. According to legend, the dragon will roar if you clap your hands beneath it.

Next comes Yōmei-mon, whose interior is adorned with a multitude of reliefs of Chinese sages, children, dragons and other mythical

TRANSPORT: NIKKŌ

Train The best way to visit Nikkō is via the Tōbu-Nikkō Line from Asakusa Station. The station is in the basement of the Tōbu department store (it's well signposted from the subway). All seats are reserved on *tokkyū* (premium) trains (¥2720, 110 minutes), but you can usually get tickets and reservations just before setting out. Trains run every 30 minutes or so from 7.30am to 10am; hourly after 10am. *Kaisoku* (rapid) trains (¥1320, 2½ hours, hourly from 6.20am to 4.30pm) require no reservation. (Note, passengers should ensure they ride in the first two carriages of the train as only these two go all the way to Nikkō.) For trains other than the *tokkyū*, you may have to change at Shimo-Imaichi. Travelling by JR is costly and time consuming, and is really of interest only to those who have purchased a Japan Railways (JR) Pass at home. The quickest way to Nikkō via JR is to take the *shinkansen* (bullet train) from Tokyo to Utsunomiya (¥4920, 54 minutes), where you will then change for a *futsū* (local) train to Nikkō (¥740, 45 minutes).

Bus Once you arrive in Nikkō, you can either do the 30-minute uphill (and fairly featureless) walk to the temple and shrine area, or you can hop on bus 1 or 2 (¥190).

All Nikkō Pass This economical bus and train pass (adult/child ¥4400/2210) is valid for four days and is available from Tōbu railways in Asakusa. It includes buses to Chūzenji-ko and Yumoto Onsen, round-trip train travel from Asakusa, train to Kinugawa and some discounts at attractions.

World Heritage Pass This two-day bus and train pass (adult/child ¥3600/1700) allows train travel to Nikkō, local buses, train travel to Kinugawa and attraction discounts.

creatures. So much effort and skill went into the gate that its creators worried that its perfection might arouse the anger and envy of the gods. To appease their predicted wrath, the final supporting pillar on the left side was placed upside down as a deliberate error intended to express humility.

Through Yōmei-mon and to the right is Nemuri-neko (Sleeping Cat; admission ¥520; 8am-4.30pm). This small feline carving is easy to miss – look to the beam above your head just before you begin the climb to Ieyasu's Tomb. Sakashita-mon here opens onto a path that climbs up through towering cedars to Ieyasu's Tomb, a relatively simple affair (but with lots of stairs to climb) considering the boundless ambition of the person entombed. If you are using the combination ticket (see the boxed text, p233), it will cost an extra ¥520 to see the cat and the tomb. To the left of Yōmei-mon is Jinyōsha, a storage depot for Nikkō's *mikoshi* (portable shrines carried during festivals), which come out and bring the temple ground to life during Nikkō's merry May and October festivals. The Honden (Main Hall) and Haiden (Hall of Worship) can also be seen in the enclosure.

OTHER SIGHTS

Near Tōshō-gū is Futarasan-jinja, dedicated to Nantai-san, the tall mountain that rises above Chūzenji-ko, its consort Nyotai and their mountainous progeny Tarō. Also in the vicinity is Taiyūin-byō, which enshrines Ieyasu's grandson Iemitsu (1604–51) and is a smaller

version of the grander Tōshō-gū. The smaller size gives it a less-extravagant air, and some consider it more aesthetically worthy than its larger neighbour.

The Nikkō Tamozawa Imperial Villa Memorial Park (日光田母沢御用邸記念公園; ☎ 0288-53-6767; 8-27 Honchō; adult/child ¥500/250; 9am-5pm Apr-Oct, 9am-4.30pm Wed-Mon Nov-Mar) is a splendidly restored royal mansion of more than 100 rooms showcasing superb craftsmanship, with parts dating from the Edo, Meiji and Taishō eras. It's about 1km west of Shin-kyō bridge.

To take a break from the colour and the crowds, take a 20-minute walk over to Gammanga-Fuji Abyss, which houses an interesting collection of statues of *Jizō* (patron of travellers, children and the unborn). One of the statues, Bake-jizō, mocks travellers foolish enough to count the number of statues (it's said to be constantly changing to frustrate such attempts).

A bit further afield, and ideal on a quiet day if you've thoroughly explored Nikkō, is the 50-minute bus trip up to a large lake, Chūzenji-ko (¥1100) along a winding road; buses depart from either Nikkō or Tōbu Nikkō train stations. There's some beautiful scenery, including the 97m-high waterfall Kegon-no-taki; an elevator (¥530 return) drops down to a platform where you can observe the full force of the waterfall. Also worth a visit is the third of the trio of Futarasan-jinja, complementing those near Tōshō-gū and on Nantai-san.

For a relaxing soak, check out the area's onsen (see opposite).

INFORMATION

Kyōdo Center tourist information office (日光郷土セ
ンター; ☎ 0288-53-3795; 591 Gokomachi; ⏱ 9am-
5pm) Providing lots of useful pamphlets and maps, the office also has helpful English-speaking staff. Internet access
costs ¥100 per 30 minutes. Call to ask for tours of Nikkō in
English, providing them with your time and date.

Nikkō post office (日光郵便局; ☎ 0288-54-0101;
896-1 Nakahatsuishi-chō) Three blocks northwest of the
Kyōdo Center tourist information office, this post office has
an international ATM.

Tōbu Nikkō station information centre (日光駅構内
観光案内所; ☎ 0288-53-4511; ⏱ 8.30am-5pm) At
the Nikkō train station, there's a small information desk
where you can pick up a town map and get help in English
to find buses, restaurants and hotels.

ONSEN

Although Nikkō is not generally thought of as
a place to hit the hot springs, it does have its
own little pocket of thermal activity.

Yashio-no-yu Onsen (やしおの湯温泉; ☎ 0288-
53-6611; 1726-4 Kiyotakiwa-no-shiromachi; adult/child ¥500/
free; ⏱ 10am-9pm Fri-Wed), a modern hot-spring
complex, has open-air baths, saunas and a
large indoor bath. Take a Chūzenji-bound
bus from either train station in Nikkō; it's a
12-minute ride to the Kiyomizu-itchōme stop.
Walk back towards Nikkō, under the bypass
and across the bridge.

One of Nikkō's best soaks, **Ogurayama Onsen**
(小倉山温泉; ☎ 0288-54-2487; 2823 Tokorono; admission ¥800; ⏱ 2pm-2am), is a jazzy, modern onsen
with indoor and outdoor baths. A cafe-bar
serves up beer and sake from ¥500. It's in the
foothills past the Nikkō Chirifuri Ice Arena,
east of Tōshō-gū.

Yumoto Onsen (湯元温泉; admission to Yumoto
Onsen-ji baths ¥500) is a quiet onsen, with several
hotel baths as well as those at Yumoto Onsen-
ji temple about 30 minutes from Chūzenji-kō
by bus (¥840) and can be a good way to wrap
up a day spent trudging between temples and
shrines.

EATING

Takumi-an (たくみ庵; ☎ 0288-53-6323; 7-46 Takumi-chō; mains ¥650-1200; ⏱ lunch Wed-Mon) This
bustling lunch eatery beside the Tamozawa
Imperial Villa serves hearty soba (buckwheat
noodles) dishes, noodle and tempura set
meals, as well as *kamo namban* (soba topped
with duck and leeks; ¥1050).

Hippari Dako (ひっぱり凧; ☎ 0288-53-2933; 1011
Kami-hatsuishichō; dishes ¥800; ⏱ 11am-7pm) Good,
cheap *yakitori* (skewers of grilled chicken) and
yaki-udon (fried noodles) and friendly staff
have made Hippari Dako a favourite travellers' spot for years. The walls are papered with
business cards and testimonies to the virtues
of hot sake.

Gyōshintei (尭心亭; ☎ 0288-53-3751; 2339-1 Sannai;
dishes from ¥4389; ⏱ 11.30am-7pm) Set in the garden grounds of Meiji-no-Yukata, Gyōshintei
serves elegant Buddhist vegetarian cuisine. In
the same complex, restaurants Meiji no Yakata
(明治の館) and Fujimoto (ふじもと) offer
exquisitely prepared Western cuisine.

SLEEPING

Nikkō Park Lodge (日光パークロッジ; ☎ 0288-53-
1201; www.nikkoparklodge.com; 2825 Tokorono; dm/d from
¥3990/5990; 🖳) This cosy, unpretentious pension in the foothills east of the shrine complex
is run by English-speaking yoga and Buddhism enthusiasts who can pick up guests
at the train station between 3pm and 5pm.
Breakfast/dinner is ¥3395/1800.

Turtle Inn Nikkō (タートルイン日光; ☎ 0288-
53-3168; www.turtle-nikko.com/turtle/index_en.html; 2-16
Takumi-chō; s w/with/without bathroom from ¥5750/4950; 🖳)
The most popular of Nikkō's pensions, this
cosy place is located by the river and beyond
the shrine area. To get here from the station,
take a bus to the Sōgō-kaikan-mae bus stop,
backtrack around 50m to the fork in the road
and follow the river for around five minutes.

Nikkō Pension (日光ペンション; ☎ 0288-53-
3636; www.nikko-pension.jp; 10-9 Nishi-Sandō; r per person
with/without breakfast & dinner ¥9800/5800, single guests add
¥1000; 🖳) A Tudor-style mansion with funky
old decor near the temples. There's a large
Japanese cypress bath open 24 hours.

Nikkō Cottage Inn Fūsha (日光コテージイン風
舎; ☎ 0288-54-2206; www.fu-sha.co.jp; 8-22 Takumi-chō;
rental for 2 people from ¥12,000) If you'd like added
privacy or you're travelling as a family, this
renovated, cosy Japanese-style house can sleep
up to six. Beds are on raised tatami mats, and
the bath facilities are modern. The friendly
proprietors live across the road.

Annex Turtle Hotori-An (アネックスタートル
ほとり庵; ☎ 0288-53-3663; www.turtle-nikko.com; 8-
28 Takumi-chō; r per person from ¥6650; 🖳) This place,
with mostly tatami rooms, is to the west of
Turtle Inn Nikkō, over the river but on the
same road. The bathhouse looks out onto the
forest surrounding the inn.

Nikkō Kanaya Hotel (日光金谷ホテル; ☎ 0288-54-0001; www.kanayahotel.co.jp/english/nikko/index.html; 1300 Kami-Hastuishi-machi; tw from ¥17,325; 🖳) Overlooking Shin-kyō-bashi, Nikkō's classiest hotel is decent value if you feel like a little civilised splendour. During peak holiday periods the rates nearly double.

HAKONE 箱根

If the weather cooperates and Mt Fuji is clearly visible, the Hakone region can make a memorable day trip from Tokyo. You can enjoy cable-car rides, visit an open-air museum, soak in hot-water springs and cruise Ashi-no-ko (Lake Ashi). A paradise for hikers, divers and onsen lovers, Fuji-Hakone-Izu National Park is a grab-bag of tourist sights taking in Mt Fuji (3776m), the surrounding five lakes, the Izu Peninsula and the Izu Islands.

Once you've arrived at Hakone-Yumoto Station, you might want to stop in at the Hakone Tourist Information Centre (p238) in front before you start exploring. It's possible to board the delightful two-car mountain train that slowly winds through the forest to Gōra. Between Odawara and Gōra on the toy-train Hakone-Tōzan Line is the Hakone Open-Air Museum (箱根彫刻の森美術館; ☎ 0460-82-1161; www.hakone-oam.or.jp; 1121 Ni-no-Taira; admission with/ without Hakone Freepass ¥1400/1600; 🕑 9am-5pm). This art museum is a short walk from Chōkoku-no-mori Station, just before Gōra. As well as paintings, the museum has a 70,000-sq-metre outdoor sculpture park that features works by artists such as Auguste Rodin and Henry Moore. The outdoor bronzes are particularly lovely in the winter under a light blanket of snow.

GŌRA TO ASHI-NO-KO

Gōra is at the end of the Hakone-Tōzan Line and the start of the funicular and cable-car trip to Tōgendai on the shore of Ashi-no-ko. There's nothing to see at Gōra, and you'll probably want to wander on. Further up the hill, 10 minutes from Gōra Station, is the Hakone Museum of Art (箱根美術館; ☎ 0460-82-2623; www.moaart.or.jp/english/hakone/index.html; 1300 Gora; admission ¥900; 🕑 9am-4.30pm Fri-Wed Apr-Nov, 9am-4pm Dec-Mar), which has an interesting moss garden and a collection of ceramics from Japan and across Asia.

Once finished with the museum, take the funicular from Gōra up Sōunzan (10 minutes). If you don't have a Hakone Freepass (see below), you'll need to buy a ticket (¥410) at the booth to the right of the platform exit. Sōun-zan is the starting point of a dramatic 4km cable-car ride

---

TRANSPORT: HAKONE

There are three ways to get to the Hakone region: the Odakyū express bus service, departing from the bus terminal on the west side of Shinjuku Station; JR service, which runs regularly from Tokyo Station; and the private Odakyū train line, which departs from Shinjuku Station.

Train JR trains run on the Tōkaidō Line between Tokyo Station and Odawara Station. *Futsū* trains (¥1450, 80 minutes) run every 15 minutes or so, while *tokkyū* trains (¥2660, one hour) leave less frequently. Shinkansen (¥3440, 35 minutes) leave Tokyo Station every 20 minutes, but you'll need to make sure you're on the train that stops at Odawara (the Kodama does, others do not). Trains also run to Odawara from Shinjuku Station on the Odakyū Line. The quickest and comfiest option is the Romance Car (¥2020, 1¼ hours), which leaves every half-hour. There's also a *kyūkō* service (¥1150, two hours). At Odawara, you can change to the Hakone-Tōzan Line, a two-car toy train that will eventually deposit you at Gōra (¥650, one hour). Alternatively, if you are already on the Odakyū Line, you can continue on to Hakone-Yumoto and change to the Hakone-Tōzan Line (¥390 to Gōra, 40 minutes) by crossing the platform.

Bus The Odakyū express bus service has the advantage of running directly into the Hakone region, to Ashi-no-ko (Lake Ashi) and to Hakone-machi (¥1950, two hours). The disadvantage is that the bus trip is much less interesting than the combination of Romance Car, toy train (Hakone-Tōzan Line), funicular, cable car (ropeway) and ferry. Buses leave from bus stop 35 in front of Odakyū department store on the west side of Shinjuku Station.

Hakone Freepass The Odakyū Line offers a Hakone Freepass (two-/three-day validity ¥5000/5500); this excellent ticket allows you to use seven modes of transport within the Hakone region and provides discounts on some of the major sights. The fare between Shinjuku and Hakone-Yumoto Station is also included in the pass, although if you're seeking the comforts of the Romance Car, you'll have to pay a surcharge (¥870). If you have a JR Pass, you'd be advised to buy a Freepass in Odawara (¥3900/4400). Altogether it's a good deal for the Hakone circuit.

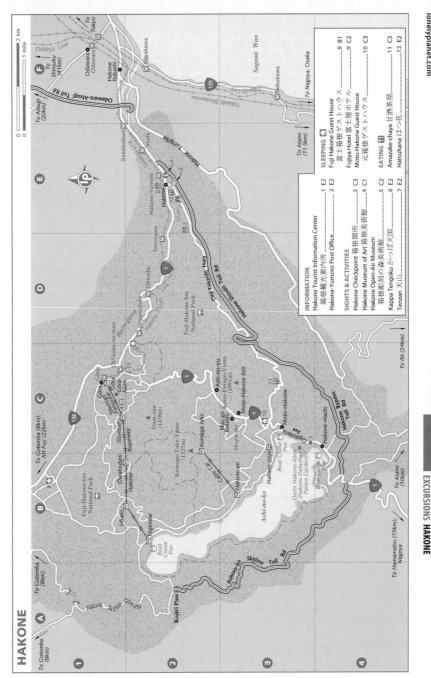

HAKONE

To Gotemba (8km)

To Shin-Juku

To Tokyo

To Atsugi (20km)

To Atami (11.5km)

To Atami (10km)

To Itō (24km)

To Nagoya; Osaka

To Hamamatsu (15km); Nagoya

To Gotemba (8km); Mt Fuji (22km)

To Gotemba (8km)

Odakyū Line

Odawara-Atsugi Toll Rd

Sagami Wan

Tōkaidō-Shinkansen

Hayakawa

Odawara

Odawara

Hakone Itabashi

Kazamatsuri

Iriuda

Odakyū Line

Hakone-Yumoto

Hakone-Yumoto

Hakone

Hakone Turnpike

Tōnosawa

Ohiradai

Hakone-tozan Line

Sōunzan Funicular

Gōra

Gōra

Gōra Kōen

Chōkoku-no-mori

Kiyomizudera

Miyanoshita

Fuji-Hakone-Izu National Park

Old Tōkaidō Toll Rd

Hakone Shindō Toll Rd

Ashi-no-yu

Ōwakudani

Sōunzan Ropeway

Kami-Futago-Yama (1091m)

Moto-Hakone Jizō

Moto-Hakone

Moto-Hakone

Hakone-machi

Hakone Bypass Toll Rd

Sōun-zan (1438m)

Komaga-take-Yama (1327m)

Komagatake

Hakone-en

Shōjin-ike

Ashinoko-Skyline Toll Rd

Togendai

Togendai

Ubako

Boat Cruise Pier

Ashi-ko

Boat Cruise Pier

Onshi Hakone-kōen (Hakone Detached Palace Gardens)

Cryptomeria Ave

Old Tōkaidō Hwy

Kojiri Pass

Hakone Skyline Toll Rd

Fuji-Hakone-Izu National Park

Hakone-jinja

INFORMATION
Hakone Tourist Information Center
 箱根観光案内所..........................1 E2
Hakone-Yumoto Post Office......2 E2

SIGHTS & ACTIVITIES
Hakone Checkpoint 箱根関所.......3 C3
Hakone Museum of Art 箱根美術館....4 C1
Hakone Open-Air Museum
 箱根彫刻の森美術館..................5 C2
Kappa Tengoku かっぱ天国........6 E2
Tenzan 天山...................................7 E2

SLEEPING
Fuji Hakone Guest House
 富士箱根ゲストハウス...............8 B1
Fujiya Hotel 富士屋ホテル..........9 C2
Moto-Hakone Guest House
 元箱根ゲストハウス..................10 C3

EATING
Amazake-chaya 甘酒茶屋...........11 C3
Hatsuhana はつ花......................12 E2

to Tōgendai. On the way, the car passes through Ōwakudani, which you'll know you're approaching when you catch the first eggy whiff of sulphur. You can get out at this point and take a look at the volcanic hot springs where the steam continually rises. The water from these hot springs is responsible for the black shells of many a boiled egg. If the weather is clear, there are grand views of Mt Fuji, both from the gondolas and from Ōwakudani. The journey from Gōra to Tōgendai costs ¥1330/2340 one way/return; make sure to hold on to your ticket if you pause at Ōwakudani. From Ōwakudani, the car continues to Ashi-no-ko (Lake Ashi), a pretty lake that on clear days serves as a reflecting pool for majestic Mt Fuji, which rises imperiously above the surrounding hills. The best way to take in the views and cross the lake is to board one of the incongruous black Ashi-no-ko Pirate Ships (cruise ¥970) at Tōgendai. These kitschy ships cruise the length of Ashi-no-ko in 30 minutes.

Near where the boats dock in Hakone-machi is the old Hakone Checkpoint, run by the Tokugawa regime from 1619 to 1869 as a means of controlling the movement of people and ideas in and out of Edo. The present-day checkpoint is a recent reproduction of the original, and can be interesting for history buffs.

From here, buses run from Moto-Hakone back to Odawara (¥1070, 50 minutes).

ONSEN

There are many bathing options in Hakone's numerous onsen areas. Along with a multitude of onsen there are also many *onsen ryokan*, some of which welcome day visitors.

Just up the hill from Hakone-Yumoto Station, Kappa Tengoku (かっぱ天国; ☎ 0460-85-6121; 777 Yumoto; adult/child ¥750/400; ⏰ 10am-10pm) is a nice *rotemburo* (outdoor bath) if it's not crowded.

Tenzan (天山; ☎ 0460-86-4126; 208 Yumoto-Chaya; admission ¥1200; ⏰ 9am-10pm) This large, popular bath is 2km southwest of town; weekends and holidays can be busy. A free shuttle bus runs from the bridge near Hakone-Yumoto Station. After soaking in *rotemburo* of varying temperatures and designs (one is constructed to resemble a natural cave), the 20-minute walk back down the hill along the river is invigorating.

INFORMATION

Hakone Tourist Information Center (箱根観光案内所; ☎ 0460-85-8911; 698 Yumoto; ⏰ 9am-5pm) Located in front of Hakone-Yumoto train station.

Hakone-Yumoto post office (郵便局; ☎ 0460-85-5681; 383 Yumoto; ⏰ 9am-6pm Mon-Fri)

EATING

Amazake-chaya (甘酒茶屋; ☎ 0460-83-6418; amazake & snacks from ¥400; ⏰ 7am-5.30pm) Since the Edo era, this tea house has been serving up *amazake* (warm, sweet sake) and light snacks. It's about 550m up the Old Tōkaidō Hwy from Moto-Hakone.

Hatsuhana (はつ花; ☎ 0460-85-8287; 635 Yumoto; mains ¥750-1100; ⏰ 10am-7pm) Slurp some soba at this pleasant eatery along the Haya-gawa (Haya River). Hang a left on the next main street after passing the tourist information centre in Hakone-Yumoto; it's over the bridge on the left.

SLEEPING

Hakone's popularity with Japanese weekenders in search of the ultimate spa experience is reflected in the high price of most accommodation in the area. With the exception of two youth hostels and a couple of ryokan, there are few budget and midrange options, although those that exist are comfortable and convenient for hiking and hot-spring hopping.

Fuji-Hakone Guest House (富士箱根ゲストハウス; ☎ 0460-84-6577; www.fujihakone.com; 912 Sengokuhara; r per person from ¥5400; 🖥) This guest house has clean, airy Japanese-style rooms and access to a hot spring bubbling up directly from the Owakudani Volcano. A natural hot spa is available for private bathing, and night-time soaks are a treat, especially when the weather cools. To get here take a bus from stand 4 of Odawara Station to the Senkyōrō-mae bus stop (¥1020, 50 minutes). There's an English sign nearby.

Moto-Hakone Guest House (元箱根ゲストハウス; ☎ 0460-83-7880; www.fujihakone.com; 103 Moto-Hakone; r per person from ¥5000; 🖥) This homey, rather pleasant guest house is located near Ashi-no-ko. From the bus terminal at Odawara Station, catch a bus from lane 3 to Ōshiba bus stop. The guest house is well signposted from there. Breakfast is available for ¥800.

Hakone Sengokuhara Youth Hostel (箱根仙石原ユースホステル; ☎ 0460-84-8966; www.theyh.com; 912 Sengokuhara; dm members/nonmembers ¥3510/4140, r ¥5000) This friendly youth hostel is located just behind Fuji-Hakone Guest House. Check-in is from 4pm to 6pm. For directions on how to get here, see Fuji-Hakone Guest House (opposite).

Fujiya Hotel (富士屋ホテル; ☎ 0460-82-2211; www.fujiyahotel.jp; 359 Miyanoshita; d from ¥21,400) The posh, wood-trimmed Fujiya Hotel, which has the rustic feel of a 19th-century hunting lodge, is famous as one of Japan's earliest Western-style hotels, and is highly rated on all fronts. The hotel is a five-minute walk from Miyanoshita Station on the Hakone-Tōzan Line; if you phone from the station, someone will be able to give you directions in English.

A WISE MAN'S CLIMB *Tony Wheeler*

I started out on a hot August night. At 10pm the temperature had been around 27°C (80°F), but by 4am it was below freezing and the wind was whistling past at what felt like hurricane speed. With a surprising number of other *gaijin* (foreigners) and a huge number of Japanese, I reached the top of Mt Fuji.

Climbing Mt Fuji is definitely not heroic: in the two-month 'season', as many as 180,000 people get up to the top – 3000-odd every night. Nor is it that much fun – it's a bit of a dusty slog, and when you get to the top it's so cold and windy that your main thought is about heading down again. But the climb and the views aren't really what you do it for. To Japanese Fuji climbers, it's something of a pilgrimage; to *gaijin*, it's another opportunity to grapple with something uniquely Japanese.

Like many other climbers, I made my Fuji climb overnight. At 9.30pm I got off the bus at the Kawaguchi-ko 5th Station, which is where the road ends and you have to start walking. Surprisingly, about half the passengers on my bus were *gaijin*, most of them a group of Americans planning to convert the Japanese to Mormonism! I'd bought a litre of the isotonic drink Pocari Sweat and a packet of biscuits at a 7-Eleven in the town of Kawaguchi-ko, and wearing a shirt and a coat, I was all set. The night was clear but dark, and I was glad I'd bought some new batteries for my torch before I left Tokyo.

My experience of climbing holy mountains is that you always get to the top too early – you work up a real sweat on the climb and then you freeze waiting for dawn. So I hung around for a while before starting out.

Despite the hordes climbing the mountain, I managed to lose the path occasionally. By the time I reached 2390m I'd already stopped to unzip the lining from my coat. By 11pm I was past 2700m and thinking it was time to slow down if I wanted to avoid arriving too early. By midnight it was getting much cooler, and I zipped the jacket-lining back in place and added more clothes to my ensemble. I was approaching 3000m – virtually halfway – and at this rate I was going to be at the top by 2.30am, in line with the four hours and 35 minutes the tourist office leaflet said it was supposed to take! In Japan, even mountain climbing is scheduled to the minute.

Although I'd started on my own, some of the faces I met at rest stops were becoming familiar by this point, and I'd fallen in with two Canadians and a Frenchman.

Huts are scattered up the mountainside; some stations have a number of huts, and others have none. The proprietors are very jealous of their facilities, and prominent signs, in English and Japanese, announce that even if it is pouring with rain, you can stay outside if you aren't willing to fork over the overnight fee. Fortunately, at 1.30am we were virtually swept into one hut, probably in anticipation of the numerous bowls of *rāmen* (noodles in broth) we would order. We hung out in this comfortable 3400m-high hideaway until after 3am, when we calculated that a final hour and a bit of a push would get us to the top just before the 4.30am sunrise.

We made it and, looking back from the top, we saw hordes of climbers heading up towards us. It was no great surprise to find a souvenir shop (there is absolutely no place in Japan where tourists won't find a souvenir shop waiting for them). The sun took an interminable time to rise, but eventually it poked its head through the clouds, after which most climbers headed straight back down. I spent an hour walking around the crater rim, but I wasn't sorry to wave Fuji-san goodbye. The Japanese say you're wise to climb Fuji, but a fool to climb it twice. I've no intention of being a fool.

If you decide to go, Fuji-san's 5th station, where most climbers from Tokyo begin their evening hike, can be reached via Keiō Dentetsu bus (☎ 03-5376-2217; ticket ¥2600), which takes 2½ hours and departs from the long-distance bus station on the west side of Shinjuku Station. The mountain is also accessible via a more-expensive and circuitous train route that takes at least two hours and involves hopping the JR Chūō Line for Ōtsuki (*tokkyū/futsū* ¥2980/1280), where you will then need to cross the platform to catch the local train to Kawaguchi-ko (¥1110, 70 minutes). If you're a glutton for punishment you can start at the base of Fuji-san and climb all the way up Fuji via the Yoshida route. Keep in mind that the official climbing season starts on 1 July and ends on 31 August (although it is possible – but not advised – to go at other times). And, of course, remember common-sense hiking precautions: take water unless you intend to buy it during your climb, and make sure you pack gear that is appropriate for cold and wet weather – conditions can vary wildly between the bottom and top of the mountain.

KAMAKURA 鎌倉

Kamakura had a spell of glory as the nation's capital from 1192 to 1333 when Japan's seat of power temporarily relocated here from Kyoto. The Minamoto and later the Hōjo clans ruled Japan from Kamakura for more than a century, until finally in 1333, weakened by the heavy cost of maintaining defences against the threats of attack from Kublai Khan in China, the Hōjo clan fell from power at the hands of the forces of Emperor Go-Daigo. Although the restoration of imperial authority was somewhat illusory, the capital nevertheless shifted back to Kyoto, and Kamakura disappeared temporarily from the history books.

Today Kamakura's wealth of notable temples and elegant shrines makes it one of Tokyo's most rewarding day trips, and one that is often undertaken by locals. The city is best in spring and autumn, when the weather is temperate, but ocean views and old-fashioned shops are a delight year-round. Be sure to stroll up Komachi-dōri from Kamakura Station, where you can stop by the Tourist Information Centre (p243) for a bit of local information in English. Then jump on the Enoden Line for a rickety ride through Kamakura's backstreets to Hase Station, which is near the awesome *Daibutsu* (Great Buddha) and Hase-dera temple.

TEMPLES & SHRINES

Kamakura has a wealth of ancient temples and shrines, making it a very worthwhile destination if you can't make it to Kyoto. These sanctuaries make for an ideal weekend stroll as many can be comfortably visited on foot.

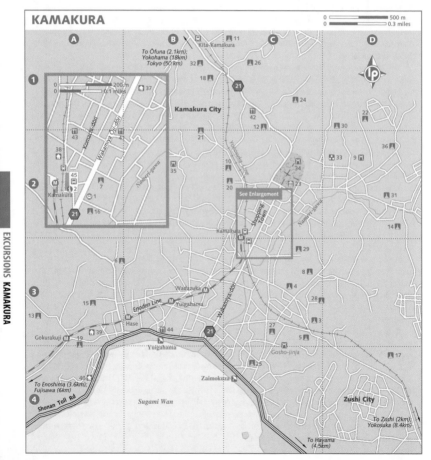

A pleasant walk from Kamakura Station, Tsurugaoka Hachiman-gū (鶴岡八幡宮; ☎ 0467-22-0315; 2-1-31 Yukinoshita; admission free, exhibition hall ¥200; 🕑 9am-4pm, closed last Mon each month) is a carnival-esque Shintō shrine that was established by the Genji family, founders of the Kamakura shōgunate. It is dedicated to a deity who is both the god of war and the guardian of the Minamoto clan. You'll see a steeply arched bridge that was once reserved for the passage of the shōgun alone.

Inside Hase-dera (長谷寺; ☎ 0467-22-6300; 3-11-2 Hase; admission ¥300; 🕑 8.30am-5pm Apr-Sep, 9am-4.30pm Oct-Mar), a temple overlooking the bay, is a 9m-tall, gold-leafed Kannon statue, said to have washed up from the sea in the early 8th century. The statue represents the Buddhist goddess of mercy whose compassion is often invoked as a source of succour to the bereaved and aggrieved. In the gardens here are thousands of small jizō. Mothers who have miscarried or aborted foetuses, or lost their children, often dress jizō in warm clothing or offer toys or food as offerings in supplication for helping those lost children negotiate the underworld.

Kenchō-ji (建長寺; ☎ 0467-22-0981; 8 Yamanouchi; admission ¥300; 🕑 8.30am-4.30pm), the first and grandest of Kamakura's Zen temples, is home to gnarled cypress trees that arose from seeds brought from China by founding priest Lah-hsi Tao-lung 700 years ago. The main hall is from Kyoto and the Buddha Hall (Butsuden) from Tokyo, but the temple bell is the only artefact that was actually made here.

One of the five main Rinzai Zen temples in Kamakura, Engaku-ji (円覚寺; ☎ 0467-22-0487; 453 Yamanouchi; admission ¥200; 🕑 8am-5pm Apr-Sep, 8am-4pm Oct-Mar) dates from 1282 and has a majestic main gate from the 1780s. The temple's main treasure, one of Buddha's teeth, is enshrined up the hill but is off-limits to the public (although you can peer into the courtyard).

For 600 years Tōkei-ji (東慶寺; ☎ 0467-22-1663; 1367 Yamanouchi; admission ¥100; 🕑 8.30am-5pm Mar-Oct, 8.30am-4pm Nov-Feb) was known as the Divorce Temple, the only place in Japan where abused or disgruntled wives could seek refuge from unhappy marriages. The main object of worship here is a statue of Shaka Nyorai (the Enlightened Buddha). The statue is believed to date back to the 14th century and, according to temple records, it escaped a great fire in 1515.

Founded in 1283 by Hojo Morotoki, Jōchi-ji (浄智寺; ☎ 0467-22-3943; 1402 Yamanouchi; admission ¥150; 🕑 9am-4pm) is the fourth of Kamakura's five great Zen temples. The main gate's bell on the 2nd floor of the belltower was cast in 1340. Nearby is Kanro-no-ni, one of Kamakura's 10 revered wells. The interest in this muddy little pond, whose name translates to 'Sweet Water', is mostly historical, but photographers still swarm its edges looking for the perfect shot.

Ennō-ji (円応寺; ☎ 0467-25-1095; 1543 Yamanouchi; admission ¥200; 🕑 9am-4pm Apr-Oct, 9am-3pm Nov-Mar) is distinguished by its statues depicting the judges of hell. According to the Juo concept of Taoism, which was introduced to Japan from

KAMAKURA

TRANSPORT: KAMAKURA

Train From Tokyo Station, the JR Yokosuka Line runs to Kamakura (¥890, 56 minutes) and Kita-Kamakura (¥780) Stations. On clear days, you may be able to catch intermittent glimpses of elusive Mt Fuji. Once here, you can continue on to Enoshima via the scenic Enoden (Enoshima Dentetsu) Line from Kamakura Station or by bus from stop No 9 in front of the station. The train (¥250, 24 minutes) is the simpler and cheaper option. The JR Kamakura-Enoshima Excursion Ticket (from Tokyo/Yokohama ¥1970/1130) is valid for two days and covers the trip to Kamakura from Tokyo or Yokohama, as well as trains around Kamakura including the Enoshima Enoden Line. The Odakyū Enoshima-Kamakura Free Pass (from Shinjuku/Machida ¥1430/990) is valid for one day, but goes to Katase-Enoshima Station and Fujisawa Station, not Kamakura Station.

Bus The transportation hub here is the Kamakura train station, from which most of the local buses depart. A lack of English-language signposting makes the bus network hard to use, but the station's Tourist Information Centre has the latest details on which boarding spots serve which destinations.

Cycling Mountain bikes are perfect for touring Kamakura's far-flung temples. Get wheels at Grove Kamakura (☎ 0467-23-6667; www.rentalmtb.com; 2-1-13 Yuigahama; per day from ¥2310; ☼ noon-8pm Thu, Fri, Mon & Tue, 10am-8pm Sat & Sun), located just past Geba intersection on the road to Yuigahama beach. ID is required.

China during the Heian period (794–1185), these 10 judges decide the fate of souls, who, being neither truly good nor truly evil, must be assigned to spend eternity in either heaven or hell. Presiding over them is Emma (Yama), a Hindu deity known as the gruesome king of the infernal regions.

Kakuon-ji (覚園寺; ☎ 0467-22-1195; 421 Nikaidō; admission with tour ¥300; ☼ 10am-4pm Sep-Jul) features a charming thatched Buddha Hall and hourly tours; the last one starts at 3pm.

Zuisen-ji (瑞泉寺; ☎ 0467-22-1191; 710 Nikaidō; admission ¥100; ☼ 9am-4.30pm) is best known for its perennial flowers and relaxing strolls through gardens laid out by founder Musō Kokushi during the Kamakura era (1185–1333).

If you feel like exploring some of Kamakura's more-remote temples and shrines, the following are good options.

Students come to Egaraten-jinja (荏柄天神社; ☎ 0467-25-1772; 74 Nikaidō; admission free; ☼ 8.30am-4.30pm) to pray for academic success. Like other Tenjin shrines, Egara is dedicated to the memory of Michizane Sugawara, a Kyoto scholar of noble birth who was born in the middle of the 9th century. Students write their aspirations on *ema* (small votive plaques), which are then hung to the right of the shrine. Buses taken from stop 6 in front of Kamakura Station run out to Egara Tenjinja; get off at Tenjin-mae.

Sugimoto-dera (杉本寺; ☎ 0467-22-3463; 903 Nikaidō; admission ¥200; ☼ 8am-4.30pm), Kamakura's oldest temple, is said to have been established by Empress Komei around the mid-8th century. The famous ancient steps lead to ferocious guardian figures (*niō*) poised at the

entrance. The main hall houses three Kannon statues that are said to have miraculously escaped a 12th-century fire by hiding behind a tree. Take a bus from bus stop 5 in front of Kamakura Station and get off at Sugimoto-dera.

Situated down the road from Sugimoto-dera, Hōkoku-ji (報国寺; ☎ 0467-22-0762; 2-7-4 Jōmyoji; admission to garden ¥200; ☼ 9am-4pm) has quiet landscaped gardens where you can relax under a parasol with a cup of green tea. This Rinzai Zen temple is known for its forest of vibrant, perennial bamboo. It regularly holds *zazen* (meditation) classes for beginners.

GREAT BUDDHA & MUSEUM

Kamakura's most famous sight, Daibutsu (鎌倉大仏; Great Buddha; Kotoku-in, 4-2-28 Hase; admission ¥200; ☼ 7am-6pm Mar-Nov, 7am-5pm Dec-Feb) was completed in 1252. Once housed in a huge hall, the statue of Buddha today sits in the open, as a result of its home having been washed away by a tsunami in 1495. Cast in bronze and weighing close to 850 tonnes, the statue is 11.4m tall. Its construction was inspired by the even bigger *Daibutsu* in Nara, although it is generally agreed that the Kamakura bronze is artistically superior. If you're not claustrophobic, you can enter the Buddha's belly through a small door that opens from his side. The privilege will cost you a measly ¥20.

The Kamakura National Treasure Museum (鎌倉国宝館; Kamakura Kokuhōkan; ☎ 0467-22-0753; 2-1-1 Yukinoshita; admission ¥300; ☼ 9am-4.30pm Tue-Sun) displays an excellent collection of Kamakura art. Some are the typically peaceful *jizō*, although the collection also houses a number of compelling sculptures that are energetic and carnal, and sometimes gruesome.

INFORMATION

Kamakura post office (郵便局; ☎ 0467-22-1200; 1-10-3 Komachi; 🕐 9am-7pm Mon-Fri, 9am-3pm Sat) Has ATMs inside.

Tourist Information Centre (鎌倉観光案内所; ☎ 0467-22-3350; 1-1-1 Komachi; 🕐 9am-5.30pm Apr-Sep, to 5pm Oct-Mar) Located just outside the east exit of Kamakura Station.

EATING

Milk Hall (ミルクホール; ☎ 0467-22-1179; 2-3-8 Komachi; dishes ¥600-1500; 🕐 11.30am-10.30pm) This retro antique shop and bar-restaurant in the alleys off Komachi-dōri dishes up light meals like curry rice and cake sets (¥1200). From Kamakura Station, go down Komachi-dōri for two blocks, then take a left and another left down the first alley.

Chaya-kado (茶屋かど; ☎ 0467-23-1673; 1518 Yamanouchi; mains from ¥900; 🕐 10am-5pm) Serving up hot, hearty soup, this humble soba spot is conveniently located on the route from Kita-Kamakura to Kamakura, just before you reach Kenchō-ji. The restaurant may close without

notice, and during the low season, may only open for lunch.

Bowls Donburi Café (鎌倉どんぶりカフェ bowls; ☎ 0467-61-3501; 2-14-7 Komachi; meals from ¥980; 🕐 11am-midnight; 💻) Donburi (rice bowls) are perfected in this jazzy spot along Wakamiya-oji, topped with everything from pork and miso paste to roasted tuna.

Seedless Bar (シードレスバー; ☎ 0467-24-9115; 4-9-1 Yuigahama; mains ¥1000; 🕐 4pm-4am). Roll up to this 2nd-floor surfers' bar facing Yuigahama beach along Route 134 and munch on pizzas, tacos and sandwiches. It's a just short walk from Yuigahama Station on the Enoden Line.

SLEEPING

Kamakura Hase Youth Hostel (鎌倉はせユースホステル; ☎ 0467-24-3990; www1.kamakuranet.ne.jp/hase_yh; 5-11 Sakanoshita; dm member/nonmember ¥3000/4000) Three minutes from Hase-dera and Yuigahama beach, this hostel has bunk beds with a tatami room and a capacity of 12. Breakfast and dinner are available. It's closed between 10am and 4pm daily.

Classical Hotel Ajisai (クラシカルホテルあじさい; ☎ 0467-22-3492; www.hotel-ajisai.com; 1-12-4 Yuki-noshita; s from ¥5780) This is an affordable option with simple Western-style rooms and views of Tsurugaoka Hachiman-gū.

BUDDHISM IN KAMAKURA

Although Buddhism came to Japan in the 6th century, it was 500 years later, during the Kamakura period (1185–1333), that Buddhism finally spread throughout the country. Initially the Kamakura period was marked by secular disillusionment with Buddhist institutions and the monastic orders, and a widespread belief that the world had entered Mappō (the Later Age), a period of Buddhist decline when individuals would no longer be able to achieve enlightenment through their own efforts alone. This led to the flourishing of alternatives to established Buddhist doctrine – notably Zen and the Jōdō (Pure Land) school of Buddhism.

The Jōdō school preached that in the Later Age, salvation could be achieved only through devotion to the transcendent Amida Buddha – all who called on him sincerely would achieve salvation in the Pure Land after death. This populist stroke opened up Buddhism in Japan to the masses, who had previously been largely excluded from the more esoteric branches of Buddhism. This also contrasted with Zen, which sought Buddhahood through meditative practice aimed at the empty centre of the self.

With its rigorous training and self-discipline, Zen found support among an ascendant warrior class and made a considerable contribution to the samurai ethic. Differences on the question of whether *satori* (enlightenment) could be attained suddenly or whether it was a gradual process accounted for Zen breaking into the Rinzai and Sōtō sects.

The contending schools of Jōdō and Zen, along with the views of charismatic leaders, such as the influential 13th-century priest Nichiren, led to the revitalisation of Buddhism within Japan during the Kamakura period. The major Japanese Buddhist sects can trace their antecedents to that era.

You will find numerous temples around Kamakura, including: Ankokuron-ji, Chōshō-ji, Daigyō-ji, Daihō-ji, Eishō-ji, Gokuraku-ji, Hongaku-ji, Hosshō-ji, Jufuku-ji, Kaizō-ji, Kūhin-ji, Myōchō-ji, Myōhon-ji, Myōhō-ji and Raigō-ji. Anyō-in is a temple known for its azalea blooms in spring; Joju-in is another temple known for its blooms in May; Meigetsu-in is a 13th-century temple; and Zeniarai-benten is a Shintō shrine famed for its ability to double money washed in its spring.

Hotel New Kamakura (ホテルニューカマクラ; ☎ 0467-22-2230; www.newkamakura.com, in Japanese; 13-2 Onarimachi; s/d from ¥6000/11,000) Reservations are recommended at this friendly, wood-floored hotel near the station. Both Western- and Japanese-style rooms are available. Rates go up on weekends.

Kamakura Park Hotel (鎌倉パークホテル; ☎ 0467-25-5121; www.kamakuraparkhotel.co.jp; 33-6 Sakanoshita; s/tw from ¥12,705/24,200) This breezy Western-style hotel by the sea has plush 1980s decor, but rooms have been renovated recently. Large rooms have ocean views. There's a weekday shuttle bus to Kamakura Station, or it's a 12-minute walk to Hase Station on the Enoden Line.

ENOSHIMA 江ノ島

Unless you're a surfer and plan on being in the water for most of the day, it's best to avoid this popular beach at weekends, when its sand is completely packed with day-tripping escapees from Tokyo. At the end of the beach is a bridge to Enoshima Island, where Enoshima-jinja (江ノ島神社; ☎ 0466-22-4020; ☒ 9am-4pm) is reached by an outdoor escalator, although it is possible, and pleasant, to walk the whole way. The shrine houses a *hadaka-benzaiten* – a nude statue of the Indian goddess of beauty. Other sights around the island include the Enoshima Samuel Cocking Garden (江の島サムエル・コッキング苑; ☎ 0466-23-0623; adult/child ¥200/100; ☒ 9am-4.30pm) and some sea caves on the far side of the island.

Enoshima's beaches are good for some meditative wandering, particularly around the rocky headlands on the southern side of the island. On fair days, Mt Fuji is clearly visible from the south and west sides of the island. In the late afternoon, you can stop for a drink at one of the cliffside restaurants, where couples often come to watch the sun set over the mountain.

IZU-HANTŌ 伊豆半島

About 80km southwest of Tokyo, Izu-hantō, with its abundant onsen and rugged coastline, is one of Japan's most popular resort destinations and cottage areas. It can get very crowded at weekends and holidays, particularly in summer. Luckily, once you get past the touristy resort of Atami, the crowds usually thin out. And over on the west coast, where transport is by bus only, things are always a lot quieter.

SHUZEN-JI ONSEN 修善寺温泉

Inland Shuzen-ji Onsen is Izu-hantō's most-charming town, a hot-spring village in a lush valley bisected by the rushing Katsura-gawa. Some of Japan's finest *onsen ryokans* are here as well. There are some gorgeous paths to stroll along, as well as a free outdoor public footbath. The tourist information office (☎ 0558-55-0412; ☒ 8.30am-5pm) is at Shuzen-ji Station, which links to Mishima via the Izu-Hakone Tetsudō railway (¥500, 35 minutes). To get to Mishima, board a Tōkaidō Line *shinkansen* at Tokyo (Kodama *shinkansen*, ¥4400, one hour). One of the best inns to stay at here, indeed in all of Japan, is the Arai Ryokan (☎ 0558-72-2007; www.arairyokan.net; 970 Shuzen-ji; r per person incl 2 meals from ¥24,300), which dates from 1872. Its preserved woodcraft interiors and exquisite indoor and outdoor baths are perfectly matched to the seasons, especially when autumn leaves are ablaze outside.

SHIMODA 下田

A quiet seaport, Shimoda is famous as the residence of the American Townsend Harris, the first Western diplomat to set up house in Japan. The Treaty of Kanagawa, which resulted from Commodore Matthew Perry's visit (p25), ended Japan's centuries of self-imposed isolation by forcing the nation to open the ports of Shimoda and Hakodate to US ships. An American consulate was established in Shimoda in 1856.

About 700m south of Izukyū Shimoda Station is Ryōsen-ji (了仙寺; ☎ 0558-22-0657; www.izu.co.jp/~ryosenji; 3-12-12 Shichiken-chō, Shimoda; admission free; ☒ 8.30am-5pm), which is now famous as the site where Commodore Perry and representatives of the Tokugawa shōgunate signed a treaty whose conditions (favourable to the US, of course) supplemented those outlined in the Treaty of Kanagawa, which was signed, in 1854. Located next to the temple is the Ryōsen-ji Treasure Museum (admission ¥500), displaying exhibits relating to the arrival of Westerners in Japan. These include pictures depicting Okichi-san, a courtesan who was forced to give up the man she loved in order to attend to the needs of the brutal barbarian, Harris. When Harris left Japan five years later, Okichi-san was stigmatised for having had a relationship with a foreigner and she

TRANSPORT: SHIMODA

Train Shimoda is as far as you can go by train on Izu-hantō. You can take the Izu Kyūkō Line from Itō (¥1570, one hour) or the Odoriko *tokkyū* from Tokyo Station (¥5480, 2¾ hours).

Bus Tōkai Bus services from Izukyū Shimoda Station run to Dōgashima (¥1360, 50 minutes) and Shuzen-ji (¥2140, two hours, one daily).

Ferry You can board a ferry near the bottom of Shimoda's Perry Road for four of the beach- and onsen-rich Izu-shotō islands (Kōzu-shima, Shikine-jima, Nii-jima, and To-shima). Shinshin Kisen (神新汽船; ☎ 0558-22-2626; ☼ 7.30am-5pm Thu-Tue) services run daily except Wednesday (tickets from ¥4140, two to five hours).

was eventually driven to drink and suicide. Next door to Ryōsen-ji is Chōraku-ji (長楽寺; admission ¥200; ☼ 8.30am-5pm), a pleasant little temple that is worth a quick look. Nearby Hōfuku-ji (宝福寺; ☎ 0558-22-0960; 1-18-26 Shimoda; museum admission ¥300; ☼ 8am-5pm) has a museum that commemorates the tragic life of Okichi-san. Her grave is also here. Nearby Perry Road is a picturesque collection of old buildings housing antique shops, restaurants and bars along a stream. It makes for great leisurely exploring.

Other ways to take in Shimoda include taking the Shimoda Ropeway (☎ 0558-22-1211; return fare incl mountaintop park admission ¥1200) up 200m-tall Nesugata-yama, walking along one of the many beaches, or taking one of the Black Ship cruises (☎ 0558-22-1151; adult/child ¥1000/500) around the bay. These cruises take about 20 minutes and depart from Shimoda Harbour every 30 minutes. There are three boats per day (9.40am, 11am and 2pm) that leave on a course for Iro-zaki. You can leave the boat at Iro-zaki (one way ¥1530, 40 minutes) and travel by bus northwards up the peninsula, or stay on the boat to return to Shimoda. Note: three boats per day leave on Monday, Friday, Saturday and Sunday; during holiday seasons the schedule is daily.

WESTERN IZU-HANTŌ 伊豆半島西部

From Shimoda's bus stop 5 in front of Izukyū Shimoda Station, it's a very scenic bus journey to Dōgashima, a small, charming fishing town on the western side of the peninsula. Along the way is Matsuzaki, a cape recommended for its traditional-style houses and quiet sandy beach. The bus to Dōgashima takes about 50 minutes (¥1360).

The main attractions at Dōgashima are the dramatic rock formations that line the seashore. The park situated just across the street

from the bus stop has some of the best views. It's also possible to take a 20-minute boat trip (☎ 0558-52-0013; tickets ¥1100) from the nearby jetty to visit the town's famous shoreline cave, which has a natural window in its roof that allows the light to pour in. You can look down into the cave from paths in the aforementioned park.

INFORMATION

Main post office (下田郵便局; ☎ 0558-22-0602; 2-4-26 Shimoda; ☼ 10am-5pm) Has an international ATM.

Shimoda Tourist Information (下田市観光案内所; ☎ 0558-22-1531; 1-1 Sotogaoka; ☼ 9am-5pm) Has maps and brochures in English. It's located at the first corner after taking a right out of Izukyū Shimoda Station. Call to ask about English-language tours of Shimoda, as well as hotel reservations.

EATING

Musashi (むさし; ☎ 0558-22-0934; 1-13-1 Shimoda; mains from ¥630; ☼ lunch Wed-Mon) Musashi serves most Japanese favourites, including tempura soba.

Page One (ぺいじわん; ☎ 0558-23-0292; 3-14-30 Shimoda; mains from ¥1000; ☼ 11am-7pm Fri-Wed) Tucked away in a row of old shops on Perry Rd, shop-eatery Page One sells women's clothing along with pizza and pastas such as the *watarigani no tomato kurīmu sōsu pasuta* (Japanese blue crab pasta with tomato sauce) ¥1600).

Sushi Take (寿司竹; ☎ 0558-22-2026; 2-4-6 Shimoda; set meals from ¥1200; ☼ lunch daily, dinner Fri-Wed) Try the excellent sets at this friendly spot near Perry Road such as the *jizakana sushi setto* (local-fish sushi set, ¥1500). There's a picture menu, and a green-and-white sign outside.

Gorosaya (ごろさや; ☎ 0558-23-5638; 1-5-25 Shimoda; lunch/dinner ¥1575/3150; ☼ 11.30am-2pm & 5-9pm Fri-Wed) This slightly upscale restaurant serves very good seafood; look for the wooden fish at the entrance.

SLEEPING

Ōizu Ryokan (大伊豆旅館; ☎ 0558-22-0123; 3-3-25 Shimoda; r per person ¥3500) With a tiny hot-spring bath and small, simple Japanese-style rooms, this popular ryokan is situated on the south side of Shimoda. It is located two blocks north of Perry Rd and four from the waterfront.

Yamane Ryokan (やまね旅館; ☎ 0558-22-0482; 1-19-15 Shimoda; r per person from ¥4630) Conveniently located between the station and Perry Rd, this recently rebuilt inn has tidy Japanese-style rooms, shared bathrooms and a friendly manager. Breakfast is available for ¥1000.

Shimoda Bay Kuroshio (下田ベイクロシオ; ☎ 0558-27-2111; www.baykuro.co.jp; 4-1 Kakisaki; s/d from ¥15,750/21,000) This futuristic hotel gleams above Shimoda-wan. Huge Japanese and Western-style rooms are done in funky decor, with relics, shells and fossils. There are outdoor and indoor onsen, a sauna and buffet dining options.

Shimoda Tōkyū Hotel (下田東急ホテル; ☎ 0558-22-2411; www.shimoda-r.tokyuhotels.co.jp; 5-12-1 Shimoda; s/d from ¥16,200/18,400; 🖳 🖭) About 2km south of Shimoda, this posh hotel has an onsen and a swimming pool (summer only), and boasts a cliffside location with ocean views. Rates include a free shuttle to and from the station.

TRANSPORT

Hyper-efficient, sparkling clean and virtually crime-free, Tokyo's public transport system is the envy of the world. The Tokyo area is a hub for international, domestic and regional travel, so whether you're headed across town or across the globe, you'll be able to get literally anywhere you want to go.

Most residents and visitors use the railway system far more than any other means of transport. It is reasonably priced and frequent (generally five minutes at most between trains on major lines in central Tokyo), and many stations have conveniences such as left-luggage lockers for baggage storage. Most places worth visiting are conveniently close to a subway or East Japan Railway Company (JR or JR East) station or, in some cases, a station on smaller suburban rail line. Where the rail network lets you down (though it really shouldn't), there are usually bus services – although using these can be challenging if you can't read kanji.

Avoiding Tokyo's rush hour is a good idea, but might be impossible if you're on a tight schedule. Commuter congestion tends to ease between 10am and 4pm, when travelling around Tokyo – especially on the JR Yamanote Line – can actually be quite pleasant. Before 9.30am Monday to Friday and from about 4.30pm onward there'll be cheek-to-jowl crowds on all major train and bus lines.

About the biggest drawback to the system is that it shuts down at midnight or 1am and doesn't start up again until 5am or 6am. If you don't plan carefully, you may face an expensive taxi ride home or have to wait for the first morning train – though depending on your perspective this could work to your advantage! Check schedules posted in stations for the last train on the line if you plan to be out late, and make sure it goes all the way to your destination – the last trains of the day sometimes stop mid-route.

Flights, tours and rail tickets can be booked online at www.lonelyplanet.com/travel_services.

AIR

Tokyo is a major hub of world aviation. In addition to the flights that originate and terminate here, many international travellers, chiefly between North America and the rest of Asia, make connections here at Narita International Airport, Japan's main gateway to the world. Tokyo is also the hub of air travel within Japan, where the aviation network is extensive, reliable and safe. In many cases, flying is faster and not significantly more expensive than riding the *shinkansen* (bullet train) to some of the country's most far-flung destinations, such as Hokkaido and Kyūshū. Flying is the only way to reach Okinawa from Tokyo.

Airports

Tokyo has two airports: Narita, which handles most international traffic, and Haneda, which is primarily for domestic flights. Customs and immigration procedures are usually straightforward, although they're more time-consuming for foreigners than for Japanese. Non-Japanese visitors are fingerprinted and photographed on arrival. A neat appearance will speed your passage through passport control and customs.

Narita Airport (☎ flight information 0476-34-5000; general information 0476-32-2802; www.narita-airport.jp/en) is 66km east of Tokyo, but aside from its inconvenient location, it's an excellent, modern airport with a plethora of services. It is divided into two terminals, which are connected by a free shuttle-bus service. From Terminal 1 board this bus at stop 6, and from Terminal 2 board at stops 8 and 18. The airport website lists which airlines use which terminal.

THINGS CHANGE...

The information in this chapter is particularly vulnerable to change. Check directly with the airline or a travel agent to make sure you understand how a fare (and ticket you may buy) works and be aware of the security requirements for international travel. Shop carefully. The details given in this chapter should be regarded as pointers and are not a substitute for your own careful, up-to-date research.

Everything at Narita Airport is clearly signposted in English. At both terminals there are post offices, currency-exchange counters (rates are the same as those in town), ATMs, plenty of restaurants, duty-free shops, left-luggage services and baggage-courier services (see right). The travel-weary (and -dirty) will find showers and day-rooms for napping, and free children's playrooms available to departing passengers who have completed emigration formalities, with computer games and well-designed play areas.

There are several information counters in both terminals, and the staff speaks English. The airport Tourist Information Centres (TIC; ☎ 0476-34-6251; ⊙ 9am-8pm) are a key stop if you haven't yet booked any accommodation. While you're there, pick up a subway map and the *Tourist Map of Tokyo*. There's a TIC on the 1st floor in each terminal. Narita Airport also has JR offices in each terminal, where you can make bookings and exchange your Japan Rail Pass (p254) voucher for a pass, if you're planning to start travelling straight away.

If you are going to Narita Airport by land, note that passports are inspected for everyone entering Narita Airport, even if they're not travelling; keep yours handy. Check-in procedures are usually very efficient, but you should arrive at the airport at least two hours before your departure time. Passport control and security procedures are similarly efficient. Bring your embarkation card, which should have been stapled into your passport upon arrival; if you don't have one, you can get a blank form before going through passport control.

Haneda Airport (☎ information 5757-8111; www.tokyo -airport-bldg.co.jp/en) is the airport seasoned Tokyo expats wish was still Tokyo's main air hub. It's a fraction of the distance from central Tokyo and smaller and easier to navigate. Haneda doesn't have Narita's services infrastructure, but there are post offices, banks, restaurants, left-luggage services and baggage-shipping companies. Nor does Haneda have a dedicated English-language information counter, although there is usually someone who can answer your questions in English.

Haneda is Tokyo's main airport for flights within Japan, so if you're arriving into Narita you may well find yourself transferring to Haneda for your connection. As we went to press, the only international flights served

Seoul, Beijing, Hong Kong and Shanghai, but that was all scheduled to change following the completion of a brand new runway in 2010.

Baggage Shipment

Baggage couriers provide next-day delivery of your large luggage from Narita and Haneda Airports to any address in Tokyo (around ¥2000 per large bag). This fabulous service can also deliver luggage to points beyond Tokyo so you don't have to haul it through trains and stations all over the countryside. With the exception of trains and buses serving the airports, it is rare to find storage for large luggage on public transport. Plus, train and subway stations may have only stairs when you need an elevator or escalator for that heavy bag, and taxis may have smaller trunks than you're used to. Baggage service counters are located on the arrival levels of each terminal.

Couriers can also pick up luggage for delivery to the airport, but be sure to call two days before your flight to arrange a pick-up. The companies listed here have some operators who speak English:

ANA Sky Porter (☎ toll free 0120-007-952)

JAL ABC (☎ toll free 0120-919-120, in Tokyo 03-3545-2800; www.jalabc.com)

Getting To/From the Airports
NARITA AIRPORT

Getting into central Tokyo from Narita Airport can take anything from 50 minutes to a couple of hours, depending on your mode of transport. Because the two terminals at Narita are fairly distant from one another, be sure to get off your train or bus at the correct terminal – all airport transport prominently displays lists of airlines and the terminal they use.

Both the Japan Railways (JR East) and the independent Keisei Line connect Narita Airport and Tokyo. Conveniently, trains depart from stations beneath the airport terminals.

On the Keisei Line (☎ 0476-32-8501; www.keisei .co.jp), two services run between Narita Airport and Tokyo: the comfortable, fast Skyliner service (¥1920, 36 minutes), which runs nonstop to Nippori and Ueno Stations (Map

CLIMATE CHANGE & TRAVEL

Climate change is a serious threat to the ecosystems that humans rely upon, and air travel is the fastest-growing contributor to the problem. Lonely Planet regards travel, overall, as a global benefit, but believes we all have a responsibility to limit our personal impact on global warming.

Flying & Climate Change

Pretty much every form of motorised travel generates CO_2 (the main cause of human-induced climate change) but planes are far and away the worst offenders, not just because of the sheer distances they allow us to travel, but because they release greenhouse gases high into the atmosphere. The statistics are frightening: two people taking a return flight between Europe and the US will contribute as much to climate change as an average household's gas and electricity consumption over a whole year.

Carbon Offset Schemes

Climatecare.org and other websites use 'carbon calculators' that allow travellers to offset the level of greenhouse gases they are responsible for with financial contributions to sustainable travel schemes that reduce global warming – including projects in India, Honduras, Kazakhstan and Uganda.

Lonely Planet, together with Rough Guides and other concerned partners in the travel industry, support the carbon offset scheme run by climatecare.org. Lonely Planet offsets all of its staff and author travel.

For more information, check out our website: www.lonelyplanet.com.

---

p78); and the *tokkyū* (premium train) service (limited express; ¥1000, 1¼ hours). Ueno Station is on both the JR Yamanote Line and the Hibiya and Ginza subway lines. If you're travelling to Ikebukuro or Shinjuku, it's more convenient to get off one stop before Ueno at Nippori Station, also on the JR Yamanote Line.

Going to the airport from Ueno, the Keisei Ueno Station is right next to the JR Ueno Station. You can buy advance tickets here for the Skyliner service, or purchase tickets for the Keisei *tokkyū* service from the ticket machines. JR Nippori Station has a clearly signposted walkway to the Keisei Nippori Station.

Japan Railways (JR East; ☎ in English 3423-0111; www .jreast.co.jp) runs Narita Express (N'EX; ¥2940, 53 minutes) and JR *kaisoku* (rapid express; ¥1280, 85 minutes) services into Tokyo Station (Map p52), from where you can change for almost anywhere.

N'EX is swift, smooth and comfortable, but it doesn't operate as frequently as the Keisei Line. N'EX trains depart Narita approximately every half-hour between 7am and 10pm for Tokyo Station, and they also run less frequently into Shinagawa (Map p119; ¥3110, 65 minutes), Shibuya (Map p102; ¥3110, 73 minutes), Shinjuku (Map p110; ¥3110, 80 minutes) and Ikebukuro (Map p116; ¥3110, 86 minutes), or to Japan's second-largest city, Yokohama (¥4180, 1½ hours), which is con-

venient if you are heading to Izu or Hakone (see p229). All seats are reserved, but tickets can usually be bought just before departure. Japan Rail and JR East Passes (p254) are valid on N'EX trains, but you must obtain a seat reservation (no extra charge) from a JR ticket office.

JR *kaisoku* service is part of the local transit network and so stops at many local stations. This service is the slowest and cheapest into Tokyo Station, leaving about once an hour.

Friendly Airport Limousine (☎ 3665-7220; www .limousinebus.co.jp/en; 1-way fare ¥3000) operates scheduled, direct, all-reserved transport between Narita Airport and major hotels and train stations in Tokyo. Don't get too excited about the name – they're ordinary buses, and sometimes they make stops at other stations and hotels along the same route before reaching your destination. The journey takes 1½ to two hours depending on traffic and other stops.

Purchase tickets at clearly marked counters on the arrival level. If your hotel is not directly served (or if you don't feel like waiting for the next departure), you may purchase a seat aboard a limousine bus to a nearby hotel or station and travel the rest of the way via public transport or taxi. Direct buses between Narita and Haneda airports (¥3000 one way) take about 1¼ hours, traffic permitting.

In case you're wondering, a taxi to Narita Airport from Tokyo will sey you back approximately ¥30,000 and, battling traffic all the way, will usually take longer than the train.

HANEDA AIRPORT

The most simple and cheapest way to get from Haneda Airport to central Tokyo is to hop on the Tokyo Monorail (www.tokyo-monorail.co.jp/english; ¥470, 18 minutes) from Hamamatsuchō Station on the JR Yamanote Line. Trains depart every 10 minutes. Limousine buses also connect Haneda with Tokyo City Air Terminal (TCAT; Map p122; ¥900, 30 minutes) and hotels around central Tokyo; buses to Ikebukuro and Shinjuku, for example, cost ¥1200 and take about one hour, while the fare to Shibuya is ¥1000. Taxis to central Tokyo will set you back around ¥7000.

Tickets

If you're planning on booking flights in Japan for domestic or overseas travel, you'll find a number of travel agencies in Tokyo where English is spoken. Note that prices fluctuate wildly depending on season, availability and fuel prices. Typical travel agency hours are 10am to 6pm Monday to Friday, 11am to 4pm Saturday, closed Sunday.

Across Traveller's Bureau (www.across-travel.com); Ikebukuro (Map p116; ☎ 5391-3227; 3rd fl, 1-11-1 Higashi-Ikebukuro, Toshima-ku); Shibuya (Map p102; ☎ 5467-0077; 3rd fl, 1-14-14 Shibuya, Shibuya-ku); Shinjuku (Map p110; ☎ 3340-1633; 2nd fl, 1-19-6 Nishi-Shinjuku, Shinjuku-ku)

No 1 Travel (www.no1-travel.com); Ikebukuro (Map p116; ☎ 3986-4690; 4th fl, 1-16-10 Nishi-Ikebukuro, Toshima-ku); Shibuya (Map p102; ☎ 3770-1381; 6th fl, 1-20-1 Dogenzaka, Shibuya-ku); Shinjuku (Map p110; ☎ 3205-6073; 7th fl, 1-16-5 Kabukichō, Shinjuku-ku)

STA Travel (www.statravel.co.jp); Ikebukuro (Map p116; ☎ 5391-2922; 7th fl, 1-16-20 Minami-Ikebukuro, Tōshima-ku); Takadanobaba (Map p116; ☎ 5287-3543; 1-32-13 Takadanobaba, Shinjuku-ku)

BICYCLE

Despite the tangled traffic and often narrow roads, bicycles are still one of the most common forms of transport in Tokyo. Theft does happen, especially of cheap bicycles, so go ahead and lock up your bike. Ride with your bag or pack on your person, as opportunists on motorbikes do swipe stuff from those front-mounted baskets.

Some ryokan (traditional Japanese inns) and hotels rent bicycles to their guests. Also see p205 for location-specific leisure-ride bike rentals.

BOAT

Water taxis are one of the most dramatic ways to take in the city. For more information on cruises down Sumida-gawa, see p65.

BUS

The vast majority of Tokyoites and resident expats seem never to have set foot on a bus as the rail and subway system is convenient and incredibly comprehensive. However, on rare occasions, it can sometimes be quicker to get between two destinations on a bus.

Bus fares are ¥200/100 per adult/child for Tokyo Metropolitan (Toei) buses; you can pick up a copy of the *Toei Bus Route Guide,* including a route map and timetable, at any Toei subway station. Deposit your fare into the box next to the driver as you enter the bus; you can get change for ¥1000 notes and coins. A tape recording announces the name of each stop as it is reached, so listen carefully and press the button next to your seat when yours is announced.

The one-day Tokyo Combination Ticket (see p253) can be used on Toei buses as well as the subway and JR railway lines.

CAR & MOTORCYCLE
Driving

Driving yourself around Tokyo is by no means impossible, but the entire experience is somewhat akin to stabbing yourself in the eye with a chopstick. Parking space is limited and expensive, traffic moves in slow-mo, traffic lights are posted virtually every 50m, and unless you've lived here for a while and can read Japanese, expect to get lost. Trust us: you're much better off taking advantage of Tokyo's excellent public transport.

However, if you intend to drive in Japan, pick up a copy of the useful *Rules of the Road* (¥1000) available from the Japan Automobile Federation (www.jaf.or.jp/e/index.htm). Also, you will need a Japanese driver's licence, or an International Driving Permit, which must be arranged in your own country before you leave.

A large number of Tokyoites and resident expats have motorcycles. It's a good way to get around town, especially after the trains have stopped running. The best place to take a look at what's available and get some information in English is the area of motorcycle shops on Korinchō-dōri, near Ueno Station (Map p78) – some of the shops there have foreign staff.

If you buy a motorcycle, you will need a motorcycle licence (for motorcycles up to 400cc, your foreign licence is transferable) and your bike will need to be registered. Bikes up to 125cc are registered at your local ward office, while bikes of more than 125cc are registered with the Transport Branch Office. Further information can be obtained through the service offered to foreign residents living in Tokyo by the Tokyo Metropolitan Government (p109).

Hire

Car-hire agencies in Tokyo will rent you one of their vehicles upon presentation of an international driving licence. Small cars average ¥8000 per day. Some rental agencies that usually have English-speaking staff on hand:

Nippon Rent-a-Car (☎ 3485-7196)

Toyota Rent-a-Car (☎ 5954-8008)

TAXI

Visitors to Tokyo are uniformly impressed by the taxis: white gloved drivers, seats covered with lace doilies, doors that magically open and close.

However, that service comes at a price. Fares start at ¥710, which buys you 2km (after 11pm it's 1.5km), then the meter rises by ¥80 every 275m (every 220m or so after 11pm). You also click up about ¥80 every two minutes while you relax in a typical Tokyo traffic jam.

It's generally quite simple to hail a taxi, and hotels and train stations usually have orderly queues. Taxi vacancy is indicated by a red light in the corner of the front window; a green light means there's a night-time surcharge; and a yellow light means that the cab is on call.

If you have to get a taxi late on a Friday or Saturday night, be prepared for long queues and higher prices. The same applies any day of the week for the first hour or so after the last trains run.

Tokyo taxi drivers rarely speak any English – if you don't speak Japanese, it's a good idea to have your destination written down in Japanese – or better yet, a map (most hotels and businesses have one). Even if your destination has an English name, it is unlikely the driver will understand your pronunciation. Many, but not all, taxis have GPS devices.

TRAIN

Tokyo's trains are a wonder. Although the train map looks like a bowl of *rāmen*, inside it's about the most orderly bowl of *rāmen* you'll ever see. Trains arrive and depart precisely on time, and even a minute's delay elicits apologies from conductors. Passengers, meanwhile, queue up at indicated points, and the trains stop right there.

The Tokyo train system can be a bit daunting at first, but most visitors get the hang of it soon enough. Much initial confusion arises from the fact that Tokyo is serviced by a combination of train lines, private and municipal inner-city subway lines and independently operated suburban lines. This sometimes means switching between different train and subway systems, though it's not as bad as it sounds since the lines are well integrated.

Station names are clearly marked in both Japanese and English on platform signs and/or posts, and electronic signs inside most trains indicate the next station in Japanese and English. Additionally, announcements are made both inside the trains and at the station when the doors open. Train lines are colour-coded and subway stations are also letter- and number-coded, which can be useful for visitors (for example, Tokyo Station is 'M17', the 17th stop on the Marunouchi Line). In reality, however, most locals don't know these numbers, and most visitors ultimately find it easier to learn the station names.

Perhaps the most confusing part of riding the rails is figuring out where to exit the station. Most stations have many exits, which are numbered, and using the wrong exit can lead to utter disorientation – even for Tokyoites. When getting directions, always ask which exit to use. Individual listings in this book give this information. See p254 at the end of this chapter.

Although it is generally not an issue in central Tokyo, if you head toward the suburbs you may encounter express services.

TIP

Unlike on many other train systems throughout the world, Japanese trains require you to swipe your ticket or store-value card upon both entering and leaving the train system. Keep your ticket in a safe place during your journey! If you've purchased a single-journey ticket, it will be collected when you exit.

The fastest 'regular' trains (ie slower than the *shinkansen* bullet trains) are the *tokkyū* (特急; limited express services) and the *kyūkō* (急行; ordinary express), which usually stop at only a limited number of stations. Local trains, which stop at all stations, are called *futsū* (普通). There is usually a board on the platform indicating exactly which trains stop at which stations, in both English and Japanese.

Tokyo's train system is remarkably safe and crime-free, but groping male hands have long been a problem for women when trains are packed. In response, most Tokyo train lines now reserve women-only carriages at peak times. The carriages are marked with signs (usually pink) in both Japanese and English, or in some cases by illustrations showing the silhouette of a man standing outside of a women-only carriage. Boys older than 12 are not allowed on women-only carriages.

Subway

Tokyo's subway system is indispensable for getting around the city centre. The city is home to no fewer than 13 subway lines, of which nine are operated by the company Tokyo Metro and four are Toei (municipal) lines. The two companies' services are essentially the same and have good connections from one to the other, although they do operate under separate ticketing systems and serve different destinations; Toei lines are also marginally pricier. Most subway fares within central Tokyo cost between ¥160 and ¥210.

Colour-coding and regular English signposting make the system easy to use. For instance, you'll quickly learn that the Ginza Line is orange and that the Marunouchi Line is red. A large number of lines intersect at Nihombashi, Ōtemachi and Ginza, making it possible to get to this part of town from almost anywhere.

Japan Railways (JR) Lines

The lines of the former Japan National Railway (privatised a few decades ago) are mostly above-ground trains and are integrated with train lines to pretty much anywhere else in Japan, including the *shinkansen*. Here are some useful JR trains within the city.

YAMANOTE LINE

The most important train line in Tokyo, both in usefulness and cultural significance, the Yamanote Line makes a 35km loop around central Tokyo. It's named for the 'high city' that once functioned within. A ride on the Yamanote Line makes a great introduction to the city. Buy the cheapest fare (¥130), grab a seat, and an hour later you'll disembark at the same station where you started with a solid overview of Tokyo's main areas of interest. JR Yamanote Line trains are silver with a green stripe.

CHŪŌ & SŌBU LINES

The JR Chūō Line (Map p110) cuts its way across the centre of the JR Yamanote Line between Shinjuku and Tokyo Stations in about 13 minutes. Trains on this line are coloured orange. This line is contiguous with the JR Sōbu Line until Ochanomizu Station where the lines split – the Chūō heading down to Tokyo Station and the Sōbu heading out to the eastern suburbs. Chūō Line trains typically run express, while the Sōbu Line runs local. Sōbu Line cars have a yellow stripe.

OTHER LINES

The JR Yokosuka Line runs south to Kamakura (see p242) from Tokyo Station via Shimbashi and Shinagawa Stations. The JR Tōkaidō Line also travels in the same direction from Tokyo Station, providing access to Izu-hantō (p244).

SUBWAY LOGIC

Riding the rails in Tokyo is a fantastic cultural study. See if you notice your fellow passengers doing the following:

- Texting – by far the most popular pastime.
- Reading – manga-mania is alive and well in Tokyo's trains.
- Sleeping – don't be surprised to find some salaryman or OL's head on your shoulder. Amazingly, Tokyoites never seem to sleep through their stop.
- Talking – actually, this is something you probably won't encounter much of. On most trains you can hear a pin drop. Mobile phone conversations are definitely frowned upon. See Sleeping, above.
- Eating – again, notable for its absence on subways. Perhaps that's how the cars stay so clean. By contrast, on inter-city trains, eating is practically a commandment.

PASSES & COMBINATION TICKETS

Here are some options to reduce your travel costs into and around Tokyo:

Available at Train Stations

- Tokyo Metro One-Day Open Ticket (¥710) Unlimited rides on Tokyo Metro subway lines only. Purchase at Tokyo Metro stations.
- Common One-Day Ticket for Tokyo Metro and Toei subway lines (¥1000) Valid on all 13 lines operating underground in Tokyo. Purchase at Tokyo Metro or Toei stations.
- Tokyo Round Tour Ticket (*Tokyo Furii Kippu*, ¥1580) Unlimited same-day rides on Tokyo Metro, Toei and JR Lines operating in Tokyo. Purchase at *midori-no-madoguchi* at JR stations.

For Passengers Coming from Narita Airport

- Limousine & Metro Pass (¥3100) One-way ticket on Friendly Airport Limousine (p249) and one-day pass on Tokyo Metro subway lines. Purchase at Airport Limousine counters or at Tokyo Metro pass outlets.
- N'EX & Suica (¥3500) One-way ride on Narita Express into the city, plus a Suica (p254) worth ¥2000 (¥1500 in value, plus deposit).
- Skyliner & Metro Pass (one/two days ¥2100/2480) Covers one-way ticket on Keisei Skyliner (p248) from Narita Airport plus a one- or two-day pass on Tokyo Metro subway lines. Available at Keisei counters at Narita Airport.
- Tokyo Metro One- or Two-Day Open Ticket (¥600/980) Unlimited rides on Tokyo Metro subway lines. Purchase at Narita Airport Railway/Bus Ticket Counter (Terminal 1) or Entertainment Ticket/Cell Phone Counter (Terminal 2).

Private Lines

The Yurikamome Line, which services Odaiba (Map p127), is a driverless, elevated train that departs from Shimbashi, just south of Ginza, crosses the Rainbow Bridge, and terminates at Toyosu, on the Tokyo Metro Yūrakuchō Line. The Shimbashi terminal is above ground and on the eastern side of JR Shimbashi Station. See p126 for details on the Yurikamome.

Most other private lines service suburban areas outside Tokyo. The ones you are most likely to use are Shibuya's Tōkyū Tōyoko Line, which runs south to Yokohama; the Keiō Inokashira Line from Shibuya to Kichijōji via Shimo-Kitazawa; Shinjuku's Odakyū Line, which runs southwest out to Hakone (p236); and Asakusa's Tōbu Nikkō Line, which goes north to Nikkō (p231).

Tickets & Passes
VENDING MACHINES/PURCHASING

For all local journeys, tickets are sold at vending machines called *kippu jidō hanbaiki*. Above the vending machines are rail maps with fares indicated next to the station names. Unfortunately for visitors, the names on the map are often in kanji only. The best way around this problem is to put your money in the machine and push the lowest fare button (¥130 on JR, ¥160 to ¥170 on subway lines) and settle the difference on arrival (see p254).

If the ticket machine has a touch screen (as opposed to push-buttons), there will be an option to switch the language to English.

All vending machines for all lines accept ¥1000 notes and most accept ¥10,000 (there are pictures of the bills accepted on the machines). Don't forget to pick up the bills you get in change. Credit cards are not accepted for local transit tickets.

Two buttons on the machine could come in handy if you completely bungle the operation. First is the *tori-keshi* (取り消し; cancel) button, which is usually marked in English. The second is the *yobidashi* (呼び出し; call) button, which will alert a staff member that you need assistance (staff sometimes pop out from a hidden door between the machines – it can be surprising).

You'll need different tickets for the two subway systems, but the automated ticket machines sell transfer tickets (¥70), which allow you to transfer from one system to another without buying another full-price ticket. The button for this ticket is usually marked only in Japanese (乗り換え; *norikae*). To save yourself time and hassle, don't bother with transfer tickets – buy a store value card or Tokyo Combination Ticket instead (see above).

In the case of JR stations, there will be signs (sometimes but not always in both English and Japanese) indicating the *midori-no-madoguchi* (緑の窓口; green window) ticket counter. Here you can buy bullet-train tickets, make reservations and buy special passes; in smaller stations this is where you ask for information as well.

FARE ADJUSTMENT

If you've purchased the base fare and think you might need to pay more, you have two options. At an attended exit gate, simply hand over your ticket and the attendant will inform you of the additional fare, which you can pay on the spot. A fare-adjustment machine, usually near the exit turnstiles, is just as simple and saves time if the gate is congested. Insert your ticket, and the screen will tell you how much to insert, then spit out your change (if any) and a new ticket. Insert this ticket into the exit turnstiles, and off you go. Fare-adjustment machines usually have English instructions.

STORE-VALUE CARDS

Those planning to spend an extended period of time in Tokyo should strongly consider getting either a Suica (sold at JR stations) or a Pasmo (sold at Tokyo Metro and Toei stations) smart card. Either card works on virtually all trains and buses within Tokyo, and Suica is also valid on JR lines in other regions of Japan. Either card has an initial purchase price of ¥2000/1000 (Suica/Pasmo, including a ¥500 deposit). Wave the card over the wicket and your fare is automatically deducted at the end of a journey. You can replenish the value of the card as needed at stations. You can even use it to pay for items in stores, vending machines and baggage lockers in stations. When you return your Suica or Pasmo card at a station office, you'll be refunded the ¥500 deposit, minus a ¥210 service fee.

Many visitors to Japan purchase a Japan Rail Pass (www.japanrailpass.net), for travel on JR trains throughout the nation. A seven-day pass costs ¥28,300 and must be purchased *before* arriving in Japan; 14-day and 21-day passes are also available. The regional JR company, JR East (www.jreast.co.jp), also offers the JR East Pass for unlimited travel on its trains in eastern Honshu and into the Japan Alps, costing from ¥20,000 for either five consecutive days or four days of your choosing with a 30-day period; the JR East Pass can be purchased in Japan. That said, if you're planning on spending most of your time in Tokyo, neither of these passes will benefit you.

Stations

Navigating your way around train stations in Tokyo can be confusing, particularly at some of the more gigantic and complex stations such as Shinjuku Station. The key is to know where you're going before you get to the station. Most stations have adequate English signposting, with large yellow signs on the platforms posting exit numbers and often including local destinations, such as large hotels, department stores and embassies. When possible, find out which exit to use when you get directions to a destination. Street maps of the area are usually posted near each exit.

Since each station will usually have several different exits, you should get your bearings and decide where to exit while still on the platform. If you have your destination written down, you can go to an attended gate and ask the station attendant to direct you to the correct exit. To help you along we've included in this guidebook exit details for each listing where possible.

Modern Japanese spend a good part of their lives on trains, a fact that is reflected in the wide range of services available at most stations. Most stations have left-luggage lockers, which can hold medium-sized bags. These lockers often come in several sizes and cost from ¥200 to ¥600. Storage is good for 24 hours, after which your bags will be removed and taken to the station office.

All train stations have toilets, almost all of which are free of charge. Bring pocket tissues, though, as toilet paper is not always provided (this is why advertising in the form of tissue packets handed out on street corners is big business). It's also a good idea to pick up a handkerchief at the ¥100 shops as paper towels and hand driers are also not always available.

At the majority of JR stations and major subway stations, you can also find several options for food. The smallest of these are kiosks, which sell snacks, drinks, magazines, newspapers etc. Next up are stores selling *ekiben* (train-station boxed lunches), which are obligatory if you truly want to experience the sophistication of Japanese long-distance rail travel, and *tachi-kui* (stand-and-eat) noodle restaurants. Most of these places require that you purchase a food ticket from a vending machine, which you hand to an attendant upon entry (most machines have pictures on the buttons to help you order). Finally, large stations might also have a choice of several sit-down places, most of which will have plastic food models displayed in the front window, or picture menus.

DIRECTORY

BUSINESS HOURS

Banks are normally open Monday to Friday from 9am to 3pm (some until 5pm). Shops and supermarkets are usually open from 10am to 8pm daily. Museums typically open at 9am or 10am and close at 5pm, with the last entry between 4pm and 4.30pm; the most common closing day for museums is Monday. Restaurants are generally open for lunch from 11.30am or noon to 2.30pm or 3pm and for dinner from 6pm or 6.30pm to 9pm or 10pm, with last orders taken about half an hour before closing. Bars typically open around 5pm and stay open until the wee hours.

CHILDREN

Tokyo, like the rest of Japan, is unreservedly child-friendly. Despite the occasional meltdown, you'll find that the majority of Japanese tots are quite reserved and well-mannered in public. In addition to loads of kid-centred activities (see the boxed text, p81), the city also offers numerous playgrounds and parks where children, and parents, can unwind. If you're travelling with small children, common items such as nappies (diapers) can be found at any pharmacy. Baby formula and other special dietary needs will, of course, be labelled in Japanese, so bringing such items from home could save time and frustration. If travelling with the little ones, consider Lonely Planet's *Travel with Children* (www.lonelyplanet.com/shop).

Babysitting

Listed are a few recommended services providing English-speaking sitters. Although some of these organisations require an annual membership fee, they may waive it if you ask for introductory or trial rates. Prices vary considerably depending on the number of children, time required and your location in Tokyo.

Japan Baby-Sitter Service (☎ 3423-1251; www .jbs-mom.co.jp, in Japanese) One of Japan's oldest – and considered one of its most reliable – services.

Poppins Service (☎ 3447-2100; www.poppins.co.jp/ english/index.html) Nannies versed in early-childhood development and first aid can also speak English, French, German or Italian.

Alternatively, if you're staying at a hotel, staff there might be able to refer you to a reliable babysitter.

CLIMATE

Tokyo kicks off its year with cold winter days and the odd snowfall. Although temperatures occasionally drop below freezing, generally clear skies make winter (December to February) usually quite tolerable provided you have the right kind of clothes. Spring (March to May) brings pleasant, warm days and, of course, cherry blossoms (see the boxed text, p18) – early April is usually the best time to view the blooms, although of course this varies with the temperature. Late June typically brings *tsuyu* (rainy season), when torrential rains leave the city hot and sticky, peaking in August. Expect the occasional late-season typhoon in September, and as late as early October. Apart from spring, autumn (late September to November) is the most pleasant season as temperatures cool down to a cosy level and days are often clear and fine. November also generally means the return of the dramatic foliage season, when the parks and green areas of the city mellow into varying hues of orange and red. For more information, see p16.

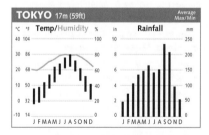

CUSTOMS REGULATIONS

Customs allowances include the usual tobacco products plus three 750mL bottles of alcohol, 57g of perfume, and gifts and souvenirs up to a value of ¥200,000 or its equivalent. You must be older than 20 years to qualify for these allowances. The penalties for importing illegal drugs are extremely severe.

Although the Japanese are no longer censoring pubic hair in domestically produced pornography, customs officers will still confiscate any pornographic materials in which pubic hair is visible, and child pornography is strictly prohibited.

Passengers carrying in excess of ¥1 million are required to declare it upon arrival. The exportation of foreign currency is also unlimited, but there is a ¥5 million export limit for Japanese currency. Visit the website of Japan Customs (www.customs.go.jp/english/) for more information on Japan's customs regulations.

ELECTRICITY

Japanese plugs are the type with two flat pins, which are identical to two-pin North American plugs. The Japanese electric current is 100V AC, an odd voltage found almost nowhere else in the world (appliances with a two-pin plug made for use in North America will work without an adaptor, but may be a bit sluggish). Tokyo and eastern Japan are on 50Hz, western Japan is on 60Hz. Transformers are easy to find at one of Japan's plentiful electronics shops.

Check www.kropla.com for detailed information on matters of voltage and plugs.

EMBASSIES

Australia (Map p92; ☎ 5232-4111; www.australia .or.jp/english/; 2-1-14 Mita, Minato-ku)

Belgium (Map p60; ☎ 3262-0191; www.diplomatie .be/tokyo; 5-4 Nibanchō, Chiyoda-ku)

Canada (Map p88; ☎ 5412-6200; www.canadainter national.gc.ca; 7-3-38 Akasaka, Minato-ku)

France (off Map p92; ☎ 5798-6000; www.ambafrance -jp.org; 4-11-44 Minami-Azabu, Minato-ku)

Germany (Map p92; ☎ 5791-7700; www.tokyo.diplo.de; 4-5-10 Minami-Azabu, Minato-ku)

India (Map p60; ☎ 3262-2391; www.embassyofindia japan.org; 2-2-11 Kudan-Minami, Chiyoda-ku)

Ireland (Map p60; ☎ 3263-0695; www.irishembassy.jp; 2-10-7 Kōjimachi, Chiyoda-ku)

Italy (Map p92; ☎ 3453-5291; www.ambtokyo.esteri.it; 2-5-4 Mita, Minato-ku)

Malaysia (off Map p102; ☎ 3476-3840; www.kln.gov .my/perwakilan/tokyo/; 20-16 Nanpeidaichō, Shibuya-ku)

Netherlands (Map p92; ☎ 5776-5400; www.oranda .or.jp; 3-6-3 Shiba-kōen, Minato-ku)

New Zealand (off Map p102; ☎ 3467-2271; www .nzembassy.com; 20-40 Kamiyamachō, Shibuya-ku)

South Korea (Map p92; ☎ 3452-7611; www.jpn-tokyo .mofat.go.kr; 1-2-5 Minami-Azabu, Minato-ku)

UK (Map p60; ☎ 5211-1100; www.UKinJapan.fco.gov.uk; 1 Ichibanchō, Chiyoda-ku)

USA (Map p88; ☎ 3224-5000; http://tokyo.usembassy .gov; 1-10-5 Akasaka, Minato-ku)

EMERGENCY

Although most emergency operators you'll reach in Tokyo don't speak English, the operators will immediately refer you to someone who does. Japan Helpline is a service that provides assistance to foreigners living in Japan.

Ambulance (☎ 119)

Fire (☎ 119)

Japan Helpline (☎ 0120-46-1997)

Police (☎ 110, English-language line 3501-0110)

GAY & LESBIAN TRAVELLERS

With the possible exception of Thailand, Japan is Asia's most enlightened nation with regard to the sexual orientation of foreigners. Tokyo in particular is a tolerant city where the bars and clubs host folks of all predilections. Tokyo has an active gay scene and a small but very lively, gay quarter (Shinjuku-nichōme). Note that some bars are 'members clubs' and not at all welcoming of outsiders, while others, called *gai-sen*, are all about welcoming foreigners; see (p182) to get you started.

Same-sex couples probably won't encounter many problems travelling in Tokyo, although some travellers have reported being turned away or grossly overcharged when checking into love hotels with a partner of the same sex. Outside Tokyo, you'll find it difficult to break into the local scene unless you spend considerable time in a place or have local contacts; Japanese would tell you much the same of their experiences in a new city.

Apart from this, it's unlikely that you'll run into difficulties. There are no legal restraints on same-sex sexual activities in Japan apart from the usual age restrictions. One note: Japanese of any sort do not typically engage in public displays of affection.

Cineastes visiting in summer should check the local listings for screenings of the annual Tokyo International Lesbian & Gay Film & Video Festival (☎ 6475-0388; www.tokyo-lgff.org).

The following are useful websites that are well worth perusing when planning your travels:

Fridae (www.fridae.com)

Utopia Asia (www.utopia-asia.com)

HEALTH Dr Trish Batchelor

As a developed city, Tokyo enjoys an excellent standard of medical care. Air pollution is one health issue, but this is unlikely to affect most travellers, apart from those with chronic lung conditions. Travellers have a low risk of contracting infectious diseases but should ensure that their basic vaccinations are up to date and that they carry a basic medical kit to deal with simple problems such as respiratory infections, minor injuries and stomach upsets.

It's also a good idea to consult your government's travel-health website before departure:

Australia (www.smartraveller.gov.au)

Canada (www.travelhealth.gc.ca)

New Zealand (www.safetravel.govt.nz)

UK (www.phac-aspc.gc.ca)

USA (wwwn.cdc.gov/travel/)

Medical Services

A national health-insurance plan covers Japanese who wish to visit a doctor, as well as foreign residents who are legally employed. When seeking medical care, be sure to bring proof of your travel or health insurance that clearly indicates that you're covered for any treatment you receive. If you arrive without insurance, it's possible to see a doctor at either a hospital or a clinic, but you will be expected to pay in full at the time of service.

If your health insurance doesn't cover you for all medical expenses incurred abroad, you should consider purchasing supplemental travel insurance before leaving home. Evacuations in an emergency can cost well over US$100,000.

Travellers should be aware that medical services in Japan are often handled differently than in other developed nations. For simple complaints, you should be fine; for emergencies, you might have no choice. For elective procedures and anything else that can wait until you get home, we suggest you do just that.

Most hospitals and clinics do not have doctors and nurses who speak English, but we've listed a few good ones that do:

CLINICS

National Center for Global Health and Medicine (Map p116; ☎ 3202-7181; www.ncgm.go.jp/rese/top/e/info .html, in English; 1-21-1 Toyama, Shinjuku-ku; ☺ Toei Ōedo Line to Wakamatsu-kawada, main exit) Operators on the phone speak English.

National Medical Clinic (Map p92; ☎ 3473-2057; www .nmclinic.net; Suite 202, 5-16-11 Minami-Azabu, Minato-ku; ☺ Hibiya Line to Hiro-o, exits 1 & 2) English-speaking physicians practise general medicine here, and there are also a few specialised services.

Tokyo British Clinic (Map p96; ☎ 5458-6099; www .tokyobritishclinic.com; 2nd fl, Daikanyama Y Bldg, 2-13-7 Ebisu-Nishi, Shibuya-ku; ☽ emergency service 24hr; ☺ Hibiya or JR Yamanote Line to Ebisu, west exit) Founded and run by a British physician, this clinic also offers paediatric, obstetric/gynaecological and referral services.

Tokyo Medical & Surgical Clinic (Map p92; ☎ 3436-3028, emergency 3432-6134; www.tmsc.jp; 2nd fl, Mori Bldg, 32, 3-4-30 Shiba-kōen, Minato-ku; ☽ emergency service 24hr; ☺ Hibiya Line to Kamiyachō, main exit) This well-equipped clinic is staffed with English-speaking Japanese and foreign physicians.

EMERGENCY ROOMS

Japanese Red Cross Medical Centre (Map p92; ☎ 3400-1311; www.med.jrc.or.jp; 4-1-22 Hiro-o, Shibuya-ku; ☽ 24hr; ☺ Hibiya Line to Hiro-o, exits 1 & 2)

Seibo International Catholic Hospital (Map pp48–9; ☎ 3951-1111; www.seibokai.or.jp, in Japanese; 2-5-1 Nakaochiai, Shinjuku-ku; ☺ JR Yamanote Line to Mejiro, main exit)

St Luke's International Hospital (Map p57; ☎ 3541-5151; www.luke.or.jp; 9-1 Akashichō, Chūō-ku; ☽ 24hr; ☺ Hibiya Line to Tsukiji, exits 3 & 4)

PHARMACIES

Pharmacies are located throughout Tokyo, although a bit of Japanese helps in getting the medication or item you need, as most pharmacists only speak basic (if any at all) English. Although Japanese law prohibits pharmacists from selling medications from other countries, they will generally be able to help you find a Japanese medication that is either identical or similar to the one you take at home. The pharmacies listed here cater to English-speaking customers.

National Azabu Supermarket Pharmacy (Map p92; ☎ 3442-3495; 4-5-2 Minami Azabu, Minato-ku; ☺ 9.30am-7pm; ⊕ Hibiya Line to Hiro-o, exit 2) Inside the National Azabu supermarket (p169).

Tomod's American Pharmacy (Map p52; ☎ 5220-7716; www.tomods.jp, in Japanese; basement 1st fl, Marunouchi Bldg, 2-4-1 Marunouchi, Chiyoda-ku; ☺ 9am-9pm Mon-Fri, 10am-9pm Sat, 10am-8pm Sun & holidays; ⊕ JR Yamanote or Marunouchi Line to Tokyo, Marunouchi exits) The American Pharmacy in the Marubiru is staffed by English-speaking pharmacists, and credit cards are accepted. There are other branches throughout town.

Recommended Vaccinations

No vaccinations are required for Japan. Your routine vaccinations should be up to date, though travellers at special risk should additionally consider the following:

Japanese B encephalitis There is no risk in Tokyo, but there is risk in rural areas of all islands. The risk is highest in the western part of the country from July to October.

Tick-borne encephalitis This is present only in the wooded areas of Hokkaidō and is transmitted between April and October. The vaccine is readily available in Europe but can be difficult to find elsewhere.

Diseases

HIV/AIDS & STDS

HIV/AIDS and other STDs can, of course, be contracted anywhere in the world. People carrying STDs often show no signs of infection. Always insist on using a condom with a new partner; however, some diseases such as herpes and warts cannot be prevented even by using condoms. If, after a sexual encounter, you develop any rash, lumps, discharge, or pain when passing urine, seek medical attention immediately. If you have been sexually active during your travels, have a check-up on your return home.

Rates of HIV infection in Japan have increased significantly in the last couple of years. It is predicted that this trend will continue, due in part to unsuccessful government awareness programs. The majority of cases in Japan are contracted via sexual contact, and more than 60% of newly infected people are under 25 years of age.

Condoms are widely available in Tokyo, but generally only locally produced varieties, which tend to be on the small side. If you think you're going to need them, it's a good idea to bring your own, since foreign-made condoms can be difficult to find.

DIARRHOEA

Tokyo is a low-risk destination, and the tap water is safe to drink. You could still be unlucky, however, so carrying some antidiarrhoea medication in your medical kit is a good idea.

HEPATITIS B

Hepatitis B is a virus spread via bodily fluids, eg through sexual contact, shared needles or unclean medical facilities. It is also the only sexually transmitted disease that can be prevented by vaccination. In the short term, hepatitis B can cause the typical symptoms of hepatitis – jaundice, tiredness, nausea – but long-term consequences can include liver cancer and cirrhosis. Long-term travellers or those who might be exposed to bodily fluids should be vaccinated.

INFLUENZA

Influenza (the flu) is primarily transmitted from November to April. The flu is caused by a virus and gives you a high fever, general body aches and generalised respiratory symptoms such as cough, a sore throat and runny nose. If you do happen to get the flu you should rest up and take a symptomatic treatment such as pain killers – antibiotics won't help. All high-risk individuals should ensure that they have been vaccinated before travelling, and all travellers should consider the vaccine if visiting in the winter months. Under some circumstances your doctor might recommend taking antiviral drugs to treat the flu.

JAPANESE B ENCEPHALITIS

Japanese B encephalitis (JBE) is not present in Tokyo, but is found in the rural areas of all of the islands, particularly in the west. It is a viral disease transmitted by mosquitoes and is present during the months of July to October. If you are intending to spend more than a month in an affected rural area, you should consider getting vaccinated. JBE is a serious disease without any specific treatment – 30% of those infected will die and around one-third will suffer permanent brain damage.

Environmental Hazards

AIR POLLUTION

Air pollution is a problem in Tokyo, although the government is taking steps to improve the situation. If you have a lung condition such as asthma or chronic airways disease, speak to your doctor before you travel, and ensure that you have enough of your regular medication with you.

FUGU (PUFFER FISH)

This famous delicacy (also known as blowfish or globefish) is strictly controlled, and there have been no deaths related to its ingestion for more than 30 years.

Medications

Some medications cannot be taken into Japan. If you take any regular medication, you should check with your local Japanese embassy whether there is any restriction on taking it into the country.

Traditional Medicine

If you decide to have any traditional medical treatments, make sure you tell your practitioner if you are taking any Western medicines. The two best-known forms of traditional Japanese medicine are *reiki* and shiatsu.

REIKI

Reiki claims to heal by charging the life force *(ki)* with positive energy, thus allowing it to flow in a natural, healthy manner. In a standard treatment, reiki energy flows from the practitioner's hands and into the client. The practitioner places their hands on or near the client's body in a series of positions that are each held for between three and 10 minutes. People only become practitioners after receiving an 'attunement' from a reiki master.

SHIATSU

Shiatsu is a form of manual therapy incorporating gentle manipulations and stretches derived from physiotherapy and chiropractic, combined with pressure techniques exerted through the fingers or thumbs. The philosophy underlying shiatsu is similar to many traditional Asian medical systems and involves the body's vital energy *(ki)* flowing through the body in a series of channels known as meridians. If the *ki* is blocked from flowing freely, illness can occur; hence shiatsu is used to improve the flow of *ki*. Shiatsu was officially recognised by the Japanese government in 1955 as a therapy in its own right.

HOLIDAYS

Japan has 15 national public holidays, and the days after or in between often become days off as well. You can expect travel and lodgings to be fully booked during Shōgatsu (New Year; 29 December to 3 January, which many extend until 6 January), Golden Week (29 April to 5 May) and the O-Bon festival in mid-August; see p16 for more information on festivals. A new holiday called Silver Week was introduced in 2009, extending the autumnal equinox in September by a couple of days. If a holiday falls on a Monday, most museums that typically close on Mondays will be open for the holiday and close Tuesday that week instead. Most businesses and many shops and restaurants shut down during holidays. Particularly during Shōgatsu, about the only places open are convenience stores and fast-food joints; if you don't want to survive on potato chips and fries, make appropriate preparations.

Japan's national public holidays are as follows:

Ganjitsu (New Year's Day) 1 January

Seijin-no-hi (Coming-of-Age Day) Second Monday in January

Kenkoku Kinen-bi (National Foundation Day) 11 February

Shumbun-no-hi (Spring Equinox) 20 or 21 March

Midori-no-hi (Green Day) 29 April

Kempō Kinem-bi (Constitution Day) 3 May

Kokumin-no-Saijitsu (Adjoining Holiday Between Two Holidays) 4 May

Kodomo-no-hi (Children's Day) 5 May

Umi-no-hi (Marine Day) Third Monday in July

Keirō-no-hi (Respect-for-the-Aged Day) Third Monday in September

Shūbun-no-hi (Autumn Equinox) 23 or 24 September

Taiiku-no-hi (Health and Sports Day) Second Monday in October

Bunka-no-hi (Culture Day) 3 November

Kinrō Kansha-no-hi (Labour Thanksgiving Day) 23 November

Tennō-no-Tanjōbi (Emperor's Birthday) 23 December

INTERNET ACCESS

No surprise that Tokyo is a very wired city. In this book, the internet symbol (🖥) in lodging listings indicates internet access of some kind, either from a shared computer in a lobby or business centre, or from your own room.

In all but the most budget accommodation, internet access with your own laptop is possible from your room, and usually it is included in room rates. Wi-fi is rare in hotels. Rather, internet access is typically via LAN cable operating over a DSL or ADSL system. Most hotels supply LAN cables for free. If yours does not and if the hotel cannot rent or sell you one, electronics shops carry them for about ¥500.

Free wi-fi access is scattered around Tokyo in cafes, public buildings and JR stations – check the Freespot access map (www.freespot.com/users/map_e.html) for locations offering fee-free wi-fi, broken down by *ku* (ward) within Tokyo.

If you haven't brought your own laptop, you'll find an abundance of internet cafes in every major neighbourhood in Tokyo. Rates vary, usually ranging from ¥200 to ¥500 per hour, and most connections are fast DSL or ADSL.

LEGAL MATTERS

Japanese police have extraordinary powers compared with their Western counterparts. For starters, Japanese police have the right to detain a suspect without charging them for up to three days, after which a prosecutor can decide to extend this period for another 20 days. Police also have the authority to choose whether to allow a suspect to phone their embassy or lawyer or not, although, if you do find yourself in police custody, you should insist that you will not cooperate in any way until allowed to make such a call. Your embassy is the first place you should call if given the chance.

Police will speak almost no English; insist that a *tsuyakusha* (interpreter) be summoned; police are legally bound to provide one before proceeding with any questioning. Even if you are able to speak Japanese, it is best to deny it and stay with your native language.

For legal counselling in English and some other languages, seek out these resources:

Human Rights Counseling Center for Foreigners (☎ 5689-0518; 🕐 1-4.30pm Tue & Thu) Free consultation and English–Japanese translation on problems regarding human rights.

Tokyo English Life Line (TELL; ☎ 5774-0992; 🕐 9am-11pm) Free, anonymous telephone counselling.

Tokyo Foreign Residents Advisory Center (☎ 5320-7744; 🕐 9.30am-noon & 1-4pm Mon-Fri)

MAPS

Stop by the Tourist Information Center of the Japan National Tourism Organization (JNTO; p265) to pick up a free copy of its superb *Tourist Map of Tokyo*. To successfully interpret and navigate Tokyo's challenging address system, longer-term visitors might consider looking up Kodansha's *Tokyo City Atlas,* a bilingual guide stocked by larger bookshops. Both Kodansha and Shobunsha (Japanese publishers) publish bilingual atlases and fold-out maps (prices start at ¥700) that are available at most of Tokyo's bookshops (see p58 for listings).

Tokyo Metro Company publishes the free *Tokyo Metro Guide,* with English-language explanations on buying tickets and special deals. Find these near the ticket machines and turnstiles in most subway stations.

MONEY
Cash

Although quite modern in most ways, cash is still king in Tokyo. One should always keep at least several thousand yen on hand for local transport, inexpensive restaurants and shops, and even some moderately priced restaurants and shops.

The currency in Japan is the yen (¥), and banknotes and coins are easily distinguishable. There are ¥1, ¥5, ¥10, ¥50, ¥100 and ¥500 coins; and ¥1000, ¥2000, ¥5000 and ¥10,000 banknotes (the ¥2000 note is very rarely seen). The ¥1 coin is a lightweight aluminium coin; the bronze-coloured ¥5 and silver-coloured ¥50 coins both have a hole punched in the middle. Prices may be listed using the kanji for yen (円). In most cases, prices are in Arabic numerals, but occasionally they are in traditional kanji; see p269 for a guide.

ATMs

Most Japanese ATMs do not accept foreign-issued cards. Even if they display Visa and MasterCard logos, most accept only Japan-issued versions of these cards. Also, 24-hour ATMs are exceedingly rare.

Fortunately, Citibank operates 24-hour international ATMs in major areas including Roppongi, Harajuku, Omote-sandō and Shinjuku. Better still, ATMs at Japanese post offices are linked to the international Cirrus and Plus cash networks (and some credit-card networks), making life a breeze for travellers to Tokyo. Most larger post offices (🕐 9am-5pm Mon-Fri,

9am-noon Sat) have postal ATMs. Press the handy button marked 'English Guidance' for English instructions. 7-Eleven convenience stores also have ATMs that accept overseas cards.

Changing Money

In theory, banks and post offices will change all major currencies. In practice, some banks refuse to exchange anything but US-dollar cash and travellers cheques. Note also that the currencies of neighbouring Taiwan (New Taiwan dollar) and South Korea (won) are not easy to change, so you should change these into yen or US dollars before arriving in Japan.

With a passport, you can change cash or travellers cheques at any Authorised Foreign Exchange Bank (signs are displayed in English), major post offices, some large hotels and most big department stores. Note that you receive a better exchange rate when withdrawing cash from ATMs than when exchanging cash or travellers cheques in Tokyo. Be aware that many banks place a limit on the amount of cash you can withdraw in one day (often around US$300).

Exchange rates are listed on the inside front cover of this guide.

Credit Cards

For businesses that do take credit cards, Visa is most widely accepted, followed by Master-Card, American Express and Diners Club. Getting a cash advance using your foreign-issued credit card is nearly impossible, but Sumitomo Mitsui banks (SMBC) give cash advances if you bring your passport with you. The main credit-card companies all have offices in Tokyo.

American Express (☎ 0120-02-0120; ☺ 24hr)

MasterCard (☎ 5728-5200)

Visa (☎ 00531-11-1555; ☺ 24hr)

NEWSPAPERS & MAGAZINES

The three English-language daily newspapers listed here serve the city's international community and are sold at most of the big train-station kiosks. Three English magazines, the weekly *Metropolis*, the monthly *Japanzine*, and the quarterly *Tokyo Journal*, round out English-language coverage of local news, dining and entertainment. Look for these magazines available for free at music venues and nightlife spots and other locations that get a lot of overseas visitors.

Asahi Shimbun/International Herald Tribune (www.asahi.com/english)

Daily Yomiuri (www.yomiuri.co.jp/dy)

Japan Times (www.japantimes.co.jp)

ORGANISED TOURS

Though exploring Tokyo on your own offers distinct pleasures, it can be daunting at first. Listed are several touring companies that can help introduce you to the metropolis by land, sea, air or even on foot. Most have websites in English, as well as English-speaking staff. All prices quoted in this section are per person.

Boat

If you've come with a gang and want a very Japanese experience, Komatsuya (☎ 3851-2780; www.komatsuya.net, in Japanese; tours ¥10,000-20,000) arranges for groups of 15 and up to cruise the city's waterways while enjoying Japanese cuisine in a tatami-room setting on a Japanese-style boat, called *yakatabune*. Even the website is in Japanese.

Tokyo Cruise (☎ 3841-9178; www.suijobus.co.jp; 1-way ¥200-1220) offers reasonably priced rides aboard the *suijō bus* (water bus) under the 12 bridges up and down the Sumida-gawa and across Tokyo Bay to Odaiba. Its main ports are Hinode Pier near Hamamatsuchō station on the JR Yamanote Line, the former feudal garden Hama Rikyū (p65), Azumabashi Pier near Asakusa and Odaiba. Most fares are under ¥800 but are highest between Asakusa and Odaiba; the boat, *Himiko*, connects Asakusa and Odaiba nonstop for ¥1520. It was designed especially for the water bus by the cartoonist Matsumoto Reiji and looks like a bug from the future.

Symphony (☎ 3798-8101; www.symphony-cruise.co.jp; tours adult ¥1500-3800, child ¥750-1900; ☻ JR Yamanote Line to JR Hamamatsucho, south exit) offers two-hour day and evening cruises around the bay, departing from Hinode Pier. If you lunch or dine on board, you'll pay from ¥5000 to ¥21,000 (including passage) depending on the type of meal you choose.

The restaurant boat Vingt-et-un (☎ 3436-2121; www.vantean.co.jp; lunch/sunset/dinner cruises from ¥5100/7100/10,200; ☻ Yurikamome Line to Takeshiba), departing from Takeshiba Pier, has lunch, sunset and dinnertime cruises accompanied by multicourse French meals. The route covers the Tokyo waterfront, Rainbow Bridge, and Odaiba and head downriver toward Haneda Airport before returning. Reservations essential.

Bus

The well-established commercial tour operators recommended here all have an extensive line-up of tours, including many in English. While buses are their stock in trade, some also offer boat and walking tours.

Without getting fancy, Gray Line (☎ 3595-5948; www.jgl.co.jp/inbound/index.htm; tours ¥4000-9700) buses chug along to places such as the Imperial Palace, Asakusa, Sensō-ji and the National Diet buildings. Tours run for either a morning, afternoon or full day and some include meals, usually at traditional Japanese restaurants. Many of the locations are just drive-throughs, but at least you'll be familiar with them when you return. Pick-up and drop-off are available at dozens of hotels.

One of the longest-standing tour operators is Hato Bus Tours (☎ 3435-6081; www.hatobus .com; tours ¥3500-14,000), which offers a dizzying variety of half-day, full-day and night-time tours around the city. It hits big spots such as Sensō-ji and Tsukiji Central Fish Market, as well as some less visited spots by tourists including Akihabara and the Higashi Gyōen (Imperial Palace East Garden, p51) or a *kaiseki* dinner with geisha. Transport options include bus, boat, subway and on foot.

Hato also operates a variety of tours aboard the double-decker Hello Kitty Bus (adult/child from ¥1300/760) departing from Tokyo Station. Programming is pretty typical tour-bus fare, although the bus itself is decorated with the cat with no mouth. There are a few different routes that cover variations on the basics like Nihombashi, Akihabara and Asakusa. Guides narrate in Japanese only; English narration is available via headphones.

Within the city, the offerings of Sunrise Tours (☎ 5796-5454; www.jtbgmt.com/sunrisetour; Tokyo tours ¥3800-14,000) are not much different from those of the other tour companies, but as a subsidiary of Japan Travel Bureau (JTB), the country's largest travel company, it boasts an extensive roster of day trips and tours in other parts of Japan. Some are return trips from Tokyo, while others originate in other big Japanese cities.

Helicopter

Excel Air (☎ 047-380-5555; www.excel-air.com; Urayasu Heliport; flights adult/child from ¥8500/4250; ⏱ 2pm-dusk; ◉ JR Keiyo Line to Urayasu then 15min by taxi) offers 15- and 20-minute flights, which are a dramatic way to take in the skyline of Ginza, the Imperial Palace or Akihabara during the day, at sunset or after dark. Helicopters fly up to eight people. Saturday and Sunday flights cost about 25% more. Flights depart from Urayasu city, east of Tokyo in Chiba Prefecture. Reserve a seat in advance.

PHOTOGRAPHY

Digital photographers will find all manner of memory media, batteries and digital cameras widely available. Japan's photo shops also offer a wide range of services for digital photographers, including high-quality prints from digital files.

Most photo-processing shops, as well as department stores and even 7-Eleven convenience stores, can also transfer digital shots onto CD for you.

Tokyo is one of the best places in the world to buy photographic equipment, including some of the latest technologies by Japanese makers. There are camera stores in all of the major commuter hubs, including Shinjuku (p149), Ikebukuro (p150) and the Tokyo Station/Yūrakuchō area, as well as in Akihabara Electric Town (p66). Bic Camera, Sakuraya and Yodobashi Camera are some of the stores of note. Be aware that most products have Japanese operating menus, although some of the larger electronics stores stock export models with English-language systems. Try these stores also for print film.

Photo processing in Japan is fast and economical and standards are usually high.

Serious photographers might want to pick up a copy of Lonely Planet's *Travel Photography*.

POST

Japan Post Service Co, Ltd (www.post.japanpost.jp) is reliable and efficient and, for regular postcards and airmail letters, has rates similar to those of other developed countries. The symbol for post offices is a red T with a bar across the top on a white background (〒). For information on courier services, see p248.

Opening Hours

District post offices (the main post office in a ward) are open 9am to 7pm Monday to Friday and 9am to 3pm Saturday, and most are closed Sunday and public holidays. Local post offices are open 9am to 5pm Monday to Friday and are closed Saturday, Sunday and public holidays. Main post offices in Tokyo, Shibuya, Shinjuku and Ikebukuro have an after-hours window open 24 hours.

Postal Rates

The airmail rate for postcards is ¥70 to any destination abroad; aerograms cost ¥90. Letters less than 25g cost ¥90 to other countries within Asia, ¥110 to North America, Europe or Oceania (including Australia and New Zealand) and ¥130 to Africa and South America. One peculiarity of the Japanese postal system is that you will be charged extra if your writing runs over onto the address side (the right side) of a postcard.

Receiving & Sending Mail

Although any post office will hold mail for collection, the poste restante concept is not well known and can cause confusion in smaller neighbourhoods. Letters are usually held for only 30 days before being returned to sender. When inquiring about mail for collection ask for 'kyoku dome yūbin'.

Mail can be sent to, from or within Japan when addressed in Roman script (rōmaji), but it should, of course, be written as clearly as possible.

TAXES & REFUNDS

Japan's consumption tax is 5%, which is figured into the price of items. Often pre-tax prices are shown in parentheses next to the full prices. At some shops, visitors from overseas may be entitled to purchase items tax free, provided the item costs over ¥10,000 and they have their passports with them. Since the tax is not charged, there is no need to collect a refund when leaving the country. See the boxed text, p140, for details.

TELEPHONE

The country code for Japan is 81: Tokyo's area code is 03, although some outer suburbs have different area codes (for listings in this book, the area code is 03 unless otherwise noted). Following the area code, 03 numbers consist of eight digits. The area code is not used if dialling within the same area code from a landline.

If you're calling Tokyo from elsewhere in Japan, dial 03 and then the eight-digit number. When dialling Tokyo from abroad, do not dial the first 0; rather, dial the international access code of the country from which you are calling, then 81-3.

The area code for mobile phones anywhere in Japan is 090 or 080, plus an eight-digit

---

number. Calls to mobile phones are significantly more expensive than local calls. If calling from overseas, dial, for example, 81-90 and then the number. If dialling from a mobile phone, you must dial all digits including area codes.

Toll-free numbers begin with 0120, 0070, 0077, 0088 and 0800. For local directory assistance, dial 104 (cost ¥105). For international directory assistance in English, dial 0057.

Mobile Phones

For an extended stay in Japan, a mobile (cell) phone is vital. The Japanese spend every waking hour of the day texting their friends from their phones, and it's virtually impossible to stay connected to people if you don't have one.

Japan has recently switched to a 3-G network, so overseas phones with 3-G technology will work in Tokyo, often better than they do at home. If your phone does not have 3-G technology, it will not work in Japan, and SIM cards are not widely available. Check with your telephone carrier as to whether your phone will work in Japan and how much you will be charged. After factoring in roaming and per-minute charges, it may be less expensive to rent or even purchase a phone in Japan. On Japanese mobile phones, incoming calls are free, though calling rates vary according to your plan and can be very dear indeed. A good way around this is to use pay phones for outgoing calls and your mobile for incoming.

Several telecommunications companies in Japan specialise in short-term mobile-phone rental, which includes delivery and return of the phone within Japan. These include:

Mobile Phone Japan (☎ 090-4284-7176; www .mobilephonejp.com) Mobile phone rentals start at ¥2900 per week. Outgoing calls use SoftBank prepaid cards, which work out to about ¥90 per minute.

Rentafone Japan (☎ 090-9621-7318, toll free within Japan 0120-746-487; www.rentafonejapan.com) Rentals start at ¥3900 per week. Domestic calls (¥35 per minute) are less expensive than Mobile Phone Japan's, but require that you dial a code before each call.

You may even find that it costs less to purchase a prepaid phone than to rent one. Mobile-phone shops dot virtually every street in Tokyo, and larger mobile-phone shops like the Omote-Sando location of SoftBank (☎ 03-6406-0711; www.mb.softbank.jp/en; 1-13-9 Jingumae, Shibuya-ku; ⏰ 10am-10pm) usually have English-speaking staff, or at least English-language pamphlets, explaining the various options.

Public Phones

The Japanese public telephone system is very well developed; there are public phones in most public places and they work almost 100% of the time. If you are going to be making a significant number of calls, it's worth purchasing a *terehon kādo* (telephone card). These stored-value cards are available from vending machines, station kiosks and convenience stores in ¥500 and ¥1000 denominations (the latter throws in an extra ¥50 in calls) and can be used in grey or green pay phones; phones display the remaining value of your card when it is inserted. They come in a myriad of designs and – this being Tokyo – people even collect them.

If you are using coins to call, carry plenty of them. Local calls cost ¥10 per minute. For long-distance calls, you will have to keep inserting coins as the call progresses; unused ¥10 coins are returned after the call is completed but no change is given on ¥100 coins. Domestic rates fall outside the standard business hours. Charges for calls to mobile phones vary depending on the region.

International Calls

International calls are best made using a prepaid international phonecard. You can also call abroad on grey international ISDN phones, usually found in phone booths marked 'International & Domestic Card/Coin Phone'. Unfortunately, these are rare; look for them in the lobbies of top-end hotels and at airports.

Calls are charged by six-second units, so if you don't have much to say, you can make a quick call home for the minimum charge of ¥100. If you find a public phone that allows international calls, it's more convenient to use a phonecard rather than coins. Reverse-charge (collect) international calls can be made from any pay phone.

You can save money by dialling late at night. Economy rates apply 11pm to 8am throughout the year; these discounts also apply to domestic calls.

To place an international call through the operator, dial ☎ 0051 (KDDI operator; most international operators speak English). To make the call yourself, dial ☎ 001 010 (KDDI), ☎ 0041 010 (SoftBank Telecom) or ☎ 0033 010 (NTT), followed by the country code, area code and local number. Although these companies compete for overseas service from Japan, there's very little difference in their rates.

Prepaid international calling cards like KDDI Superworld Card, NTT Communications World Card and SoftBank Telecom Comica Card are available at convenience stores and can be used at regular pay phones.

TIME

Tokyo local time is nine hours ahead of Greenwich Mean Time (GMT). When it's noon in Tokyo, it's 7pm (the day before) in Los Angeles, 10pm in Montreal and New York, 3am (the same day) in London, 4am in Frankfurt, Paris and Rome, 11am in Hong Kong, 3pm in Melbourne and 5pm in Wellington. Japan does not observe daylight-savings-time, so remember to subtract one hour when working out the time difference with a country using daylight-savings-time.

TIPPING & BARGAINING

Despite the high quality of customer service in Japan, it is not customary to tip, even in the most expensive restaurants and bars. Bargaining is not customary either, with the exception of outdoor markets, such as Ameyoko in Ueno (see p81).

However, particularly in higher end restaurants and hotels, a 10% service fee is added to the bill.

TOILETS

Toilets in Tokyo run the gamut from heated-seat thrones that wash and dry your most intimate of areas at the touch of a button (in fancy hotels), to humble porcelain squat toilets in the floor (typically in public places like train stations).

Deciphering the Japanese instructions on the techie loos can be a bit of a challenge; sit down before you begin pressing buttons, or you run the risk of having an inadvertent shower!

For using squat toilets, the correct position is facing the hood, away from the door; take care that the contents of your pockets don't spill out. If you just can't bear a squat toilet, look for the characters 洋式 (yō-shiki, Western style) on the stall door, and handicapped washrooms are always Western style. The most common words for toilet in Japanese are トイレ (pronounced 'toire') and お手洗い ('o-tearai'). 女 (female) and 男 (male) will probably also come in helpful!

Toilet paper isn't always provided in public washrooms, so always graciously accept those small packets of tissue handed out on the street, a common form of advertising. These same loos will probably not have paper towels or hand-driers either, so Japanese carry a handkerchief for use after washing their hands.

In many bathrooms in places like homes and restaurants where you take off your shoes at the entrance, separate toilet slippers are typically provided just inside the toilet door. These are for use in the toilet only, so remember to shuffle out of them when you leave.

It's quite common to see men urinating in public – the unspoken rule is that it's acceptable at night-time if you happen to be drunk. Public toilets are free and can usually be found in or around most train stations.

TOURIST INFORMATION

Japan's tourist information services (観光案内所, kankō annai-sho) are first rate, and the Tokyo branch of the Japan National Tourism Organization (JNTO; www.jnto.go.jp) is the best of the bunch.

JNTO is the main English-language information service for foreign travellers to Japan and produces a great deal of useful literature, which is available from its offices abroad and its Tourist Information Centers (TICs) inside Japan. Most publications are available in English and, in some cases, other Asian and Asian languages. JNTO's website is extremely useful for planning your journey.

JNTO operates two main TICs in Tokyo:

Narita (☎ 0476-34-6251; 1st fl, Terminals 1 & 2, Narita Airport, Chiba; ☼ 9am-8pm)

Tokyo (Map p57; ☎ 3201-3331; 10th fl, Kōtsū Kaikan Bldg, 2-10-1 Yūrakuchō, Chiyoda-ku; ☼ 9am-5pm Mon-Fri, 9am-noon Sat; ☻ JR Yamanote Line to Yūrakuchō, exit A8)

TIC staff cannot make transport bookings; they can, however, direct you to agencies that can, such as the Japan Travel Bureau (JTB; Map p110; ☎ 5321-3077; 1st fl, Tokyo Metropolitan Government Building No 1; ☼ 9.30am-6.30pm, closed year-end & New Year period).

In addition to its main offices listed, JNTO operates 111 English-language Tourist Information Centers throughout Japan. The centres are usually found in the main train stations of major Japanese cities. Look for the red question mark with the word 'information' printed beneath it.

Other helpful places about town include the following:

Japan Guide Association (☎ 3213-2706; www.jga21c .or.jp) Can put you in contact with licensed, professional guides.

Tokyo Convention & Visitors Bureau (TCVB; Map p52; ☎ 3287-7024; 1st fl, 3-2-2 Marunouchi, Chiyoda-ku; ☼ 10am-5pm Mon-Fri, 10am-4pm Sat, Sun & holidays; ☻ Chiyoda, Hibiya or Toei Mita Lines to Hibiya, exit B7)

Tokyo Tourist Information Center Keisei Ueno Station (TIC; Map p78; ☎ 3836-3471; Keisei Ueno Station)

Tokyo Tourist Information Center Tochō (TIC; Map p110; ☎ 5321-3077; Tokyo Metropolitan Government Offices, North Tower, 1st fl, 2-8-1 Nishi-Shinjuku, Shinjuku-ku; ☻ Toei Ōedo Line to Tochōmae, exit A4)

Tourist Offices Abroad

JNTO has a number of offices abroad, including the following:

Australia (☎ 02-9279-2177; www.jnto.org.au; Level 7, 36-38 Clarence St, Sydney, NSW 2000)

Canada (☎ 416-366-7140; www.ilovejapan.ca; Suite 306, 481 University Ave, Toronto, Ontario M5G 2E9)

France (☎ 01 42 96 20 29; www.tourisme-japon.fr; 4 rue de Ventadour, 75001 Paris)

Germany (☎ 069-20353; www.jnto.de; Kaiserstrasse 11, 60311 Frankfurt am Main)

UK (☎ 020-7398-5670; www.seejapan.co.uk; 5th fl, 12 Nicholas Lane, London EC4N 7BN)

USA (www.japantravelinfo.com); Los Angeles (☎ 213-623-1952; Suite 302, Little Tokyo Plaza, 340 E 2nd St, Los Angeles, CA 90012); New York (☎ 212-757-5640; 19th fl, 11 W 42nd St, New York, NY 10036)

TRAVELLERS WITH DISABILITIES

Many new buildings in Tokyo have access ramps, traffic lights have speakers playing melodies when it is safe to cross, train platforms have raised dots and lines to provide guidance and some ticket machines have Braille. Some attractions also offer free entry to travellers with disabilities and their companion. A fair number of hotels, from the higher end of midrange and above, offer a 'barrier-free' room or two. Still, Tokyo can be rather difficult for travellers with disabilities to negotiate, especially visitors in wheelchairs who are often forced to make a choice between negotiating stairs or rerouting.

For more information, check the following websites:

Accessible Japan (www.tesco-premium.co.jp/aj/index .htm) Details the accessibility of hundreds of sites in Tokyo, including hotels, sights and department stores, as well as general information about getting around Japan.

Japanese Red Cross Language Service Volunteers (Map p92; ☎ 3438-1311; http://accessible.jp.org; 1-1-3 Shiba Daimon, Minato-ku, Tokyo 105-8521) Has loads of useful information, and it also produces an excellent guide called *Accessible Tokyo*, which can be requested by email, mail or telephone – or found on its website.

VISAS

Generally, visitors who are not planning to engage in income-producing activities while in Japan are exempt from obtaining visas and will be issued a *tanki-taizai (*temporary visitor visa) on arrival.

Stays of up to six months are permitted for citizens of Austria, Germany, Ireland, Mexico, Switzerland and the UK. Citizens of these countries will almost always be given a 90-day temporary visitor visa upon arrival, which can usually be extended for another 90 days at immigration bureaus inside Japan (see Visa Extensions, right).

Citizens of the USA, Australia and New Zealand are granted 90-day temporary visitor visas, while stays of up to three months are permitted for citizens of Argentina, Belgium, Canada, Denmark, Finland, France, Iceland, Israel, Italy, Netherlands, Norway, Singapore, Spain, Sweden and a number of other countries.

Japanese law requires that visitors to the country entering on a temporary visa possess an ongoing air or sea ticket or evidence thereof. In practice, few travellers are asked to produce such documents, but to avoid surprises it pays to be on the safe side.

For additional information on visas and regulations, contact the nearest Japanese embassy or consulate in your country, or visit the website of the Japan Ministry of Foreign Affairs (www .mofa.go.jp), where you can check out the Guide to Japanese Visas, read about working-holiday visas and find details on the Japan Exchange and Teaching (JET) program, which sponsors native English speakers to teach in the Japanese public-school system. You can also contact the Immigration Information Center (外国人在留総合インフォメーションセンター; Tokyo Regional Immigration Bureau; Map pp48–9; ☎ 5796-7112; www.moj.go.jp/ ENGLISH/; 5-5-30 Kōnan, Minato-ku; ☒ 9am-noon & 1-4pm Mon-Fri; ◉ Tokyo Monorail or Rinkai Line to Tennozu Isle).

Alien Registration Card

Anyone – and this includes tourists – who stays for more than 90 days is required to obtain a *gaikokujin torokushō* (Alien Registration Card). This card can be obtained at the municipal office of the city, town or ward in which you're living. Moving to another area requires that you re-register within 14 days.

You must carry your Alien Registration Card at all times as the police can stop you and ask to see the card. If you don't have it, you could be hauled off to the police station to wait until someone fetches it for you – providing you have one.

Visa Extensions

With the exception of those nationals whose countries have reciprocal visa exemptions and can stay for six months, the limit for most nationalities is 90 days. To extend a temporary visitor visa beyond the standard limit, apply at the Immigration Information Center (Tokyo Regional Immigration Bureau; see above). You must provide two copies of an Application for Extension of Stay (available at the immigration office), a letter stating the reasons for the extension and supporting documentation as well as your passport. There is a processing fee of ¥4000.

Many long-term visitors to Japan get around the extension problem by briefly leaving the country, usually by going to South Korea. Be warned, however, that immigration officials are starting to wise up to this practice, and many 'tourist visa returnees' are turned back at the entry point.

Work Visas

Ever-increasing demand has prompted much stricter work-visa requirements than previously. Arriving in Japan and looking for a job is quite a tough proposition these days, though people still do it and occasionally succeed in finding sponsorship. With that said, there are legal employment categories for foreigners that specify standards of experience and qualifications.

Once you find an employer in Japan who is willing to sponsor you, it is necessary to obtain a Certificate of Eligibility from your nearest Japanese immigration office. The same office can then issue your work visa, which is valid for either one or three years. This procedure can take two to three months.

Generally speaking, it is recommended that you arrange your job in Japan prior to arrival. In this case, your employer will arrange your visa in advance, which will save you the hassle of having to enter as a tourist and subsequently change your status.

Working-Holiday Visas

Citizens of Australia, Canada, France, Germany, Korea, New Zealand and the UK can apply for a working-holiday visa if they're between 18 and 30 (the upper age limit for UK citizens is officially 25, but this is negotiable). This visa allows a six-month stay and two six-month extensions. The visa is designed to enable young people to travel extensively during their stay; thus, employment is supposed to be part-time or temporary. In practice, many people work full-time.

A working-holiday visa is much easier to obtain than a work visa and is popular with Japanese employers. Single applicants must have the equivalent of US$2000 of funds, a married couple must have US$3000, and all applicants must have an onward ticket from Japan. For details, enquire at the nearest Japanese embassy or consulate (see p256).

WOMEN TRAVELLERS

Japan is one of the safest countries in the world for women travellers in terms of physical crime. Compared with the West, Japan has a much lower incidence of violent crime, including rape. As a result, women should have no problem walking alone down the streets of Tokyo, even at night. Of course, as with any unfamiliar destination, it's best to use your discretion and keep your guard up at all times.

It's worth mentioning, however, that women who have spent a considerable amount of time in Japan have probably experienced some form of sexual harassment including verbal harassment and prying questions. Jam-packed trains can provide opportunities for the roving hands of *chikan* (gropers). A loud complaint usually shames the perpetrator into retreating. To avoid the possibility altogether, ride in the women-only train carriages during rush hour.

If you do experience a problem and find the local police unhelpful, call the Human Rights Counseling Center for Foreigners (see p260).

Finally, an excellent resource for any woman setting up in Japan is Caroline Pover's book *Being A Broad in Japan;* find it in bookshops or order from her website (www .being-a-broad.com).

WORK

Finding work in Tokyo is possible, but it's not as easy nor as lucrative as it used to be. Teaching English is still the most common job for Westerners, but bartending, hostessing, modelling and various other jobs are also possible.

Whatever line of work you choose, it is essential to look neat and tidy for interviews – appearances can make or break you in Japan. You'll also need to be determined, and you should have a sizable sum of money to float on while you're looking for work, and possibly to get you out of the country if you don't find any (it happens). Foreigners who have set up in Japan over the last few years maintain that a figure of around US$5000 or more is necessary to make a go of it. People do it with less, but they run the risk of ending up penniless and homeless before they find a job.

Be advised that business cards *(meishi)* carry much more weight in Japan than they do in the West. Information about a person's status and, perhaps even more importantly, their connections can be obtained from business cards, which are ritually exchanged on first meeting. Business cards should be kept neat – many Japanese have entire business card files. It's good form to keep yours in a business-card holder (not a wallet), present and accept business cards with both hands, and examine them. If attending a meeting, the card should be left on the table until the end of the meeting, and only afterwards be respectfully put away.

Bartending

In the tourist-friendly entertainment district of Roppongi (p90), foreign bartenders are the rule rather than the exception. As little as five years ago, it was not necessary to have a valid work visa to work in Roppongi as the majority of establishments were perfectly willing to pay tourists under the table. Of course, bartenders were expected to work 80-plus hours a week for little more than pocket change (there are no tips in Japan), though when you're down and out, a job is a job.

Following a recent crackdown on illegal workers, however, the Roppongi nightlife scene is slowly turning legit. Today, few establishments are willing to take a chance by hiring a tourist, though the upside is that wages have slightly increased. Although you cannot expect a bar to sponsor a work visa, mixing cocktails in the evenings is a great way to supplement the meagre pay of an English teacher.

English Teaching

Teaching English has always been the most popular job for native English speakers in Japan. While it's a fairly common option, competition for the good jobs is very tight since many English schools have failed as a result of Japan's weakened economy.

A university degree is an absolute essential as schools cannot sponsor you for a work visa without one (be sure to bring the actual degree with you to Japan). Teaching qualifications and some teaching experience will be of huge advantage when job hunting.

Travellers without a degree who can take advantage of the Japanese working-holiday visa (p267) are in a much better position than those who cannot. Schools are happier about taking on unqualified teachers if it means that they don't have to bother with sponsoring a teacher for a work visa.

For job listings, start with the following:

Dave's ESL Café (www.eslcafe.com)

ELT News (www.eltnews.com)

GaijinPot (www.gaijinpot.com)

Japan Times (www.japantimes.co.jp) Publishes the bulk of its classified listings in the Monday print edition.

Hostessing

Hostess clubs, which are a common feature of Japan's entertainment industry, employ female staff to serve men drinks, and engage them in conversation. Unlike strips clubs or brothels, hostesses are not forced to remove their clothes or engage in sex with customers, though they can be encouraged to meet clients (and perform favours) outside of working hours.

Hostessing is a popular employment option among young foreign women in Japan as few places require valid visas, and salaries can sometimes reach hundreds of dollars per hour. Particularly attractive or popular hostesses can also receive gifts from clients, such as jewellery, clothing, trips and even cars.

Of course, there are dangers. In 1992 Carita Ridgeway, an Australian hostess, was drugged and killed after a paid date. In 2000 Lucie Blackman, an English hostess, was abducted, raped and murdered by a customer.

Hostessing has inherent dangers, which is why we cannot recommend that anyone consider the job as a viable and sustainable form of employment in Japan. With that said, if you do decide to accept a hostessing job, be sure that you understand the nature of your employment, and know the extent of your personal boundaries.

Modelling

As one of the world's greatest fashion capitals, Tokyo is a lucrative place to live if you were born with beautiful looks, perfect posture and a healthy dose of poise. Although there's no denying the beauty of Japanese models, foreigners are all the rage these days, and it's not difficult to find the faces of your favourite Hollywood actors selling everything from mobile phones to canned coffee.

Modelling is a legitimate business that can pay extremely well, but you will need to be in possession of a valid work visa. Although there are literally hundreds of agencies in Tokyo, the following list should get you started:

Agence Presse (www.agencepresse.com)

Bravo Models (www.bravomodels.net)

Switch (www.switchmodels.co.jp)

World Top (http://worldtop.co.jp)

LANGUAGE

Japanese is spoken by more than 125 million people. While it bears some resemblance to Altaic languages such as Mongolian and shows grammatical similarities to Korean, it has no clear link to any related languages. Written Japanese is a combination of three scripts: kanji (Chinese ideographic characters), and the indigenous hiragana and katakana scripts, in which each character represents a syllable.

It's not hard to get a basic grip on the language. Japanese pronunciation is easy to master – unlike some Asian languages, it has no tones – and the grammar is fairly simple. Japanese uses various registers of speech to reflect social and contextual hierarchy, but these can be simplified to the form most appropriate for a wide range of situations – which is exactly what we've done in this chapter.

To learn more Japanese than what we've included here, pick up a copy of Lonely Planet's comprehensive and user-friendly *Japanese* phrasebook.

PRONUNCIATION

Pronounce double consonants with a slight pause before them. Vowels are pronounced individually, and vowel length affects meaning, so make sure you distinguish your short and long vowels clearly. The long vowels are represented in our pronunciation guide with a horizontal line on top of them.

Certain vowel sounds (like u and i) aren't pronounced in some words, but are included as part of the official Romanisation system (which employs a literal system to represent Japanese characters). In the following words and phrases these 'silent' letters are shown in square brackets to indicate that they aren't actually pronounced.

a	short, as the 'u' in 'run'
ā	long, as the 'a' in 'father'
e	short, as in 'red'
ē	long, as the 'ei' in 'rein'
i	short, as in 'bit'
ī	long i, as in 'marine'
o	short, as in 'pot'
ō	long, as the 'aw' in 'paw'
u	short, as in 'put'
ū	long, as in 'rude'

SOCIAL
Meeting People

Hello./Hi.
こんにちは。 konnichi wa
Goodbye.
さようなら。 sayōnara

Yes.
はい。 hai
No.
いいえ。 īe
Please.
(if offering something)
どうぞ。 dōzo
(if asking a favour or making a request)
お願いします。 onegai shimas[u]
Thank you (very much).
（どうも）ありがとう (dōmo) arigatō
（ございます）。 (gozaimas[u])
You're welcome.
どういたしまして。 dō itashimash[i]te
Excuse me.
(to get attention or to get past)
すみません。 sumimasen
Sorry.
ごめんなさい。 gomen nasai

Could you please …?
…くれませんか？ … kuremasen ka
  repeat that
  繰り返して kurikaeshite
  speak more slowly
  もっとゆっくり motto yukkuri
  話して hanash[i]te
  write it down
  書いて kaite

What's your name?
お名前は何ですか？
o-namae wa nan des[u] ka
My name is …
私の名前は…です。
watashi no namae wa … des[u]

Do you speak English?
英語が話せますか?
eigo ga hanasemas[u] ka

Do you understand?
わかりましたか?
wakarimash[i]ta ka

Yes, I do understand.
はい、わかりました。
hai, wakarimash[i]ta

No, I don't understand.
いいえ、わかりません。
īe, wakarimasen

What's on …?
…は何が   … wa nani ga
ありますか?   arimas[u] ka

locally
近所に   kinjo ni

this weekend
今週の週末   konshū no shūmatsu

today
今日   kyō

tonight
今夜   konya

Where can I find …?
どこに行けば…   doko ni ikeba …
がありますか?   ga arimas[u] ka

clubs
クラブ   kurabu

gay venues
ゲイの場所   gei no basho

Japanese-style pubs
居酒屋   izakaya

places to eat
食事が   shokuji ga
できる所   dekiru tokoro

pubs
パブ   pabu

Is there a local entertainment guide?
地元のエンターテインメントガイドは
ありますか?
jimoto no entāteinmento gaido wa
arimas[u] ka

PRACTICAL
Question Words

How?
どのように?   dono yō ni

How much does it cost?
いくらですか?   ikura des[u] ka

What?/What is this?
何?/なに?   nan/nani

Which?
どちら?   dochira

When?
いつ?   itsu

Where?
どこ?   doko

Who?
だれ?/どなた?   dare/donata (inf/pol)

Numbers

0	ゼロ/零	zero/rei
1	一	ichi
2	二	ni
3	三	san
4	四	shi/yon
5	五	go
6	六	roku
7	七	shichi/nana
8	八	hachi
9	九	ku/kyū
10	十	jū
11	十一	jūichi
12	十二	jūni
13	十三	jūsan
14	十四	jūshi/jūyon
15	十五	jūgo
16	十六	jūroku
17	十七	jūshichi/jūnana
18	十八	jūhachi
19	十九	jūku/jūkyū
20	二十	nijū
21	二十一	nijūichi
22	二十二	nijūni
30	三十	sanjū
40	四十	yonjū
50	五十	gojū
60	六十	rokujū
70	七十	nanajū
80	八十	hachijū
90	九十	kyūjū
100	百	hyaku
200	二百	nihyaku
1000	千	sen

Days

Monday	月曜日	getsuyōbi
Tuesday	火曜日	kayōbi
Wednesday	水曜日	suiyōbi
Thursday	木曜日	mokuyōbi
Friday	金曜日	kinyōbi
Saturday	土曜日	doyōbi
Sunday	日曜日	nichiyōbi

Banking

I'd like to …
…をお願いします。 … o onegai shimas[u]

cash a cheque
小切手の現金化 kogitte no genkinka

change money
両替 ryōgae

change a travellers cheque
トラベラーズ toraberāz[u]
チェックの現金化 chekku no genkinka

Where's …?
…はどこですか? … wa doko des[u] ka

an ATM
ATM ētīemu

a foreign exchange office
外国為替 gaikoku kawase
セクション sekushon

Post

Where is the post office?
郵便局はどこですか?
yūbin kyoku wa doko des[u] ka

I want to send a/an …
…を送りたいの … o okuritai no
ですが。 des[u] ga

letter
手紙 tegami

parcel
小包 kozutsumi

postcard
はがき hagaki

I want to buy a/an …
…をください。 … o kudasai

envelope
封筒 fūtō

stamp
切手 kitte

Phones & Mobiles

I want to …
…たいのですが。 … tai no des[u] ga

buy a phonecard
テレフォンカード terefon kādo
を買い o kai

call (Singapore)
（シンガポール） (shingapōru)
に電話し ni denwa shi

make a (local) call
（市内）に電話し (shinai) ni denwa shi

reverse the charges
コレクトコールで korekuto-kōru de
電話し denwa shi

I'd like a …
…をお願いします。 … o onegai shimas[u]

charger for my phone
携帯電話の keitai-denwa no
充電器 jūdenki

mobile/cell phone for hire
携帯電話の keitai-denwa no
レンタル rentaru

prepaid mobile/cell phone
プリペイドの puripeido no
携帯電話 keitai-denwa

SIM card for your network
SIMカード shimukādo

Internet

Where's the local internet cafe?
インターネットカフェはどこですか?
intānetto-kafe wa doko des[u] ka

I'd like to …
…したいのですが。 … shitai no des[u] ga

check my email
Eメールをチェック īmēru o chekku

get internet access
インターネット intānetto
にアクセス ni akuses[u]

Transport

When's the … (bus)?
…（バス）は … (bas[u]) wa
何時ですか? nan-ji des[u] ka

first
始発の shihatsu no

last
最終の saishū no

next
次の tsugi no

What time does it leave?
何時に出ますか?
nan-ji ni demas[u] ka

What time does it get to …?
…に何時に着きますか?
… ni nan-ji ni tsukimas[u] ka

Is this taxi available?
このタクシーは空車ですか?
kono tak[u]shī wa kūsha des[u] ka

Please stop here.
ここで停めてください。
koko de tomete kudasai

How much is it to …?
…までいくらですか?
… made ikura des[u] ka

Please take me to (this address).
（この住所）までお願いします。
(kono jūsho) made onegai shimas[u]

EMERGENCIES

Help!
たすけて！　　　　　tas[u]kete

It's an emergency!
緊急です！　　　　　kinkyū des[u]

Call the police!
警察を呼んで！　　　keisatsu o yonde

Call a doctor!
医者を呼んで！　　　isha o yonde

Call an ambulance!
救急車を呼んで！　　kyūkyūsha o yonde

Please help.
たすけてください。　tas[u]kete kudasai

Where's the police station?
警察署は　　　　　　keisatsusho wa
どこですか？　　　　doko des[u] ka

HEALTH

Where's the nearest …?
この近くの…　　　　kono chikaku no …
はどこですか？　　　wa doko des[u] ka

  (24-hour) chemist
  （24時間営業の）　（nijūyojikan eigyō no）
  薬局　　　　　　　yakkyoku
  doctor
  医者　　　　　　　isha
  hospital
  病院　　　　　　　byōin

I need a doctor (who speaks English).
（英語ができる）お医者さんが必要です。
（eigo ga dekiru) o-isha-san ga hitsuyō des[u]

I'm allergic to …
私は…　　　　　　　watashi wa …
アレルギーです。　　arerugī des[u]

  antibiotics
  抗生物質　　　　　kōsei busshitsu
  aspirin
  アスピリン　　　　as[u]pirin
  bees
  蜂　　　　　　　　hachi
  nuts
  ナッツ類　　　　　nattsurui
  penicillin
  ペニシリン　　　　penishirin

Symptoms

I have (a) …
私は…　　　　　　　watashi wa …
があります。　　　　ga arimas[u]

  diarrhoea
  下痢　　　　　　　geri
  headache
  頭痛　　　　　　　zutsū

  nausea
  吐き気　　　　　　hakike
  a pain
  痛み　　　　　　　itami

FOOD & DRINK

breakfast	朝食	chōshoku
lunch	昼食	chūshoku
dinner	夕食	yūshoku
snack	間食	kanshoku
to eat	食べます	tabemas[u]
to drink	飲みます	nomimas[u]

Can you recommend a …?
どこかいい…　　　　doko ka ī …
を知っていますか？　o shitte imas[u] ka

  bar
  バー　　　　　　　bā
  cafe
  カフェ　　　　　　kafe
  restaurant
  レストラン　　　　res[u]toran

Is service included in the bill?
サービス料込みですか？
sābis[u] ryō komi des[u] ka

A table for (two/five) people, please.
（二人/五人）お願いします。
(futari/go-nin) onegai shimas[u]

Do you have an English menu?
英語のメニューがありますか？
eigo no menyū ga arimas[u] ka

Can you recommend any dishes?
おすすめの料理がありますか？
osusume no ryōri ga arimas[u] ka

Is this self-service?
ここはセルフサービスですか？
koko wa serufu sābis[u] des[u] ka

I'm full.
お腹がいっぱいです。
o-naka ga ippai des

Cheers!
乾杯！
kampai

Bon appetit!
いただきます！
itadakimas[u]

Delicious!
おいしい！
oishī

Thank you. (said after a meal)
ごちそうさまでした。
gochisō sama deshita

Please bring (a/the) …
…をお願いします。 … o onegai shimas[u]

bill
お勘定 o-kanjō
chopsticks
おはし o-hashi
fork
フォーク fōku
glass (of water)
コップ koppu
（一杯の水） (ippai no mizu)
knife
ナイフ naifu
spoon
スプーン supūn

I can't eat meat.
肉は食べられません。
niku wa taberaremasen
I can't eat chicken.
鶏肉は食べられません。
toriniku wa taberaremasen
I can't eat pork.
豚肉は食べられません。
butaniku wa taberaremasen
I can't eat seafood.
シーフードは食べられません。
shīfūdo wa taberaremasen
I'm a vegetarian.
私はベジタリアンです。
watashi wa bejitarian des[u]
I'm allergic to (peanuts).
私は（ピーナッツ）アレルギーです。
watashi wa (pīnattsu) arerugī des[u]

Food Glossary
SUSHI & SASHIMI

ama-ebi 甘海老
sweet shrimp
awabi あわび
abalone
ebi 海老/エビ
prawn or shrimp
hamachi はまち
yellowtail
ika いか
squid
ikura イクラ
salmon roe
kani かに
crab
katsuo かつお
bonito
maguro まぐろ
tuna

tai 鯛
sea bream
tamago たまご
sweetened egg
toro とろ
the choicest cut of fatty tuna belly
unagi うなぎ
eel with a sweet sauce
uni うに
sea urchin roe

NOODLES

chānpon-men ちゃんぽんメン
noodles in meat broth with toppings
chāshū-men チャーシューメン
rāmen topped with slices of roast pork
kake かけ
soba/udon in broth
kitsune きつね
soba/udon with fried tofu
miso-rāmen 味噌ラーメン
rāmen with miso-flavoured broth
shio-rāmen 塩ラーメン
rāmen with salt-flavoured broth
shōyu-rāmen 醤油ラーメン
rāmen with soy sauce–flavoured broth
soba そば
buckwheat-based noodles
tempura 天ぷら
soba/udon with tempura shrimp
tsukimi 月見
soba/udon with egg on top
udon うどん
thick, white wheat noodles
wantan-men ワンタンメン
rāmen with meat dumplings
zaru ざる
cold *soba*/udon served on a bamboo mat, with nori

IZAKAYA

agedashi-dōfu 揚げだし豆腐
deep-fried tofu in a fish-stock soup
aspara-batā アスパラバター
buttered asparagus
chīzu-age チーズ揚げ
deep-fried cheese
hiya-yakko 冷奴
cold block of tofu with soy sauce and spring onions
jaga-batā ジャガバター
baked potatoes with butter
kata yaki-soba 固焼きそば
hard fried noodles with meat and vegetables
niku-jaga 肉じゃが
beef and potato stew
pīman ピーマン
small green peppers

poteto furai　　　　ポテトフライ
French fries

sashimi mori-awase　刺身盛り合わせ
selection of sliced sashimi

shītake　　　　　　しいたけ
Japanese mushrooms

shio-yaki-zakana　　塩焼魚
whole fish grilled with salt

shishamo　　　　　ししゃも
pregnant smelts, grilled and eaten whole

tebasaki　　　　　手羽先
chicken wings

tsukune　　　　　　つくね
chicken meatballs

tsuna sarada　　　ツナサラダ
tuna salad over cabbage

yaki-onigiri　　　焼きおにぎり
triangle of grilled rice

yaki-soba　　　　　焼きそば
fried noodles with meat and vegetables

yakitori　　　　　焼き鳥
skewers of grilled chicken

yasai sarada　　　野菜サラダ
mixed vegetable salad

TEMPURA

kakiage　　　　　　掻き揚げ
tempura cake of shredded vegetables

kakiage-don　　　　掻き揚げ丼
kakiage served over a large bowl of rice

shōjin age　　　　精進揚げ
vegetarian tempura

tempura mori-awase　天ぷら盛り合わせ
selection of tempura

ten-don　　　　　　天丼
tempura shrimp and vegetables over a large bowl of rice

SUKIYAKI, SHABU-SHABU & YAKINIKU

buta　　　　　　　豚
pork

gyūniku　　　　　　牛肉
beef

harami　　　　　　ハラミ
tender meat from around the diaphragm

karubi　　　　　　カルビ
short ribs without the bones

reba　　　　　　　レバ
beef liver

rōsu　　　　　　　ロース
beef tenderloin

tan　　　　　　　　タン
beef tongue, served with salt and lemon

toriniku　　　　　鶏肉
chicken

yasai　　　　　　　野菜
vegetables, typically carrots, mushrooms, onions

OKONOMIYAKI

gyū okonomiyaki　　牛お好み焼き
beef *okonomiyaki*

ika okonomiyaki　　イカお好み焼き
squid *okonomiyaki*

mikkusu-yaki　　　ミックス焼き
mixed fillings of seafood, meat and vegetables

modan-yaki　　　　モダン焼き
okonomiyaki with *yaki-soba* and a fried egg

negi okonomiyaki　ネギお好み焼き
thin *okonomiyaki* with spring onions

SHOKUDŌ

donburi-mono　　　丼物
large bowl of rice topped with egg or meat

karē-raisu　　　　カレーライス
rice topped with ingredients in curry sauce

niku-don　　　　　肉丼
rice topped with thin slices of cooked beef

omu-raisu　　　　　オムライス
rice flavoured with ketchup, served inside a thin omelette

oyako-don　　　　　親子丼
rice topped with egg and chicken

TONKATSU

hire katsu　　　　ヒレカツ
tonkatsu (crumbed pork) fillet

katsu-don　　　　　カツ丼
tonkatsu and egg on rice

kushi katsu　　　　串カツ
deep-fried pork and vegetables on skewers

minchi katsu　　　ミンチカツ
minced pork cutlet

rōsu katsu　　　　ロースカツ
fattier cut of pork (which some consider more flavourful)

tonkatsu teishoku　トンカツ定食
set meal of *tonkatsu*, rice, *miso shiru* and shredded cabbage

UNAGI

kabayaki　　　　　蒲焼
skewers of grilled eel without rice

unadon　　　　　　うな丼
grilled eel over a bowl of rice

unagi teishoku　　うなぎ定食
full-set *unagi* meal with rice, grilled eel, eel-liver soup and pickles

unajū　　　　　　　うな重
grilled eel over a flat tray of rice

FUGU

fugu chiri　　　　ふぐちり
stew made from *fugu* and vegetables

fugu sashimi　　　ふぐ刺身
thinly sliced raw *fugu*

fugu teishoku　　　ふぐ定食
set course of *fugu* served several ways, plus rice and soup

yaki fugu　　　　　　焼きふぐ
fugu grilled on a *hibachi* (small earthenware grill) at your table

ALCOHOLIC DRINKS
akai-wain　　　　　　赤いワイン
red wine
bīru　　　　　　　　ビール
beer
chūhai　　　　　　　チューハイ
shōchū with soda and lemon
mizu-wari　　　　　　水割り
whiskey, ice and water
nama bīru　　　　　　生ビール
draught beer
onzarokku　　　　　　オンザロック
whiskey with ice
oyu-wari　　　　　　お湯割り
shōchū with hot water
rōku-de　　　　　　　ロックで
to serve a liquor on the rocks
shiroi-wain　　　　　白いワイン
white wine
shōchū　　　　　　　焼酎
distilled grain liquor
sutoraito　　　　　　ストライト
to serve a liquor straight
whiskey　　　　　　ウィスキー
whiskey

NONALCOHOLIC DRINKS
american kōhī　　　　アメリカンコーヒー
weak coffee
burendo kōhī　　　　ブレンドコーヒー
blended coffee, fairly strong
kafe ōre　　　　　　カフェオレ
café au lait, hot or cold
kōcha　　　　　　　紅茶
black, British-style tea
kōhī　　　　　　　　コーヒー
regular coffee
mizu　　　　　　　　水
water
orenji jūsu　　　　　オレンジジュース
orange juice
oyu　　　　　　　　お湯
hot water
uron-cha　　　　　　烏龍茶
traditional Chinese tea

JAPANESE TEA
bancha　　　　　　　番茶
ordinary-grade green tea, brownish in colour
matcha　　　　　　　抹茶
powdered green tea used in the tea ceremony
mugicha　　　　　　麦茶
roasted barley tea
o-cha　　　　　　　お茶
green tea
sencha　　　　　　　煎茶
medium-grade green tea

agaru – north of

ageya – traditional banquet hall used for entertainment, which flourished during the Edo period

Amida Nyorai – Buddha of the Western Paradise

ANA – All Nippon Airways

bashi – bridge (also *hashi*)

ben – dialect, as in *Kyoto-ben*

bentō – boxed lunch or dinner, usually containing rice, vegetables and fish or meat

bosatsu – a bodhisattva, or Buddha attendant, who assists others to attain enlightenment

bugaku – dance pieces played by court orchestras in ancient Japan

bunraku – classical puppet theatre that uses life-size puppets to enact dramas similar to those of *kabuki*

chadō – tea ceremony, or 'The Way of Tea'

chanoyu – tea ceremony; see also *chadō*

chō – city area (for large cities) sized between a *ku* and *chōme*

chōme – city area of a few blocks

dai – great; large

Daibutsu – Great Buddha

daimyō – domain lords under the *shōgun*

dera – temple (also *ji* or *tera*)

dōri – street

fugu – poisonous pufferfish, elevated to *haute cuisine*

futon – cushion-like mattress that is rolled up and stored away during the day

gagaku – music of the imperial court

gaijin – foreigner; the contracted form of gaikokujin (literally, 'outside country person')

gawa – river (also *kawa*)

geiko – Kyoto dialect for *geisha*

geisha – a woman versed in the arts and other cultivated pursuits who entertains guests

gū – shrine

haiden – hall of worship in a shrine

haiku – 17-syllable poem

hakubutsukan – museum

hanami – cherry-blossom viewing

hashi – bridge (also *bashi*); chopsticks

higashi – east

hiragana – phonetic syllabary used to write Japanese words

honden – main building of a shrine

hondō – main building of a temple (also *kondō*)

ikebana – art of flower arrangement

irori – open hearth found in traditional Japanese homes

ITJ – International Telecom Japan

izakaya – Japanese pub/eatery

ji – temple (also *tera* or *dera*)

jingū – shrine (also *jinja* or *gū*)

Jizō – bodhisattva who watches over children

JNTO – Japan National Tourist Organization

jō – castle (also *shiro*)

JR – Japan Railways

kabuki – form of Japanese theatre that draws on popular tales and is characterised by elaborate costumes, stylised acting and the use of male actors for all roles

kaiseki – Buddhist-inspired, Japanese *haute cuisine*; called *cha-kaiseki* when served as part of a tea ceremony

kaisoku – rapid train

kaiten-zushi – automatic, conveyor-belt sushi

kamikaze – literally, 'wind of the gods'; originally the typhoon that sank Kublai Khan's 13th-century invasion fleet and the name adopted by Japanese suicide bombers in the waning days of WWII

kampai – cheers, as in a drinking toast

kanji – literally, 'Chinese writing'; Chinese ideographic script used for writing Japanese

Kannon – Buddhist goddess of mercy

karaoke – a now famous export where revellers sing along to recorded music, minus the vocals

karesansui – dry-landscaped rock garden

kawa – river

kayabuki-yane – traditional Japanese thatched-roof farmhouse

KDD – Kokusai Denshin Denwa

ken – prefecture, eg Shiga-ken

kimono – traditional outer garment that is similar to a robe

kita – north

KIX – Kansai International Airport

Kiyomizu-yaki – a distinctive type of local pottery

ko – lake

kōban – local police box

kōen – park

koma-inu – dog-like guardian stone statues found in pairs at the entrance to *Shintō* shrines

kondō – main building of a temple

koto – 13-stringed zither-like instrument

ku – ward

kudaru – south of (also *sagaru*)

kura – traditional Japanese warehouse

kyōgen – drama performed as comic relief between *nō* plays, or as separate events

kyō-machiya – see *machiya*

kyō-ningyō – Kyoto dolls

kyō-obanzai – see *obanzai*

kyō-ryōri – Kyoto cuisine

Kyoto-ben – distinctive Japanese dialect spoken in Kyoto

LDP – Liberal Democratic Party

live house – a small concert hall where live music is performed machi – city area (for large cities) sized between a *ku* and *chōme*

machiya – traditional wooden town house, called *kyō-machiya* in Kyoto

maiko – apprentice geisha

maki-e – decorative lacquer technique using silver and gold powders

mama-san – older women who run drinking, dining and entertainment venues

matcha – powdered green tea served in tea ceremonies

matsuri – festival

mikoshi – portable shrine carried during festivals

minami – south

minshuku – Japanese equivalent of a B&B

minyō – traditional Japanese folk music

Miroku – Buddha of the Future

mizu shōbai – the world of bars, entertainment and prostitution (also known as *water trade*)

momiji – Japanese maple trees

momiji-gari – viewing of the changing autumn colours of trees

mon – temple gate

mōningu setto – morning set of toast and coffee served at cafés

mura – village

Nihon – Japanese word for Japan; literally, 'source of the sun' (also known as *Nippon*)

ningyō – doll (see also *kyō-ningyō*)

niō – temple guardians

Nippon – see *Nihon*

nishi – west

nō – classical Japanese mask drama performed on a bare stage

noren – door curtain for restaurants, usually labelled with the name of the establishment

NTT – Nippon Telegraph & Telephone Corporation

o- – prefix used as a sign of respect (usually applied to objects)

obanzai – Japanese home-style cooking (the Kyoto variant of this is sometimes called *kyō-obanzai*)

obi – sash or belt worn with *kimono*

Obon – mid-August festivals and ceremonies for deceased ancestors

okiya – old-style *geisha* living quarters

onsen – mineral hot spring with bathing areas and accommodation

o-shibori – hot towels given in restaurants

pachinko – vertical pinball game that is a Japanese craze

Raijin – god of thunder

ryokan – traditional Japanese inn

ryōri – cooking; cuisine (see also *kyō-ryōri*)

ryōtei – traditional-style, high-class restaurant; *kaiseki* is typical fare

sabi – a poetic ideal of finding beauty and pleasure in imperfection; often used in conjunction with *wabi*

sagaru – south of (also *kudaru*)

sakura – cherry trees

salaryman – male employee of a large firm

sama – a suffix even more respectful than *san*

samurai – Japan's traditional warrior class

san – a respectful suffix applied to personal names, similar to Mr, Mrs or Ms but more widely used

sen – line, usually railway line

sencha – medium-grade green tea

sensu – folding paper fan

sentō – public bath

setto – set meal; see also *teishoku*

Shaka Nyorai – Historical Buddha

shakkei – borrowed scenery; technique where features outside a garden are incorporated into its design

shakuhachi – traditional Japanese bamboo flute

shamisen – three-stringed, banjo-like instrument

shi – city (to distinguish cities with prefectures of the same name)

shidare-zakura – weeping cherry tree

shinkaisoku – special rapid train

shinkansen – bullet train (literally, 'new trunk line')

Shintō – indigenous Japanese religion

shiro – castle

shodō – Japanese calligraphy; literally, 'the way of writing'

shōgun – military ruler of pre-Meiji Japan

shōjin-ryōri – Buddhist vegetarian cuisine

shokudō – Japanese-style cafeteria/cheap restaurant

shukubō – temple lodging

soba – thin brown buckwheat noodles

tatami – tightly woven floor matting on which shoes should not be worn

teishoku – set meal in a restaurant

tera – temple (also *dera* or *ji*)

TIC – Tourist Information Center (usually refers to Kyoto Tourist Information Center)

tokkyū – limited express train

torii – entrance gate to a *Shintō* shrine

tsukemono – Japanese pickles

udon – thick, white, wheat noodles

ukiyo-e – woodblock prints; literally, 'pictures of the floating world'

wabi – a Zen-inspired aesthetic of rustic simplicity

wagashi – traditional Japanese sweets that are served with tea

wasabi – spicy Japanese horseradish

washi – Japanese paper

water trade – see *mizu shōbai*

yakuza – Japanese mafia

yudōfu – bean curd cooked in an iron pot; common temple fare

Zen – a form of Buddhism

BEHIND THE SCENES

THIS BOOK

This 8th edition of *Tokyo* was written by Andrew Bender and Timothy N Hornyak; Timothy and Matthew Firestone wrote the 7th edition. This guidebook was commissioned by Lonely Planet's Oakland office and produced by the following:

Commissioning Editor Emily K Wolman

Coordinating Editor Justin Flynn

Coordinating Cartographer David Kemp

Coordinating Layout Designer Frank Deim

Managing Editors Imogen Bannister, Laura Stansfeld, Sasha Baskett

Managing Cartographer David Connolly

Managing Layout Designer Celia Wood

Assisting Editors Pete Cruttenden, Jeanette Wall, Susan Paterson

Assisting Cartographers Andras Bogdanovits, Csanad Csutoros

Cover Research Pepi Bluck, lonelyplanetimages.com

Internal Image Research Jane Hart, lonelyplanet images.com

Project Manager Chris Love

Language Content Laura Crawford

Thanks to Heather Dickson, Emma Gilmour, Lisa Knights, Katie O'Connell, Nigel Chin, Raphael Richards

Cover photographs *Aka choochin* (red lanterns), Antony Giblin, Lonely Planet Images (top), Woman in traditional dress talking on a mobile phone, Lucinao Lepre, Photolibrary (bottom)

All images are copyright of the photographer unless otherwise indicated. Many of the images in this guide are available for licensing from Lonely Planet Images: www .lonelyplanetimages.com.

THANKS

ANDREW BENDER

First thanks to Yohko Scott and Minako Aoshima at the JNTO Los Angeles office and Keiko Garrison of the TCVB for their always excellent support. On the ground, key helpers included Honma Yūko, Saitō Mayumi, Joan Stein, Nishi Keiko, Yoneyama Yoshiko, Dave Mori, Dave Tropp, Sakai Isao, Katherine Melchior Ray, Nancy Craft and Steve Beimel. In-house thanks go to Emily Wolman for the opportunity, guidance and good cheer, Chris Love, Rebecca Lalor and, last but not least, to Tim Hornyak for being such a great collaborator.

TIMOTHY N HORNYAK

A big *arigato* to my colleagues Andy Bender, Emily Wolman, Matthew Firestone and other LP staff, as well as Mamiko Hokari, Rumiko Morinaga, Ari Taira, Aya Shimada for her insights into Shinagawa, Susan Bigelow and Max Sato for putting me up in their lovely cottage, Akamon, in Nikkō, Andree Dufleit, Nacio 'Skip' Cronin at the Imperial Hotel, Giles Murray, Charles Spreckley and Nicole Fall of Bespoke Tokyo, Yoshimi Nakagawa and Tracey Glass for helping me on a long detour to Ayabe in northwest Kyoto, my Kagurazaka drinking buddy Toshie Niida, James LePoidevin and Yohan Passos, Akiko Moorman, and Umeyo Sato of the Shimoda Tourist Office. My sincere thanks to Eugene Shim and Joohee Kim for lots of tea, kimchee and laughs during the write-up, and my family for their unflagging support, enthusiasm and patience.

THE LONELY PLANET STORY

Fresh from an epic journey across Europe, Asia and Australia in 1972, Tony and Maureen Wheeler sat at their kitchen table stapling together notes. The first Lonely Planet guidebook, *Across Asia on the Cheap*, was born.

Travellers snapped up the guides. Inspired by their success, the Wheelers began publishing books to Southeast Asia, India and beyond. Demand was prodigious, and the Wheelers expanded the business rapidly to keep up. Over the years, Lonely Planet extended its coverage to every country and into the virtual world via lonelyplanet.com and the Thorn Tree message board.

As Lonely Planet became a globally loved brand, Tony and Maureen received several offers for the company. But it wasn't until 2007 that they found a partner whom they trusted to remain true to the company's principles of travelling widely, treading lightly and giving sustainably. In October of that year, BBC Worldwide acquired a 75% share in the company, pledging to uphold Lonely Planet's commitment to independent travel, trustworthy advice and editorial independence.

Today, Lonely Planet has offices in Melbourne, London and Oakland, with over 500 staff members and 300 authors. Tony and Maureen are still actively involved with Lonely Planet. They're travelling more often than ever, and they're devoting their spare time to charitable projects. And the company is still driven by the philosophy of *Across Asia on the Cheap*: 'All you've got to do is decide to go and the hardest part is over. So go!'

BEHIND THE SCENES

SEND US YOUR FEEDBACK

We love to hear from travellers — your comments keep us on our toes and help make our books better. Our well-travelled team reads every word on what you loved or loathed about this book. Although we cannot reply individually to postal submissions, we always guarantee that your feedback goes straight to the appropriate authors, in time for the next edition. Each person who sends us information is thanked in the next edition and the most useful submissions are rewarded with a free book.

To send us your updates — and find out about Lonely Planet events, newsletters and travel news — visit our award-winning website: lonelyplanet.com/contact.

Note: We may edit, reproduce and incorporate your comments in Lonely Planet products such as guidebooks, websites and digital products, so let us know if you don't want your comments reproduced or your name acknowledged. For a copy of our privacy policy visit lonelyplanet.com/privacy.

OUR READERS

Many thanks to the travellers who used the last edition and wrote to us with helpful hints, useful advice and interesting anecdotes:

Karen Albright, Susan Baker, Diego Coruña, Kylie Crawley, Biljana Davcheva, Andrew Dye, Petra Ederer, Katarina Hue-mer Fredriksen, Bryan Hollar, Simon Kennedy, Jeff Liddell, Daniel Madrid, Norelle Oneill, Orhan Ozerhan, Astuti Pitarini, Pakorn Pongpoonsuk, Jane Powell, Tom Royal, Gordon Smith, Lydia Tong

ACKNOWLEDGMENTS

© 2009 Tokyo Metro and Bureau of Transportation Tokyo Metropolitan Government. Tokyo Metro Co., Ltd. approved (Approval Number 21-A006)

Notes

Notes

INDEX

INDEX

INDEX

INDEX

MAP LEGEND

ROUTES

.... Tollway
.... Freeway
.... Primary
.... Secondary
.... Tertiary
.... Lane
.... Under Construction
.... Unsealed Road
.... One-Way Street

.... Mall/Steps
.... Tunnel
.... Pedestrian Overpass
.... Walking Tour
.... Walking Tour Detour
.... Walking Trail
.... Walking Path
.... Track

TRANSPORT

.... Ferry
.... Metro
.... Monorail
.... Bus Route
.... Private Rail

.... Rail
.... Rail (Underground)
.... Tram
.... Cable Car, Funicular
.... Rail (Fast Track)

HYDROGRAPHY

.... River, Creek
.... Intermittent River

.... Canal
.... Water

BOUNDARIES

.... International
.... State, Provincial
.... Disputed

.... Regional, Suburb
.... Ancient Wall
.... Cliff

AREA FEATURES

.... Airport
.... Area of Interest
.... Beach, Desert
.... Building
.... Campus
.... Cemetery, Christian
.... Cemetery, Other
.... Forest

.... Land
.... Mall
.... Market
.... Park
.... Reservation
.... Rocks
.... Sports
.... Urban

POPULATION

○ **CAPITAL (NATIONAL)**
● **Large City**
○ Small City

◉ .... CAPITAL (STATE)
● .... Medium City
○ .... Town, Village

SYMBOLS

Information
⊜ .... Bank, ATM
🛈 .... Embassy/Consulate
✚ .... Hospital, Medical
ⓘ .... Information
@ .... Internet Facilities
☺ .... Police Station
✉ .... Post Office, GPO
☏ .... Telephone
🚻 .... Toilets

Sights
⛱ .... Beach
卍 .... Buddhist
🏰 .... Castle, Fortress
✝ .... Christian
🏛 .... Confucian
🗼 .... Monument

🏛 .... Museum, Gallery
● .... Point of Interest
🏛 .... Ruin
♨ .... Sento Public Hot Baths
⛩ .... Shinto
🦅 .... Zoo, Bird Sanctuary

Shopping
🛍 .... Shopping

Eating
🍴 .... Eating

Entertainment
🎭 .... Entertainment

Drinking
🍷 .... Drinking
☕ .... Café

Sports & Activities
🏊 .... Pool

Sleeping
🛏 .... Sleeping

Transport
✈ .... Airport, Airfield
🚏 .... Border Crossing
🚌 .... Bus Station
🚲 .... Cycling, Bicycle Path
🅿 .... Parking Area
⛽ .... Petrol Station
🚕 .... Taxi Rank

Geographic
🚨 .... Lighthouse
👁 .... Lookout
▲ .... Mountain, Volcano
🌲 .... National Park
→ .... River Flow
🌊 .... Waterfall

Published by Lonely Planet Publications Pty Ltd
ABN 36 005 607 983

Australia (Head Office)
Locked Bag 1, Footscray, Victoria 3011,
☎03 8379 8000, fax 03 8379 8111, talk2us@
lonelyplanet.com.au

USA 150 Linden St, Oakland, CA 94607,
☎510 250 6400, toll free 800 275 8555,
fax 510 893 8572, info@lonelyplanet.com

UK 2nd fl, 186 City Rd, London, EC1V 2NT, ☎020
7106 2100, fax 020 7106 2101,
go@lonelyplanet.co.uk

© Lonely Planet 2010
Photographs © as indicated 2010

Printed by Hang Tai Printing Company, Hong Kong
Printed in China